GU01218406

Critical Approaches to International Criminal Law

Drawing on the critical legal tradition, the collection of international scholars gathered in this volume analyse the complicities and limitations of International Criminal Law. International Criminal Law has recently experienced a significant surge in scholarship and public debate; individual criminal accountability is now firmly entrenched in both international law and the international consciousness as a necessary mechanism of responsibility. *Critical Approaches to International Criminal Law: An Introduction* shifts the debate towards that which has so far been missing from the mainstream discussion: the possible injustices, exclusions, and biases of International Criminal Law.

This collection of essays is the first dedicated to the topic of critical approaches to international criminal law. It will be a valuable resource for scholars and students of international criminal law, international law, international legal theory, criminal law, and criminology.

Christine Schwöbel is Lecturer in Law at the University of Liverpool. She specializes in international law, particularly the narratives surrounding global constitutionalism, global governance, international criminal law, and international human rights law. Her publications include *Global Constitutionalism in International Legal Perspective* (Martinus Nijhoff/Brill, 2011).

Critical Approaches to International Criminal Law

An Introduction

Edited by
Christine Schwöbel

LONDON AND NEW YORK

First published 2014
by Routledge
2 Park Square, Milton Park, Abingdon, Oxfordshire OX14 4RN

and by Routledge
711 Third Avenue, New York, NY 10017

First issued in paperback 2015

a GlassHouse Book

Routledge is an imprint of the Taylor & Francis Group, an informa business

© 2014 Christine Schwöbel

British Library Cataloguing in Publication Data
A catalogue record for this book is available from the British Library

Library of Congress Cataloging-in-Publication Data
Critical approaches to international criminal law : an introduction / edited
by Christine Schwöbel.
pages cm
ISBN 978-0-415-72704-4 (hardback) – ISBN 978-1-315-85594-3 (ebk)
1. International criminal law. I. Schwöbel, Christine E. J., author editor of
compilation.
KZ7050.C75 2014
341–dc23
2013048745

ISBN-13: 978-1-138-65976-6 (pbk)
ISBN-13: 978-0-415-72704-4 (hbk)

Typeset in Baskerville
by Cenveo Publisher Services

Contents

Notes on the editor and contributors

Christine Schwöbel (*Staatsexamen* (Heidelberg), LLM (City University London), GDL (BPP), PhD (King's College London)) is Lecturer in Law at the University of Liverpool. She specializes in international law, particularly the narratives surrounding global constitutionalism, global governance, international criminal law, and international human rights law. Her publications include *Global Constitutionalism in International Legal Perspective* (Martinus Nijhoff/Brill, 2011).

Grietje Baars is a Lecturer in the City Law School with experience as a corporate lawyer and a human rights/law of armed conflict advisor in the Middle East. She is interested in critical and Marxist theory of law, and class, ideology and the corporation in global governance. She has published on the regulation of the global economy and on the political economy of international criminal law.

Michelle Burgis-Kasthala is a Lecturer in Public International Law at the University of Edinburgh School of Law. Previously, she was Lecturer in International Law and Middle East Studies in the School of International Relations at the University of St Andrews. Michelle has degrees from the University of Sydney (BA(Hons)/LLB(Hons)) and the Australian National University (PhD). She is an expert on the role of international law in the Arab world, especially in relation to the Palestinian–Israeli conflict and international tribunals. She is the author of *Boundaries of Discourse in the International Court of Justice: Mapping Arguments in Arab Territorial Disputes* (Martinus Nijhoff, 2009).

Michelle Farrell is a Lecturer in Law at the School of Law and Social Justice, University of Liverpool. Michelle writes on international law, counter-terrorism and states of emergency from historical, theoretical and human rights perspectives. She is the author of *The Prohibition of Torture in Exceptional Circumstances* (Cambridge University Press 2013).

Johannes C.S. Frank is a writer, translator and publisher, and is the programme director of the Ernst Ludwig Ehrlich Scholarship Fund. Johannes is the co-initiator and organizer of the Zeitkunst Festival, an international arts festival. He is also the editor and founder of the Berlin-based independent publishing house Verlagshaus J. Frank. His publications include *Märchenland:Die Gebrüder Grimm in Israel* (2010) and *Remembrances of Copper Cream* (2012).

Christopher Gevers is a Lecturer in the School of Law, University of KwaZulu-Natal, where he teaches human rights, public international law and international criminal law. His research interests include international criminal law, international legal theory and African studies.

Emily Haslam is Senior Lecturer in International Law at the University of Kent and a member of the Centre for Critical International Law at Kent. She publishes in the fields of international law, international criminal law and civil society.

Sara Kendall is a researcher at the Grotius Centre for International Legal Studies at Leiden University. She completed her doctorate at the University of California at Berkeley on issues of legitimacy and jurisdiction at the Special Court for Sierra Leone. Her current research focuses on the social and political effects of International Criminal Court interventions.

Tor Krever is a PhD candidate in Law at the London School of Economics and Political Science and assistant editor of the *London Review of International Law*. He writes in the areas of international law, political economy and international development.

Heidi Matthews is a doctoral candidate at Harvard Law School, where she is also a Fellow at the Institute for Global Law and Policy. Her research lies at the intersection of criminal law, the law of war, and human rights.

Frédéric Mégret is an Associate Professor at the Faculty of Law, McGill University, where he holds the Canada Research Chair in the Law of Human Rights and Legal Pluralism and is the Associate-Dean for Research. He has interests in many of the theoretical and practical dimensions of international criminal justice.

Gerry Simpson holds the Sir Kenneth Bailey Chair of Law at Melbourne Law School. His latest books, *The Margins of International Law* (a collection of his essays) and *Hidden Histories* (with Kevin Heller), were published by Cameron and May and Oxford respectively in 2013. Gerry currently is working on a book about the literary life of international law.

Immi Tallgren, LL.D., is Research Fellow at the Erik Castrén Institute of International Law and Human Rights, University of Helsinki, and Chercheuse associée, Saint-Louis University, Brussels. Her professional background is in the government and international organizations, working on international law. She now publishes and teaches on international criminal law, international cooperation in criminal matters and human rights.

Acknowledgements

This book is a selection of edited papers presented at the inaugural Critical Approaches to International Criminal Law (CAICL) conference, held in Liverpool in December 2012. The conference came about through the efforts of the then newly formed CAICL research network. Funding and support were generously provided by the University of Liverpool as well as an Institute for Global Law and Policy (IGLP) grant.

Fiona Beveridge, Head of the School of Law and Social Justice at the University of Liverpool, was exceptionally supportive of the conference and of the first steps in bringing a research network together.

The IGLP at Harvard Law School has been central for the conceptualizing of the CAICL network and conference. Many of the contributors in this volume have taken part in IGLP events and it was at the IGLP Workshop in Harvard in summer 2012 that the idea for the CAICL network first took on form. Michelle Burgis-Kasthala, Paul Clark, Tor Krever, Heidi Matthews, John Reynolds and myself were the recipients of the IGLP Collaborative Research Grant. On behalf of the network, I would like to thank David Kennedy, Director of IGLP, and Neal O'Connor, Administrative Director, for their generous support – not only of the conference but of the idea behind CAICL. The IGLP provides an important forum for scholars from across the world, particularly to support research which might not otherwise find funding through the usual channels.

On behalf of the network, my thanks to those who have not been able to contribute to this collection but whose scholarship and enthusiasm for critique has been crucial for its production. Their work is referenced in almost all chapters. This includes Sarah Nouwen, John Reynolds, Thomas Skouteris and Wouter Werner.

My heartfelt thanks to the contributors who have dared to embark with me on the exploration of CAICL. It is an honour to have worked with some of the most eminent and most promising scholars in the field of ICL. I am proud and thankful that the process of the production of this book has not only produced what you hold in your hands but also treasured friendships.

I would like to acknowledge the Lauterpacht Centre for International Law at the University of Cambridge, which allowed me to undertake a visiting research fellowship in the summer of 2013. Sarah Nouwen, fellow at the Centre and valued friend, was particularly supportive in many ways: in making me feel welcome at the Centre, by engaging in stimulating and probing conversations on ICL, and in organizing a take-them-a-meal scheme after the birth of our son, which helped free some time for childcare as well as writing and editing. My thanks also to Michael Dougan, Head of Department at the Liverpool Law School, and Fiona Beveridge for granting me this time away from law school duties.

It is a pleasure to thank the Routledge editor Colin Perrin, and editorial assistant Rebekah Jenkins, for their support, and, above all, patience. Their enthusiasm and optimism throughout the process have been crucial for this collection coming together.

Inevitably, an edited collection makes (unfair) demands on family life and I am particularly lucky to have a family who tolerates these demands with grace. My husband Axit was exceptionally supportive, particularly in light of the arrival of our son Nilu, born during the production of the manuscript. Axit and I find that Nilu's perfection defies even the most critical of approaches.

List of abbreviations

ASP	Assembly of State Parties to the Rome Statute
CLS	Critical Legal Studies
ICC	International Criminal Court
ICJ	International Criminal Justice
ICT	International Criminal Tribunal
ICTR	International Criminal Tribunal for Rwanda
ICTY	International Criminal Tribunal for the former Yugoslavia
IMT	(Nuremberg) International Military Tribunal
IMTFE	(Tokyo) International Military Tribunal for the Far East
NATO	North Atlantic Treaty Organization
NGO	Non-Governmental Organization
OTP	Office of the Prosecutor
P5	Permanent Five (Member States in the UNSC)
Rome Statute	The Rome Statute of the International Criminal Court
STL	Special Tribunal for Lebanon
TWAIL	Third World Approaches to International Law
UK	United Kingdom
UN	United Nations
US	United States of America
UNSC	United Nations Security Council

Introduction

Christine Schwöbel

A critique is not a matter of saying that things are not right as they are. It is a matter of pointing out on what kinds of assumptions, what kinds of familiar, unchallenged, unconsidered modes of thought the practices that we accept rest …

(Foucault 1988)

Commencing on a journey

This collection of essays is the first dedicated to the topic of critical approaches to international criminal law by a group of scholars who set out to engage in a common critical project. The essays are selected from papers presented at the inaugural Critical Approaches to International Criminal Law Conference in Liverpool in December 2012. The conference marked the first time that scholars had come together to explore critical approaches to international criminal law under the acronym CAICL, each with a view as to what this may encompass. In part, it was a letter which brought these scholars together. In the summer of 2012, after testing the idea on colleagues and friends, I sent the following to some of those who would later associate themselves with the CAICL research network:

> Driven by frustration with the absence or the isolation of pockets of a meaningful body of critique of ICL, it appears necessary to both begin to engage in critique as well as pull together those people and that work which already engages in some form of critique. I believe we have all at some point encountered and experienced frustration, even a sense of crisis, at the seemingly overwhelming self-congratulatory and uncritical nature of the field of ICL. ICL is significantly connected to projects of humanitarianism on a global scale. The predominant rhetoric is one of justice, peace, law, addressing impunity, and accountability. There are only few scholars who are addressing concerns about the possible inequalities and biases produced through ICL. What of the complicity of ICL in injustice, conflict, exclusions and selective responsibility?

The idea then is to assemble a body of critical approaches to (and from within) ICL. This 'body' means a body of scholarship and of people who are working on relevant aspects of ICL critique. While an exchange with more mainstream scholars and scholarship is necessary, it seems that an initial stage could be directed towards the identification of an identity of critique within ICL. This project may take inspiration from the critical traditions and culture in the international human rights movement; this movement, although in part also problematic, appears to have established a dialectic between critique and mainstream scholarship.

Here is an initial – and tentative – list of topics or sites of critique, which I hope you will comment on and extend:

1. ICL and the political
2. ICL and neoliberalism
3. ICL and gender
4. ICL and 'afrocentricism'
5. ICL crowding out other disciplines
6. ICL and the emergence of a 'judiocracy'

… In essence this is about creating a network so I suppose the first stage is to identify who is interested in this project. Please get in touch with your respective contacts and network by forwarding this message. This should crucially not be limited to academics, but should include practitioners and anyone engaged in activist/policy projects.

The call for papers for the conference in Liverpool was modelled on this letter. In discussions with some of the speakers, and the emergent research network, it was agreed that CAICL should encompass a critique of ICL doctrine as well as a meta-critique of the field itself.

This then was the thin common ground on which the idea of Critical Approaches to International Criminal Law and its acronym CAICL emerged. We agreed that there was a surge in scholarship of ICL, in institutions, and in the public debate and we agreed that there was a 'gap'; that while individual criminal accountability is firmly entrenched in both international law and the international consciousness as a necessary mechanism of responsibility, the structures constructing international criminal law remain largely unchecked and unquestioned.

Mind the gap

Every piece of research commonly begins with a description of the gap which is being addressed by it. The gap is what legitimizes research in a particular area; it is the gap which *necessitates* the research. To the scholars who are contributing to this volume, this gap seemed a gaping one: where was the meaningful critique of the tremendously successful international criminal law?

The great speed at which international tribunals, such as the International Criminal Tribunal for the former Yugoslavia (ICTY) or the International Criminal Tribunal for Rwanda (ICTR) and of course the permanent International Criminal Court (ICC), were established had seemingly left little time to ponder the assumptions which inform international criminal justice as it is currently understood. The sense of success at arresting Slobodan Milosovic, of convicting Charles Taylor, of the referral of the situation in Libya to the ICC, had made critique largely unpopular, prompting the suspicion that those practising critique were somehow endorsing mass atrocities.

Given the significant anniversaries – the tenth anniversary of the coming into force of the constituting treaty for the ICC and the tenth anniversary of the Statute of the Special Court for Sierra Leone – 2012 appeared to be a good year not only to take stock of the successes of ICL, but crucially to place a spotlight on some of the assumptions which inform the field and thereby critically examine the central tenets of ICL. Such 'assumptions critique' is explained particularly well in the words of Foucault in the epigraph: 'pointing out on […] what kinds of familiar, unchallenged, unconsidered modes of thought the practices that we accept rest'. What seemed to be broadly missing from the mainstream debate were the possible complicities of ICL in injustice, conflict, exclusions, and biases perpetuated and created through the taking-for-granted of particular modes of thought. At the conference in Liverpool, as a research network, and in this collection, we have set out to explore some of these assumptions.

Caution is called for when a gap in research is identified, and subsequently suggestions for filling the gap are proposed. There is a clear tension between the desire to describe the necessity and timeliness of the scholarship (the gap, its 'newness'), and the danger of overstating this very gap. In regard to the seeming gap here, I am therefore not claiming that there is *no* critique; I am, however, claiming that the most common critique is largely one which focuses on effectiveness and the strengthening of the existing structures. Notwithstanding the examination of critical motifs of the international criminal justice project (Mégret, Chapter 1), the careful analysis of critique and its etymology in the word 'crisis' (Kendall, Chapter 2), and the insightful distinction between critique and criticism (Tallgren, Chapter 3), it seems important to briefly illustrate the difference between 'effectiveness critique' and the type of 'assumptions critique' pursued in this collection.

Effectiveness arguments in ICL are commonly made somewhere along the following lines: if the International Criminal Court is not functioning as well as it could be, then it must be strengthened; if peace is not yet achieved through tackling impunity, then there must be more accountability; if the US or Israel are appearing to pursue military or economic interests prompted by their sense of exceptionalism, they should ratify the Rome Statute; if the current focus of international criminal justice is on African individuals, it should be extended to include, say, George W. Bush or Tony Blair.

To exemplify this further: a contemporary object of critique is the criminal investigation of sitting heads of state – a debate enflamed by recent demands made by Kenya's President and Deputy-President. President Uhru Kenyatta and Deputy-President William Ruto have both been charged by the ICC with crimes against humanity committed during Kenya's post-election violence of 2007–08 and have requested that the investigations be suspended while they are in power. At its summit in Ethiopia in October 2013, the African Union passed a resolution stating that no sitting African head of state should appear before an international court, contravening provisions of the Rome Statute. Prior to the summit there had also been calls for a mass walk-out from the jurisdiction of the ICC of the 34 of the 54 African states which are also part of the African Union. The typical (effectiveness) commentary in response to this has been around the ICC expanding its work outside of the African continent. Commentators have urged African states to continue the fight against impunity and have appealed to the ICC not to focus exclusively on African states (for example, Amnesty International 2013). The critique is therewith directed towards the strengthening and effectiveness of the ICC. An assumptions critique, on the other hand, may, for example, examine why African states were so enchanted with the ICC ten years ago and now feel disenchanted – why did they believe they would benefit from signing the Rome Statute, including provisions regarding the accountability of sitting heads of state? And why have those expectations not been met? Rather than advocating for the strengthening of the existing structures (the language, institutions, advocates), an assumptions critique questions who benefits in the existing parameters, who loses through the given legal structures, and why.

Further, in regard to the 'gap' in research and practice, this collection does not wish to claim that we are beginning 'assumptions critique' from scratch; we draw on already existing work inside and outside the field of ICL. Indeed there was, arguably, already a defined CAICL canon, even before the acronym came to mean anything. This can be identified through a glance at the bibliographies at the end of each chapter in this collection. Almost all contributors have referenced Sarah Nouwen and Wouter Werner's piece 'Doing Justice to the Political' (Nouwen and Werner 2011). David Kennedy, Martti Koskenniemi, Frédéric Mégret, Gerry Simpson, Thomas Skouteris and Immi Tallgren are international law scholars whose work also features prominently. The works of political theorists Hannah Arendt, Michel Foucault and Judith Shklar are, judging by the chapter bibliographies, also part of the CAICL canon. The common bibliography is something worth noting as it is the awareness of existing work and its preferences or biases which informs a more nuanced understanding of our own positions.

Roadworks ahead

From the outset, we were aware that there may be significant tensions, dangers and pitfalls setting the limits as to what critique as an orientation can achieve. One of these has already been named as the possible strategic overstating of the gap in research. Further issues which I am wary of for this project – worries which are shared by several of the contributors to this collection and are reflected in a number of the chapters – are (a) the danger of losing the ICL perspective; (b) the danger of introspection; (c) the danger of complicity; and (d) the danger of instrumentalizing the object of critique. The following chapters take these concerns on in a careful and scholarly fashion; I simply sketch out, with a broad-brush approach, what these tensions, dangers, and pitfalls may encompass.

The danger of losing the ICL perspective

The danger of losing the ICL perspective is given if a certain type or tradition of critique is employed as a blueprint, thereby ignoring or sidelining the specificity of ICL. CAICL is undoubtedly associated with critical legal studies (CLS), new approaches to international law (NAIL), third world approaches to international law (TWAIL), and similar critical legal theory traditions and movements. Yet, CAICL is also distinct from these traditions, not only in regard to its subject matter. The named critical traditions all employ the above-mentioned technique of questioning assumptions in regard to legal claims.[1] They share the idea that within legal claims are embedded moral, epistemological and empirical assumptions; and they share the aim of examining these assumptions in terms of how they operate in the specific setting in which the legal claim is made, particularly to expose the interest of a stakeholder.[2] There are variations in terms of which frame should be employed to understand that or those who have been privileged. For example, an ideology critique, a class critique, a political economy critique, a feminist critique, or a combination of these.

While the literature and tradition drawn on is inspired by the critical traditions in international law and law in general, these traditions should neither be viewed as having authoritative power on determining what is critical, nor be viewed as setting the agenda for a critique of ICL. As Tallgren states in Chapter 3: 'Critical genealogies are likely to have their own empty spaces and silences.' Undoubtedly, the unearthing of the assumptions on which the practices that we accept rest, brings the question of the role of law itself to the fore. Yet, if we (as those associating with CAICL) allow the object of critique to be determined through a general critique of law and society, we may miss important sites of critique which are particular to ICL, and we may also miss the possibilities which lie within ICL. In addition, employing a blueprint of critique risks the community of critical scholars being viewed as academic vultures picking one by one on the carcasses of (international) legal fragmentation. International criminal law today, international investment law tomorrow, then international environmental law. Being aware of the danger of losing perspective hopefully reminds us what it is specifically about ICL that needs to be critiqued, but also why it is worthwhile critiquing ICL.

I would like to suggest that what makes it worthwhile is that there are possibilities within ICL: opportunities for justice. These opportunities still seem vague and blurry to me, but there are some moments in which the view appears to sharpen. For example, Frédéric Mégret argues that despite the problematic bias towards individual reparations, one can make a case for collective reparations before the ICC, and therewith potentially evoke a rethinking of the distribution of goods within ICC reparations awards. He argues that collective reparations would be 'awarded to a group or category of persons as such (e.g. a particular ethnic, racial, political, religious group, or "civilians"), quite independently of the group or category's legal existence' (Mégret 2014). The relative newness of the discipline, the few reparations awards so far, and the little case law on the matter could allow for mechanisms which defy the ideological and cultural bias for individualism. Mégret explains that collective reparations provide an opportunity, 'an opportunity to construct the "collective" in a manner that is sound from the point of view of international criminal justice' (2014: 6). In the first chapter of this collection, Mégret sets out some additional possibilities for international criminal justice.

It therewith emerges that an assumptions critique is not simply about rejectionism, it is also about a political project. In other words, the critical project is not simply about negating, but rather about '*understanding international criminal justice differently*' (Mégret, Chapter 1, emphasis added). Such commitment is tremendously difficult, particularly since it takes one down the slippery terrain of doctrine and normativity, and ultimately (maybe) hypocrisy and complicity. Yet, a 'critical approach' is and should also openly be a political project; political here refers to decisions concerning the allocation of available goods and opportunities. This suggests that the testing of assumptions from the epigraph is therefore perhaps the first step rather than the destination. The political project arguably *begins* with an understanding of critique noted in the epigraph.

The danger of introspection

The other extreme to losing the ICL perspective, namely an orientation which narrows the understanding of ICL, presents a further danger: the danger of introspection. Trying to come to grips with what critique means, working on an identity, maybe even wanting to establish a 'movement' from within ICL, could lead to a detachment from the contexts within which we are working. There are two possible scenarios of introspection. First, there seems to be a gravitational pull towards internal politics of a 'movement' taking prominence over external politics; and second, introspection could lead to the furthering and establishment of a separate discipline within the discipline of ICL, condemning critique to remain trapped in the minds of academics–never to be lived.

It was already evident in Liverpool that the scholars present understood themselves as belonging to different 'schools of thought'. Essentially, the 'crits' were at loggerheads with the 'non-crits'. And within the crits, there was a mutual suspicion of the political agenda pursued. Identities were already set. This in itself is and should be neither surprising nor problematic. Yet, the hardening and institutionalization of such identities could be problematic. A high degree of introspection (an obsession with international politics, if you will) can lead to the institutionalization of critique. In 1990, Mark Tushnet stated in regard to CLS: 'the project of critical legal studies does not have any essential intellectual component' (Tushnet 1991: 1516). Yet, that statement was arguably proved wrong. CLS has become increasingly institutionalized and therewith, although partly vigorously disputed, undoubtedly has an essential intellectual component. It has developed a language which allows those who speak it to be part of it, and those who do not to be excluded. There are particular journals, institutions and academic commanders who set the parameters and boundaries of the movement. Arguably, this is inevitable of any movement, even one which has 'indeterminacy' and 'class' as its critical foci. A critical research project, also one on the Left, must therefore be wary of the possible emphases and exclusions it creates. The objective is for the CAICL research project to be allowed to grow organically; as a forum which offers scholars and practitioners a space to drift in and out of depending on their current interest or grievance in ICL. Yet, organic does not necessarily mean elusive and impalpable. If CAICL is to have an impact and a longer-lasting resonance, some parameters must be defined. Akbar Rasulov has commented that the effect of a tradition of thought over time depends in part on the creation of sufficiently steady social networks (Rasulov 2012). Sufficiently steady social networks require at the very least a loose common understanding. This in turn engages the risk of essentializations and slippage into a branding language which operates through simplified messages and sacrifices content over image (Schwöbel, Chapter 12).

A further danger relating to introspection is if the expression of critique is located exclusively within the legal academy. Richard W. Bauman noted his dissatisfaction with the CLS tradition's creation of a paradox in 'the form of critical legal authors calling for an appreciation of law as deeply political while refusing on principle to disclose in detail their substantive political views' (Bauman 2002: 124). It appears crucial that the political project of CAICL should be animated before it is silenced through the creation of an inanimate sub-discipline of ICL.

The danger of complicity

Engagement and political projects bring with them the danger of complicity (Farrell, Chapter 4). In how far does an engaged critique (a dialectic between practice and theory) strengthen precisely those structures which it aims to unsettle? Undoubtedly, doctrinal arguments are often informed by and disguise ideological thinking. Indeed, Gerry Simpson commented (partly in jest) that the most radical approach for a CAICL project would be to stop the project immediately. How does the critic avoid a failure to see their own role in creating and perpetuating the structures of repression?

In addition to complicity, employing critique as a methodology, an orientation or an agenda may lead to critics' hubris. Critics could be tempted to view themselves as outside of the very context they are interrogating: the academic in the ivory tower. Although such an academic will argue against an 'objective' standpoint in the law, they view themselves as able to adopt an 'objective' view.

In how far, then, do we need to find a way of navigating complicity and hubris? I do not purport to have a definitive answer to this. Constantly testing one's assumptions, revealing one's agenda, and a sustained discomfort with prescription are, in my view, the means to address inevitable complicity (Schwöbel 2013). For CAICL, this involves a continuous questioning of the political project, an awareness of the silences which it may foster, and the exclusions – or gaps – which it creates (Odumosu 2008: 475, in regard to TWAIL). Such a self-reflective attitude towards critique is 'meant to foreground our own stakes in this work rather than adopting a removed, "objective", "scientific" standpoint' (Kendall, Chapter 2).

The danger of instrumentalizing the object of critique

A further danger in critique is the possible instrumentalizing of those 'we' want to speak for. If academics, practitioners, and civil society members speak for the Other, be that victims of international crimes, women who are disadvantaged by the gendered language of ICL, or the accused, it is important to be wary of instrumentalizing tendencies. There is a temptation to overstate, to essentialize, to provoke, or to shock in order to make a point. Those practising critique are often in a privileged position, living in comfortable circumstances, able to travel, enjoying institutional support for their work – this is by and large true for the contributors to this collection. In my view, this does not mean that we cannot practise critique; but it does require great sensitivity. We need to be aware of the narratives which we create and the stories we spin. Too often, African victims of mass crimes, or even simply Africans, are portrayed with the clichéd AK-47, prominent ribs, naked breasts (Wainaina 2012). These make 'good' victims – they are vulnerable and fearful. Yet this generalization is not only patronizing, it also risks the creation of a market of victims, in which each victim is assessed according to their value: the more vulnerable and fearful the higher their value (Green 2007: 112). Such commodification of victims solidifies an essentialized view of victimhood and locks victims in a marketplace in which business and agencies compete for the best-value victim (2007: 113). The selected issues are extremely difficult to navigate. When acting as a voice for strangers' concerns, a high level of self-awareness as well as attention to context is crucial. All in all, the listed dangers highlight that being on the side of the critics is not to be equated with being on the side of the angels.

Roadmap

Part I of the book examines the need for critique and the agenda of critique in international criminal law. Frédéric Mégret begins the section and this collection with an outline of a critical research agenda. Mégret analyses ten critical motifs, outlining in turn the critical charge, the liberal response, the questions of a critical project, and finally further directions for rethinking international criminal justice. He concludes with some thoughts on the dialectics of irrelevance/absorption of the critic, asking how one can keep a critical distance yet not forfeit the desire for change.

Chapter 2 enquires into critique as an ethical orientation for addressing international criminal law. Sara Kendall directs the critical lens to one of the field's central institutional sites of production, namely the ICC. She calls for a focus on who and what is excluded in the wider field of international criminal justice, a focus on who has suffered but falls outside institutional frameworks of redress, as well as the uncovering of the political and material conditions which allow for 'great criminality' to happen.

In Chapter 3, Immi Tallgren asks the question of who 'we' are in international criminal law. She first examines the 'ICL we' which speaks in relation to a higher subject, often 'humanity'. She then turns her attention to the 'critical we' in ICL, articulating a certain discomfort with the possible assumption that the 'critical we' could, in contrast to the 'ICL we', be power-neutral, sincere, egalitarian and simply correct.

Chapter 4 by Michelle Farrell delves deeper into the question of where the critic stands *vis-à-vis* the critique. How far are they complicit in the reproduction of those structures which they purport to overcome? Is it possible to practise critique without complicity? Does practising critique itself create suffering?

The second part of the book engages with the politics of international criminal law, endeavouring to go further than simply stating that 'international criminal law is political'. Indeed Tor Krever, in Chapter 5, begins this part by enquiring whether the statement 'international criminal law is political' in fact acts as a screen, exhausting all possible forms of critique and preventing further investigation into the deeper political meaning of a trial. He illustrates that the critique of the political nature of ICL assumes that ICL *can* and *should* be apolitical, and therefore reproduces the image of a neutral trial.

The next chapter, by Heidi Matthews, applies the critique of depoliticization to the Special Tribunal for Lebanon, in particular to the tribunal's *Ayyash* case. In this case, the Appeals Chamber (upholding the Trial Chamber decision) held that it was incompetent to review UN Security Council resolutions and therewith refused to review the establishment of the tribunal. Matthews argues that this refusal is employed as a technique by which the tribunal attempts to formally distance its work from political questions, thereby upholding a strategic and artificial distinction between law and politics.

Part III of the collection revisits the discipline's accepted history with a critical eye. Gerry Simpson examines the historical narratives which are privileged through international criminal tribunals. These biases include individualized historical narratives (a 'Great Man' theory of history) over structural histories; linear over fragmentary or chaotic histories; and hegemonic histories which celebrate agency over counter-hegemonic, social, accounts. He examines how moments of institutional decision provide an 'official' narrative of geopolitical trends or national struggle or the very meaning of the 'international'.

Chapter 8, by Emily Haslam, picks up on some of these biases, noting them as 'silences' in the way in which the history of the discipline is told. She argues that popular historical accounts gloss over questions regarding African agency in the development of international criminal law as well as the relationship between European colonialism and ICL. Haslam employs the example of a nineteenth-century trial of a slave trader Joseph Peters to demonstrate the multifaceted and complex narratives of abolition. It is suggested that writing abolition litigation into international criminal legal histories can transform the dominant progressive and linear accounts of victims' rights in ICL into a complex account of potential continuities and ruptures.

Grietje Baars closes this section of the book with an examination of how lawyers congeal capitalism through the production of knowledge, and here specifically ICL knowledge. She begins with a typology of four mainstream approaches of ICL's foundational narrative. In doing so, she evokes the possible sites of critique which are trapped within their respective approaches – which she calls 'pre-fab' critiques. This forecloses any critique which could reach beyond these approaches, in particular a critique which would expose the function of ICL in neoliberal governance and the capitalist mode of production.

The fourth and final part of the collection employs some of the above themes of the politics of international criminal law as well as its accepted history to reflect on what is commonly rendered visible and what is rendered invisible in ICL. In Chapter 10, Christopher Gevers questions the individualism of the international criminal law project, particularly in reference to concerns of African states. He examines the centrality of individualism in regard to the field's histories, purpose and its 'performance', contextualizing each aspect through an African perspective. Gevers demonstrates how the 'politics of individualism' blunts, misrepresents, distorts or dismisses African states' concerns about the international criminal justice project.

In the next chapter, Michelle Burgis-Kasthala considers the purview of international criminal law through the lens of the establishment of the Special Tribunal for Lebanon. She examines how and why the killing of Lebanon's former Prime Minister Rafiq Hariri prompted the establishment of an international tribunal. She argues that internationalization, depoliticization and naturalization are employed as international law narrative devices to transform political events; these devices allow for some things to be *seen* and others to remain *unseen.*

In the final chapter, I aim to make visible the underlying neoliberal logic of ICL. I argue that the field is committed to growth (its market culture) and branding (its marketing culture), both central paradigms of neoliberalism. Parallels are drawn between the means and methods of growth of capital and of ICL. In terms of branding, I demonstrate how ICL has placed undue emphasis on image at the expense of substance. Finally, I argue that this commitment to neoliberalism is strengthening big power-players, while at the same time claiming to fight them. The very group in whose interest the fight is supposedly being fought (the victims of international crime) is seemingly losing out.

The epilogue to the book is a poem by Johannes C.S. Frank, presented at the conference in Liverpool. 'Bella. A Love Song for War' touches on the themes of violence, gender bias, hegemony and exclusions through a poetic form. The poem not only resonates with the themes explored in the above chapters; it also offers an alternative mechanism for entering into critique.

Common ground

In this collection, there are some common themes which emerge for CAICL. It is worth noting these common themes in order to gain a sense of the self-understanding of those scholars associating with CAICL. As Michael Fakhri wrote of TWAIL, CAICL itself has no agency – it cannot do anything itself (2012: 10). It is a forum to speak *in* as well as *from*. Yet, while each contributor has their own research and political commitments, agendas and trajectories, there is some kind of 'glue'. This common ground is not set in stone; it is temporary, contingent, and carries different meanings for each participant. However, for this collection, it is distinctive.

First, there is a common theme of sensitivity to ideology. Several chapters highlight that the universals employed in international criminal law are determined through the dominant ideology – whether one may call that liberalism, neoliberalism or capitalism. There is a common wariness in regard to absolute moral sentiments which emanate from ICL's centre, The Hague, the scholars and practitioners from the Global North. In this collection, such moral sentiments and their seemingly naturalized meanings are both questioned and unsettled.

Second, a common theme is the suspicion of popular historical narratives. In particular, a suspicion of historical accounts which treat the past and present as part of a progress narrative can be discerned. Not only in Part III of this collection, which is dedicated to history, is this suspicion voiced. The contributions share the intention to unsettle the assumption that the present is part of a pattern in which the past has been overcome. Presenting the present as a culmination of continuous achievements of law and lawyers is self-serving of those in the centre in that it paints their history as one of success. It condemns those in the periphery to remain in the sidelines – or to assimilate to the centre if they wish to be a part of the success story.

There is also a common literature evident, as already briefly mentioned above. While reading through the contributions in the editing process, I was struck by just how much overlap between the sources and references there is. Naturally, there is going to be a certain common bibliography due to the collaborative nature of this collection, not to mention the bibliography which was compiled for the CAICL website;[3] however, the relatively small CAICL canon is striking. Whether this is testament to the – as yet – relatively small available commentary on critical approaches to ICL, or whether this is due to a more reified common ground and orientation than we would like to admit, is up to the reader to decide. Notwithstanding the previous point about the common literature, the chapters in this collection draw from various disciplines, including political theory, anthropology, philosophy, criminology and fiction; and the approaches are wide-ranging, drawing from historical sources, interviews from field research and anecdotes. The relatively little doctrinal law is notable (although not surprising).

Then, there is a common attitude which should be highlighted: all contributions are self-conscious, even anxious, about the employment of a 'critical approach' and what this means. Although we have gathered under an acronym, we are not quite comfortable with this association. However, there is also an appeal to the acronym. Susan Marks observed in regard to the 'naming' of Global Administrative Law, there is 'something about the act of naming that seems to work a kind of magic' (Marks 2005: 995). And this is certainly true for CAICL. The acronym allows us to highlight the 'systemic significance of events' (2005: 995) in ICL – the systemic use of absolute moral sentiments which remain untested, the systemic rhetoric of a division between law and politics, the systemic silencing of voices which ought to be heard. Further, it allows the mobilization of a 'constituency for investigation, action, and institutional change' (2005: 995). This may be a scholarly intervention, interventions through litigation, or civil society mobilization. However, there are also downsides to 'naming', in the gathering under an acronym, which the contributors to this collection are all too aware of. The possible reifying effects of pinning down sites of interrogation can lead to (unintended) privileging of some issues and the exclusion of others. This can simply occur through the participants' respective expertise. In this collection, issues of political economy have, for example, been emphasized due to the contributors' expertise in this area. This is not to say that a class, race or gender critique is less important. Thankfully, Marks states that '[t]hese reifying effects are not inevitable'; however, she adds that 'it does take a conscious effort to keep conflict and contingency in view' (2005: 996). Indeed, viewing them as inevitable would have a paralysing effect. Duncan Kennedy's words resonate with me here:

> It is crucial to form coalitions based on relatively vague consensus that things should be different, and it is a mistake to carry programmatic thinking to the point of hardness where it excludes potential allies. But it is never too early to start building a much sharper consensus about what we would do if we could.
>
> (Kennedy 1982: 613)

Routes ahead

In the closing paragraphs of this opening piece, it should be emphasized that this is an 'Introduction' to CAICL; the possible themes explored are not comprehensively represented in this collection; and the contributors welcome and look forward to further engagement with the themes that they have introduced here. To me, the organic nature of CAICL (its body of scholarship and its body of scholars) is and ought to be one of its main attributes. This is part and parcel of the conscious effort 'to keep conflict and contingency in view' (Marks 2005: 996).

Importantly, the scholarly contributions in this collection invite not only other themes but also other and further forms of intervention. This collection comprises scholarly visions of critical approaches to international criminal law, which can no less be understood as political interventions. They are interventions, first and foremost, in knowledge production. What further political projects may entail remains to be determined – it could mean interventions through litigation, discussions with practitioners, thinking critically about teaching ICL and the impact teaching has on the next generation of international lawyers, interventions in the mainstream media, activism. All this is for the future and goes beyond the remit of what we were trying to achieve with an 'Introduction'. But, I think those associating with CAICL would agree with me that CAICL comprises both a scholarly community and a political project.

Notes

1   Interestingly, both CLS and NAIL have been proclaimed 'dead'.
2   The origins of the CLS movement are sometimes placed as beginning with Duncan Kennedy at Harvard Law School and Mark Tushnet at Georgetown University Law Centre, sometimes as beginning with the first Conference on

Critical Legal Studies at the University of Wisconsin at Madison (1977). The British CLS movement is often placed with thinkers and in scholarship at Birkbeck, particularly with the establishment of the annual Critical Legal Conference.

3   www.caicl.org.

Bibliography

Amnesty International (2013) 'African States Must Reject Calls to Withdraw from the ICC'. Available at: www.amnesty.org/en/news/african-states-must-reject-calls-with-draw-icc-2013-10-10.

Bauman, R.W. (2002) *Ideology and Community in the First Wave of Critical Legal Studies*, Toronto: University of Toronto Press.

Fakhri, M. (2012) 'Introduction – Questioning TWAIL's Agenda', *Oregon Review of International Law* 14: 1–15.

Foucault, M. (1988) 'Practicing Criticism' (trans. A. Sheridan *et al.*) in L.D. Kritzman (ed.) *Politics, Philosophy, Culture: Interviews and Other Writings, 1977–1984*, New York: Routledge, pp. 152–8.

Green, S. (2007) 'Crime, Victimisation and Vulnerability', in S. Walklate (ed.) *Handbook of Victims and Victimology*, Cullompton: Willan Publishing, pp. 91–117.

Kennedy, D. (1982) 'Legal Education and the Reproduction of Hierarchy', *Journal of Legal Education* 32: 591–613.

Marks, S. (2005) 'Naming Global Administrative Law', *New York University Journal of International Law and Politics* 37: 995.

Mégret, F. (2014) 'The Case for Collective Reparations Before the ICC', in J.-A. Wemmers (ed.) *Reparations for Victims of Crimes Against Humanity*, Oxford: Routledge (forthcoming).

Nouwen, S. and Werner, W. (2011) 'Doing Justice to the Political', *European Journal of International Law* 21: 941–65.

Odumosu, I.T. (2008) 'Challenges for the (Present/) Future of Third World Approaches to International Law', *International Community Law Review* 10: 467–77.

Rasulov, A. (2012) 'New Approaches to International Law: Images of a Geneology', in J.M. Beneyto and D. Kennedy (eds), *New Approaches to International Law: The European and the American Experiences*, The Hague: TMC Asser-Springer, pp. 151–91.

Schwöbel, C. (2013) 'The Comfort of International Criminal Law', *Law and Critique* 24: 169–91.

Tushnet, M. (1991) 'Critical Legal Studies: A Political History', *Yale Law Journal* 100: 1515–46.

Wainaina, B. (2012), 'How to Write about Africa', *Granta*. Available at: www.granta.com/Archive/92/How-to-Write-about-Africa/Page-1 (accessed 27 November 2013).

Part I

Critique as an agenda

Chapter 1

International criminal justice

A critical research agenda

Frédéric Mégret

Introduction: situating critical approaches to international criminal justice

This chapter seeks to outline the broad contours of what might be described as a critical project in international criminal justice. This is a delicate exercise because it is hardly clear that there is a unified critical project when it comes to international criminal justice. Moreover, there is always a risk of being either over-inclusive or under-inclusive. In the former case, the specificity of the critique risks being minimized; in the latter case, more or less arbitrary distinctions are made that will exclude worthwhile intellectual ventures.

Perhaps a good starting point is that there is such a thing as an international criminal justice project. That project is both political and legal and has occupied a very distinctive place in the history of international law, international relations and of particular societies in the last 25 years. Although diverse and not without its contradictions, it includes a series of recognizable features, including the centrality of individual guilt, the need to respect the rights of the defence both procedurally and substantively, a commitment to international institutions of criminal justice, and a rhetoric that foregrounds the needs of 'humanity' over sovereignty. Thinking about a parallel 'critical' project, then, may be a way of better understanding the sort of reactions and contextualizations that international criminal justice has engendered.

There has been much support for institutions of international criminal justice, so that a great deal of the commentary on the issue can be said not to be particularly critical in any way, sometimes even celebratory. A typical conceit in the field is the idea that the 'problems' that international criminal justice faces come above all from outside it, notably state sovereignty. The movement itself is pure, free of the compromises of power, sure of its mission. As time has passed, however, and as the need to uphold the requirement for international criminal justice at all costs in order to adopt the Rome Statute has receded, it is only normal that actual, institutionalized international criminal justice has come in for more criticism. An early point worth making is that at a certain level, almost everyone is 'critical' of international criminal justice in some way or other. That is, there are few pure apologists, nor could one be a consistent apologist without running into contradictions, for there have been all kinds of forms of international criminal justice, some of which must surely be less worthy of praise than others. Certainly, scholarship on international criminal justice is almost always critical of something about its operation, or it would not be of much interest.

But there is a risk that if 'critical' just becomes another word for 'analytical' or 'opinionated', then the word will lose much of its relevance. Not all critical points evidence a significantly critical stance. Much of the criticism directed at international criminal justice is, in fact, rather pragmatic, instrumental and policy-oriented. It is part of a rolling exercise that is constantly updated based on the concern of the moment. Much of this type of criticism is in a very traditional legal vein, to the effect that international criminal tribunals have got the law wrong, or at least not as right as they could have. There are some, for example, who will criticize the International Criminal Tribunal for the former Yugoslavia (ICTY) for engaging in judge-made law, when reviewing the legality of its own creation or extending international crimes to non-international armed conflicts based on a shaky concept of custom (Milanovic 2012). Another body of criticism targets international tribunals' perceived lack of 'efficiency' (Meernik and King 2001). Tribunals come in for regular reproach for not doing enough of something, for example not having prosecuted enough individuals quickly enough. Finally, there is much policy criticism of various decisions by international criminal prosecutors, for example of going for prioritizing relatively 'small fish' in a way that does not seem to make sense of scarce resources or for relying on secondary sources for investigations (Stuart 2008).

This is, in other words, criticism aimed at making institutions of international criminal justice 'the best that they can be'. This is the most internal, even intimate, type of criticism in that it pictures itself as a sort of adjunct of international criminal justice, much in the same way that doctrinal commentators have often thought of themselves in relation to the main body of legal developments. It typically takes the 'big questions' as answered and works from within the limitations that are more or less taken for granted and not even necessarily seen as problematic. It is a useful form of 'accompaniment criticism', a pragmatic engagement with the difficult exercise of making practice conform to ambitions, of wrestling with the world's complexity and the challenge of any institution building. But to describe it as a critique in the deeper sense might be misleading, because of the way in which the criticism is so invested in being part of what it criticizes. It is often tempted by a managerial discourse in which certain typical policy prescriptions ('the tribunals should ensure consistency', 'more efforts should be undertaken to outreach', 'the nullum crimen principle should be strictly adhered to', 'tribunals should be independent/impartial') are suggested time and time again as the way to solve existing problems. Noticeably, such criticism engages in forms of discourse that are not fundamentally different from those of tribunals themselves.

At a more systemic level, one might highlight the existence of two strands of critique that evidence a clearer conceptual ambition: the realist and the liberal. There is, and has long been, to begin with, a realist critique of international criminal justice, both in law and international relations.[1] Even though that critique has in practice become much more muted when it comes to institutions like the International Criminal Court (ICC), it still often seems to act as an implicit reference point in many discussions about the court. The realist critique is part of a broader tradition of scepticism, particularly about international judicial institutions. It is typically sceptical that international criminal tribunals can be created at all; if they are created that they stand for the lofty ideals that they claim to stand for; and whether they are desirable at all. The deeper point that an international criminal law 'cannot be said to exist' in a world of states was made energetically for a long time (Schwarzenberger 1950). Although it is less convincing with the emergence of several international criminal tribunals, it does raise interesting questions about the nature of these tribunals that will be further discussed in this chapter. For example, some have argued that the ICC is essentially futile given how improbable it is that states likely to commit international crimes would become parties to the Rome Statute (Goldsmith 2003).[2] The normative argument on the undesirability of international criminal justice has been made by various realists. For Kissinger, writing on universal jurisdiction, international criminal justice introduces a dangerous moralizing element in international law, and risks interfering with the practice of diplomacy (Kissinger 2001). Although that argument is quite wedded to a conservative view of the world, it is interesting for the purposes of this chapter because of the way it more generally challenges international criminal justice's implicit claim to a monopoly of international ethics.

Much more dominant than the realist critique and in part a response to it is a fairly popular *liberal* critique of international criminal justice. From early critiques of 'victors' justice', to detailed concerns with almost every conceivable aspect of international criminal tribunals' operation, the liberal critique of international criminal justice is very much alive. It is a critique that has targeted every facet of international criminal law: international, criminal procedural and criminal substantive. Internationally, the reproach has long been that international criminal justice is too wedded to political power and must be emancipated from it. International tribunals must be independent and impartial, as must those working for them; the preference is for permanent rather than ad hoc institutions. Procedurally, every conceivable critique has been levelled at international criminal tribunals from the days when the ICTY started hearing anonymous witnesses, to the failure of the tribunals to honour the highest evidentiary standards, through problems of representation, preventive detention, presumption of innocence, right to a trial within a reasonable delay, and so on. Substantively, there is by now a well-developed but nonetheless lively debate on the substantive justice of international criminal law, particularly focused on modes of imputation of responsibility.

This is an evidently necessary type of criticism and the temptation of thinking that international criminal tribunals will engage in liberal practices simply because they emerged from broadly liberal premises should be strongly resisted. In fact, there is every reason to believe that international criminal tribunals have been singularly illiberal in some instances, even though there is occasionally an element of holier-than-thou in some of the complaints against them that seems to idealize the functioning of domestic criminal justice. Yet precisely because it seems to adopt many of the same starting assumptions that the international criminal justice project at least explicitly endorses (Fichtelberg 2008), the strength of its critical thrust remains relatively limited. The liberal critique of international criminal justice is essentially a critique of international criminal tribunals not striving enough to be their liberal selves, of not 'being more like themselves' as they should be. It is typically, moreover, what one might call an optimistic or at least existentially serene critique ('insightful (but) not structural' as Mark Drumbl once put it) (Drumbl 2005: 1304) in that it does not point to anything fundamentally wrong with the project that cannot be fixed through continuous attention to rules and policies. Its attempt to pose as an external critique quickly collapses and makes it appear as little more than a principle-oriented version of the more pragmatic variant of criticism outlined earlier.

Together, the realist and liberal critiques have been very central historically to the development of the international criminal justice project. One might even argue that, in tandem, they have framed a range of acceptable critiques that may have made it harder for other critical traditions to manifest themselves. The sort of critical project this chapter is interested in is neither liberal nor realist. It is at a distance from the liberal critique because although it is not necessarily illiberal (in the sense, for example, that it would exhibit a Churchillian preference for war criminals being shot), and may certainly concede that international criminal trials may as well occur in ways that respect the rights of the accused, it considers that part of the problem of international criminal justice lies precisely in its excessive embeddedness within the liberal paradigm. It is at a distance from the realist critique because while it is quite willing to acknowledge that there is more to international criminal justice than the liberal tales that are spun about it and has some sympathy with the notion of the state as a bulwark against internationalist imperialism, it does not think that international judicial institutions' constraining of sovereignty or nationhood is the most relevant or incisive critique to be made about the project. In contrast to realism, this chapter will consider that the power of institutions of international criminal justice is very real; in contrast to liberalism, it will consider that this power is not merely restrained but in fact also enabled by liberal rules.

So what is it that characterizes the particular project that this chapter seeks to examine? It may be that the common point is a particular tone, one that is best described as ambivalent, sceptical, or uneasy about some aspects of international criminal justice. It is therefore not as dismissive as the realist but certainly not as optimistic as the liberal. Where the latter sees novelty, progress, transcendence and better tomorrows, the critical project is likely to see repetition, stagnation, reproduction and ideology. The project is also less concerned than liberals with issues of legal consistency and predictability, and wary of what typically passes for positivism. It typically sees the problems with international criminal justice as not of the type that can be fixed by further attention to details, but that may go to the heart of some of the project's premises. In other words, it tends to view the trouble with international criminal justice as inherent to the project itself, or at least running quite deep in the particular historical configuration within which international criminal justice has existed and continues to exist.

Critique is a project that exhibits a certain aesthetics of suspension. Although it does not shun normative judgment, it is critical of even its own normative judgment; although it does not shun action, it is wary of the normalized appetite for action; although it is not without beliefs, it spends a lot of time dealing with its sense of disbelief. The critical project is not, essentially, an *alternative* project understood as a fully developed anti-hegemony, and thus in a sense has nothing to 'offer' in the rather brutally limited sense that the expression is often understood. Rather than 'improving', it is interested in 'understanding', and more specifically in 'understanding understanding' or understanding 'the relation of knowledge to power such that our epistemological certainties turn out to support a way of structuring the world that forecloses alternative possibilities of ordering' (Butler 2004). In other words, what is at stake is international criminal justice's politics of truth and the political economy of its knowledge production (who gets to define the doxic debate, through what journals and publications, with a view to convincing who). The project, in Foucault's terms, is one of 'how not to be governed' (Foucault 1990) in a particular way, which in the world this book and its authors inhabit might mean something like 'how not to be governed by the rules and fantasies of a globalized criminal legal mind and its stranglehold on progressist imaginations'. Its tools include those, in no particular order, of epistemological deconstruction, historicization, law and literature and law and popular culture, interdisciplinarity, and field analysis.

In the following, ten critical motifs are examined with a view to providing a simultaneously panoramic and multilayered view of the richness of the critical project in international criminal justice (for a similar exercise in international human rights law, see Mégret 2013a). The headings of the sections draw loosely on a style popularized by David Kennedy, who has been a considerable influence (although by no means the only one) on several involved in developing critical themes in international criminal justice, and certainly on this author (Kennedy 2002). In each case, I outline the heart of the critical charge, what a liberal response to it might be and how it differs from this project, as well as some key references and further directions for rethinking international criminal justice. Some of the ideas have been extensively developed and correspond to well-known situated strands of critique, and others less so. I make no pretence that the views presented exhaust the critique, or indeed that these different strands are fully or even at all reconcilable. Indeed, names will be dropped who might be surprised to be in each other's company, who may self-describe as critical or not (needless to say, one may be critical without endorsing any 'crit' label), and in some ways at odds with each other. The general aim is to be more rather than less inclusive. It is hoped that the chapter can in the process shed light on the subtlety of the critique, its potential and its limitations, as well as help bring some of its salient themes to new audiences.

The chapter is also more incidentally an opportunity to synthesize and reflect on some of my own academic work in the last 15 years, since working as a minor intern to the French delegation at the ICC conference, an opportunity that provided me with invaluable insights on the cuisine that goes into cooking an international treaty, as well as intimate knowledge of the lost luggage section of Fiumiccino airport. Since an early rant on what I perceived as the flaws of the ICC (Mégret 2002), I have been interested in seeking to understand what the significance of international criminal justice is for international law and relations, seeking to both keep my distance from the project and engage with it.

International criminal justice is a form of power that does not say its name

Perhaps the starting point in the critique of international criminal justice is the extent to which it is, irrepressibly so, a form of power. To this day, this is counter-intuitive for many proponents of international criminal justice who see it as threatened by the powers that be (sovereigns, the Security Council, even international civil society), and have become accustomed to portraying international criminal tribunals as outliers in international relations. It is certainly the case that international criminal tribunals remain susceptible to the power of others. But while international criminal tribunals may not have quite the power that some of their more cosmopolitan proponents would want them to have, it should by now be clear that the project has accumulated significant symbolic capital, and wields, in fact, quite considerable power. If not the power to keep others entirely at bay, it is at least the power to engage other powers on terms that are partly set by institutions of international criminal justice themselves.

The realization that international criminal justice is a form of power, then, is perhaps the most fundamental entry point for critique, for there would certainly be little point in critiquing a movement that was powerless. It is, as yet, only a partial form of critique because there is nothing necessarily wrong *per se* with power. What makes the exercise of that particular power a cause for critique is, aside from various possible uses that the rest of this chapter will detail further, the extent to which it does not say its name, does not reveal itself as such. Deep down in the international criminal justice mystique is the idea that, since international criminal justice is itself an attempt to constrain power, then it cannot be a form of power itself, or at least not of a similar kind.

It would be wrong, of course, to claim that international criminal justice enthusiasts do not have a concept of its power, but it is one that is essentially benign. The question is whether international criminal tribunals have the power to truly contribute to 'international peace and security', or 'post-conflict reconstruction', or 'reconciliation'. If they do not, then they can be faulted for 'not doing enough' or 'not doing well enough', but not for 'doing'. In the dominant view, there are no nefarious uses of international criminal justice's power. The only power that the liberal mind is keenly aware that it exercises is over individual defendants, so that excesses must be checked by appropriate protections and safeguards. But this power is understood in a typically narrow fashion, as if international trials were merely domestic trials, in isolation from the way in which prosecutions of individuals may have considerable consequences domestically and internationally. To sum up, minute attention to due process *vis-à-vis* individuals (in the best liberal case, of course) is simply not matched by attention to the other forms of power that international criminal tribunals may wield.

One of the essential and most urgent tasks for the critical project is to understand the nature of that power. I can only suggest a few leads here. Perhaps fundamentally, it is the power to frame certain problems as criminal law problems. In that respect, one has to recognize the quite remarkable success of international criminal lawyers in prompting many to view problems that were traditionally seen as problems of balance of power or of international peace and security or of domestic politics as essentially problems involving the criminal mind at work, and the need to sanction it through the use of certain elaborate penalization techniques. Although that transformation is by no means complete, it has seen the Security Council repeatedly speak the language of criminal accountability in the last 20 years, to the point of almost reinventing itself. It is no small feat, then, that even if for reasons that have to do with the council's own agenda, the international criminal justice project is both a consequence and a cause of significant semantic evolutions in international legal discourse.

The power of international criminal justice, moreover, is the power to designate the criminal. Even with broad agreement on the crimes, there remains considerable work to be done to identify who is actually worthy of condemnation or not. Of the thousands of cases that the ICC could prosecute in theory, the Prosecutor has to select a handful each year. Such a designation, moreover, has considerable implications not only for those accused, but for the lives of entire nations. For whatever the efforts to make individual responsibility appear just that, it is almost always likely to appear locally as based on particular reading of the relative guilt of different groups supporting the individuals in question (Mégret 2011a). In effect, the consequences of prosecutorial decisions to investigate or charge often go far beyond the individuals in question, and can have significant effect on conflict and post-conflict dynamics. Moreover, the decision about who to prosecute is almost as important for what it tells us about who is not being prosecuted (for example, Hirohito, Kagame, Bush).

Finally, and less symbolically, the power of international criminal justice is the power to inflict political costs to those who oppose it and, in the most extreme of cases, to unleash violence against the deviants (Mégret 2011b). That power is not unlimited, but nor is it negligible, especially as will be seen when it works in tandem with other sources of power. In that respect, international criminal justice manifests a renewed hegemonic ambition in international law, one that may unleash further considerable violence in the name of a new 'humanitarian order' (Mamdani 2008). Alongside arrest warrants come travelling limitation, financial sanctions, political ostracism, and the occasional kidnapping. Seeing these as manifestations of power rather than as legal techniques, then, can help problematize them as uses of power.

Beyond the goals of power, a critical project in international criminal justice will seek to understand how the power of international criminal tribunals is manifested, wielded and maximized. It would put at the heart of such a study a series of practices operating on the margin of the law, and which include the consolidation of the field, alliances, and shaming tactics (Peskin 2009). It will explore the extent to which power is, for example, never as strong as when it need not be used, and weak to the point of collapse when it relies only on legal injunction. In many ways, it would see international criminal tribunals as occasionally quite adept at exercising power and less despondent than the conventional image (Miller *et al.* 2011), even as that power then creates conundrums of its own.

International criminal justice ultimately expresses a form of politics that is remarkably rule-unbound

Potentially the one saving grace of international criminal justice as an otherwise considerable form of power is that it claims to be thoroughly rule-bound, so that its power is, in the end, a legal rather than a political one. It is true that international criminal trials give rise to carefully orchestrated legal rituals that emphasize almost scrupulous adherence to rules. In fact, the element of showcasing this adherence is arguably essential to the performative function of international criminal justice, and its ability to build up credibility, as evidenced in particular in increasingly lengthy and detailed judgments. International criminal justice is nothing if not rule-bound.

Yet there are reasons to believe that rules hardly have the last word in international criminal justice, or at least that their operation is impossible to understand without a significant background in the political dynamics of tribunals. The seemingly unmoored nature of much international criminal jurisprudence is often particularly decried in one context: that of sentencing, which regularly defies expectations in its seeming randomness (Holá 2012). Ultimately, it seems sentencing is extremely hard to pin down because of the element of hunch and intuition about the convicted involved, but also because of persistent uncertainties about the very goals and functions of international criminal justice that manifest themselves when the time comes to condemn individuals.

Yet rather than view sentencing's discretionariness as the exception, and rule bindingness as the norm, one might see the former as setting the tone for much of the practice of international criminal justice, even when it comes down to as central an issue as the determination of guilt or innocence. This is particularly true of substantive international criminal law. It goes further, moreover, than the usual argument about the 'novelty' of international criminal law engendering some temporary unpredictability in the law that is nonetheless quickly resolved after a few decisions. Rather, all major international offences are essentially constantly evolving and unstable categories, largely because of persistently unresolved underlying issues about the authority, nature and source of international criminal law. Take the meaning of as central an offence as genocide, for example. It is constantly subject to interpretation and disagreement. Which groups are protected? Can only states commit genocide? How should one evidence special intent? Can genocide be committed by killing only one individual? Of course, actual, 'authoritative' answers are arrived at. But these answers are never arrived at merely by inference from the rules; rather, they flow from a bizarre assemblage of traditional international sources reasoning, commitment to and faith in international criminal law, and subsuming of verdicts under overall implicit theories of what is at stake in international trials (Mégret 2014a).

More importantly, what defines the work of international criminal tribunals is not so much what happens in the courtroom as who ends up in the courtroom in the first place. The (apparent) legal normality of the trial, in the end, is derived from and almost entirely conditioned by the very exceptionality of the discretion over who should stand trial. The creation of a permanent ICC was supposed to have marginalized that element of discretion: instead, it has simply displaced it from some external political actor to the heart of the tribunal's operation. The exceptional power to decide who stands trial has become the rule. That element alone suggests a considerable space for a politics of international criminal justice that is hardly amenable to a legal formula. It implicitly portrays the ICC Prosecutor, for example, as a sort of sovereign, with the unique 'decisionist' ability to lay the foundations for the ongoing order of international criminal justice, in the context of a never-ending situation of emergency.

There has, of course, been a distinct (albeit relatively slow to express itself) liberal concern about the extent to which international criminal justice is hard to define through its rules. The apparent idiosyncrasy of prosecutorial decisions is combatted with suggestions about how prosecutorial policy could be more transparent and consistent. The emphasis on those 'most responsible for the worst crimes' provides a formula around which many will rally (Danner 2003). The Prosecutor of the ICC herself has shown a significant resolve to adopt guidelines outlining the sort of considerations that she will take into account in making decisions to prosecute. Yet aside from the factual challenge of determining, in advance of a trial, who is indeed most guilty, the point is that for all the apparent consensus on international crimes as categories, that consensus does collapse as soon as the question is asked who in particular was responsible for what in what context.[3] Given the only few dozen cases that international criminal tribunals can realistically hope to prosecute during their lifespan, the process by which courts sift through thousands if not hundreds of thousands of suspects is highly indebted to particular constructions of what are the worst crimes and the worst ways of participating in them that is ultimately so unconstrained as to be purely political.

For a 'crit', for whom rule-scepticism is almost second nature, this element of radical discretion as the very basis for the existence of ordered trials is not as troublesome as it is for the liberal mind. It may in fact herald a realization that politics and law cannot but move together, in ways that need to be better understood. But it does militate for accepting the politics of international criminal justice for what they are, and possibly for having a conversation about what these politics ought to be. There is room for a contextualization of international criminal law within politics that is neither fetishistic nor naively instrumental (Corten 2004; Snyder and Vinjamuri 2004). One should be wary of attempts to portray the problem of discretion under a technocratic light, merely as a problem that can be tackled by adopting appropriate guidelines. Contra the popular view that the prosecutor of an international criminal tribunal ought not to be political, a critical vision might on the contrary urge it to be political in ways that are emancipatory and progressive (Mégret 2014b). Generally, there is much need for scholarship, notably of an ethnological or anthropological sort, that seeks to better understand what is actually going on in international criminal tribunals beyond the dominant fascination with rule-following (Eltringham 2008, 2012; Mégret 2013b; Meierhenrich 2013).

International criminal justice rests on a precarious legitimacy

If not its adherence to rules, then the question of the ultimate foundation of international criminal justice is bound to be asked. Simply invoking the gravity of the crimes involved and the sacred consensus surrounding their condemnation will not suffice as everyone becomes aware that there is a considerable distance between the general denunciation of criminal categories and the highly connoted work of designating who will stand for trial. International criminal justice is thus on a constant search for legitimacy, one which nonetheless turns out to be forever unsatisfactory.

A very tempting way of grounding the legitimacy of international criminal tribunals is through the tried and tested route of state consent. The movement is always prompt to point out that states have ratified the Rome Statute and therefore in a sense brought upon themselves the calamities that they may subsequently complain of. Even in the case of the ICTY, which faced evident hostility from some dismembered former Yugoslav entities, much was made of the consent of Yugoslavia to the UN Charter more than four decades earlier – as if that had some sort of direct connection to the creation of the tribunal. But state consent of this kind is rather artificial. Even the formal consent of, say, African states to become parties to the Rome Statute may be the result of subtle and not so subtle pressures to ratify, and have been based on expectations that the court would behave quite differently. Ratification will suffice legally, but it can hardly be the end of the debate if a state manifests clear displeasure with prosecutions despite having ratified. Moreover, the invocation of ratification may be awkward in dictatorships or ill-functioning democracies where ratification is really *pro forma*. More importantly, there are well-known problems with invoking state consent to ground an enterprise as moralizing as international criminal justice (Koskenniemi 1990). Torture really ought to be an international crime even if a state has not ratified the torture convention or even if no conventional route could be found to establish its customary character.

Grounding international criminal justice in some higher demand of humanity or the laws of nature remains a strategy that is resorted to regularly, even if not quite explicitly. It was evident in the slightly quirky interest for the Martens clause in the 1990s, in particular by authors with significant responsibilities at the ICTY (Cassese 2000; Meron 2000), or in the tendency for some judges to engage in broad teleological jurisprudence that seemed to assume that we knew unproblematically what the *telos* of international criminal justice was. Certainly, the international community has never seemed as close to holding something to be an absolute truth that genocide is prohibited and is the gravest international crime today. But, as already seen, this apparent unanimity on empty vessels such as 'genocide', 'torture' or 'terrorism' is prone to break down rapidly under the pressure of concretization. Although international criminal justice thrives on the language of transcendence and faith (Tallgren 2002), it can only in the end preach to the converted in that language, and must make do with the rest of the world in terms that are much more characteristic of an older international law tradition.

There remains one possible source of legitimacy which international criminal justice cannot really invoke, namely its democratic character. There are always ways in which one can imagine oneself as having received a popular mandate from particular countries to try some of their nationals. That may well be in some cases, but the truth is that international criminal justice makes no particular effort to actualize these supposed manifestations of popular will and engage with the societies on the receiving end of international criminal justice in ways that would underscore a real accountability to them. International criminal tribunals largely consider themselves, instead, to be accountable to their parent bodies (states, the UN, the Security Council). In fact, one could argue that international criminal justice is ultimately deliberately anti-democratic, at least in the sense that it foregrounds an absolute obligation to prosecute certain crimes regardless of societies' complex deliberations on the issue. As such, international criminal justice replaces a principle of political and, ideally, democratic debate by one that is expert and law based. It risks foreclosing the possibility of transitional processes such as the South African one on the basis that they do not rise up to the obligation to prosecute rigidly understood. This is evidently a debated issue doctrinally but at any rate the significance of the change is that judges ultimately are called upon to arbitrate such life and death national decisions. Although there is some talk of making prosecutors accountable, this is typically never for the consequences of their most important political decisions.

After a while, international criminal justice may find itself drifting to legitimacy expedients such as the occasional manifestation of repentance by the accused (Mégret 2014c) or, more plausibly, the conveniently vague but pathos-inducing figure of the 'victim'. The victim has emerged as the ultimate bulwark of international criminal justice (Findlay 2009) in a context where international criminal tribunals cannot simply claim to be protecting an international public order. Victims are convenient in that many words and wishes can be attributed to them, even though the category is, at heart, problematic (what of victims that are also perpetrators? child soldiers?), and victims' wishes may be more complex than appears (what of victims who do not seek justice?) (see Michelle Farrell, Chapter 4 in this book). In fact, international criminal justice's commitment to victims is more to abstract than to concrete victims, the latter often appearing as a reminder of the messiness of concrete life and its disruptive potential for the narrativization of international criminal justice (Kendall and Nouwen 2013).

Ultimately, the temptation may be strong to conclude that the only real legitimacy of international criminal justice is the one that it manages to build for itself as a result of its particular power as a field and its ability to claim a certain degree of expertise (Glasius 2002) or pose as the arbiter of different forms of knowledge about crime, international relations and justice (Dixon and Tenove 2013). It thus tends naturally towards a self-referential and elite legitimacy, one driven by the needs of the discipline within which it is embedded.

International criminal justice reduces complex political and moral questions to simplistic legal formulas

There has long been a strand of discontentment with international criminal justice's tendency to reduce complex political and moral questions to simple legal formulas. In particular, international criminal justice's legal individualism may be at odds both with the need to account historically for atrocities and with moral exigencies (Mégret 2013c). International criminal justice is evidently committed to a strong idea of individual responsibility, linked to certain conceptions about human agency and volition, as well as a perceived need to avoid collective stigmatization (see Christopher Gevers, Chapter 10 in this book). This tendency is, if anything, reinforced by liberal principles regarding fair trial, and the efforts to disaggregate cases individually (Mégret 2011c). To those who take it to task for its weak historicization it typically retorts that its goal is not to tell history but simply – typically, more modestly – to ascertain individual guilt or innocence. But there are questions about whether it can even do one without the other and, at any rate, whether in doing the latter it is not inevitably participating in the former.

The problem is that international crimes are in essence mass crimes. They most often require considerable societal implication and almost always a heavy state or state-like organization. Considerable tensions arise between the emphasis on individual responsibility and the necessary systemic component of international crime commission. First, a series of complex legal and criminological problems complicate the task of adjudication. International criminal justice's emphasis on individual guilt in practice is in tension with the need to establish various 'policy' elements that seem to perpetually challenge its initial individualism. Although guilt may be individualizable, the idea that reparations for a particular crime are owed by a single individual to all its victims seems to lay blame excessively on one individual (Mégret 2010a).

Second, international criminal justice's individualism may hamper its ability to 'represent' the crimes that occurred from a historical and moral point of view (Mégret 2005b). The common confusion between guilt (with its *de minimis* causal threshold: X contributed in however small a manner to the genocide) and responsibility more generally (one is *responsible* for the genocide) may give the impression that a handful of individuals were guilty of much more than they can realistically be blamed for. International criminal justice is thus always at risk of confusing its normatively necessary presuppositions (freedom, individual agency) for analytically and descriptively pertinent propositions. As a result, it may end up producing a telling of history that endows individuals with larger than life characteristics (Simpson 2012), at the risk of regular Eichmannian counter-climaxes (Erdemovic, Akayesu, Lubanga, etc.). It will also perform individual guilt in a way that makes it seem to spring from some reservoir of evil, rather than misplaced political passions (extreme ethno-nationalism comes to mind) whose role in the production of atrocities is considerable.

As a consequence, international criminal justice may occasionally let states and society off the hook too easily and even delay a necessary realization of collective faults. This is paradoxical given how international criminal justice is typically conceived, in liberal terms, as a formidable incursion into state sovereignty; yet there is also something to the idea that individual responsibility in international criminal law is a way of relegating the issue of state responsibility and effectively protecting states by bypassing them altogether (Mégret 2001). A focus on individual responsibility may be appropriate in cases where individual agency was indeed essential, but it may obscure reality in cases where individuals received massive, sometimes democratic popular support. Although the Versailles treaty is often justly criticized for the broad opprobrium with which it painted the Germans, it seems that Nuremberg's focus on individuals also paved the way for the idea in post-war German public opinion that the Nazis had misled and betrayed the population (Burchard 2006).

International criminal justice's focus on individual agency may also lead to the marginalization of explanations of international crime that foreground the role of the international community. The international community is often the great absentee of international trials, except, of course, as the symbolic accuser. It is often as if it had no conceivable part in the occurrence of crimes. Hence questions of historical injustice, alliances and support of dictatorships, or failure to intervene are all carefully sidelined by the operation of international trials. Finally, international criminal justice is also weak on structural factors that would too directly contradict the notion of individual agency. In that context, problems of land distribution, urbanization, demographics, environmental degradation, systemic discrimination, alienation or class struggle are typically given short thrift.

There are, of course, some sophisticated mainstream answers to these dilemmas. More room can be made procedurally, for example, for persons and entities indirectly affected by indictments (Damaška 2012); considerable thought has gone into how to manage the essential *litispendance* of individual and collective responsibility in some cases (Nollkaemper 2003), to the point of suggesting that all individual responsibility in international law is a form of state responsibility (Maison and Leben 2004). Critical strands in international criminal justice might more resolutely challenge the very idea of individual responsibility, at least as an increasingly hegemonic feature of the international legal order by emphasizing the extent to which collectives are often quite good at finding the individuals they need to inflict harm and should shoulder a greater share of responsibility. The work of George Fletcher (2002), Mark Drumbl (2002), Larry Backer (2003), Kirsten Ainley (2006), or Andre Nollkaemper (2010) comes to mind.

International criminal justice is excessively universalistic/centralized and oblivious to pluralism

Few lines of inquiry have been as productive for the critique of international criminal justice than the concern that it is excessively universalistic and centralized. International criminal justice is at heart – like the international humanitarian and human rights projects from which it draws – a universalistic regime. Although it is not nonsensical to think of a regional criminal law (Burke-White 2003), the ambition behind the notion of 'crimes against humanity' is surely that these are crimes committed against the whole of mankind in at least some meaningful metaphorical sense. Moreover, albeit perhaps more reluctantly, international criminal justice is also a centralizing, centripetal project. It posits that the universality of international criminal justice will be best rendered by the existence of at least some central institutions of international criminal law, and is often contrasted, for example, with the 'second best' device of universal jurisdiction (Langer 2012). Much of the progress of international criminal justice, in fact, can be recounted as a tale of the gradual centralization of criminal repressive resources into international bodies. For all the talk of complementarity, there is a suspicion that many international criminal lawyers are, at heart, 'primacists' (David 1998).

Yet there inevitably arises a distance between such grand, overarching concepts and the proposal for their centralized promotion on the one hand, and the continuing reality of the world's pluralism on the other. International criminal justice is forever caught between the cosmopolitanism that the existence of its constitutive offences posits, and the reality of the international legal system within which it operates. Moreover, it is caught between the need to legitimize itself through appeals to a universal in order to argue against reluctant sovereigns, but equally to be seen as acceptable to the state and local populations by 'speaking their language'.

There are many angles from which these tensions can be envisaged. These include a tendency to view 'atrocities' in excessively universalistic fashion; for example, to see the Holocaust and the Rwandan genocide as part of the same, a-temporal phenomenon (genocide) in ways that minimize relevant differences between the two (Chrétien 1995). Another way of looking at the tension is as putting in play the rather contradictory perceptions of local constituencies (public opinion, victims) and the international community. The latter is tempted to see international crimes as above all crimes committed against an international public order rather than against actual constituted communities. This in turn exposes international criminal justice to persistent misunderstandings (Alvarez 1999). These may occur in the courtroom as witnesses confront an unfamiliar international legal system which they perceive as instrumentalizing them; or they may confront defendants who face accusations under modes of liability that are unfamiliar to them domestically; or they could occur at the sentencing stage when those convicted by international criminal tribunals face penalties that are significantly less severe than those they would have faced had they been condemned domestically. Institutionally, debates are at stake on what should be the limits of the ICC's tolerance, under its complementarity regime, for unorthodox judicial practices.

These tensions have attracted increased interest from scholars, notably from the point of view of the 'fragmentation' debate (Herik and Stahn 2012). The main response has commonly been to suggest better outreach to explain decisions (rather than change them) to relevant populations; or to occasionally praise hybridity at least insofar as it may help bridge the gap between international and local communities. None of these responses seems to propose to do more than manage the tension and correct some of its more glaring dimensions. By contrast, a critical project in international criminal justice would emphasize the degree to which the centralization and universalism of international criminal justice is part and parcel of processes of hegemony (Mégret 2010b). It might go much further in arguing against tribunals' centralizing and somewhat arrogant distance by taking a systematic stance for the pluralization of international criminal justice and the existence of a significant margin of appreciation in implementing it. The work of Mark Drumbl (2007), Sasha Greenawalt (2011), Jenia Turner (2005), Eric Blumenson (2006), Jaya Ramji-Nogales (2010), Harmen van der Wilt (2008) and Elies Van Sliedregt (2012) comes to mind, among no doubt many others. I have also argued with Marika Giles Samson for a very flexible understanding of complementarity when it comes to societies in transition whose human rights practices, shocking as they may be, still should not exclude a country's ambition to enforce its criminal law (Mégret and Samson 2013).

International criminal justice is ultimately apologetic and prone to serve as a powerful exculpatory device

While great hopes typically accompany international criminal justice's gradual ascent to power in terms of reordering international law and relations, there is also much reason to think that it heralds a continuation of patterns of symbolic domination, perhaps even their obfuscation and reinforcement. The particular mechanics by which that which claims to transcend ends up merely reproducing are an enduring concern of critical theory (Mégret 2014d). Of course, international criminal justice as a project develops a power of its own, but that power does not simply emerge from the moral aura and awe projected by it. Rather it comes as a result of a subtle interaction – osmosis, even – with various sources of power. Historically, international criminal justice has only come about as a result of its ability to interact productively with such sources. Time and again it has converged towards powerful patrons: leading states, states speaking through international bodies such as the Security Council, states *tout court*. Of course, this is just another way of saying that states have only supported international criminal justice to the extent that they have seen it as conducive to their national interest. In that respect, the realist critique of international criminal justice rather misses out the degree to which some states, at least objectively, benefit from their association with international criminal justice.

The relationship to power is obviously not something that the liberal critique of international criminal justice has missed. But because it sees power as operating from outside international criminal tribunals, it typically contents itself with reassurances that international tribunals are indeed independent, and have grown much more so. The project is tempted to focus on the formal dimensions of independence, and makes much of the fact that international criminal tribunals have gone from being created by a coalition of allies, to the Security Council, to being created by a treaty.

As a result, however, there is a risk of underestimating the extent to which the relationship to power suffuses the operation of international criminal justice in ways that are not reducible to external compulsion and that go to the heart of international criminal practice. The source of the conundrum is fairly self-explanatory. It is often deplored, in the international criminal justice literature, that states cooperate insufficiently with international tribunals. What is minimized, however, is the degree to which international tribunals have been willing to accommodate states in order to be able to obtain some cooperation and thus wield some power. Sophisticated international criminal justice practitioners know better than to retrench themselves behind the invocation of some supposedly absolute obligation to cooperate, a move which, in its strident legalism, may expose their weakness (the obligation is, in practice, at best a rhetorical trope as part of a multi-prong strategy to get states to actually cooperate, in which the 'law' serves merely as a referential function). In fact, international criminal tribunals, confronted with the choice of glorious irrelevance or corrupted relevance, have rather emphatically chosen the latter.

The point is that international criminal prosecutors do not need to be told what to do; they very much know what they ought to do in a world of states to maximize the successful trajectory of the tribunals whose powers they exercise. The constraint, in short, is not external but internal. As already seen, there is nothing necessarily wrong with the exercise of judicial power in a world of power relations. But there should be no illusion that the resulting justice will, for the foreseeable future at least, do much more than reinscribe and perhaps even amplify existing power relations.

There is a long history of the justice of international tribunals being a justice rendered more or less enthusiastically in the shadow of power. This was evident at Nuremberg where the tribunal conscientiously followed the terms of its Charter excluding the *tu quoque* defence. It was especially clear in the case of the International Criminal Tribunal for Rwanda (ICTR), where the prosecutorial practices of the tribunal – both never prosecuting anyone from the FPR and never exercising primacy over Rwandan jurisdictions – can only be understood as a function of the internalization of a realistic bottom line, which was that the tribunal would be led to close down if it offended the Rwandan government. It was hoped that the ICC's permanence and more voluntary base would move it away from this proximity to state power. However, in many ways, very little has changed. The challenge of cooperation remains, not to mention that of legitimacy. The ICC is keen not only to get states that cooperate with it, but states that seem to offer their caseload on a silver tray. Hence state self-referrals have emerged as probably the single most important prong of successive prosecutors' strategy.

The danger is that the court will be at risk of trying only those cases that states want it to try.[4]

International criminal tribunals also have a very strong record of not biting the hand that feeds them. From accepting to go ahead with the Soviet push to punish the German defendants for the Katyn massacre, to not launching prosecutions for NATO bombings in Kosovo or British treatment of prisoners in Iraq, international tribunals seem to have deeply internalized the need not to cross red lines. Of course, there are always reasonable reasons not to launch prosecutions in such cases, but these typically betray a vision of international justice that is deeply indebted to a particular view of what is most deserving of prosecution (see below). All in all, rather than a constraint on states' power, international tribunals, *ad hoc* or not, have arguably acted as an extension of the power of at least some states; rather than speaking truth to power, they can legitimately be suspected of having spoken a certain truth *of* power, namely that one ignores it at one's cost. It may seem ironic that international criminal justice, as the great allocator of international guilt, may end up powerfully exculpating. Yet, arguably, international criminal justice is not only about condemning; it is also about, implicitly, 'innocenting'. For the stigma of prosecutions flows not only from the prosecuting to the condemned but, in the reverse, from the condemned to the prosecuting: he who judges implicitly sees himself as innocent of that which he judges the other for.

In other words, far from being the sort of radical cosmopolitan revolution in international law it has often been described as, the ICC is better understood as at best a very subtle amelioration of well-tried inter-state themes (Economides 2003), most likely along the lines of a Grotian *via media* (Mégret n.d.). In addition to uncovering these biases, a critical project of international criminal justice would seek to imagine the conditions under which an anti-hegemonic prosecutorial policy might emerge, one devoted to challenging established hierarchies, perhaps based on an understanding that different states or non-state actors commit different types of crimes (genocide, torture, terrorism). In this perspective, the goal would be to 'give each their due' rather than simply retreating behind a supposedly self-evident hierarchy of international crimes.

International criminal justice is a manifestation of Western neo-colonialism

When it comes to fleshing out how exactly the power of international criminal justice is exercised in ways that would warrant criticism, perhaps no critique has echoed internationally more than the one that international criminal justice is increasingly turning into a manifestation of Western neo-colonialism. If one includes the ICTR and the Special Court for Sierra Leone, the fact that the ICC has famously (so far) only indicted Africans is troubling. On the side of the accusers, perhaps more importantly, European states with deep historical involvement in colonialism have often featured prominently. With some exceptions, universal jurisdiction has tended to be exercised by 'north-ern' states over 'southern' crimes. The critique, moreover, has been given credence through being proffered by a variety of politicians and international actors, as well as some academics (Mamdani 2008).

In its simplest neo-colonial form, however, the critique may be worth taking with a pinch of salt. Indeed, there have been more scholars, including scholars from the South, who have taken up the African Union challenge to the ICC to refute it (albeit subtly) than scholars who have by and large sided with it (Jalloh *et al.* 2011; Manirabona 2011). The liberal defence of international criminal justice is on relatively strong grounds when it claims that there is nothing in it that directs it specifically towards Africa except circumstances. Indeed, the critique is a somewhat bizarre twist for international criminal justice, given the way in which it has historically been targeted first towards the West towards itself (Nuremberg) and towards a significantly Westernized and never colonized other (Tokyo), and towards what is at least the West's close periphery (the Balkans). This is not to mention countless domestic trials for war crimes organized in Europe after the Second World War that dealt with Europeans. Although a bit tired, the argument that the African continent, for a wide variety of reasons, has been the site of particularly gruesome and extensive atrocities in the last decade is hard to dismiss.

There are in fact many arguments as to why the portrayal of international criminal justice as colonial simply because more Africans have been targeted is not entirely convincing. These include the presence of many Africans at the tribunals, significant African public opinion and civil society support for their action (which the 'crit' cannot dismiss lightly in order to make an anti-colonial argument without itself resorting to paternalistic tropes) and, indeed, from African states themselves. In fact, the simplistic 'anti-imperialist' view that African states were 'coerced' into joining the Rome Statute or were not aware of the consequences may paradoxically smack of condescension. All in all, so-called 'Twailers' have been fairly balanced in their critique of international criminal justice, being in effect as critical of governments trying to escape its reach as they have been of the ICC and some of its choices (Gathii 2011, 42).

If anything, rather than a critique of how international criminal justice interferes with the sovereignty of Global South states, the TWAIL (Third World Approaches to International Law) critique addresses the way in which *both* international criminal justice and Global South states, in subtle conjunc-tion, may perpetuate patterns of symbolic confiscation of the aspirations of peoples (and not just 'victims'). Rather than strictly neo-colonial, then, the critique of international criminal justice's imperialism is at its best when it adopts a post-colonial lens, one that sees the continuity of the colonial in more subtle manifestations than simply the number of cases coming from the region. TWAIL critiques, in particular, can emphasize how international criminal justice is part and parcel of processes of 'otherization', in which Africa is repeatedly and subtly portrayed as a site of a-political savagery, a truly dark continent.

The choice of Lubanga of all people as the first person tried by the court, and the fact that he was prosecuted only for child recruitment (even though the Ituri population would have wanted him prosecuted for various other crimes), is probably a fairly telling example of the considerable emphasis on crimes that are by and large seen as emblematically African. This sort of representation is all the more ironic given the role of colonial armies in introducing practices of child soldiering. The 'criminality' of Africans powerfully feeds into the 'savages, victims and saviours' metaphor popularized by Makau Mutua (2001). Mixed in with a gendered component, international criminal justice is arguably never far from a 'white men and women saving black women and children from black men' motif that has, of course, a long and rather infamous history.

Critical approaches to international criminal justice inspired by TWAIL might seek to counter the post-colonial gaze on Africa. At a deeper level, the post-coloniality of international criminal justice ought to be situated in a *temps long* of the Western colonial encounter with Africa as it has been mediated by the criminal law, seen as a vehicle of civilization, to counter local normative traditions (Mégret 2013d); it would more systematically tell the story of how behind every African genocide or 'genocide' lies a complex story of colonial construction of ethnicity that cannot be reduced to a simple background fact (Mamdani 2008), as well as the continued geo-political effects of resource competition (Clarke 2010); it might seek to show how the portrayal of the African continent, reconnecting as it does with century-old stereotypes, echoes some of the ways in which the anti-slavery discourse in its day was also a way of legitimizing and justifying the exercise forms of judicial and political tutelage over the continent (Mégret 2013e); or it might seek to emphasize the degree to which African states and political actors exercise agency *vis-à-vis* international criminal justice in ways that belie the notion that they are merely its recipients (Mégret 2013f; Reinold 2012).

International criminal justice reinforces gendered and racialized stereotypes

International law has long exhibited a number of blind spots as a result of its origin in a particular vision of humanity. Perhaps none has been clearer historically than the exclusion of women, or more generally the gendered construction of international law. International criminal justice did not initially escape that fate, arguably reproducing in the process some of the very sources of international law's gendered exclusions. However, international criminal justice has also provided an opportunity to seek to update international law, notably by emphasizing the extent to which international criminal violence specifically targets women.

Here again, there is both a reformist and a more radical critique. Feminism is no stranger to liberalism (and vice-versa), and it is perfectly possible to incorporate feminist concerns within an overall liberal framework. Much feminist work has gone on during the last 20 years, in particular into seeking to encourage international prosecutors to include sexual violence charges and generally make the issue more prominent through incorporation into legal texts and case law (Askin 2004). This effort is complemented by a renewed attention to the situation of victims of sexual violence both as witnesses and, increasingly in the ICC context, as victims entitled to reparation and rehabilitation. Moreover, it has not gone without some more institutional changes, such as an effort made to build a bench that is more broadly representative of gender diversity (Lehr-Lehnardt 2001). Although it seems that more progress could always be made and there is an ongoing concern about the relative lack of success of sexual violence charges in individual cases, it is clear that the situation has changed quite considerably, with sexual violence now routinely considered to be an instrument of war and genocide (rather than a merely incidental product thereof).

However, this effort has, as it has in other realms of international law, notably human rights (Kapur 2006; Otto 2010), also generated a measure of discomfort among some feminists, which has in turn engendered probably some of the richest and most sophisticated literature on international criminal justice's potential for unintended consequences. In fact, the story of feminist strategic interaction with international criminal justice and the incorporation of feminist concerns has for many been one of active engagement followed in rapid succession by bewilderment at the gains obtained, and ultimately a striking disenchantment about some of the costs of this apparent entrenchment. Feminist critique, then, has been turned against various forms of feminist gains in successive waves, challenging the seemingly progressive as effectively conservative, and making it in the process the most internally complex and multilayered of the strands of critique reviewed in this chapter.

The very exercise of defining and representing gender violence for the purposes of international criminal law may subtly and not so subtly reproduce gendered stereotypes, and thus 'reiterate' or 'reinscribe' some of the very sources of oppression that it seeks to combat (Henry 2013). For example, prosecutions of sexual violence by international criminal tribunals may represent women as passive victims deprived of much agency, who can only be in denial if they claim they were not raped and could never have consented to sexual relations in war (Engle 2005). This in turn tends to exculpate women from participation in and encouragement of international crimes including sexual violence (despite a notable line of female offenders including female concentration camp guards, Pauline Nyiramasuhuko, Biljana Plavisc or female soldiers in Abu Ghraib), while laying the blame entirely on men. Moreover, it inevitably feeds into powerful international interventionist agendas to 'protect' women from sexual violence which, paradoxically, seem to reproduce some of the paternalism which feminism had sought to combat. Moreover, the courtroom has been assessed as a poor forum to adjudicate issues of sexual violence (Buss 2011).

Considerable attention, moreover, has been devoted to how prosecutions before international tribunals may send contradictory or even misleading signals about the causes, nature and consequences of sexual violence. Prosecuting rape as genocide (MacKinnon 1994), for example, may in some cases be the only way of doing justice to the fact that genocide has, in fact, occurred; but there has also been a suspicion that the meshing of accusations of sexual violence and genocide has occasionally been more opportunistic, simply reflecting an implicit calculus that this would give most publicity to issues of sexual violence. If the latter is the case, it may come at considerable cost to feminist values. For example, to ensure that rape is prosecuted as genocide involves portraying rape as fundamentally an instrument of genocidal intent (the same goes *mutatis mutandis* for crimes against humanity and war crimes). Linking rape to genocide in a sense upgrades its status by associating it with what is generally seen as the worst international crime; but it may also paradoxically devalue it in portraying sexual violence as 'not its own' crime, one that only strikes the international imagination if it is committed as part of something broader. In the process, it may be that the pervasiveness of everyday sexual violence against women will be downplayed as a result of an emphasis on the exceptionality of 'war' or 'genocide', and that the element of criminality against women specifically will be minimized (Copelon 1994). Perhaps the portrayal of rape as an instrument of war or genocide even gets the equation reversed: it is not rape that is an instrument of war and genocide but genocide and war that are instruments of sexual violence, essentially providing opportunistic macro-public outlets for a form of systemic androcentric violence against women.

It may be, however, that the vision of rape as genocide is on the decline, which may bring a new wave of soul searching. According to Janet Halley, and at least at the level of rules, the ICC now seems to stand for the proposition that sexual violence in war is primarily directed at women as such, and is therefore merely a manifestation of a deeper structural gendered oppression rather than an instrument of some other, non-gendered design. The problem with this latest tilt is that it may occasionally be descriptively wrong. Pushing the notion of a war-against-women in the context of armed conflict may even 'reproduce in reverse the blind-spotted moral vision that (feminism) contests' (Halley 2008a, 123; 2008b). More generally, a critical race angle on feminist debates about violence in armed conflict might insist on the degree to which the international debate largely reproduces divisions internal to a particular Western, Anglophone, even North American debate on gender, race and identity (Jaleel 2013).

A feminist jurisprudence of international criminal justice, then, might move beyond these contradictions in a variety of ways. It has already led, for example, to a refocus on the question of gender as opposed to an exclusive focus on women's rights. Without putting into question the undeniable element of patriarchy and violence against women in armed conflict and genocidal situations, the attention to the gendered nature of violence also brings attention to the existence of female perpetrators (of, typically, violence against other women) (Alison 2007; Sperling 2005) and of male victims (Lewis 2009; Sivakumaran 2007), as well as the persecution of homosexuals (Johnson 2009; Plant 2011). Rather than the simple portrayal of women as victims and men as perpetrators, a gendered concept of sexual violence would emphasize how, beyond sex, violence is the product of the normalized assumption of certain sexualized roles for each sex (which would include, notably, pressures on men to perform their heterosexuality through rape and the disempowerment of women as agents of positive change as a result of the inability to see them as active subjects in war at all).

Feminist ideas on criminal justice have also been criticized as doing little to upset the dominant forms of criminal justice, except through a change of focus on women (Daly 1989). The main thrust of the feminist challenge to international criminal justice effort does often appear to have been to 'mainstream' women's concerns within international prosecutions, much more than to challenge the very idea of international prosecutions on feminist grounds. In fact, the drive to include more charges for sexual violence often seems to include a strong quantitative, almost productivist element. The result is a concern that the feminist agenda will be enthusiastically co-opted by institutions of international criminal justice to cement their legitimacy, both as worthwhile institutions of penality and as institutions that 'save' women (Bumiller 2008, ch. 6). The investment by traditionally marginalized groups in the repressive apparatus, then, may culminate in a form of 'carceral feminism' (Bernstein 2010) or even 'queer necropolitics' (Lamble 2013), which must at least be a source of interrogation.

In this context, one of the more significant outcomes of feminist jurisprudence, beyond the better taking into account of sexual and gender concerns within an otherwise enduringly male-defined criminology, would be a contribution to the redefinition of criminal justice itself (in the same way that the feminist critique of international law is adamant that it is not about an otherwise unreformed international law simply taking more 'account' of women) (Charlesworth et al. 1991). Rather than a form of feminist cheerleading of criminal repression, then, feminism might, as it has domestically, form the core of a critique of androcentric criminological and criminal justice constructs (Masters and Smith 1998; Simpson 1989), typically although not inevitably in a more victim-centred (SáCouto 2011) and restorative direction not just for women (Van Wormer 2009) but also for female (Failinger 2005) and male (Ward and Salmon 2011) perpetrators.

The charge that international criminal justice also has a tendency to reinforce racialized stereotypes is a more complex one to make, and one that has clearly received less attention than the gender element. Although I cannot develop it in detail here, I would like to contribute a few thoughts. International criminal justice has developed in a direction where the element of targeting particular groups, notably ethnic or racial groups, is a pre-eminent concern. This is evidence in the crime of genocide, obviously, as well as persecution as a crime against humanity. In the process, however, international criminal justice has had to enter the fraught terrain of defining what constitutes, notably, ethnic groups. Few questions have been as complex and controversial as this one.

The problem is that the notion that races or ethnic groups 'exist' in a sort of objective, immanent sense is a very dated notion, heavily indebted to nineteenth-century raciology. Race and ethnicity are much better seen as constructed categories. This is a turn that international criminal tribunals have taken quite deftly, redefining, for example, Tutsi ethnicity as largely subjective, in the eyes of the beholder. Yet several paradoxes ensue. First, 'race' and 'ethnicity' only seem to have been constructed in the nineteenth century to support and buttress projects of colonization and domination (the 'Nilotic Tutsis' against the 'dumb Bantu'). If 'races' or 'ethnicities' only really exist as rather nefarious social constructs, then it is open to question whether international law should be protecting them as such, except as something quite different from what they are traditionally understood as being (e.g. as historically constructed communities of victimhood). Here the legacy of the Rwandan genocide is particularly enlightening. In a highly paradoxical and little remarked way, it has confirmed the very claim so central to the colonial enterprise and the genocide itself, namely that the Tutsis are an ethnic group, albeit for very different ends, and by subjectifying and updating the notion. Although considerable effort has been poured into prosecuting the perpetrators of the genocide and in a sense protecting the 'Tutsi' group, the post-genocide government has done its very best to erase all traces of ethnicity in a way that suggests that ethnicity was seen as the very source of the problem (Eltringham 2011).

Finally, the intersection of gender and ethnicity probably represents one of the most interesting areas for critical thinking about international criminal justice. For example, accusations of sexual violence and depravity have long had a role in stigmatizing certain communities, shaping their perception and rendering them vulnerable to violence. The risk is that charges of sexual violence will be used to delegitimize one side of the conflict only and attend to the needs of only one type of victim (Buss 2009), that rape will even be 'weaponized' (Halley 2008b). This is something that feminists cannot be oblivious to, or risk being manipulated by various nationalist causes. Or consider the more vexing problem of how international criminal tribunals may, as a result of seeking to protect certain groups, unwittingly reinforce traits within these groups that are in themselves oppressive (and which may not be that anchored in the first place). For example, the idea that the Tutsi or Bosnian Muslims as groups were destroyed by the use of rape because raped women from these groups would be shunned by their community, or because transmission of ethnicity is patrilineal, seems to reify characteristics that surely discriminate against women within the group. In some cases the only inference may be that the target group's disintegration is partly the result of endogenous practices that lead a group to effectively partake in its own destruction through a sort of faulty cross-gender cohesiveness that effectively amplifies the designs of the *génocidaires*. To focus on such characteristics as naturalized elements of a particular ethnicity may make them harder to challenge, as a result of having been integrated in a narrative of victimization. Moreover, it may caricature both ethnicity and masculinity to portray 'all Tutsi men' or 'all Bosnian Muslim men' as necessarily shunning victims of rape or all children resulting from 'forced impregnation' to be of the father's ethnicity whatever the mothers may have had to say on the matter.

International criminal justice represents a subtly biased view of what is wrong in the world

International criminal justice has emerged over the last decades as an evolving project of ranking what most threatens international society. At any given time, this ranking reflects the evolution of dominant prejudices about what international society ought most to protect itself from. Uncovering these hierarchies and challenging them as reflective of certain biases is a necessary component of a critical approach to international criminal justice.

The early tilt of international criminal law towards interstate violence, as exemplified in Nuremberg's focus on crimes against peace, could be faulted for misunderstanding the specificity of the Holocaust as a crime that was in many ways more quintessentially atrocious and not inherently dependent on aggression. The interstate element of international criminality thus arguably served to obscure forms of cosmopolitan horror. By the same token, international criminal justice almost seems to have moved too far in the opposite direction. Indeed, one of the most spectacular developments of the last decades is aggression's spectacular fall from grace (despite its rather uncertain inclusion in the Rome Statute) as the 'crimes of crimes', and its replacement by genocide and crimes against humanity as the ultimate taboos of the international order. Not only that, but the two seem correlated: aggression is much less aggression if it is designed to prevent a genocide (Murphy 2009), and there is a push to make sure this is well understood in the ICC context (DeNicola 2008) so that the international criminal law regime might even be understood as encouraging the use of force. The sidelining of aggression as a cardinal crime and the emphasis on war crimes as the regime of choice to regulate armed conflicts thus coincides with and accompanies the increased weakening of *jus ad bellum* safeguards.

Another direction that international criminal justice has taken is the foregrounding of 'proper', 'core' international crimes at the expense of a range of international offences that are considered more peripheral. This dichotomy is relatively new and closely tied to the development of international criminal tribunals in the 1990s. It is often reinforced by doctrinal arguments to the effect that only the core crimes are really 'international crimes', because they are susceptible to being judged by international tribunals. However, this is slightly specious since there is no reason in principle why a range of other crimes might not be judged internationally (terrorism, for one, has been). More significantly, it reflects a typical foregrounding of 'public' crimes as opposed to 'private' ones, in ways that emphasize the centrality of 'atrocities' at the expense of various other forms of violence, and of violence over forms of harm (Michels 2009). It is also linked to a disciplinary emphasis on 'crisis' endemic to international law (Charlesworth 2002) that has been denounced as taking attention away from 'extraordinary crimes at ordinary times' (Starr 2007). It also goes hand in hand with a potentially misleading emphasis on crimes committed as part of armed conflict rather than in 'peacetime'.

The implicit downgrading of crimes linked to transnational flows (trafficking in human beings, environmental crimes, slavery) – particularly flows of an economic nature most associated with globalization – then, aside from likely being at odds with a great part of the world's everyday experience of crime (both as victims and authors), reflects a particular political economy of international criminal law that deserves to be questioned. Rather than the typical prescription of including transnational crimes in the Rome Statute (Coracini 2008; Paulose 2012), the more interesting challenge is whether the study of transnational criminal law can be re-energized in ways that challenge the dominance of supra-criminal law. Moreover, the particular mechanics by which certain crimes become relatively disqualified, the nature of the argument that states do not desire to prosecute some crimes such as drug-trafficking offences internationally when some clearly do, or the use of arguments based on indeterminacy to discredit certain attempts to criminalize rather than others, all merit further study.

International criminal justice encapsulates an impoverished concept of justice

A final strand of critique is concerned with the idea that international criminal justice represents a rather dismal project of justice. If anything, international criminal justice has focused on a fairly restrictive, largely retributive view of criminal justice. It often seems as if its justice is evaluated entirely in relation to whether the defendant's right to a fair trial has been respected. Largely missing from liberal accounts of international criminal justice, until very recently at least, is the extent to which, for example, it might become more restorative. Indeed, the gap between accused and victims' rights advocates does not seem remotely close to being bridged. A critical approach to international criminal justice, conversely, would seek to transcend this sterile opposition by understanding how it is the very concept of criminal justice that needs to change.

Indeed, international criminal justice might be criticized for being part of a broad rehabilitation of criminal justice internationally, when by any measure criminal justice globally is – to use a 'Koskenniemian' refrain – 'a disaster'. Again, the liberal drive to constrain an international criminal justice system, useful as it has been historically and continues to be, has stopped at a fairly limited, highly legalized concept of the justice of international justice. It has always had trouble contextualizing the operation of criminal justice within an environment in which gender, race or class all have powerfully structuring roles (Beale 1997; Coker 2003). It has notably had trouble dealing aggressively with the way in which the criminal justice system unevenly impacts minorities (Davis 2007), the interaction of the criminal law and cultural difference, or the very massive recourse to criminal justice.

A critical project in international criminal justice, by contrast, might be more focused on the political economy of penalization/depenalization, underlining the extent to which international criminal justice fits within a broader agenda of resort to criminal law on a global plane. Rather than the almost compulsive reflex to criminalize more behaviour, it might be at the forefront of an international depenalization agenda. It might also help imagine ways of thinking differently about international criminal trials beyond liberal sacred cows – for example, as 'expressivist' (Sloane 2007) or 'show' trials (Koskenniemi 2002; Osiel 1999) – and of thinking beyond international criminal trials altogether.

Moreover, if anything, international criminal justice typically thinks of itself as primarily a form of *criminal* justice. Yet this is clearly not the way in which most populations at which its messages are directed understand it. Eluded or minimized are the extent to which international criminal justice might be viewed as a form of transitional justice. Although international criminal justice and transitional justice are often assimilated in public discourse, it is also clear that the former has tended to colonize the latter, implicitly relegating various tools of transitional justice (truth commissions, lustration, etc.) to secondary status (Aukerman 2002).

Finally, international criminal justice arguably has a role in the marginalization of other non-criminal forms of *international* justice. It is striking that the last decades of political and moral thought on issues of global justice have almost never even alluded to international criminal justice (Pogge 2008; Rawls 2001; Walzer 2006). Conversely, it now seems as if for many international lawyers international criminal justice is the ultimate test of global justice, a unique hope of redemption for the international legal order. One cannot be oblivious to the fact that international criminal justice, with its somewhat limited ambitions but considerable hold on imaginations, is in fact powerfully displacing other thinking about justice – most notably distributive justice, forever the neglected branch in international designs. It has not escaped many commentators, moreover, that international criminal justice can act as a fig leaf for the absence or poverty of various forms of international political engagement.

Conclusion: critique – dialogue or struggle?

This chapter has sought to show how the critique is not simply a way of negat-ing, but a way of *understanding* international criminal justice differently, with its potential and limitations. More could be gained from weaving different strands of critique together to produce a more compelling, overarching critique than each strand of critique can achieve alone. Questions of violence, power, repre-sentation, justice, selectivity all frame these central dilemmas in ways that are tenacious and cannot simply be wished away by the day-to-day practice of international criminal law, whatever its ability to move unperturbed.

In this conclusion I want to offer a few thoughts on the relationship of different critiques to each other, and of critique to what it critiques. All share many more subterranean connections than meet the eye and are part of a dense competition for symbolic capital within the field of international crimi-nal justice. There are uses to criticism and critique: they are, ultimately, subtle ways of elevating the status of the author of critique in relation to others. Criticism of international criminal justice does not always escape a degree of posturing. For example, critique is frequently tempted to produce a series of dichotomies that enhance its profile: between 'criminalists' or 'criminologists' v. 'internationalists' (Roberts and McMillan 2003); 'human rights' v. 'criminal law' (Danner and Martinez 2005; Fletcher and Ohlin 2005; Robinson 2008); 'criminal justice v. transitional justice', 'critique v. criticism', and so on.

Of course, the particular critical sensitivity described in this chapter can no more claim to escape this tug-and-pull than others. The critique may well be itself, ultimately, part of the project of constituting international criminal justice. Indeed the relationship of critique to its object is surprising, an often oddly intimate one (see Farrell, Chapter 4, this volume). The critique is para-doxically dependent on what it claims to critique; in fact, it is always at risk of being sucked into the very things that it criticizes. As to international criminal justice, it is not necessarily adverse to the sort of contestation that provides it with opportunities to reaffirm its legitimacy, in a context where it is unlikely to be fundamentally unsettled. Criticism of international criminal tribunals, most of the time, hardly makes a dent in their ideological armour, even assuming it was intended to.

Moreover, the critique inevitably becomes blunted through its interaction with its object over time. This is because the novelty of the critique quickly wears off, requiring investment in new ways of delivering critical charges; it is also because over time the project incorporates parts of the critique in ways that fundamentally deflect it. For example, the criticism that international criminal justice is too universalist will lead to at least some effort to engage in outreach; the critique that international criminal justice is selective will lead to renewed attention to how guidelines might constrain the hand of the pros-ecutor. Every critique, it seems, can be met by some liberal response that does not take it entirely to heart but promises to go to work on the issues. This is why after a while it may be impossible to distinguish the mainstream and critique in that the former will inevitably develop its own savvy discourses that acknowledge everything yet concede nothing.

The international criminal justice project can be seen to exercise its own subtle gravitational pull on the field, in ways that safeguard its pre-eminent hold on imaginations. For all its limitations, it does implicitly set the research agenda of both followers and contradictors. To be too radical, for example, is to consign oneself to a form of academic irrelevance. Practitioners may grant that the critique is 'interesting', but will underline how irrelevant it is to the micro-institutional dynamics and everyday life of international criminal justice. This in turn raises questions for would-be critics about what sort of social actors they want to be within the field, and what they ultimately stand for. There can be something sanctimonious about critiquing a thing from a position of self-assigned irrelevance. There will be subtle pressures, conversely, to frame one's criticism in a particular way; to produce 'useful', 'constructive' scholarship, to frame one's critique in the language of the project, is to experience the thrill of relevance. There are positions waiting to be filled, honours waiting to be bestowed, and more generally symbolic rewards to those who make themselves indispensable.

The dialectics of irrelevance/absorption, then, must frame any critical thinking about the critical project itself. What is it to both engage the world that international criminal justice makes and yet to not simply become absorbed by it? How can one keep a critical distance yet not forfeit the desire for change? The ambition of critique must be perpetually readjusted in light of this dilemma. It is a dilemma that is particularly familiar to feminists who have grappled with it for the better part of two decades in the international human rights sphere, alternating between the need to put theoretical rifts behind them to effect a tentative 'move to institutions', and the occasionally painful realization that 'coalition-building' may sometimes come at too high a cost, the cost of co-optation. The temptation of a certain superb isolation is a recurring one for the critique, as is engagement. At a certain level the question is whether the critique is merely interested in being scholastic or whether it aspires to truly unsettle. It is also about who the critique wants to talk to and with, and whether it thinks of itself as ultimately engaged in dialogue or struggle. Finally, it is about the decisions and compromises that one makes as part of living meaningful political lives individually and collectively.

One way to think of the work of critique that safeguards both its radicality and real-world relevance, then, might be to see it as a form of intellectual guerrilla. The debate on international criminal justice is not a level playing field. International criminal justice, in this day and age, concentrates too much real and symbolic capital. Moreover, where the project of international criminal justice is a coherent, organized whole, the critique is divided, hesitant, prompt to turn its critical tools against itself. The critique should resist being drawn onto the battlefields that the mainstream project of international criminal justice wants to draw it to, and where it can be, as it were, slaughtered in the open. The ability to define the intellectual battlefield and the type of engagement is crucial. If anything, the critique should harass the discipline whenever it is engaging in hubris; infiltrate its lines to destabilize defensive certainties; instil fear where it becomes hegemonic; use the arms of the powerful against it when it can, and unconventional tactics when it must; and retreat and regroup when it has little to contribute to the debate save its own uncertainties.

The challenge, at any rate, is to upset international criminal justice's balance, expose some of its contradictions, increase its anxiety, and situate it within a larger horizon of possibilities. As a result, it may be that the critique must be less fixated on some grand counter-horizon than willing to draw the field into tactical skirmishes. In the end, it would be ironic if attention to the inevitability of power ended up as a project to shun power's exercise rather than capturing it for more emancipatory outcomes. This entails an ability to navigate against yet close to the wind. The struggle is in a sense a struggle *for* international criminal justice rather than against it.

Ultimately, however, the most potent critique of international criminal justice may be one that does not obsessively focus on some of its shortcomings, but rather seeks to draw attention away from international criminal justice altogether by opening entirely new fronts, at a distance from what it criticizes. It is a critique based on doing rather than simply thinking, of opening new fronts in ways that resist the disciplinary shackles that come from proceeding, for example, as an 'international criminal lawyer'. The critique of international criminal justice, then, must be thought of as an embodiment of the transgressive potential of critical theory, a living incarnation of the refusal to become pigeonholed.

Notes

1 Note that realists need not necessarily be critical of international criminal justice, and I have certainly long thought that there could be a realist case for drawing on international criminal tribunals to project various forms of soft power. For example, it is very possible that the US would, in fact, wield more not less international power as a result of being a party to the Statute and incurring the very marginal risk of prosecutions of its nationals for the quite considerable benefit of being in a position to better influence the court from within. Perhaps luckily for the court, however, realists have been almost too busy stubbornly looking at how the court might negatively affect their state's national interest if it were to operate independently and impartially, rather than devising ways in which it could maximize their state's national interest if they were more actively engaged with it. At any rate, it seems that the US is now getting the best of both worlds, keeping outside the court to safeguard some of its national interest while orienting its fate with sufficient precision via the Security Council.
2 It seems nonetheless possible to chart a path by which states might want to become parties to the Statute even when they see themselves as potentially committing crimes (Mégret 2005a).
3 Of course, this depends on who one considers ought to be privy to the consensus. If the consensus is only among international elites involved in the operation of

institutions of international criminal justice, then the consensus may be relatively greater than if one opens up the equation globally.
4 Even when the ICC prosecutor has used her *proprio motu* powers, she has tended to do so against relatively 'easy targets,' i.e. in circumstances where she would not encounter significant resistance.

Bibliography

Ainley, K. (2006) *Rethinking Agency and Responsibility in Contemporary International Political Theory* (PhD) London School of Economics. Available at: http://etheses. lse.ac.uk/332/1/Ainley_Rethinking%20agency%20and%20responsibility.pdf.

Alison, M. (2007) '"Wartime Sexual Violence: Women's Human Rights and Questions of Masculinity', *Review of International Studies* 33(1): 75–90.

Alvarez, J. (1999) 'Crimes of States/Crimes of Hate: Lessons from Rwanda', *Yale Journal of International Law.*

Askin, K.D. (2004) 'A Decade of the Development of Gender Crimes in International Courts and Tribunals: 1993 to 2003', *Human Rights Brief* 11(3): 5.

Aukerman, M.J. (2002) 'Extraordinary Evil, Ordinary Crime: A Framework for Understanding Transitional Justice', *Harvard Human Rights Journal* 15: 40.

Backer, L. (2003) 'The Fuhrer Principle of International Law: Individual Responsibility and Collective Punishment', *Penn State International Law Review* 21(3): 509–67.

Beale, S.S. (1997) 'What's Law Got To Do With It? The Political, Social, Psychological and Non-Legal Factors Influencing the Development of (Federal) Criminal Law', *Buffalo Criminal Law Review* 1(1): 23–66.

Bernstein, E. (2010) 'Militarized Humanitarianism Meets Carceral Feminism: The Politics of Sex, Rights, and Freedom in Contemporary Antitrafficking Campaigns', *Signs* 36(1): 45–71.

Blumenson, E. (2006) 'The Challenge of a Global Standard of Justice: Peace, Pluralism, and Punishment at the International Criminal Court', *Columbia Journal of Transnational Law* 44(3): 801–74.

Bumiller, K. (2008) *In an Abusive State: How Neoliberalism Appropriated the Feminist Movement against Sexual Violence*, Durham, NC: Duke University Press Books.

Burchard, C. (2006) 'The Nuremberg Trial and its Impact on Germany', *Journal of International Criminal Justice* 4(4): 800–29.

Burke-White, W.W. (2003) 'Regionalization of International Criminal Law Enforcement: A Preliminary Exploration', *Texas International Law Journal* 38: 729.

Buss, D. (2009) 'Rethinking "Rape as a Weapon of War"', *Feminist Legal Studies* 17(2): 145–63.

Buss, D. (2011) 'Performing Legal Order: Some Feminist Thoughts on International Criminal Law', *International Criminal Law Review* 11: 409–23.

Butler, J. (2004) 'What is Critique? An Essay on Foucault's Virtue', in S. Salih (ed.) *The Judith Butler Reader*, London: Wiley-Blackwell.

Cassese, A. (2000) 'The Martens Clause: Half a Loaf or Simply Pie in the Sky?', *European Journal of International Law* 11(1): 187.

Charlesworth, H. (2002) 'International Law: A Discipline of Crisis', *The Modern Law Review* 65(3): 377–92.

Charlesworth, H., Chinkin, C. and Wright, S. (1991) 'Feminist Approaches to International Law', *American Journal of International Law* 85: 613.

Chrétien, J.-P. (1995) 'Un "Nazisme tropical" au Rwanda? Image ou logique d'un génocide', *Vingtieme siecle: Revue d'histoire*.

Clarke, K. (2010) 'Rethinking Africa through its Exclusions: The Politics of Naming Criminal Responsibility', *Anthropological Quarterly* 83(3): 625–51.

Coker, D. (2003) 'Foreword: Addressing the Real World of Racial Injustice in the Criminal Justice System', *Journal of Criminal Law and Criminology (1973–)* 93(4): 827.

Copelon, R. (1994) 'Surfacing Gender: Reconceptualizing Crimes Against Women in Time of War', *Mass Rape: The War Against Women in Bosnia-Herzegovina*.

Coracini, A. (2008) '"Amended Most Serious Crimes": A New Category of Core Crimes within the Jurisdiction but out of the Reach of the International Criminal Court?', *Leiden Journal of International Law* 21(3): 699–718.

Corten, O. (2004) 'De quel droit? Place et fonction du droit comme registre de légitimité dans le discours sur la "compétence universelle"', *Annales de droit de Louvain* 64: 51–82.

Daly, K. (1989) 'Criminal Justice Ideologies and Practices in Different Voices: Some Feminist Questions about Justice', *International Journal of the Sociology of Law* 17(1): 1–18.

Damaška, M. (2012) 'Unacknowledged Presences in International Criminal Justice', *Journal of International Criminal Justice* 10(5): 1239–56.

Danner, A.M. (2003) 'Enhancing the Legitimacy and Accountability of Prosecutorial Discretion at the International Criminal Court', *American Journal of International Law* 97(3): 510.

Danner, A.M. and Martinez, J.S. (2005) 'Guilty Associations: Joint Criminal Enterprise, Command Responsibility, and the Development of International Criminal Law', *California Law Review* 93(1): 75–169.

David, E. (1998) 'The International Criminal Court: What is the Point?', in K.C. Wellens (ed.) *International Law: Theory and Practice, Essays in Honour of Eric Suy*, The Hague: Martinus Nijhoff.

Davis, A.J. (2007) 'Racial Fairness in the Criminal Justice System: The Role of the Prosecutor', *Columbia Human Rights Law Review* 39: 202.

DeNicola, C.P. (2008) 'Shield for the Knights of Humanity: The ICC Should Adopt a Humanitarian Necessity Defense to the Crime of Aggression', *University of Pennsylvania Journal of International Law* 30: 641.

Dixon, P. and Tenove, C. (2013) 'International Criminal Justice as a Transnational Field: Rules, Authority and Victims', *International Journal of Transitional Justice*, p. ijt015.

Drumbl, M.A. (2002) 'Restorative Justice and Collective Responsibility: Lessons for and from the Rwandan Genocide', *Contemporary Justice Review* 5(1): 5–22.

Drumbl, M.A. (2005) 'Review: Pluralizing International Criminal Justice', *Michigan Law Review* 103(6): 1295–328.

Drumbl, M.A. (2007) *Atrocity, punishment, and international law*, Cambridge University Press. Available at: www.loc.gov/catdir/toc/ecip073/2006035762.html; www.loc.gov/catdir/enhancements/fy0703/2006035762-d.html; www.loc.gov/catdir/enhancements/fy0729/2006035762-b.html.

Economides, S. (2003) 'The International Criminal Court: Reforming the Politics of International Justice', *Government and Opposition* 38(1): 29–51.

Eltringham, N. (2008) '"A War Crimes Community"?: The Legacy of the International Criminal Tribunal for Rwanda Beyond Jurisprudence', *New England Journal of International and Comparative Law* 14: 309.

Eltringham, N. (2011) 'The Past is Elsewhere: The Paradoxes of Proscribing Ethnicity in Post-genocide Rwanda', in S. Straus and L. Waldorf (eds) *Remaking Rwanda: State Building and Human Rights after Mass Violence*, Madison: University of Wisconsin Press.

Eltringham, N. (2012) 'Spectators to the Spectacle of Law: The Formation of a "Validating Public" at the International Criminal Tribunal for Rwanda', *Ethnos* 77(3): 425–45.

Engle, K. (2005) 'Feminism and its (Dis)Contents: Criminalizing Wartime Rape in Bosnia and Herzegovina', *American Journal of International Law* 99(4): 778–816.

Failinger, M.A. (2005) 'Lessons Unlearned: Women Offenders, the Ethics of Care, and the Promise of Restorative Justice', *Fordham Urban Law Journal* 33: 487.

Fichtelberg, A. (2008) 'Liberal Values in International Criminal Law: A Critique of Erdemović', *Journal of International Criminal Justice* 6(1): 3–19.

Findlay, M. (2009) 'Activating a Victim Constituency in International Criminal Justice', *International Journal of Transitional Justice* 3(2): 183–206.

Fletcher, G.P. (2002) 'The Storrs Lectures: Liberals and Romantics at War: The Problem of Collective Guilt', *The Yale Law Journal* 111(7): 1499–573.

Fletcher, G.P. and Ohlin, J.D. (2005) 'Reclaiming Fundamental Principles of Criminal Law in the Darfur Case', *Journal of International Criminal Justice* 3(3): 539–61.

Foucault, M. (1990) 'Qu'est-ce que la critique? (Critique et Aufklärung)', *Bulletin de la Société française de philosophie* 84(2): 35–63.

Gathii, J.T. (2011) 'TWAIL: A Brief History of Its Origins, Its Decentralized Network, and a Tentative Bibliography', *Trade, Law and Development* 3: 42.

Glasius, M. (2002) 'Expertise in the Cause of Justice: Global Civil Society Influence on the Statute for an International Criminal Court', *Global Civil Society*, Oxford: Oxford University Press.

Goldsmith, J. (2003) 'The Self-defeating International Criminal Court', *University of Chicago Law Review* 70(1): 89–104.

Greenawalt, A.K. (2011) 'Pluralism of International Criminal Law', *Indiana Law Journal* 86: 1063.

Halley, J. (2008a) 'Rape at Rome: Feminist Interventions in the Criminalization of Sex-Related Violence in Positive International Criminal Law', *Michigan Journal of International Law* 30: 1.

Halley, J. (2008b) 'Rape in Berlin: Reconsidering the Criminalisation of Rape in the International Law of Armed Conflict', *Melbourne Journal of International Law* 9: 78.

Henry, N. (2013) 'The Fixation on Wartime Rape: Feminist Critique and International Criminal Law', *Social and Legal Studies*, doi: 0964663913499061.

Herik, L. van den and Stahn, C. (2012) *The Diversification and Fragmentation of International Criminal Law*, The Hague: Martinus Nijhoff.

Holá, B. (2012) 'International Sentencing: A Game of Russian Roulette or Consistent Practice?', *European Journal of Criminology* 9(5): 539–52.

Jaleel, R. (2013) 'Weapons of Sex, Weapons of War', *Cultural Studies* 27(1): 115–35.

Jalloh, C.C., Akande, D. and Du Plessis, M. (2011) 'Assessing the African Union Concerns about Article 16 of the Rome Statute of the International Criminal Court', *African Journal of Legal Studies* 4(1): 5–50.

Johnson, D.K. (2009) *The Lavender Scare: The Cold War Persecution of Gays and Lesbians in the Federal Government*, Chicago: University of Chicago Press.

Kapur, R. (2006) 'Revisioning the Role of Law in Women's Human Rights Struggles', in S. Meckled-Garcia and B. Cali (eds) *The Legalization of Human Rights: Multidisciplinary Perspectives on Human Rights and Human Rights Law*, London: Routledge.

Kendall, S. and Nouwen, S. (2013) *Representational Practices at the International Criminal Court: The Gap between Juridified and Abstract Victimhood*, SSRN Scholarly Paper ID 2313094, Rochester, NY: Social Science Research Network. Available at: http://papers.ssrn.com/abstract=2313094 (accessed 14 November 2013).

Kennedy, D. (2002) 'International Human Rights Movement: Part of the Problem?', *Harvard Human Rights Journal* 15: 101–25.

Kissinger, H.A. (2001) 'The Pitfalls of Universal Jurisdiction', *Foreign Affairs*, July/August: 86–96.

Koskenniemi, M. (1990) 'The Pull of the Mainstream', *Michigan Law Review* 88(6): 1946–62.

Koskenniemi, M. (2002) 'Between Impunity and Show Trials', *Max Planck Yearbook of United Nations Law* 6(1): 1–32.

Lamble, S. (2013) 'Queer Necropolitics and the Expanding Carceral State: Interrogating Sexual Investments in Punishment', *Law and Critique* 24(3): 229–53.

Langer, M. (2012) 'The Archipelago and the Hub: Universal Jurisdiction and the International Criminal Court', in M. Minow and A. Whiting (eds) *The First Global Prosecutor: Constraints and Promises*, Ann Arbor: University of Michigan Press.

Lehr-Lehnardt, R. (2001) 'One Small Step for Women: Female-Friendly Provisions in the Rome Statute of the International Criminal Court', *BYU Journal of Public Law* 16: 317.

Lewis, D. (2009) 'Unrecognized Victims: Sexual Violence Against Men in Conflict Settings Under International Law', *Wisconsin International Law Journal* 27(1): 1–49.

MacKinnon, C.A. (1994) 'Rape, Genocide, and Women's Human Rights', *Harvard Women's Law Journal* 17: 5.

Maison, R. and Leben, C. (2004) *La responsabilité individuelle pour crime d'État en droit international public*, Brussels: Bruylant.

Mamdani, M. (2008) 'The New Humanitarian Order', *The Nation*. Available at: www.thenation.com/article/new-humanitarian-order# (accessed 15 November 2013).

Manirabona, A.M. (2011) 'Vers la decrispation de la tension entre la cour penale internationale et l'Afrique: quelques defis a relever', *Revue Juridique Themis* 45: 269.

Masters, G. and Smith, D. (1998) 'Portia and Persephone Revisited: Thinking about Feeling in Criminal Justice', *Theoretical Criminology* 2(1): 5–27.

Meernik, J. and King, K.L. (2001) 'The Effectiveness of International Law and the ICTY– Preliminary Results of an Empirical Study', *International Criminal Law Review* 1(3): 343–372.

Mégret, F. (2001) 'Epilogue to an Endless Debate: The International Criminal Court's Third Party Jurisdiction and the Looming Revolution of International Law', *European Journal of International Law* 12(2): 247–268.

Mégret, F. (2002) 'Three Dangers for the International Criminal Court: A Critical Look at a Consensual Project', *Finnish Yearbook of International Law*, p. 207.

Mégret, F. (2005a) 'Why Would States Want to Join the ICC? A Theoretical Exploration Based on the Legal Nature of Complementarity', in J.K. Kleffner and G. Kor (eds) *Complementary Views on Complementarity: Proceedings of the International Roundtable on the Complementary Nature of the International Criminal Court*, Amsterdam 25–26 June 2004, The Hague/Cambridge, TMC Asser Press/Cambridge University Press.

Mégret, F. (2005b) 'In Defense of Hybridity: Towards a Representational Theory of International Criminal Justice', *Cornell International Law Journal* 38(3): 725–51.

Mégret, F. (2010a) 'Justifying Compensation by the International Criminal Court's Victims Trust Fund: Lessons from Domestic Compensation Schemes', *Brooklyn Journal of International Law* 36: 123–337.

Mégret, F. (2010b) 'Too Much of a Good Thing? ICC Implementation and the Uses of Complementarity', in C. Stahn and M. El Zeidy (eds) *The International Criminal Court: From Theory to Practice*, Cambridge: Cambridge University Press.

Mégret, F. (2011a) 'The Legacy of the ICTY as Seen Through Some of its Actors and Observers', *Goettingen Journal of International Law* 3(3).

Mégret, F. (2011b) 'ICC, R2P and the Security Council's Evolving Interventionist Toolkit', *Finnish Yearbook of International Law*.

Mégret, F. (2011c) 'Joinder, Fairness and the Goals of International Criminal Justice', in T.W. Waters (ed.) *The Milosevic Trial: An Autopsy*, Oxford: Oxford University Press.

Mégret, F. (2013a) 'Where Does the Critique of International Human Rights Stand? An Exploration in 18 Vignettes', *New Approaches to International Law*.

Mégret, F. (2013b) 'Practices of Stigmatization', *Law & Contemporary Problems* 76(2).

Mégret, F. (2013c) 'Les angles morts de la responsabilité pénale individuelle en droit international', *Revue interdisciplinaire d'études juridiques*.

Mégret, F. (2013d) 'Justice pénale internationale et colonialisme: au-delà des évidences' (under submission).

Mégret, F. (2013e) 'Droit international et esclavage: pour une réévaluation', *African Yearbook of International Law/Annuaire africain de droit international*.

Mégret, F. (2013f) 'How States Use the ICC', presented at the International Studies Association, San Francisco.

Mégret, F. (2014a) 'Anxieties, Practices and the Construction of the International Criminal Justice Field' (submitted, under review).

Mégret, F. (2014b) 'Beyond "Gravity": For a Politics of International Criminal Prosecutions', *ASIL Proceedings*.

Mégret, F. (2014c) 'Repentance', in G. Simpson (ed.) *The Passions of International Law*, Cambridge: Cambridge University Press.

Mégret, F. (2014d) 'The Apology of Utopia: Reflections on Some Koskenniemian Themes with Particular Emphasis on Massively Institutionalized Human Rights Law', *Temple International and Comparative Law Journal*.

Mégret, F. (n.d.) 'Trois paradigmes de la justice pénale internationale', *Observateur des Nations Unies* 32.

Mégret, F. and Samson, M.G. (2013) 'Holding the Line on Complementarity in Libya: The Case for Tolerating Flawed Domestic Trials', *Journal of International Criminal Justice* 11(3): 571–89.

Meierhenrich, J. (2013) 'The Practice of International Law: A Theoretical Analysis', *Law & Contemporary Problems* 76(2).

Meron, T. (2000) 'The Martens Clause, Principles of Humanity, and Dictates of Public Conscience', *American Journal of International Law* 94(1): 78–89.

Michels, J.D. (2009) 'Keeping Dealers off the Docket: The Perils of Prosecuting Serious Drug-Related Offences at the International Criminal Court', *Florida Journal of International Law* 21: 450.

Milanovic, M. (2012) 'On Realistic Utopias and Other Oxymorons: An Essay on Antonio Cassese's Last Book', *European Journal of International Law* 23(4): 1033–48.

Miller, J., McMahon, P. and Broyhill, K. (2011) 'The ICTY as a Realist Institution: International Courts, Accountability Networks, and Transitional Justice', APSA Annual Meeting Paper.

Murphy, S.D. (2009) 'Criminalizing Humanitarian Intervention', *Case Western Reserve Journal of International Law* 41: 341.

Mutua, M. (2001) 'Savages, Victims, and Saviors: The Metaphor of Human Rights', *Harvard International Law Journal* 42: 201.

Nollkaemper, A. (2003) 'Concurrence Between Individual Responsibility and State Responsibility in International Law', *International and Comparative Law Quarterly* 52(3): 615–40.

Nollkaemper, A. (2010) 'Systemic Effects of International Responsibility for International Crimes', *Santa Clara Journal of International Law* 8: 313–52.

Osiel, M. (1999) *Mass Atrocity, Collective Memory, and the Law*, Piscataway, NJ: Transaction Publishers.

Otto, D. (2010) 'Power and Danger: Feminist Engagement with International Law through the UN Security Council', *Australian Feminist Law Journal* 32: 97.

Paulose, R.M. (2012) 'Beyond the Core: Incorporating Transnational Crimes into the Rome Statute', *Cardozo Journal of International and Comparative Law* 21: 77–195.

Peskin, V. (2009) 'Caution and Confrontation in the International Criminal Court's Pursuit of Accountability in Uganda and Sudan', *Human Rights Quarterly* 31(3): 655–91.

Plant, R. (2011) *The Pink Triangle: The Nazi War Against Homosexuals*, London: Macmillan.

Pogge, T. (2008) *World Poverty and Human Rights: Cosmopolitan Responsibilities and Reforms*, London: Polity Press.

Ramji-Nogales, J. (2010) 'Designing Bespoke Transitional Justice: A Pluralist Process Approach', *Michigan Journal of International Law* 32(1).

Rawls, J. (2001) *The Law of Peoples: with, The Idea of Public Reason Revisited*, Cambridge, MA: Harvard University Press.

Reinold, T. (2012) 'Constitutionalization? Whose Constitutionalization? Africa's Ambivalent Engagement with the International Criminal Court', *International Journal of Constitutional Law* 10(4): 1076–105.

Roberts, P. and McMillan, N. (2003) 'For Criminology in International Criminal Justice', *Journal of International Criminal Justice* 1: 315.

Robinson, D. (2008) 'The Identity Crisis of International Criminal Law', *Leiden Journal of International Law* 21(4): 925–63.

SáCouto, S. (2011) 'Victim Participation at the International Criminal Court and the Extraordinary Chambers in the Courts of Cambodia: A Feminist Project', *Michigan Journal of Gender and Law* 18: 297.

Schwarzenberger, G. (1950) 'The Problem of an International Criminal Law', *Current Legal Problems* 3(1): 263–96.

Simpson, G. (2012) 'International Criminal Justice and the Past', in G. Boas, W.A. Schabas and M.P. Scharf (eds) *International Criminal Justice: Legitimacy and Coherence*, Cheltenham: Edward Elgar.

Simpson, S.S. (1989) 'Feminist Theory, Crime, and Justice', *Criminology* 27(4): 605–32.

Sivakumaran, S. (2007) 'Sexual Violence Against Men in Armed Conflict', *European Journal of International Law* 18(2): 253–76.

Sloane, R.D. (2007) 'The Expressive Capacity of International Punishment: The Limits of the National Law Analogy and the Potential of International Criminal

Law', *Stanford Journal of International Law* 43. Available at: http://papers.ssrn.com/abstract=900641 (accessed 19 November 2013).

Snyder, J. and Vinjamuri, L. (2004) 'Trials and Errors: Principle and Pragmatism in Strategies of International Justice', *International Security* 28(3): 5–44.

Sperling, C. (2005) 'Mother of Atrocities: Pauline Nyiramasuhuko's Role in the Rwandan Genocide', *Fordham Urban Law Journal* 33: 637.

Starr, S. (2007) 'Extraordinary Crimes at Ordinary Times: International Justice beyond Crisis Situations', *Northwestern University Law Review* 101: 1257.

Stuart, H.V. (2008) 'The ICC in Trouble', *Journal of International Criminal Justice* 6(3): 409–17.

Tallgren, I. (2002) 'The Sensibility and Sense of International Criminal Law', *European Journal of International Law* 13(3): 561.

Turner, J.I. (2005) 'Nationalizing International Criminal Law', *Stanford Journal of International Law* 41: 1.

Van der Wilt, H. (2008) 'Equal Standards? On the Dialectics between National Jurisdictions and the International Criminal Court', *International Criminal Law Review* 8(1-1): 229–72.

Van Sliedregt, E. (2012) 'Pluralism in International Criminal Law', *Leiden Journal of International Law* 25(4): 847–55.

Van Wormer, K. (2009) 'Restorative Justice as Social Justice for Victims of Gendered Violence: A Standpoint Feminist Perspective', *Social Work* 54(2): 107–16.

Walzer, M. (2006) *Just And Unjust Wars: A Moral Argument With Historical Illustrations*, New York: Basic Books.

Ward, T. and Salmon, K. (2011) 'The Ethics of Care and Treatment of Sex Offenders', *Sexual Abuse: A Journal of Research and Treatment* 23(3): 397–413.

Chapter 2

Critical orientations

A critique of international criminal court practice

Sara Kendall

Introduction

A decade into the institutional life of the International Criminal Court (ICC), during a time when court proponents were celebrating 'successes' and contemplating 'lessons learned', some actors within and outside the court had already begun to discuss the ICC's departure from situation countries and the legacy they aspired to have it leave behind. At the 2012 meeting of the Assembly of States Parties, the annual ritual that gathers all member states parties to the ICC's founding treaty, a civil society-sponsored side event took up the question of the court's 'completion strategy'. There, a sitting ICC Trial Chamber judge, Registry actors from other tribunals, and state representatives discussed how to develop a strategy for the court's withdrawal from its sites of intervention.[1] Should there be general principles? Should the strategy be specific and tailored to individual situations? Will it differ according to the way in which the court has exercised jurisdiction, and whether a situation is temporally open-ended? A representative from a non-state party pointed out that the court needed to ensure that it was 'not checking in and out of a situation country like a hotel'.[2] A civil society panellist asked, perhaps rhetorically, 'Who determines what the legacy of the court should be?'[3]

I begin from this scene in The Hague, a central point of production for the field of international criminal law, because it illustrates some of the issues of power and ethics that accompany international judicial interventions. The discourses of exit, legacy and completion are remarkable in light of the fact that the ICC is the first permanent institution set up to adjudicate international crimes, unlike its *ad hoc* and hybrid contemporaries established for Rwanda, the Balkans, Sierra Leone, Cambodia and Lebanon. The above exchange illustrates some of the ongoing struggles faced by the court in circumscribing its mandate, securing the means through which to carry out its work, and generating consensus around its role as a permanent instantiation of international criminal justice. It also raises issues of agency and belonging: on whose behalf is the court seen to act, and to whom is it answerable?

Scholarship on and practice within international criminal law have moved from concerns about its existential status to emphasizing its developing jurisprudence, institutional anniversaries and discussions of legacy. This chapter takes up the volume's invitation to approach the field critically by turning to one of its central institutional sites of production. By addressing the ICC, the first permanent setting where international criminal law is shaped and performed, I read the work of this court as indexing broader dilemmas for the field and its proponents. The work of critique foregrounds the power-laden circumstances that produce certain discursive forms (such as international criminal law) and certain institutional arrangements (such as the ICC). Following social theorist Bruno Latour's call to renew an empirical dimension of critique (Latour 2004), I understand the work of critique as interrogating not only the conditions of possibility of international criminal law, but also the institutional structures and practices through which it is performed.

Although the ICC is a legal institution with a limited mandate, its social life and ethical obligations stretch further than a strict reading of its mandate would suggest. Such an understanding of the ethical obligations of institutions builds upon an approach to individual ethics that regards the human subject as embedded in a network of relations with others, which produces responsibilities that are not always the product of subjective consent (Murray 2007; Stauffer 2013). Responsibility is therefore tied to relationality; it is intersubjective rather than solely a product of an individual's own intent. Mapped onto an institutional form, this reading of ethical responsibility suggests that it is not limited to mere positivist expressions – such as the obligations contained in the ICC's statute – but extends further, as an ethical obligation to the communities where the court carries out its particular form of justice-as-accountability. As the court intervenes in domestic political contexts and conflict-affected communities, the ICC produces and reproduces discourses about justice that may not align with the views of those who are affected by its work, and its practices may lead to unintended consequences.

This chapter thus focuses on critique as an ethical orientation for addressing international criminal law. It first briefly situates its institutional object, the ICC, within the broader field of international criminal law. It then considers critique as an orientation, illustrating some of the insights from critical legal scholarship and critical theory that may contribute to this approach. I draw upon Michel Foucault's work here for its critique of the ideological underpinnings of discourses as well as of social practices. Moving into a critique at the level of *praxis*, then, the chapter considers some of the court's practices that reinscribe core–periphery relationships and produce ethical implications. In conclusion, the chapter argues that a critical *ethos* should address the unanticipated responsibilities that exceed the court's restricted legal mandate.

The ICC in context

What is the broader context or 'juridical field' (Bourdieu 1987) in which the ICC operates? There is by now an industry of international criminal law practice populated by judges, lawyers and administrators who move from tribunal to tribunal and a growing demand-driven academic response through specialized programmes, generating ever more students of mass atrocity jurisprudence for a legal market incapable of absorbing them (Skouteris 2010; Kendall 2014; Schwöbel 2013). Outside of legal scholarship and professional practice, the broad field of actors commonly referred to as civil society have increasingly adopted the ICC discourse of 'complementarity' to describe their work on rule of law initiatives in countries where the court is active (Nouwen 2013). This market of international criminal justice operates through its own recursive logic, with the ICC and other actors mirroring back a set of standards, values and terminologies through which the shared 'fight against impunity' is envisioned and enacted. This unifying norm at the centre of the struggle is indeterminate, though presumably understood by all – a kind of regulative ideal on the horizon of global justice.

For actors within this shared community, winning the 'fight' rests on increasing technical capacity and political will, which suggests that a temporal closure to impunity and a triumph of accountability is possible. Proponents place emphasis on the ongoing campaign for universal ratification taken up by NGO networks such as the Coalition for the International Criminal Court, domesticating the Rome Statute among existing state parties, and developing 'complementarity' mechanisms at the state level, such as specialized chambers or separate tribunals to try mass atrocity crimes. The ASP side event mentioned above is another example of attempting to improve and refine from within the frame, anticipating possible oversights and shortcomings in the quest to implement 'best practices' of international criminal justice.

Optimistic commentary on international criminal tribunals attempts to demonstrate their contributions to 'the justice cascade' (Sikkink 2011) or a nascent 'humanity law' (Teitel 2011) as part of a broader progress narrative where conflict and its social effects are curtailed and rectified through law. There has also been a rise in empirical efforts to chart the constructive impact of international criminal justice in extending the rule of law in post-conflict societies.[4] Many of these studies make several presumptions: first, that impact is something that can be 'measured' scientifically, and second, that power relations are held at bay through the framework of international criminal justice as an enactment of 'the rule of law'. Yet as Michel Foucault argues, juridical forms (such as states or courts or bodies of law) frequently disavow or efface the role of power in speaking the language of right. Humanity is not liberated through juridical forms, but is instead subjected to new configurations of power (Foucault 1984). The analysis of power relations is often excluded from scholarship *within* the field of international criminal law, with few exceptions (Mégret 2002; Simpson 2007; Nouwen and Werner 2010; Nouwen 2013). Much international criminal law scholarship has a positivist focus on decisions and judgments while sidestepping critical engagement, understood here as the examination of underlying presuppositions and animating forces; critical work in this sense is often left to other disciplines such as anthropology and political science (Clarke 2009; Kelsall 2009).

Yet the need for critical engagement is more acute given the developing crisis of legitimacy manifesting at the institutional sites of international criminal law production. Signs of crisis are evident from the growing assertions that the field has focused disproportionately on the African continent (Clarke 2009; Bikundo 2012). This was noted by many participants at the 2012 ICC Assembly of States Parties meeting mentioned above: at its opening session the Senegalese president emphasized that ICC proponents must ensure that it is not viewed as 'a court for the weakest', and at a side event the current prosecutor, Fatou Bensouda, acknowledged that the court's relationship to Africa has been beset by 'structural fault-lines'.[5] The court's inability to execute the arrest warrant against Sudanese president Bashir to date and African Union summit decisions on non-cooperation are among the more evident examples. Meanwhile, at the 2013 swearing-in ceremony of Kenyan president Uhuru Kenyatta, indicted by the ICC for crimes against humanity, Ugandan president Yoweri Museveni remarked:

> I want to salute the Kenyan voters on one other issue – the rejection of the blackmail by the International Criminal Court (ICC) and those who seek to abuse this institution for their own agenda. I was one of those that supported the ICC because I abhor impunity. However, the usual opinionated and arrogant actors using their careless analysis have distorted the purpose of that institution. They are now using it to install leaders of their choice in Africa and eliminate the ones they do not like.
>
> (Museveni 2013)

The ICC's exclusive focus to date on the African continent forms part of a broader set of concerns around interventions that appear to be driven by the Global North. There are ongoing contestations around 'rule of law' priorities: military interventions undertaken in the name of the 'responsibility to protect', the push for increased prosecutions of international crime at the domestic level, national 'capacity-building' and other externally driven transitional processes (Branch 2011). Indeed, a critical approach to the court's selective geographies might begin from the standpoint of viewing it in the broader context of what anthropologist James Ferguson refers to as 'transnational apparatuses of governmentality' (Ferguson 2006). Reading the court's work in this way shows how it operates as a form of governance *through* law that exceeds its formally retributive framework.

Controversy and conflict structure current discussions of the role of international criminal law, even when it comes to identifying shared definitions of key concepts such as 'complementarity' and key objectives such as the court's core mandate. These contestations stem in part from issues of identity: who forms the political community of the ICC and how that membership is established, whether through being a *de jure* signatory to the Rome Statute or whether through wielding *de facto* power. As shown through the Ugandan president's comments above, even state signatories to the Rome Statute may claim that their interests are not represented or that the court serves as a conduit of outside interests. The presence of non-state parties on the United Nations Security Council, which may refer situations to the ICC (as with Sudan and Libya), reveals an exception at the heart of this otherwise consent-based institution that further supports claims that states who determine where the court intervenes are not themselves subject to its authority. The ICC claims to carry out its work in the name of the 'international community', but this community is partial (not all states are members), inequitable (states parties do not have the same power, and some non-members enjoy considerable influence), and uneven in where it intervenes. The court's selective geography of intervention has offered support for its critics that prosecuting international crimes is an inherently political undertaking.

International criminal law harbours the view that impunity must be fought and eradicated through legal institutions such as the ICC. Within this understanding, law is thought to bring about an end to violence, yet as a lineage from Aeschylus's *Oresteia* to the work of Friedrich Nietzsche and Michel Foucault tells us, law becomes another contested forum of power and resistance. This legal field not only seeks to redress transgressions but also works as a form of governance. These insights have long been acknowledged within critical legal scholarship, yet they have been less present within the field of international criminal law. Regarding the juridical form of the ICC as a space of both power and resistance opens further avenues for critiquing its work. The crisis currently facing the field also offers critical possibilities, as the following section shows.

Critique and (a field in) crisis

Building upon the work of German historian Reinhart Koselleck, critical scholars have noted that the term 'critique' was previously connected through a shared etymology to the Greek term *krisis* (Koselleck 1988). Political theorist Wendy Brown writes,

> Nearly untranslatable from the holistic Greek context to our much more compartmentalized one, *krisis* integrates polis rupture, tribunal, knowledge, judgment, and repair at the same time that it links subject and object in practice. *Krisis* refers to a specific work of the polis on itself – a practice of sifting, sorting, judging and repairing what has been rent by a citizen violation of polis law or order. As the term winds its way into Latin and then the vernacular European languages, critique loses this many-faceted holism.
>
> (Asad *et al.* 2009: 9)

As the linguistic foundation of critique, *krisis* speaks to a broader world-view that is no longer evident in critique's modern usage, where it is often aligned with criticism and rejection. *Krisis* refers to dividing (creating a distinction), choosing, judging, and deciding. This suggests not only dissent and controversy, but also the constructive practices of reaching decision and passing judgment. As Brown notes, *krisis* is reflexive: it is the work of a political community upon itself, and is thus an immanent rather than a transcendent practice. Seyla Benhabib's account of Frankfurt School critical theorists also draws upon this earlier understanding of the term: "'critique' is the subjective evaluation or decision concerning a conflictual and controversial process – a crisis' (Benhabib 1986: 19). Also drawing upon Kosselleck, critical legal scholar Costas Douzinas notes that critique is imbricated with crisis, 'an objective historical process', and leads to political effects (Douzinas 2005). What this etymological understanding shows is that the subjective work of critique as an act of cognition takes place within a broader context of crisis – an event or set of events calling for judgments or decisions.

This understanding of crisis as a 'conflictual and controversial process' that calls for judgment and repair is a constructive orientation for critiquing the ICC. If international criminal law and its institutions are in a state of crisis, how should the work of critique be brought to bear upon the field? Unlike scientific epistemology, with its tendency to objectify, critique is thought to be part of the object-domain that it describes (Geuss 1981). It is immanent rather than transcendent and reflective rather than objectifying. The self-reflective exercise of critique is meant to foreground the critic's own stakes in this work rather than adopting a removed, 'objective', and 'scientific' standpoint. There is thus a diagnostic dimension to the work of critique, and critics are also reflexively diagnosing themselves to the extent that they engage in this work (Tallgren 1999). What orientation should be taken toward the object of critique? Is it suspicious? Corrective? Hopeful? Parasitic? This raises questions addressed elsewhere in this volume; namely, *who* is engaging in this critical work (Immi Tallgren, Chapter 3 in this volume), and on the relationship between the critic and the critique, which may entail a degree of complicity in replicating the terms and structures of critique's object (Michelle Farrell, Chapter 4 in this volume).

Another set of orienting questions concerns the purpose of critique. Critical work resists evaluating international criminal law in terms of success or failure, but instead asks about its underlying presumptions and conditions of possibility. For some critics this translates into a project of developing a more just legal field. Within international criminal law scholarship, for example, Mark Drumbl has claimed that his intention is not to abandon or 'constrict' law, but to improve it from within, 'through a sustained process of critique and reflection' (2005: 133). Yet for others this would amount to an 'efficacy critique', and more work needs to be done to reveal what the field of international criminal law is displacing during a time when it is considerably expanding, such as a focus on human rights rather than individualized criminal accountability (Schwöbel 2013).

These orienting debates about the objectives of critique have been addressed in detail elsewhere, and a critique of international criminal law can build upon this tradition. A rich history of critical legal scholarship spans three decades of efforts to unsettle the liberal sentiments of the legal field, to track its legitimating claims, to reveal its antinomies, and to show its inherent indeterminacy. Some scholars reflexively charted the approach of critical legal studies as it emerged within the legal academy (Unger 1982; Trubeck 1984; Kennedy 1985; Hunt 1986; Fitzpatrick and Hunt 1987). Critical legal scholarship drew upon insights from American legal realism as well as continental approaches of critical theory and post-structuralism to engage in what one commentator referred to as a 'critique of legal order' (Trubeck 1984: 600). Critical Legal Studies (CLS) emerging from the United States offered an internal critique of judicial reasoning and legal institutions, and was accompanied by the rise of 'law and society' scholarship that illustrated the distance between law's textual forms and its work in practice. The British critical tradition imported deconstructive textual practices combined with an attention to political context. The extent to which these strands are seen to be part of a related critical tradition is contested within the literature. Some commentators claim that the British tradition is more engaged with emancipatory political projects, while CLS in the United States is more jurisprudentially oriented (Douzinas 2005), whereas other interdisciplinary efforts within the North American academy suggest a broader critical landscape than what is traditionally identified as CLS scholarship (Brown and Halley 2002). Meanwhile, critical scholarship within the field of international law has sought to diagnose its argumentative forms and ideological structures (Marks 2003; Koskennicmi 2005). This work has informed more recent efforts to engage in an 'ideology critique' of international criminal law (Krever 2013).

These broader traditions of critical scholarship offer a number of animating questions and orientations that are relevant for a critique of international criminal law. For example, how does the legal discipline produce and reproduce its authoritative claims? What forms of power course through the discipline, and how are they obscured within and disavowed through legal discourse? Furthermore, what are the possibilities (and limits) of critique as an approach to the field of law and its institutions?

In addition to focusing on the power relations at work throughout the international criminal law project, a critique of the field interrogates its taken-for-granted understandings, or what Foucault refers to as the 'assumptions' and 'unconsidered modes of thought' that the practices we accept rest upon (Foucault 1988). Within critical legal scholarship in both its North American and British variants, for example, there has been a long history of critiquing liberal legalism (Unger 1975). Liberal legalism presumes that law can work to contain the political field and can protect individuals from the excesses of state power through a doctrine of human rights. Critiques of these presuppositions have been brought from within legal scholarship as well as in political theory. For example, writing about the rise of modern (positivist) law in the wake of decolonization, with its promise of formal equality and rights as a corrective to the disenfranchised status of colonial subjects, Samera Esmeir claims that

> liberal accounts of the modern rule of law equate its ideals with protection of the human. These accounts maintain that exclusion from the law, or assignment to an extralegal status, results in dehumanization. When the rule of law prevails upon the lives of the dehumanized, their entry into its domain occasions their rehumanization.
>
> (Esmeir 2012: 2)

Esmeir's insights concerning early twentieth-century efforts to bring former colonial subjects into the modern Egyptian state by granting them a status *within* law are relevant to the critical project taken up by this volume as well. The idea that coming within the fold of international criminal law – whether as victim, witness, perpetrator, or even (fragile) state – is a humanizing, dignifying, expiating, or equalizing experience is precisely the kind of ideo-logical presumption that critique seeks to unsettle.[6] International criminal law presumes a certain view of what justice ought to be, and it works to mould institutions to suit that image – for example, through the discourse of 'complementarity' and its attendant vision of extending prosecution of inter-national crimes to the national level. Bringing victims of crimes into the fold of international criminal law as participants in criminal trials is seen by many commentators as a progressive development within the field. Meanwhile, some academic work has begun to critique these presumptions about the progressive potential of bestowing legal recognition through the retributive frame of international criminal law (Kendall and Nouwen 2014). Indeed, legal recognition is restricted by its own limited categories, as is revealed by the field's work in practice.

This section has presented a broad account of critical possibilities drawing upon the traditions of critical theory and critical legal scholarship. I have suggested that critique may happen on both ideological and empirical regis-ters: some critical work may be directed at the field's embedded presumptions, and other work may take up how it operates in practice. Critiques of interna-tional criminal law ideology may foreground the field's liberal legalist framing, its focus on individual accountability, and its universalist presumptions. Yet there is also a need for critical approaches to international criminal law at the level of practice that considers the field's effects. As David Trubeck noted in the early years of the critical legal studies movement: 'Inquiry into practice at the field level and the micropolitics of legal consciousness would be quite consistent with the Critical studies tradition' (1984: 613). The body of Michel Foucault's work takes up both ideological and empirical approaches, and his broad consideration of the workings of power helps to orient a critique of international criminal law.

Across his body of writing, Foucault's analysis of power addressed its juridical forms – the classical model of centralized power based upon the figure of the sovereign – as well as its more diffuse manifestations in what he termed governmentality ('the conduct of conduct'), biopower (directed at the level of the population), and discipline (directed at the body). Foucault was concerned with drawing attention to 'where power surmounts the rules of right which organize and delimit it and extends itself beyond them, invests itself in institutions, becomes embodied in techniques' (Foucault 1994: 34). Without disregarding more juridical or 'sovereign' understandings of power – his later lectures acknowledge a triangle of 'sovereignty-discipline-government' (Foucault 2004: 108) – Foucault also sought to chart the workings of power 'at the extreme points of its exercise, where it is always less legal in character' (Foucault 1994: 35). This more complex and multifaceted understanding of the workings of power helps to illuminate some of the dynamics at work in ICC situation-countries, where it is not always (or solely) the court in The Hague determining priorities in 'the field'. Following Foucault, a critique of international criminal law would not only evaluate the court's exercise of juridical power emanating from its Hague-based centre (and its attendant jurisprudence), but also 'where [power] becomes capillary, that is, in its more regional and local forms and institutions' (Foucault 1994: 34). The critical frame should not restrict itself to formalist legal dimensions of the field, but should also address the *extra*-legal dimensions of international criminal law: how it produces effects in its sites of intervention.

Critiquing ICC practice

Scholarship on the ICC is frequently directed towards legal evaluations of what transpires in the space of the courtroom: witness testimony is transformed into evidence and judicial rulings are scrutinized for their relations to other ICC jurisprudence or that of the *ad hoc* tribunals. This positivist scholarship presumes a juridical model of power, where The Hague stands for the central point from which international criminal law emanates. It is focused predominantly on the court's 'sites of production' as opposed to its 'sites of reception' (Kennedy 2003: 635). The uptake of court practices (or counter-practices) at the periphery has been a more marginal feature of international criminal law scholarship. Few accounts address what happens at the court's more capillary sites of power: in field offices, in the interface between court actors and in-country groups working on the court's behalf, and in communities where ICC staff explain what is happening remotely in The Hague.

A critique of International Criminal Court practice can address the structural binarism of the court and its effects. Multiple court employees working in situation country field offices have referred to 'two courts' – one in The Hague and one in 'the field'. One staff member explained, 'I spent eight years at the ICC in The Hague, and I realized that the court is here [in Kenya].'[7] Even so, court policy is developed from The Hague and disseminated through field offices into conflict-affected communities. At times this dynamic of transmission from the core of international criminal law production to its peripheries misses the specifics of context, whether political or cultural. From this vantage point the court's institutional centre appears removed from the communities on whose behalf it claims to work, and decisions about the distribution of resources, personnel, and policy reinscribe this core–periphery relationship. This division between the 'two courts' is a binarism which ultimately reinforces the authority of The Hague, raising questions concerning who the court's constituents are and where they are located. Is the court mainly addressing itself to the 'industry' of the international criminal law field mentioned above, with its advocates and scholars, or is its primary audience the conflict-affected communities on whose behalf it frequently claims to act? Court practice, with its consolidation of staff and resources in The Hague, suggests the former despite policy statements about 'local ownership' as a driving norm.[8]

Meanwhile, far from the court's centre in The Hague where its power is more diffuse and capillary, its interventions at times appear *ad hoc* and experimental: 'haphazard', in the words of one Kenyan civil society representative.[9] This has particularly been the case with regard to the practices surrounding investigations, under the authority of the Office of the Prosecutor, and victim representation, under the Registry. The Office of the Prosecutor's decision to drive investigations from The Hague by sending investigators on field 'missions' rather than basing them in-country for longer periods has contributed to evidentiary weaknesses at trial (De Vos 2013). To address this by arguing for field-based rather than Hague-based investigations would support an efficacy critique that this volume aspires to move beyond. A different kind of critical perspective would treat this as a symptom of the consolidation of power and resources at the institution's core, with epistemological effects: the privileged site of knowledge is a Hague-centric interest in developing jurisprudence rather than in acquiring a more detailed understanding of social and political contexts. Although this is perhaps unsurprising for a court to focus on legal frameworks more than the social worlds in which they operate, this chapter argues that the ICC does so to its own detriment and to the detriment of those on whose behalf it claims to act. Meanwhile, the cursory knowledge of sites where the court is intervening leads to a kind of experimental *ethos*, where policies are crafted in the core and adjusted in the periphery to the extent that they can be adapted.

The category of the court-recognized victim provides another example of experimentation with tangible social effects, where identities are produced (and withheld) before the ICC. A court handbook for victim participants explains: 'In order to ensure that the voices of victims are heard and their interests taken into account during proceedings, victims at the ICC enjoy rights that have never before been incorporated in the mandate of an international criminal court' (ICC: 12). But how does the figure of the victim appear as a legal subject within the jurisdiction of the ICC? In his opening statement to the Assembly of States Parties, the ICC President noted the increasing number of victims to be 'assessed' and 'represented' – the active verbs of court practice oriented towards the production of victimhood as a juridical category. Yet these practices of assessment and representation are uneven across cases and situations, with understaffed and under-resourced members of the Victims Participation and Reparation Section (VPRS) focusing on clearing backlogs of incomplete participation forms. Meanwhile, individuals whose suffering does not fall within the boundaries of specific charges are not recognized as victims at all. Those who do fill in forms may wait months or even years to hear whether they have been accepted as participants, subject to the institutional vicissitudes of different ICC pre-trial and trial chamber timelines. Different rulings about modes of representation in The Hague produce effects in situation countries, where in-country staff must explain why approaches have changed and why some individuals falling under prior decisions receive differential treatment.

The process of 'juridified victimhood' that occurs within the ICC framework thus produces a subject whose own agency before the court is marginal in practice while over-determined in ICC discourse (Kendall and Nouwen 2014). Here the victim participant is a tenuous subject, seeking to exercise rights that are substantially narrowed by jurisdictional constraints and institutional practice, in a legal culture that overstates these rights and uses their theoretical existence to legitimate its own authority.

Practices of restorative justice at the ICC are also haphazard and experimental. The court's affiliated Trust Fund for Victims has a dual mandate of providing support to individuals and communities as well as reparations following a conviction. At least in theory, the work of the fund is one of the more inclusive sites of the court's work, as conflict-affected populations may receive Trust Fund-sponsored medical assistance and livelihood support through local partner organizations if they fall within the boundaries of the 'situation' – the broadest category that the court employs, in contrast to the narrower designation of a 'case'. As a former chairperson of the fund put it, through its work the fund was 'offering victims a path to the restoration of their dignity'.[10] Yet such a construction presumes that individuals are evacuated of their own agency and are left to wait passively for the judicial structure to grant them recognition and 'restore' their dignity. According to a civil society representative in Kenya, where the Trust Fund has not completed a feasibility study as of the time of writing, many individuals 'are suffering and some have even died on the basis of not having proper medical support or are living in communities that need Trust Fund assistance'.[11] Whether the Trust Fund could have made a difference through intervening earlier is unknown; what is striking here are the claims about the fund's restorative capacities set against the unpredictability of its work in practice. Meanwhile the fund appears to produce a kind of 'biopolitics' of care, in the Foucaultian sense of 'a tactic of power that takes the population as its target' (Dean 2010: 6), which in turn divides populations based upon juridical categories.

A further area of court practice that invites critical scrutiny is its dependence on the work of actors who are not directly employed by the ICC. Court officials have often stressed the limitations of the court's budget, and its Prosecutor has stated that her office 'cannot provide technical assistance and capacity-building' because 'the cuts have now reached the bones'.[12] With its restricted budget, the court has come to rely heavily on relationships with civil society actors and what it terms 'intermediaries' to support its in-country work.[13] As an intermediary in the Congolese situation observed, the ICC's limited resources negatively impact its work in the field. Another intermediary in northern Uganda expressed that working with the court's victim section (VPRS) is very difficult given resource constraints, and he has needed to sacrifice and 'preach the message of volunteerism'.[14] Meanwhile in Kenya, networks of internally displaced persons voluntarily work on the court's behalf at personal risk to themselves and their communities.[15] Those who work for the court as intermediaries are left to assume responsibility for their own security and for the security of the conflict-affected individuals that they are working with. By contrast, their ICC staff counterparts typically work (and live) in secure compounds and may enjoy UN and government assistance in carrying out their work. This disparity in the material conditions and security conditions of labour reveal a substantial gap between the institutionalized efforts to 'end impunity' from afar and grassroots concerns with accountability. These domestic concerns are often appropriated into the ICC framework without an attendant provision of resources and security from the court itself.

A consideration of some of the ICC's work in practice – investigations, victim participation, the provision of Trust Fund assistance, and the reliance upon intermediaries – thus returns us to this binary image of the 'two courts' described above. Further attention to these power differentials may build upon David Kennedy's critical call to 'revitalize' the tradition of analysing 'the role of law in the dynamic relationship between centres and peripheries' (2013: 12). This also opens further lines of inquiry about the ethical obligations that accompany international criminal law interventions.

Conclusion: towards a critical *ethos*

The gulf between promise and practice at the ICC necessitates not only political critique but also a consideration of the outcomes of its interventions. The court's work in practice raises ethical questions that do not appear within the framework of the ICC's legal mandate. The ICC Rome Statute's preambular claim that 'the most serious crimes of concern to the international community as a whole must not go unpunished' expresses the sentiments of the 'fight against impunity' – a justification for intervening in circumstances that is figured as an end in itself. What happens along the way – the by-products of international criminal interventions – fall outside the ICC's official mandate. They appear instead in an ethical register that is unrecognizable within the legalist frame of ICC practice. As a matter of law the ICC might be a strictly legal institution with a limited mandate, but its cultural life and ethical obligations stretch further, partly as a consequence of the inflated assertions it makes regarding its 'fight against impunity'.

At the level of critique, then, international criminal law scholarship can be more acutely attuned to the limits of institutional discourses, conflations between law and justice, and the exclusions (and injustices) produced through this legal frame. Justice exceeds the limits of law (Derrida 1990; Constable 2005); it is not something to be 'delivered' through the form of a tribunal, just as a victim's dignity will not be 'restored' by court recognition. Revealing the ICC's rhetorical excesses may be an initial step in instituting an immanent critique of its practice. Beyond this, there is the 'efficacy critique' of pushing the court's ethical obligations to take responsibility for how it addresses the conflict-affected communities with whom it works as well as those who work voluntarily on its behalf. The court's neoliberal concerns with 'efficiency' in carrying out its mandate further consolidate its resources for Hague-based work while subjecting in-country work to an economy of volunteerism and personal risk.

Part of what the court does – as many courts do – is to restrict its work to the purely 'legal', disavowing what falls outside of the (criminal) legal framework. Yet the practices described above suggest an ethical remainder that comes back to haunt the international criminal law project. In addition to focusing on the 'fight against impunity' and the individuals who are taken as exemplary enemies within this 'fight', a critique of ICL should focus on who and what is excluded: those who have suffered but fall outside institutional frameworks of redress, as well as the political and material conditions that make 'great criminality' possible. Such an orientation tacks between an efficacy critique and a broader critique of the very assumptions underlying the project, opening a space for critical engagement that includes both the realm of practice as well as the field's ideological underpinnings.

Notes

1 The 11th Assembly of States Parties annual meeting, side event hosted by No Peace Without Justice, 'Discussing an ICC Completion Strategy', The Hague, 17 November 2012.
2 Ibid., intervention by Stephen Rapp, US Ambassador-at-Large for War Crimes Issues, author's notes.

3 Ibid., presentation by Alpha Sesay, Open Society Justice Initiative, author's notes.
4 A report on the impact of the Special Court for Sierra Leone finds that it was widely regarded as 'effective' among members of the Sierra Leonean and Liberian populations. See No Peace Without Justice (2012) 'Making Justice Count: Assessing the impact and legacy of the Special Court for Sierra Leone in Sierra Leone and Liberia'. Notably, No Peace Without Justice had been assisting the Special Court with fundraising activities at various points throughout its operations.
5 The 11th Assembly of States Parties annual meeting, statement by the President of Senegal, The Hague, 14 November 2012, author's notes; side event on 'African efforts to end impunity: lessons for complementarity from national and regional actions', co-hosted by The Hague Institute for Global Justice and the Institute for Security Studies, The Hague, 16 November 2012, author's notes from statement by Fatou Bensouda.
6 For an account of the attendant risks of such critical work, see Farrell, Chapter 4, this volume.
7 Author's interview with employee of Kenyan field office, Nairobi, 27 November 2012.
8 The court's website describes outreach as 'a process of establishing sustainable, two-way communication between the Court and communities affected by the situations that are subject to investigations or proceedings': www.icc-cpi.int/en_menus/icc/structure%20of%20the%20court/outreach/Pages/outreach.aspx.
9 Author's interview with representative from Kenyans for Peace, Truth and Justice network, Nairobi, 2 August 2012.
10 The 11th Assembly of States Parties annual meeting, Chair of the Board of the Trust Fund for Victims Elizabeth Rehn's statement, 14 November 2012, author's notes.
11 Author's interview with representative from Kenyans for Peace, Truth and Justice network, Nairobi, 2 August 2012.
12 The 11th Assembly of States Parties annual meeting, statement by ICC Prosecutor Fatou Bensouda, 14 November 2012, author's notes.
13 The court defines an 'intermediary' as an individual or non-governmental organization which 'facilitates contact or provides a link between one of the organs or units of the Court or Counsel on the one hand, and victims, witnesses, beneficiaries of a project of the Trust Fund or affected communities more broadly on the other'. ICC, Draft Guidelines governing the Relations between the Court and Intermediaries, April 2012, p. 5.
14 Author's interview with Lira-based intermediary, Kampala, 11 November 2011.
15 Author's roundtable with ICC intermediaries, Kisumu, 30 July 2012.

Bibliography

Asad, T., Brown, W., Butler, J. and Mahoud, S. (2009) *Is Critique Secular? Blasphemy, Injury, and Free Speech*, Berkeley, CA: UC Berkeley Townsend Papers in the Humanities.

Benhabib, S. (1986) *Critique, Norm, and Utopia: A Study of the Foundations of Critical Theory*, New York: Columbia University Press.

Bikundo, E. (2012) 'The International Criminal Court and Africa: Exemplary Justice', *Law and Critique* 23: 21–41.

Bourdieu, P. (1987) 'The Force of Law: Toward a Sociology of the Juridical Field', *The Hastings Law Journal* 38: 805–53.

Branch, A. (2011) *Displacing Human Rights: War and Intervention in Northern Uganda*, Oxford: Oxford University Press.

Brown, W. and Halley, J. (2002) *Left Legalism/Left Critique*, Durham, NC: Duke University Press.

Clarke, K. (2009) *Fictions of Justice: The International Criminal Court and the Challenge of Legal Pluralism in Sub-Saharan Africa*, Cambridge: Cambridge University Press.

Constable, M. (2005) *Just Silences: The Limits and Possibilities of Modern Law*, Princeton, NJ: Princeton University Press.

Dean, J. (2010) 'Drive as the Structure of Biopolitics: Economy, Sovereignty, and Capture', *Krisis: Journal for Contemporary Philosophy* 2: 1–15.

Derrida, J. (1990) 'Force of Law: The "Mystical Foundation of Authority"', *Cardozo Law Review* 11: 919–1045.

De Vos, C. (2013) 'Investigating from Afar: The ICC's Evidence Problem', *Leiden Journal of International Law* 26: 1009–24.

Douzinas, C. (2005) 'Oubliez Critique', *Law and Critique* 16: 47–69.

Drumbl, M. (2005) 'Pluralizing International Criminal Justice', *Michigan Law Review* 103: 101–34.

Esmeir, S. (2012) *Juridical Humanity: A Colonial History*, Stanford, CA: Stanford University Press.

Ferguson, J. (2006) *Global Shadows: Africa in the Neoliberal World Order*, Durham, NC: Duke University Press.

Fitzpatrick, P. and Hunt, A. (1987) *Critical Legal Studies*, Oxford: Oxford University Press.

Foucault, M. (1984) *The Foucault Reader*, ed. P. Rabinow, New York: Pantheon Books.

Foucault, M. (1988) *Politics, Philosophy, Culture: Interviews and Other Writings, 1977–1984*, ed. L.D. Kritzman, New York: Routledge.

Foucault, M. (1994) *Critique and Power: Recasting the Foucault/Habermas Debate*, ed. M. Kelly, Cambridge, MA: MIT Press.

Foucault, M. (2003) *Society Must be Defended: Lectures at the Collège de France, 1975–76*, trans. D. Macey, New York: Picador.

Foucault, M. (2004) *Security, Territory, Population: Lectures at the Collège de France, 1977–78*, trans. G. Burchell, New York: Picador.

Geuss, R. (1981) *The Idea of a Critical Theory: Habermas and the Frankfurt School*, Cambridge: Cambridge University Press.

Hunt, A. (1986) 'The Theory of Critical Legal Studies', *Oxford Journal of Legal Studies* 6: 1–45.

International Criminal Court, *Victims Before the International Criminal Court: A Guide for the Participation of Victims in the Proceedings of the Court*. Available at: www.icc-cpi.int/en_menus/icc/structure%20of%20the%20court/victims/participation/Pages/booklet.aspx (accessed 15 September 2013).

Kelsall, T. (2009) *Culture under Cross-Examination: International Justice and the Special Court for Sierra Leone*, Cambridge: Cambridge University Press.

Kendall, S. (2011) 'Donors' Justice: Recasting International Criminal Accountability', *Leiden Journal of International Law* 23: 585–606.

Kendall, S. (2014) 'Marketing Accountability at the Special Court for Sierra Leone', in *The Sierra Leone Special Court and its Legacy: the Impact for Africa and International Criminal Law* (Cambridge: Cambridge University Press).

Kendall, S. and Nouwen, S. (2014) 'Representational Practices at the International Criminal Court: the Gap between Juridified and Abstract Victimhood', *Law and Contemporary Problems* 76(3–4).

Kennedy, D. (1985) 'Psycho-Social CLS', *Cardozo Law Review* 6: 1013–31.

Kennedy, D. (2003) 'Two Globalizations of Law & Legal Thought: 1850–1968', *Suffolk University Law Review* 36: 631–79.

Kennedy, D. (2013) 'Law and the Political Economy of the World', *Leiden Journal of International Law* 26: 7–48.

Koselleck, R. (1988) *Critique and Crisis: Enlightenment and the Pathogenesis of Modern Society*, Cambridge, MA: MIT Press.

Koskenniemi, M. (2005) *From Apology to Utopia: The Structure of International Legal Argument*, Cambridge: Cambridge University Press.

Krever, T. (2013) 'International Criminal Law: An Ideology Critique', *Leiden Journal of International Law* 26: 701–23.

Latour, B. (2004) 'Why Has Critique Run out of Steam? From Matters of Fact to Matters of Concern', *Critical Inquiry* 30: 225–48.

Marks, S. (2003) *The Riddle of All Constitutions: International Law, Democracy, and the Critique of Ideology*, Oxford: Oxford University Press.

Mégret, F. (2002) 'Three Dangers for the International Criminal Court: A Critical Look at a Consensual Project', *Finnish Yearbook of International Law* 12: 195–247.

Murray, S. (2007) 'Ethics at the Scene of Address: A Conversation with Judith Butler', *Symposium: Review of the Canadian Journal for Continental Philosophy* 11: 415–45.

Museveni, Y. (2013) Statement by H.E. Yoweri Kaguta Museveni, President of the Republic of Uganda, Inauguration of H.E. Uhuru Kenyatta, Kenya's President-Elect, Nairobi, 9 April 2013, *The New Vision*. Available at: http://allafrica.com/stories/201304091224.html (accessed: 28 June 2013).

Nouwen, S. (2013) *Complementarity in the Line of Fire: The Catalysing Effect of the International Criminal Court in Uganda and Sudan*, Cambridge: Cambridge University Press.

Nouwen, S. and Werner, W. (2010) 'Doing Justice to the Political: the International Criminal Court in Uganda and Sudan', *European Journal of International Law* 21: 941–65.

Schwöbel, C. (2013) 'The Comfort of International Criminal Law', *Law and Critique* 24: 169–91.

Sikkink, K. (2011) *The Justice Cascade: How Human Rights Prosecutions are Changing World Politics*, New York: W.W. Norton.

Simpson, G. (2007) *Law, War and Crime: War Crime Trials and the Reinvention of International Law*, Cambridge: Polity Press.

Skouteris, T. (2010) *The Notion of Progress in International Law Discourse*, The Hague: TMC Asser Press.

Stauffer, J. (2013) 'Speaking Truth to Reconciliation: Political Transition, Recovery, and the Work of Time', *Humanity* 4: 27–48.

Tallgren, I. (1999) 'We Did It? The Vertigo of Law and Everyday Life at the Diplomatic Conference on the Establishment of an International Criminal Court', *Leiden Journal of International Law* 12: 683–707.

Teitel, R. (2011) *Humanity's Law*, Oxford: Oxford University Press.

Trubeck, D. (1984) 'Where the Action Is: Critical Legal Studies and Empiricism', *Stanford Law Review* 36: 575–622.

Unger, R. (1975) *Knowledge and Politics*, New York: Free Press.

Unger, R. (1982) 'The Critical Legal Studies Movement', *Harvard Law Review* 96: 561–675.

Chapter 3

Who are 'we' in international criminal law? On critics and membership

Immi Tallgren[1]

Roadmap

This article is devoted to trying to understand those daring to approach critically the project of international criminal law (ICL) that stands for the survival of mankind, justice and peace, at its centre the ICC that 'is likely to become the central pillar in the world community for upholding fundamental dictates of humanity' (Cassese 2002: 18). I start by briefly presenting the rhetoric and doctrinal 'we-talk' in ICL. I then turn to my focus: are there critical voices separate from the 'ICL we' up to a point of forming a 'critical we'? If so, where do the voices of the 'critical we' emanate from and what do they say? I try to situate them in time, space and discourses of the field, and tentatively identify the critics' zones of comfort, as well as the shady backyard of unease. This manner of presenting patterns of thought and positions of actors as fantomatic collectivities has its limits: I will not be able to solve the fundamental issue of why and how do any human 'we's of identification, desire, political will, or disciplinary approach to the world come about and thereby also form their 'them, other'. I am merely flagging questions to be anxious about anytime you or I pronounce a 'we': How to engage responsibly without being oppressive and patronizing? How to live the concern and commitment without constructing blind alleys of expertise and ownership? How to look and see further than ourselves?

We-talk in international criminal law

'There is a pleasure to say we and not I,' Emile Durkheim confessed (1963: 203). This is a pleasure often enjoyed in the context of international criminal law (ICL): '*We* must never forget that the record on which *we* judge these defendants today is the record on which history will judge *us* tomorrow,' stated the American chief prosecutor Justice Robert H. Jackson solemnly in the Nuremberg trials in 1945 (1947: 101). But who is the 'we'? Whereas one 'we' may primarily refer to the victorious nations of a war, organizing trials for those accused of crimes on the defeated side, another 'we' evokes the representatives of states present in Rome to establish an international criminal court: '*We* have an opportunity to create an institution that can save lives and serve as a bulwark against evil' (Annan 1998, emphasis added). No doubt, 'we' as the plural personal pronoun stands for a variety of different things in particular uses and contexts. At the same time, the 'we' of international law – and here the 'we' of ICL, in particular – has ambiguous contours, as if implicitly encompassing more than just countries x, y and z, or a particular political or moral entity of particular adepts, currently vested in social engineering by criminal law and thus present in a particular diplomatic conference.

As in '*our* sacred task is to work to banish this great crime against humanity' (Clinton 1998, emphasis added), the 'we' of ICL frequently appears to grow towards representing a sacralized higher subject, perhaps the 'international community' that intuitively approaches a universalizing register as 'all peoples of the world' or 'humanity', of which ICL then forms an elementary building-stone. In the words of Cherif Bassiouni, chairman of the drafting committee of the ICC Statute: 'The establishment of the ICC symbolizes and embodies certain fundamental values and expectations shared by *all peoples of the world* and is, therefore, a triumph for *all peoples of the world*' (1998: xxi, emphasis added). Or, by Antony Duff: 'Some kinds of wrong should concern *us*, are properly *our* business, in virtue of *our* shared humanity with their victims (and perpetrators): for such wrongs the perpetrators must answer not just to their local communities, but to *humanity*' (2010: 601, emphasis added).

In this way, the ICC jurisdiction is at times seen as emanating from absolute moral sentiments shared internationally. These sentiments seem intrinsically related to a need of belonging to something higher, larger, and shared by all humans, bearing resemblance to the 'oceanic feeling' of religious faith that Freud saw accompanied by a 'feeling of an indissoluble bond, of being one with the external world as a whole' (Freud 1973: 1–2).[2] The species-centred discourse of 'humanity' with its aspirations to Enlightenment universalism is then overwhelmingly present and often uncontested in ICL, whereas it is suspect elsewhere.[3] The particular tones of universal voices have been made audible, for example by political theorists Ernesto Laclau (1996), Judith Butler (1996) and, in international law, Martti Koskenniemi (2005). Nevertheless, the 'we' of ICL gets lifted high above questioning by the emotions that violence in its extreme generates. That 'we' is as if inhabiting the scene: confronted with suffering, devastation, death, human beings utter the 'we' that aligns them into a collective subject of 'our' shared emotion, an epidermic humanity, and as the story goes, action. A natural, unavoidable 'we', a 'we' of survival of a civilization on Earth, as suggested by Jackson: 'The wrongs which *we* seek to condemn and punish have been so calculated, so malignant, and so devastating, that *civilization* cannot tolerate their being ignored, because it cannot survive their being repeated' (1947: 99).

The frequent 'we-talk' in ICL is then intriguing not only as such, but as a potential key in trying to understand ICL, or in broader terms international law. Could the naturalness of the 'we' account for why ICL seemingly resists as a relic of 'formal law'; when all other securities and authorities fail and human existence is at peril? A deep anxiety would explain the recent intense reliance on the conceptual frameworks of individual criminal responsibility, as well as the procedural aspects of investigations or testimonies about 'what really happened'. The search for frameworks of meanings and causalities that are putatively understandable and stable would be an instinctive reaction to expansion of the horizons in human interaction and knowledge globally, accompanied by a perceived growth and complication of risks and threats that gets referred to as 'globalization'.[4] ICL would figure among the last markers for the possibility of an (international) normative order and a control of that known order. Whereas this picture is extremely simplified, it would make some sense in explaining why the transcendence of ICL, with its *jus cogens, erga omnes,* Martens clause or other mystifications, gets so uninhibitedly celebrated, not only in popular belief but also in much of the doctrine.[5]

In the last 20 years, ICL has experienced a legislative and institutional expansion. In academia, there is a boom of new research and education programmes, dedicated chairs at universities, specialized journals, literature and conferences. Today, students are often entering international law via their interest in ICL. Those vested in the ICL in different roles in the institutions, government, academia or NGOs often manifest an affect and belonging to the field, perhaps a tendency to see and conceptualize the world with a bulk of its problems through the lens of ICL. As one indicator, they have their own jargon and referential environment in which they exchange on the prominent accused of today and of the past by their names, as well as on the prosecutors or the judges, as if characters in a shared story where only the victims appear anonymous. By the sense it makes and the faith it generates in criminal responsibility as an organizer of causalities, that story is seemingly somehow overshadowing a world of chaotic struggles for leadership and resources, of violence that technology makes constantly more efficient, of the deteriorating natural environment and the general inequality of opportunities of individuals, peoples and regions. This faith is envisaged as essential for human existence, as a common heritage of mankind to be passed from generation to generation: 'From Versailles to Rwanda, and now to the "Treaty of Rome", many have arduously labored for the establishment of a system of international criminal justice. Today *our* generation proudly, yet humbly, passes that torch on to future generations' (Bassiouni 1998: xxi, emphasis added). The expectations for international criminal justice are expressed in high ideals, to 'endeavour to seal the primacy of the rule of law, due process and human rights for future generations', in the words the ICC prosecutor in 2013.[6] Whereas recent commentaries report a sobering of tone in the rhetoric (Akhavan 2013;

Luban 2013), ICL is still firmly in the centre of what matters, as a church in the middle of the village.

But ICL is yet not the only Esperanto of international lawyers and other actors in the field. What lies outside or at the margins of the 'ICL we'? How to deal with the 'indignity of speaking for others' (Foucault–Deleuze in Bouchard 1977: 209), or in Herbert Spiegelberg's words, the '"arrogance of power" behind the patronizing usurpation of the right to speak for the "free" people of the world, when they have never been asked' (1975: 215)?[7] Does an alternative epistemic community exist? There are the critical observers who notice how the founding instruments of ICL, such as the ICC Statute, carry in explicit manner the signs of the complications at their birth. They are most visible in the blunt terms by which they direct the scrutiny from the centre to the periphery, from infrastructural, high-tech violence to its more primitive, low-tech forms, and from the responsibility of states or corporations to that of a presumably rational individual agent of large-scale criminality. There are voices who highlight how the 'we' in 'we punish serious international crimes' is clearly not a union based on equality, reciprocity and mutual respect that we-unions ideally are about (Spiegelberg 1975: 332). That the orators of the 'we' hold positions of dominance that distort the perspectives, and that this renders the 'we-union' of ICL sick, perhaps incurably (1975: 233), no matter how touchingly the charitable 'we' is dressed as the manager of the only possible moral order. There are critics who want to make it visible: that there are indeed conflicts of interest and political battles for power and influence; that they are not a temporary pathology but a persistent normality, since there is no universal agreement on shared moral or legal rules or on their application. There may even be some who believe that any 'we' or 'humanity' are just reified structures and 'thingified' social roles, elementary for mystifying the exercise of power and the oppression of the otherness, in terms of wealth, gender, North–South, religion, or on any other ground. Who are these people and what do they want? Would 'we' ever make sense with regard to them: are critics not individuals with the biggest 'I' ever? If the 'ICL we' got caricatured as hypocritical, dissymmetric and very much particular behind outspoken universal aspirations of solidarity and moral sensitivity, are those approaching ICL critically by contrast power-neutral, sincere, egalitarian and simply correct?

Voices of critical approaches

Heritages and ruptures

The 'ICL we' sketched above and 'critical approaches to ICL' have a history. Both could obviously be presented in various genealogies of ideas and actors, with continuities and breaks in time, positions and identities. I, however, desist here from finding the meanings of the tentative 'critical we' of ICL by comparing it to the recent or current CLS (Kelman 1984; Tushnet 1990–91), NAIL (Kennedy and Tennant 1994; Skouteris 1997), Newstream (Cass 1996; Kennedy 1988), TWAIL (Chimni 2006; Mutua 2000; Eslava and Pahuja 2011), the feminist approaches to international law (Orford 2002; Charlesworth and Chinkin 2000), or elaborating on Marxism and international law (Marks 2008; Mieville 2005), structuralism (Kennedy 1985–86), queer theory, the relations of critique and activism, and so on. In broad terms, there are likely to be shared approaches to be identified. Most critical people associated in meetings or journals sometimes flagging these different appellations might be able to say: 'Our work aims at destabilizing traditional conceptions of law and challenging existing institutions, often by way of a search for hidden interests, class domination and repetition of historical patterns of power behind them. We are sensitive to identities and identifications in law and by law and the inclusions and exclusions, oppression and suppression they may entail. We are open to experimental methods and our approach is often interdisciplinary. We are tolerant of differences in tones and styles of research and commentary.'

Analysing the melanges of blood in the various genealogies could be an enriching exercise, as well as a melancholic one, as David Kennedy demonstrates in 'When Renewal Repeats' (2000). It would be confusing also, not least with the classical issues of financial, linguistic and disciplinary boundaries. How to tackle, for example, the claim that today's critical 'movements' or perhaps rather 'sensibilities' just mentioned are mostly communicated in the academia of the North and published in English, even if frequently by non-native speakers, and that this focus on the English-speaking academia, with its codes of conduct and jargon, its renowned journals and publishers, is overshadowing not only other known critical corners, such as Ecole de Reims in the French-speaking world,[8] the autochthonous elements of Frankfurter school not yet imported, or *Kritische Justiz* published in German, but in particular a whole horizon of others one is even more ignorant of? Critical genealogies are likely to have their own empty spaces and silences. I desist also from explicitly addressing here the problem of my own positionality in this investigation: from what position (ivory tower?) am *I* hearing these 'voices'?

What would then be so very particular about being critical of ICL? Is it not about the same concerns, simply transposed to the context of international criminal justice? Yes and no, I think. An important particularity of being critical of ICL is the challenge of swimming in counter-flow to what is currently considered among the noblest goals to fight for, also in established critical encounters, such as some feminist commentary or TWAIL. In that sense, being critical of ICL differs from being critical of the role of multinational corporations in global liberalism or the nuclear arms race, for example. To have international law finally 'enforced' against infamous dictators or military commanders sends intrinsically powerful messages. Very few individuals outside the closest circle of affinities are defending the right of these individuals to retire peacefully. Beyond this, there is something very special about the mechanism of criminal justice in itself, in the density of cultural or religious symbols it represents: a moment of reversal of fates, a judgment of evil, a righteous infliction of pain in punishment, excommunication, redemption, grace, or expiation. Here is not the place to take this up in detail, but I do not think Emile Durkheim and his colleagues were on a false track when depicting a religious origin of criminal justice.[9] The ritual practices of criminal justice with the weight of violence, in the iconic presence of victims – that are instrumentalized as its putative *raison d'être*, as a critical voice might say – are stirring emotions, convictions and beliefs. To put it bluntly, the criminal accountability is the sacred cow. Space for critical questions, not to even mention transformative agendas, is scarce amid the distributed roles in black and white, mainly solemnly black. ICL is thus a field where a critic may find herself, contrary to the best of intentions, in the role of a dangerous heretic, subject to suspicions of cynicism and moral relativism. In the most stereotypical terms, she becomes the advocate of 'letting those guilty of genocide walk free'.

Another particularity of critical approaches to ICL originates in the peculiar relationship the international criminal justice project has both to criminal justice systems nationally and to research on criminal law, criminology or criminal policy in national contexts. Conceptually, a domestic analogy is in operation, but on an overly idealistic level: international criminal justice mimes the most perfect national criminal justice ever encountered in an existing society. In research, the *décalage* is perhaps even greater. At the national level, in societies where research and public discussion are possible, there is today little need to direct major critical energies to tear down fantasies about criminal law and law enforcement, simply because criminal justice is not seen as standing for empathy, humanitarian concern, or peace. Few express visions of criminal justice as an adequate instrument for achieving progress in societies. Nor are criminal procedures seen as establishing macro-level 'truths' or writing history. Criminal justice is rather considered as a necessary yet problematic part of the legal and institutional architecture of a society, perhaps a costly sanitary system of order and control, perhaps a slightly embarrassing steel structure of morality. Its ideological functions in maintaining hegemony or producing political sentiments and loyalties are more present in research than picturing it as a fruitful occasion for expressing and thereby reinforcing values unanimously shared, as ICL's 'utility' is often seen. A national scholar does not find particularly original the claim that criminal law is one of the focal points of conflict and struggle in modern societies, a means of legitimizing power. In international criminal law, that claim makes you a fervent radical. At a national level, criminological research demonstrates the challenges of concretizing and also of measuring positive effects of punishments, either individually or collectively, either by prevention, by retribution or by other explanations. Research is therefore animated also by desires of alleviating the damage and cost, human, societal and financial, of punishment. Victimology illustrates how deep the trauma and insecurity of victims of serious crimes may lie, how insufficient a mere trial and punishment are in alleviating them, and how both victimization and criminality often depend on socio-economic conditions. Seen from these perspectives, the ICL project with the rehearsal of a mixture of firm beliefs materializes a solemn and tightly closed mausoleum of idealized Benthamian, Kantian or perhaps Durkheimian criminal justice. As in any mausoleum, the atmosphere is heavy with respect and illusions of the great deeds of the past. Thick curtains prevent new winds from penetrating.

The critic of ICL is thus confined to operate in a demanding environment, to slide along the aisles of a church or line up at the entrance of a mausoleum. How does a critic occupy the space in between the church and the mausoleum? A tempting way to approach this would be a historical analysis: what kind of flavours have critical approaches to ICL had in the past, when understood in the broadest possible terms, to range from presenting critical questions, expressing doubts to the upright active opposition to the idea of international criminal trials and punishments? It would be a slightly aberrant approach also, digging up and dusting off the 'critics' in contemporary historiography that views the past century much in light of its pathologies as evidenced in the tragedy of the world wars which yet gave birth to the progress story of ICL: without those wars, what would one write about? To touch upon the variety of contexts would be complex, starting with the question of who should be chosen as the focal points of emitting positions. Academics? Institutional actors such as judges, prosecutors or defence lawyers? Politicians and their legal experts, international law counsellors of governments? The media, journalists, civil society activists? And what about the absent voices in the past: voices of women, the Global South, the subaltern or the proletariat? Until the 1950s or much later, any 'critical we' of ICL had the voice of a white male educated in the North. In that sense, there was no difference with the 'ICL we'. A few famous exceptions exist, such as Justice Radhabinod Pal, an Indian judge at the Tokyo Tribunal. Today, efforts are undertaken to give a standing and a voice to those who were absent or silent in international criminal justice. The challenge is how to respond to these multiple silences. With the best of intentions, there are risks of falling for retroactive retouches, remedial 'reconstruction work', as Hilary Charlesworth warns with regard to the silence of women (1999: 381).

I am here able to offer a mere skeleton of the fluctuations of positions. Close to the years of the First World War, directly opposing ICL occurred mostly in the sense of defending a certain kind of political realism one might also call *laissez-faire*. Critical approaches were expressed in the huge deception by those who had hopes for the Leipzig and Constantinople trials. There were efforts to redress these failures for the future in the League of Nations. However, the Convention for the creation of an International Criminal Court to try terrorism offences negotiated under its auspices never entered into force.[10] The seeds of establishing the crime of aggression by the Kellogg-Briand pact had virulent critics. A major change took place during and after the Second World War, when establishing criminal accountability for some of the unprecedented violence was seen as a sign of the possibility of progress of the ideas of international solidarity and collective action, after years of totalitarianism and war. Critical approaches to the efforts to organize international criminal trials were associated with either mere cynicism, or a certain political expediency, by Churchill or Stalin, for example. Or they were taken as a shameful defence of national sovereignty up to the point of a dangerous nationalism. Much of the contemporary academic discussion on legalism in the German context was put in the same basket with the defence lawyers of the accused in Nuremberg.

During the Cold War, ICL may have become too irrelevant to be critical about, for most of the time. These years are often presented as the silent years of ICL. Whether they were as silent as is often thought is one of the topics for critical research. In the chronological slot from Nuremberg and Tokyo in the 1940s to The Hague in the 1990s, major armed conflicts with atrocities and massive victimization of civilians took place, without audible efforts to entail international criminal responsibility for those responsible: Korea, Algeria, Angola, Vietnam, Cambodia, El Salvador, Nicaragua, Iran, Iraq, Afghanistan, Somalia, and the list goes on. A major exception to the silence of critics are the UN negotiations for the definition of the crime of aggression,[11] carried out in huge controversy intermittently for almost 30 years, in the tensions of decolonization and the Cold War. Likewise, national prosecutions of war crimes on the basis of the Nuremberg principles had notorious critics, such as Hannah Arendt on the trials of Eichmann or Jacques Vergès on the trials of Barbie.

According to the way the development of ICL is conventionally chronicled, it was the major violence breaking out at the end of the Cold War that stands out as special: after the decades of relative indifference towards it, ICL was rediscovered in the early 1990s faced with the wars in the former Yugoslavia and the Rwandan genocide that 'served to rekindle the sense of outrage felt at the closing stage of World War II' (Cassese 2002: 11). As 'the international community was sobered into action' (2002: 11) it became supremely progressive to insist that the perpetrators be punished, whatever their official position; that the barriers of state sovereignty be broken; that peace and development be grounded on criminal trials. Being critical of this powerful rediscovery was easily seen to fall into one of the following categories: conservative in the sense of defence of state sovereignty and non-interference; serving some particular national interests; or lacking vision and faith, being cynical, even 'post-modern'.

The criminal accountability euphoria that marked the 1990s culminated in the adoption of the ICC Statute in 1998 and its entry into force in 2002.

What happened thereafter, up to the first meeting convened under the title of the Critical Approaches to International Criminal Law in Liverpool in 2012? There are no doubt many ways to narrate those years. One way is to highlight how decisively the ICC was a product of *fin d'époque* before 9/11. In the ICC negotiations, the real-life context of reference for criminality to be suppressed had predominantly consisted of violations against civilian populations, or objectives in the context of an armed conflict of at least some systematic or large-scale violence, either by or in infamous totalitarian regimes or in chaotic situations of pure spontaneous primitiveness such as the Rwandan genocide was seen to represent at first sight. The likely theatres of these imagined crimes were at a considerable distance from the centres of power, since with 'the end of the Cold War many in America and throughout the industrialized world came to take national security for granted' (Reisman 2001: 833). These intuitive assumptions of the ICC project, on what 'the most serious crimes for the international community as a whole' (ICC Statute Preamble) could consist of, were dramatically shaken by the violence of 9/11. The large-scale victimization took place in a manner and a theatre that were disturbingly deviant from the way law and history are narrated in international law (Wright 2002). Following the shock that 'shattered the world view and, quite possibly, the emotional foundation of which the sense of security rested' (Reisman 2001: 833), nothing in the scenario of the historic examples of Nuremberg or Tokyo or the recent *ad hoc* tribunals for the former Yugoslavia or Rwanda seemed to be of use in the parts of the world that had been victimized or that felt threatened by 9/11 and other acts of terrorism associated with it.

As a consequence, the early existence of the ICC became dominated by a 'post-9/11' climate where own-handed justice by military force became omnipresent. The new judicial institution, built on sophisticated rules of international and criminal law, emphasizing due process of law and the balance of national and international law-enforcement competences, entered a confusing kaleidoscope of media images. Black gowns in the solemn ceremonies of The Hague celebrating the rule of law alternated with those of pure retaliations and wanton destruction of civilian life; of dehumanized individuals arbitrarily detained, tortured and executed, in violation of the basic norms of international law in the hands of the supposedly most developed societies of the world, on the legal cultures of which the ICC was founded. It became increasingly difficult to distinguish illegitimate violence from legitimate violence, and those who break the law from those who struggle for its respect. When a few years later it started to appear, in addition, that the ICC had a territorial and socio-economic focus on the Global South, in particular Africa, even the last of the progressive compasses were urgently recalibrated. The celebrated flagship of international law entered critical waters.

This skeleton account suggests a zigzag path where critical approaches to ICL oscillated between the international and national, the global and local, law as progress and law as politics. At times, a sense of crisis and loss of belief in an external authoritative system of order in the national sphere led to look-ing for rescue in the international, here ICL, in particular. If and when that promise became empty – state sovereignty or hegemonic alliances showed their faces lurking behind the façades of the new international instruments and institutions – the sense of crisis and loss of belief returned strengthened, lead-ing to fierce rejection and criticism of the international, and leaving the main options for the next movements as: (1) a return to faith in national systems and authorities, closer to the communities concerned and thus more authentic, sometimes up to romanticizing in the spirit of Rousseau on traditional forms of life and discovering vernacular means of problem-solving; (2) a remodelling of the ideas of the international, by other actors, with other principles, hoping to make its parameters correspond with the objectives the critics engage in, whatever they are; or (3) the static position of maintaining a critical voice for the sake of it, without engaging in reformatory proposals.

Latitudes of contestation and construction

At this point of studying a 'critical we', it is necessary to pay some attention to the terminology. Behind the words 'criticism' and 'critique', in particular, lie debates that I am not able to fully engage in here. Susan Marks's pertinent analysis on critical knowledge is very helpful in understanding the stakes (2000: 121–46).[12] I simply recall how Karl Marx distinguished criticism and critique, and how this distinction has been explained by Seyla Benhabib:

> While criticism … stands outside the object it criticizes, asserting norms against facts, and the dictates of reason against the unreasonableness of the world, critique refuses to stand outside its object and instead juxta-poses the immanent, normative self-understanding of its object to the material actuality of this object.
>
> (Benhabib 1986: 32–3)

Whereas criticism 'criticizes facts for their failure to correspond to imposed standards' (Marks 2000: 25), critique involves 'bringing out the true significance underlying [actuality]', pushing it to 'go beyond its own confines' (2000: 25, quoting Marx 1978: 14.) What then is ideology critique? For Marks, in ideology critique '[e]nquiry is motivated not only by curiosity alone, but also by a sense of injustice, a wish to break down barriers to the enjoyment of social goods' (Marks 2000: 121). Marks expresses the hope to persuade all of 'the connec-tion … between academic debates and political struggles' (2000: 122). In Marx' famous words, 'The philosophers have only interpreted the world, in various ways: the point, however, is to change it' (Marx 1969: 15).

What are then the different voices and directions of critical approaches to ICL today? In the first meeting convened under the title 'Critical Approaches to International Criminal Law' in Liverpool in 2012, a panoply of ways of understanding and practising those approaches was present. No later than the afternoon of the first day, tensions between different approaches appeared. Much related to the different latitudes of feelings of ownership towards the legal and institutional field of ICL. My impression was that the tensions culminated in the question of membership, in the terms of being inside or outside those who 'know what they are talking about', are legitimate, authentic and authorized members of the project, thus entitled to express some critical questions or recommendations. Up to a fence delimiting the area of members manifesting reasonable conduct, beyond which the critic is seen to burn her membership card: 'but you are not proposing anything, you are just destroying with cynical intellectual abstractions!' Whereas similar discussions have often taken place in other get-togethers of legal scholars and practitioners, in ICL this may have been the first time in the open. I will in the following investigate what this fence is made of and what one would find in the territories outside it. In order to go beyond enumerating the statements of 'law is political' or 'law is indeterminate' or 'legal institutions and actors are biased' and so forth as adapted to the ICL context, I explore examples of current topics in the field, with sketches of how various latitudes of critical approaches might face them. Acknowledging the risk of oversimplifications, I term the alternative positions 'criticism' and 'critique'. For the sake of clarity: I am leaving the adjective 'critical', the adverb 'critically', and the noun 'critic' for a general use.

I start the examples with critical approaches to a couple of categories of crimes in ICL, namely environmental crime and sexual violence. There the major division consists of either leaning on 'the ready-made solution' (Marx 1978: 13) of non-questioned utility and necessity of criminal trials and punishment, or rejecting it. With regard to the environmental consequences of war,[13] for example, *criticism* is likely to see as the main problem that there are far too few prosecutions for damage to environment in armed conflict. Whereas these crimes are already to some extent included in the ICC's jurisdiction, more and better international rules on environmental crimes should be enacted. The existing definitions should be enlarged to cover more acts that are disastrous to the environment and the work of the ILC on its Draft Articles on the Effects of Armed Conflict on Treaties should be supported.[14] With regard to sexual violence, a lot has changed in the last 15–20 years. This part of law and institutional practice is notable both as a success story of strong evolution since the Nuremberg and Tokyo trials, but also as a field frequently subject to critical attention. For what I call *criticism* here, the main problems lie in insufficient means or deficient legal rules to provide trials and punishment, or simply bad institutional policy. The call is for international criminal justice to pay more attention to sexual violence. The prosecutors must more often bring charges on alleged sexual violence and the judges must accord this criminality more punitive weight: that is, harsher punishments. To this end, the provisions criminalizing sexual violence must be read broadly. In order to assure more prosecutions and convictions, the institutions must be more equipped with relevant expertise in the phases of information gathering, investigations and prosecution. Special treatment, for example for witnesses, must be more broadly accorded. Counselling for victims and witnesses must be made available more systematically. For this purpose, more funds should be accorded to the institutions and relevant NGOs, for example.

What might a *critique* of environmental crime or sexual violence in ICL consist of? On environmental crime, its starting point could be, for example, how the defence and chemical industries produce arms and substances that could render the earth uninhabitable in a few moments, even without nuclear weapons; how these industries make major benefits out of this, entirely legally, and often enjoy public subventions to R&D or infrastructural investment. How developed countries sell these products and expertise to less developed countries with great profit, while their governments simultaneously engage in drafting exercises on international crimes or calls for jurisdiction, as well as policing efforts to contain the outbursts of violence. The Syrian situation would be the most concrete example of this in 2013. The critique would highlight that while punishing end-users may be important, it is secondary. The primary concern should be at the level of production and commerce. The critique would also insist on how individual criminal responsibility is not well adapted to environmental crimes with typically long-term effects on health, infrastructures and economical viability of entire regions. Corporate or state responsibility with palpable material consequences in a long-term perspective might make more sense than deprivation of liberty of few individuals.

Concerning sexual violence, critique might unveil the economic, political and social conditions in which the victims are being victimized, and that these conditions may be of a permanent nature: that is, not specifically related to armed conflict or other contexts where serious international crimes are typically committed. Critique might thus argue for attention to these conditions also after the sudden limelight of international criminal adjudication is dimmed. Critique could further remind that there are a variety of victims of sexual violence, and alarm on the ways in which an excessive focus on women in the discourse on sexual violence depicts women as vulnerable and dependent on protection, thus powerless by definition. Hereby it would not argue that sexual violence should not be treated as serious crime, but that women, even in the conflict areas, may have roles, energies and desires beyond the stereotypes of receiving gynaecological and psychological care. In exploring the multiple horizons of violence, the critique would be conscious of the history of, in Gayatri Spivak's terms, 'white men ... saving brown women from brown men' (Spivak 1999: 284), and the delicate place of white women in that history (Orford 2002: 275). It might also warn against the excitement of empathy that does not stand for long-term commitment for improvement of the living conditions of the individuals directly concerned but rather for excitement of compassion, the 'pornography of pain' (Halttunen 1995). In all this, critique would not be against criminal justice for environmental crimes or sexual violence or any improvements that could be introduced either at the level of law, institutional practice or resources. It would rather underline how insufficient and potentially distorted an exclusive attention on criminal justice can be, and beware of the smokescreen effect, giving the false impression that something sufficiently effective is already undertaken.

Another field of examples that I now turn to discuss is the relationship of international criminal justice to the Global South or 'peripheries', which at the time of writing of this chapter (October 2013) is culminating in the threats of a massive withdrawal from the ICC Statute that are to be discussed in the extraordinary summit of the African Union in Addis Ababa, at the request of Kenya who sees the ICC as 'not accountable'. Criticism and critique would start from the same parameters. The ICC statute has been ratified by over 120 states, while the major powers have chosen not to be bound by it. Its preamble underlines how 'it is the duty of every State to exercise its criminal jurisdiction over those responsible for' 'the most serious crimes of concern to the international community as a whole'. So far, the ICC prosecutor has opened investigations exclusively on alleged African crime and African criminals, using the three different trigger mechanisms of Article 13. Investigations in Uganda, Democratic Republic of the Congo, Central African Republic and Mali were triggered by state referrals. In Cote d'Ivoire and Kenya, the prosecutor acted *proprio motu*. The situations of Sudan (Darfur) and Libya were referred to the ICC by the UN Security Council. Several indictments are targeting the highest leadership, ex-presidents or presidents in office. Much of the tension focuses on the 'principle of complementarity', supposed to delimit the jurisdiction of the ICC to a complementary role only. As the current Libyan admissibility challenges demonstrate, the limit is cumbersome to draw.[15]

For what I here call *criticism*, the confrontations with some African leaders and civil society, the calls denouncing the ICC as 'neo-colonial' or a 'European court for Africa', and the proposals for a collective de-ratification of the ICC in favour of a broader competence of the African court are likely to relate to the following three factors. First, the law and its institutions are recent, so with time they will progress to reach maturity and the difficulties will ease. Second, the occasional inadequate institutional practices on the side of the states concerned or the ICC, such as the behaviour and personality of the first ICC prosecutor, for example. Third, the fact that the ICC statute is not (yet) universally ratified. Criticism would urge for patience, rectifying institutional practices, and most importantly, all states to ratify the ICC statute. With regard to questions on whether complementarity *de facto* obliges states to organize particular kind of trials, or whether the ICC should be competent to verify the respect of the fair trial guaranties by national jurisdictions as if a human rights court, criticism would be likely to point to the direction of 'positive complementarity': African states should reform their legal systems in order to bring successful complementarity challenges and try eventual international crimes in national jurisdictions. States should benefit from development programmes under the auspices of the ICC Assembly of States Parties, donor states and the NGO community, comprising external expertise and evaluations to aid developing national legislations and judicial systems to make them, by carrots and sticks, up to the standards set by the ICC statute and practice. The logic is that as soon as all states have evolved up to those standards, no problems will persist.

Critique might start by pointing out how the ICC statute is yet another international legal instrument setting up an international institution in the negotiations of which the Global South was *de facto* sidelined (Buchet and Tallgren 2012). Yet it became the territorial laboratory to test and adjust quality criteria, standards and institutional practice. It would highlight how underneath the polemics of a bias lie more fundamental issues of international law that go beyond the ICC as an institutional frame, the choices of individuals exercising power in it or the number of ratifications. Are there limits to the use of force? If those limits exist, are they universal? What kind of universality would that be, based on what? Critique might picture as axiomatic the way in which particular types or situations of use of force by some actors are understood either as tolerable or even desirable, if not sacred, while in others are considered illegal, criminal or outright incarnations of the evil. Self-defence, humanitarian intervention, responsibility to protect, and aggression could be cited as examples of the legal paradigms of justification or condemnation of violence that are inherited from an international law framed by powerful nation-states in a history which has not been a shared path to progress for everybody. Whereas built on a narrative of humanitarian convictions and universal morality applied in the legalistic frame of criminal law with its ideals of equality before the law and the measurability of crime and punishment, international criminal justice faces its own limits: the moral, political, legal and cultural foundations it is constructed on are not necessarily shared. The simplest of concrete examples on the inbuilt inequality of international criminal justice is the decisive role played by the UN Security Council. Critique might further question how 'positive complementarity' induces national legislative or institutional reforms that are determined from the outside. It would try to introduce a larger perspective: If the logic in which the ICC is functioning necessitates controlling national legal systems, how coherent is such an effort if compared to what happens outside the scope of the ICC jurisdiction, such as the international cooperation in counter-terrorism? Is there a global policy on criminal justice in general? If yes, what kind of political choices and hierarchies are involved?

One technique that critique would be likely to use to broaden the vision is historical analysis. It might try out parallels between the current policies of evaluating, controlling and complementing national legal systems with past experiences. In colonial legal administration, there were situations where 'legal regulation remained in local hands – an inevitability, given the limited penetration of imperial rule', even if the colonists, 'because of their higher position in the scale of progression', could, in the words of Peter Fitzpatrick, 'know and represent the natives better than they could themselves' (1992: 110). Critique might juxtapose the ICC Statute's provisions of 'unwilling or unable genuinely' to exercise jurisdiction as determined by evaluating 'principles of due process recognized by international law', 'independently or impartially', or 'a total or substantial collapse of unavailability of its national judicial system' (Art. 17) with the way in colonial times 'local law or custom could not be effective if found to be "repugnant to natural justice" or to "the general principles of humanity" and such – criteria intrinsic, of course, to a universal imperial project' (Fitzpatrick 1992: 110). Administering through local chiefs and through the instruction of local subjects maximized colonial presence by ensuring self-responsibility and self-management in colonized subjects. Frederick Lugard, for example, saw this as a way to obtain the best from local places and natives, while keeping them inscribed at the material and subjective level into large (international) structures of governance (Lugard 1922). As Luis Eslava demonstrates, Lugard's attempt to reconfigure the *modus operandi* of the international is patent: the international acquires a local face; what could be contested becomes familiar (Eslava 2013).

The final example concerns outreach. The institutions of international criminal justice are situated outside the territories, their populations living hundreds or thousands of 'miles away from the Tribunal ... established for their benefit' (Kirk McDonald 2004: 569). The staff members and the principal working languages are often foreign to the locals, and the law and procedures are unknown. After the negative image of the ICTY in its territorial jurisdiction, the other tribunals and the ICC have established programmes where dedicated offices and staff reach out to the populations by meetings, seminars, training programmes, publications, websites, radio programmes, and broadcasting of court proceedings on the internet. Gaining acceptance and influence in regions where international criminal justice is operating determines 'the success of these institutions and whether they can achieve their ambitious objectives' (Clark 2009: 116), to 'serve as deterrence, and thus prevent future victimization [...] bring peace and eventual reconciliation' (Bassiouni 2008: 20), as well as a closure to victims or historical records of the atrocities (Report of the Secretary-General 2004: §38). Whereas the early expectations on preventive effects have been down-scaled, a 'utilitarian' symbolism on a collective level is evoked as the most likely positive function of international criminal justice: reinforcing law and order, and expressing values of the international community.[16]

Criticism on outreach would be likely to highlight how complicated and costly all this is, and yet how essential. It might focus on the challenges of outreach when the territory is closed to the international staff, as in Sudan. It would encourage broader or better targeted programmes, more personnel and NGOs settling down in the regions concerned, all this culminating on the question of securing financing and physical security. The institutions or states should therefore accord more serious attention and budgets. More local antennae of international institutional actors should be established. Where possible, they should include local staff members. *Critique* would question the manner in which outreach and positive complementarity are advanced as projects of decentralization and heterogeneity, of consultation and local ownership, whereas a change of point of view shows them as 'imperial' instruments of extending the ICL's reach and the dominant human rights framework. It would ask whether, by seemingly focusing on localism and difference, the debate on complementarity distracts from a political discussion of structural arrangements and distributive issues, most notably those including the causes and consequences of the alleged patterns of international crimes (Nesiah 2011). It would question the priorities set from above in the material conditions of illiteracy, poverty, corruption or abusive governance, discriminations based on gender, ethnicity, or religion. It might also deplore the limited sustainability in time and the purpose-oriented nature of outreach offered in the colours of local development. Finally, it might question the ownership and educative programme of the 'moral learning' becoming 'common property of humankind', in which complementarity and outreach are supposed to be 'helping to devolve norms to local institutions' (Luban 2013: 512).

Antagonisms, parasitisms or symbiosis?

> The moment I inject discourse from my universe of discourse to your universe of discourse, the yourness of yours is diluted. The more I inject, the more you dilute …
>
> (Barthelme 1968)

'[I]f you seriously wish to be "new", it is not sufficient to cite Kant,' it was warned in a special volume on the New Approaches to International Law in 1996 (Koskenniemi 1996: 340).[17] It is not new either to turn to Kant in trying to understand how some international lawyers feel they need to make a particular set of legal rules and institutions prosper and grow, whereas others turn into critics. In the late eighteenth century it was in the conditions of absolutism confronted with Enlightenment ideologies at the wake of the French Revolution that Immanuel Kant entrusted the oversight of his ultimate political end, perpetual peace, to 'everyman a part time man of learning' (Laursen 1996: 259). For Kant, legal reforms and other enlightened developments were defined against a standard of 'publicity' – 'the public use of one's own reason […] as a scholar before the entire public of the *world of readers*' (Kant 1996a: 8:37). The 'vocational' use of reason, then, in the sense of the use which 'one may make of it in a particular *civil* post or office which he is entrusted', was seen by Kant as private. In this vocational use of reason it was 'impermissible to argue'; one behaves 'passively', as a 'part of a machine', bound by an 'artificial accord' to promote certain 'public ends' (1996a: 8:73).

Both the 'critical we' and the 'ICL we' may encompass individuals forming 'parts of a machine' (Kant 1996a, 8:37), for a part of their day. Their professional occupations may be identical. The difference would lie in the personal investment and willingness to engage in critical public arguments as 'a member […] of the society of citizens of the world' (1996a: 8:37). For Kant, officials obey, but when off duty they also argue for reform of the laws which they obey: in 'private' an army officer must follow orders, but shall be allowed to use freely his reason to publish criticisms of the 'errors of the military service' (1996a: 8:37). Public debate among scholars 'on the inadequacies of current institutions' contributes to spreading 'public insight into the nature of these things', possibly culminating in a petition to the crown for reform (1996a: 8:39).[18] In Kant's thinking, so much depends on the choice the individual subject makes on how to use his reason. But what affects that choice?

Two centuries after Kant, a legal scholar-official confesses: 'We think in prepackaged categories, clusters, reified systems. We forget the degree to which we invent the social world. We come to think that rules make us act impersonally; we often forget that we must continually choose to act impersonally' (Kelman 1987: 294). For Pierre Schlag, this is 'a repetition of the quintessentially liberal-legalist aggrandizement of the individual subject as a self-determining agent who fashions his or her world by choosing to realize *this* moral vision as opposed to *that* one' (1990–91: 1698). This (illusionary or real) freedom of choice would then be something the individual subjects engaged in ICL as their professional or intellectual occupation have in common. Would the choice to enhance and cement the 'ICL we' then be less of a genuine, independent choice than that of being critical, as the above quotes seem to suggest? How could this be explained? What sort of desires, fascinations or logics of attachment does the ICL project generate? Are 'the ICL we' acting under the charismatic authority of their own project and its emblematic figures, in Max Weber's terms (Weber 1947)? Does the 'ICL we' experience some form of Durkheimian sacredness in (international) society and law that is projected in particular on ICL? Would this, in contrast, mean that the *critical* individual subject would be more 'mature', demonstrate more individual 'responsibility' or a 'calling for politics' to be celebrated (Barnett 2002: 181)?[19] Or would it rather mean that they simply hold sacred other ideas or objects, are sensitive to other charismas or dogmas, follow alternative loyalties or affects? That behind what looks like a renouncement of references to the universal altogether, critical individuals venerate another kind of a universal reference, the 'truly universal'? That critical individuals have their mausoleums and altars too? I cannot go beyond flagging these dilemmas here. An in-depth analysis of how a disciplinary self-consciousness is constructed, to what extent that construction is a collective process or rather that of an individual 'as a competent intellectual and normative agent' (Schlag 1990–91: 1698), making conscious choices to either adhere or distance herself from a context, be it intellectual, ideological or institutional, is beyond the limits of this chapter, and perhaps my limits, too. Yet I believe these questions merit careful and unprejudiced reflection. What is crucial in that reflection, neither the individual nor the 'we' can be figured as above or outside the historical and geographical heritage of international law in general, with its roots in Europe, 'generalized into a representative of the universal' (Koskenniemi 2005: 114).[20]

If there is a 'critical we' that shares a common heritage with the 'ICL we', what is, then, their mutual relationship? In how far is the 'critical we' dependent on the 'ICL we': living out of its arguments to criticize legal instruments, jurisprudence and actions, just as a parasite devours the wood it lives in? Or is the relationship rather to be qualified as a symbiosis, in the sense that each one needs the other to define its contours, to inhabit an identification, to legitimate and institutionalize its existence in antagonisms: 'this is what we do not think, this is what we do not accept, that is what we have to fight against'? As alluded to earlier on, inclusion and exclusion as members in an intellectual or institutional project may both come at a cost. The more the 'critical we' approaches the 'ICL we', aspiring for knowledge, influence and recognition in the field, the more it faces difficulties in preserving its own voice and its (critical) objectives. Is it doomed either to assimilate up to losing its (critical) power or, on the contrary, to be marginalized on the forums of relevance up to an ultimate, autarchic solitude?

The specific context of ICL, of not dealing with investment treaties or the continental shelf, but with genocide, crimes against humanity, war crimes and aggression, may seem to point to a special responsibility. As discussed in the introduction, ICL is strongly affected by the weight of 'death and suffering which internationalism seems unable to prevent' (Orford 2006: 29). How do international lawyers relate to death and suffering as individuals? A general observation, with the wrong it no doubt causes to individual histories, would have it that many lead lives that are if not wealthy and secure, at least are at a distance from the violence and danger of the main theatres of serious international crimes. In that case the individuals share not only the professional commitment to get involved but also the position of outsiders, spectators. This position leads to dilemmas. The disparity of living conditions accentuates the problem of 'people knowing so little and feeling so much' (Rieff 1995: 42). Many remember Arundhati Roy's devastating questions concerning 'those who make a professional life off their expertise in poverty and despair … at what point does a scholar stop being a scholar and become a parasite who feeds off of despair and dispossession?' (2001: 26). A separate ethical challenge to international criminal lawyers is to ask in how far does the focus on ICL and its institutions render sensible only to the particular kind of death and suffering, whereas other types of loss of life and pain are obscured to the point of becoming indifferent. While the 'drama of justice' in ICL is analysed, admired or criticized, other tragedies and horror films proceed parallel. They just have fewer spectators.

A constructive way to understand the 'critical we' and the 'ICL we' as complementary would present itself if both the law and the institutional practice were seen as verbal constructions in a relationship comparable to that of literary fiction and the 'real world' (Waugh 1984). The 'critical we' would have the role to shake the narrative with sometimes crude intrusions to make evident the way the project is mediated and constructed, written and directed, in ways that are by no means consensual or self-evident. The critics would force themselves and others not to fall in the tempting mode of suspension of disbelief: 'Of course we *know* that what we are reading is not "real", but we suppress the knowledge in order to increase our enjoyment' (Waugh 1984: 33). While the 'ICL we' would be occupied with reinforcing the sense of a coherent reality and advancing the lines of the narrative of progress of international law, the 'critical we' would be busy finding ways of splitting it open, of exposing the mechanisms leading to what it may consider an illusion. As a counter-weight to the universalistic claims of incontestable common good by the 'ICL we', the 'critical we' would aim at creating a 'new awareness of how the meanings and values of that world have been constructed and how, therefore, they can be challenged or changed' (1984: 34). The risk that critics are enduring figures in that law's 'as if', '*comme si*', as Lenoble and Ost call it in their study on legal rationality (1980: 549),[21] may be a condition to exist in that universe, to exercise a meaningful role in it.

Another manner in which the 'ICL we' may need the 'critical we' appears by setting this question in terms of frame theory. The need for the 'critical we' could lie in the circumstance that the 'critical we' is likely to manage just a minor frame-break that the ICL project's created sense of 'reality' is capable of resisting. Minor frame-breaks may end up serving contrary aims, reaffirming the established frame, ensuring its 'continuity and viability' (Goffman 1986: 382). Similarly, rituals of contestation or protestation at times end up confirming the order they are contesting.[22] Contrary to its outspoken intentions, the 'critical we' may find that its engagement contributes to perpetuating ICL. Are there ever going to be critical approaches to ICL that break the frame and reverse the order, eroding the edifice?

Bring down those walls!

Such a scenario pushes critical approaches to the heart of their zone of discomfort, in its centre the theme of abolition that hardly anyone approaches.[23] The 'so what do you propose?' question stands for the often-heard expectations of usefulness of any disciplinary contribution or involvement, in positioning in between reformers and critics (Kennedy 2000: 461–6). Many crucial dilemmas are involved. Are critics always against, and against what? Are critics 'cynical', 'nihilistic', or rather incurably 'idealistic', and thereby so 'unrealistic'? Should critics be 'constructive', and, if yes, what should they construct and why? Do critics have agendas, and can they take political responsibility? And do the ones defending and nourishing the existing international law and institutions take responsibility for the consequences of their actions? How exactly do they do it?

Were the antagonistic, parasitic or symbiotic 'we's of ICL to come crashing down with the cement of the edifice, what would the world look like? Many other buildings might still stand steady. There would still be life on Earth. That is where the greatest challenges of any critical intellectual commitment or professional engagement in ICL may lie: how to stretch out from the 'ornamental structure' (Morgan 2007: 169) of law and its institutions, their reforms, their exciting labyrinths of ownership and expertise? How to open the windows of mausoleums, be more tolerant about one's own church and those of others? Would it be possible to reach beyond ICL for discovering other grammars to express and understand what is today anxiously experienced as a destabilization of the living conditions globally and a lack of international solidarity? Perhaps by dispersing some of the affect jam around ICL and its institutions, spaces would open to engender new directions for engaging energies.

Notes

1 I would like to thank warmly Grietje Baars, Antoine Buchet, Hilary Charlesworth, Martti Koskenniemi, Sarah Nouwen, Gerry Simpson, Thomas Skouteris, Sujith Xavier, the colleagues and friends present at the Liverpool conference in December 2012, and the editor of this volume Christine Schwöbel-Patel for their precious comments and support.
2 See also Koskenniemi (2012: 1–2), referring to a feeling that 'has frequently received expression in ethical, religious and legal doctrines that emphasize altruism, love for one's fellowmen or indeed humanity as a whole as the basis of ambitious intellectual and political agendas for world government.'
3 See, for example, A. MacIntyre, *After Virtue: A Study in Moral Theory*, Notre Dame, IN: University of Notre Dame Press, 1981; R.N. Bellah *et al.*, *Habits of the Heart: Individualism and Commitment in American Life*, Berkeley, CA: University of California Press, 1985; R. Rorty, *Contingency, Irony, Solidarity*, New York: Cambridge University Press, 1989.
4 By 'globalization' is meant both 'the inexorable integration of markets, nation-states and technologies to a degree never witnessed before – in a way that is enabling individuals, corporations and nation-states to reach around the world faster, deeper and cheaper than ever before', Friedman (1999: 7), and more diffuse evolutions towards irrelevance of geographical borders in the political, social and cultural identity.
5 See, for example, R. Teitel, *Humanity's Law*, Oxford: Oxford University Press, 2012; A.A. Cancado Trindade, *International Law for Humankind: Towards a New Jus Gentium*, The Hague: Martinus Nijhoff, 2010; P.-M. Dupuy, 'L'Unité de l'ordre juridique international: Cours général de droit international public', *Recueil des Cours*, 2002, 297.
6 Prosecutor Fatou Bensouda, presenting her fifth report concerning the situation in Libya to the UN SC, 8 May 2013.

7 See I. Tallgren, 'The We-Voice of the International: Who Is Speaking', in S. Nouwen and W. Werner (eds) forthcoming, 2014.

8 For recent discussions, see, for example, R. Bachand (ed.), *Théorie critique du droit international*, Brussels: Bruylant, 2013.

9 See E. Durkheim, *De la division du travail social*, Paris, Quadrige/PUF, 2007 [1893]; M. Mauss, *La religion et les origines du droit pénal d'après un livre récent, Oeuvres II. Représentations collectives et diversité des civilisations*, Paris: Editions de minuit, 1969 [1896]; P. Huvelin, 'Magie et droit individuel', *Année sociologique*, 1905–06, 10: 1–47.

10 Adopted on 16 November 1937. See also V.V. Pella, 'Towards an International Criminal Court', *American Journal of International Law*, 1950, 44: 37ff.

11 The General Assembly resolution 3314 (XXIX), with the Definition of Aggression annexed to it, was adopted on 14 December 1974.

12 Other essential readings are, for example, Beatrice Hanssen's analysis of the tensions between post-structuralist and critical theory (Hanssen 2000) and Robert Cox's distinction into problem-solving theory and critical theory in 'Social Forces, States, and World Orders: Beyond International Relations Theory', *Millennium*, 1981, 10: 126.

13 See, for example, A.T. Kassim and D. Barceló (eds), *Environmental Consequences of War and Aftermath*, New York: Springer, 2009; J.E. Austin and C.E. Bruch, *The Environmental Consequences of War: Legal, Economic, and Scientific Perspectives*, Cambridge: Cambridge University Press, 2000.

14 Draft Articles on the Effects of Armed Conflicts on Treaties, with Commentaries, adopted at the 63rd session of the ILC (2011). Available at: www.untreaty.un.org/ilc/texts/instruments/English/commentaries/1_10_2011.pdf.

15 Libya challenges the ICC jurisdiction in the cases of Saïf al-Islam and Abdullah Al-Senussi; for the latest development see: www.icc-cpi.int. See also S. Nouwen, *Complementarity in the Line of Fire: The Catalysing Effect of the International Criminal Court in Uganda and Sudan*, Cambridge: Cambridge University Press, 2013.

16 See, for example, I. Bantekas and S. Nash, *International Criminal Law*, Abingdon: Routledge/Cavendish, 2007. See also M. van de Kerchove, 'La dimension symbolique du droit pénal du droit pénal et les limites de son instrumentalisation', in Ch.-A. Morand (ed.) *L'Etat propulsif*, Paris: PubliSud, 1991. Generally on justifications, see M. Drumbl, *Atrocity, Punishment and International Criminal Law*, New York: Cambridge University Press, 2007; I. Tallgren, 'The Sensibility and Sense of International Criminal Law', *European Journal of International Law*, 2002, 13: 561–95. On the recent sobering of the expectations, see Akhavan (2013).

17 Koskenniemi (1996) refers to O. Korhonen's argument in 'Liberalism and International Law: A Centre Projecting a Periphery', *Nordic Journal of International Law*, 1996, 65: 481–532.

18 After bitter experiences under Frederick William II, Kant narrowed down the scope of this freedom, according the privilege of free debate only to the 'learned community' of professors. For Kant, legal scholars had to teach what they are told, whereas the scholars in the faculty of philosophy had more liberty. Legal scholars could, however, debate freely among themselves (Kant 1996b, 7:20). See also Laursen (1996); A. Perreau-Saussine, 'Immanuel Kant on International Law', in S. Besson and J. Tasioulas (eds) *The Philosophy of International Law*, Oxford and New York: Oxford University Press, 2010. On the 'subversive' purposes Kant may have had in his analysis of 'public' and 'publicity', see Michel Foucault's interpretation of Kant's enlightenment vs. critique (Foucault 1996, 386–93), and Beatrice Hanssen's analysis on this (Hanssen 2000: 30–96).

19 See also Orford's analysis of Barnett's account (Orford 2013: 179–80).

20 See A. Anghie, *Imperialism, Sovereignty and the Making of International Law*, Cambridge and New York: Cambridge University Press, 2007; M. Koskenniemi, *The Gentle Civilizer of Nations: The Rise and Fall of International Law 1870–1960*, Cambridge and New York: Cambridge University Press, 2002; W.G. Grewe, *The Epochs of International Law*, Berlin and New York: Walter de Gruyter, 2000.

21 '… tout s'y passe en effet "comme si" le droit s'assurait d'emblée l'intelligibilité complète et la validité absolue' (p. 549).

22 See, for example, David Kertzer, *Ritual, Politics, and Power*, New Haven, CT and London: Yale University Press, 1988.

23 See, however, Grietje Baars (Chapter 9 in this volume); also R. Knox, 'Strategy and Tactics', *The Finnish Yearbook of International Law*, 2012, 21: 193–229.

Bibliography

Address by the UN Secretary-General on 15 June 1998. Available at: www.un.org/icc/speeches.htm.

Akhavan, P. (2013) 'The Rise, and Fall, and Rise, of International Criminal Justice', *Journal of International Criminal Justice* 11: 527–36.

Annan, K. (1998) Address by the UN Secretary-General in the Rome Conference on 15 June 1998. Available at: www.un.org/icc/speeches.htm.

Bassiouni, M.C. (1998) *The Statute of the International Criminal Court: A Documentary History*, Ardsley, New York: Transnational Publishers.

Bassiouni, M.C. (2008) 'The Need for International Accountability', in M.C. Bassiouni (ed.) *International Criminal Law*, Vol. 3, Leiden: Brill.

Barnett, M. (2002) *Eyewitness to a Genocide: The United Nations and Rwanda*, Ithaca, NY: Cornell University Press.

Barthelme, D. (1968) *Snow White*, London: Cape.

Benhabib, S. (1986) *Critique, Nom, and Utopia: A Study of the Foundations of Critical Theory*, New York: Columbia University Press.

Bouchard, D.F. (1972) 'Intellectuals and Power: A Conversation with Michel Foucault and Gilles Deleuze', in *Language, Counter-Memory, Practice: Selective Essays and Interviews by Michel Foucault*, Ithaca, NY: Cornell University Press, 1977.

Buchet, A. and Tallgren, I. (2012) 'Sur la route de Rome – Les negotiations préalables à l'adoption du Statut de la Cour pénale international', in J. Fernandez and X. Pacreau (eds) *Commentaire du Statut de Rome de la Cour Pénale Internationale*, Paris: Pedone.

Butler, J. (1996) 'Universality in Culture', in M. Nussbaum (ed.) *For the Love of the Country: Debating the Limits of Patriotism*, Boston, MA: Beacon Press.

Cass, D.Z. (1996) 'Navigating the Newstream: Recent Critical Scholarship in International Law', *Nordic Journal of International Law* 65: 341–83.

Cassese, A. (2002) 'From Nuremburg to Rome: From Ad Hoc International Criminal Tribunals to the International Criminal Court', in A. Cassese, P. Gaeta and J. Jones (eds) *The Rome Statute of the International Criminal Court: A Commentary*, Oxford: Oxford University Press.

Charlesworth, H. (1999) 'Feminist Methods in International Law', *American Journal of International Law* 93: 379.

Charlesworth, H. and Chinkin, C. (2000) *The Boundaries of International Law: A Feminist Analysis*, Manchester: Manchester University Press.

Chimni, B.S. (2006) 'Third World Approaches to International Law: Manifesto', *International Community Law Review* 8: 3–27.

Clark, J.N. (2009) 'International War Crimes Tribunals and the Challenge of Outreach', *International Criminal Law Review* 9: 99–116.

Clinton, B. (1998) President Clinton's speech in Rwanda in March 1998. Available at: www.clintonfoundation.org/legacy/032598-speech-by-the-president-to-survivors-rwanda.htm.

Durkheim, E. (1963 [1925]) *L'Éducation Morale*, Paris: Presses Universitaires de France.

Duff, A. (2010) 'Authority and Responsibility in International Criminal Law', in S. Besson and J. Tasioulas (eds) *The Philosophy of International Law*, Oxford and New York: Oxford University Press.

Eslava, L. (2013) *Local Space, Global Life: The Everyday Operation of International Law and Development*, unpublished thesis, University of Melbourne.

Eslava, L. and Pahuja, S. (2011) 'Between Resistance and Reform: TWAIL and the Universality of International Law', *Trade, Law and Development* 3: 103–30.

Fifth Report of the Prosecutor of the International Criminal Court to the UN Security Council pursuant to UNSCR 1970 (2011).

Fitzpatrick, P. (1992) *The Mythology of Modern Law*, London and New York: Routledge.

Foucault, M. (1996) 'What is Critique?', in J. Schmidt (ed.) *What is Enlightenment? Eighteenth Century Answers and Twentieth Century Questions*, Berkeley and Los Angeles: University of California Press.

Freud, S. (1973) *Civilization and its Discontents*, London: Hogarth Press.

Friedman, T.L. (1999) *The Lexus and the Olive Tree: Understanding Globalization*, New York: Farrar, Straus and Giroux.

Goffman, E. (1986 [1974]) *Frame Analysis*, Boston, MA: Northeastern University Press.

Halttunen, K. (1995) 'Humanitarianism and the Pornography of Pain in Anglo-American Culture', *American Historical Review* 100: 303–34.

Hanssen, B. (2000) *Critique of Violence: Between Poststructuralism and Critical Theory*, London and New York: Routledge.

Jackson, R.H. (1947) in *The Trial of the Major War Criminals Before the International Military Tribunal*, Part II. Available at: www.loc.gov/rr/frd/Military_Law/NT_major-war-criminals.html.

Kant, I. (1996a [1784]) 'An Answer to the Question: What is Enlightenment?', *Practical Philosophy*, Cambridge: Cambridge University Press.

Kant, I. (1996b [1798]) 'The Conflict of the Faculties', *Religion and Rational Theology*, Cambridge: Cambridge University Press.

Kelman, M. (1987) *A Guide to Critical Legal Studies*, Cambridge, MA: Harvard University Press.

Kennedy, D. (1985–86) 'Critical Theory, Structuralism and Contemporary Legal Scholarship', *New England Law Review* 21: 209–90.

Kennedy, D. (1988) 'A New Stream of International Law Scholarship', *Wisconsin International Law Journal* 7: 1–49.

Kennedy, D. (2000) 'When Renewal Repeats: Thinking against the Box', *New York University Journal of International Law and Politics* 32: 335–500.

Kennedy, D. and Tennant, C. (1994) 'New Approaches to International Law: A Bibliography', *Harvard International Law Journal* 25: 417–60.

Kirk McDonald, G. (2004) 'Problems, Obstacles and Achievements of the ICTY', *Journal of International Criminal Justice* 2: 558–71.

Koskenniemi, M. (1996) 'Preface', *Nordic Journal of International Law* 71: 337–40.

Koskenniemi, M. (2005) 'International Law in Europe: Between Tradition and Renewal', *European Journal of International Law* 16: 113–24.

Koskenniemi, M. (2012) 'The Project of World Community', in A. Cassese, *Realizing Utopia: The Future of International Law*, Oxford: Oxford University Press.

Laclau, E. (1996) *Emancipations*, London and New York: Verso.

Laursen, J.C. (1996) 'The Subversive Kant: The Vocabulary of "Public" and "Publicity"', in J. Schmidt (ed.) *What is Enlightenment?: Eighteenth Century Answers and Twentieth Century Questions*, Berkeley and Los Angeles: University of California Press.

Lenoble, J. and Ost, F. (1980) *Droit, mythe et raison. Essai sur la dérive mytho-logique de la rationalité juridique*, Brussels: Facultés Universitaires Saint-Louis.

Luban, D. (2013) 'After the Honeymoon', *Journal of International Criminal Justice* 11: 505–15.

Lugard, F. (1922) *The Dual Mandate in British Tropical Africa*, Edinburgh and London: W. Blackwood.

Marks, S. (2000) *The Riddle of All Constitutions*, Oxford: Oxford University Press.

Marks, S. (ed.) (2008) *International Law on the Left*, Cambridge and New York: Cambridge University Press.

Marx, K. (1969) *Marx/Engels Selected Works*, Vol. 1, Moscow: Progress Publishers.

Marx, K. (1978) *The German Ideology*, reprinted in R. Tucker (ed.) *The Marx-Engels Reader*, 2nd edn, New York: W.W. Norton.

Mieville, C. (2005) *Between Equal Rights: A Marxist Theory of International Law*, Leiden: Brill.

Morgan, E. (2007) *The Aesthetic of International Law*, Toronto: University of Toronto Press.

Mutua, M. (2000) 'What is TWAIL?', *Proceedings of the 94th Annual Meeting of the American Society of International Law*, pp. 31–40.

Nesiah, V. (2011) 'Complementarity: Local Ownership of Global Governance', conference paper, International Law and Empire, Helsinki, 4–6 October.

Orford, A. (2002) 'Feminism, Imperialism and the Mission of International Law', *Nordic Journal of International Law* 71: 275–96.

Orford, A. (ed.) (2006) *International Law and its Others*, Cambridge: Cambridge University Press.

Orford, A. (2013) 'On International Legal Method', *London Review of International Law* 1: 166–97.

Reisman, M. (2001) 'In Defense of World Public Order', *American Journal of International Law* 95: 833.

Report of the Secretary-General on the Rule of Law and Transitional Justice in Conflict and Post-Conflict Societies, UN Doc. S/2004/616, 23 August 2004, § 38.

Rieff, D. (1995) *Slaughterhouse: Bosnia and the Failure of the West*, New York: Simon & Schuster.

Roy, A. (2001) *Power Politics*, Cambridge, MA: South End Press.

Schlag, P. (1990–91) 'The Problem of the Subject', *Texas Law Review* 69: 1627–743.

Spiegelberg, H. (1975) '"We": A Linguistic and Phenomenological Analysis', in *Doing Phenomenology*, The Hague: Martinus Nijhoff.

Skouteris, T. (1997) 'Fin de NAIL: New approaches to international law and its impact on contemporary international legal scholarship', *Leiden Journal of International Law* 10: 415–20.

Spivak, G.C. (1999) *A Critique of Postcolonial Reason: Toward a History of the Vanishing Present*, Cambridge, MA: Harvard University Press.

The Trial of German Major War Criminals: Proceedings of the International Military Tribunal sitting at Nuremberg, Part I, 20 Nov. 1945 to 1 Dec. 1945, p. 51.

Tushnet, M. (1990–91) 'Critical Legal Studies: A Political History', *Yale Law Journal* 100: 1515–46.

Waugh, P. (1984) *Metafiction*, London and New York: Routledge.

Weber, M. (1947) *Theory of Social and Economic Organization*, New York: Free Press.

Wright, S. (2002) 'The Horizon of Becoming: Culture, Gender and History after September 11', *Nordic Journal of International Law* 71: 215–53.

Chapter 4

Critique, complicity and I

Michelle Farrell[1]

Introduction

This chapter explores some of my unease with the premise of developing a 'critique' of international criminal law. The discussion that follows revolves around the problems of complicity and of representation and around how these problems relate to the limits of my own view of international criminal law. By the limits of my view, I do not mean that I do not know enough about the discipline of international criminal law (which is certainly true); rather, I do not know enough about what *is wanted* from international criminal law. This is partly, on the one hand, because of the indeterminacy of the field in terms of its object – justice, punishment of atrocities, putting an end to atrocities, ending impunity, promoting accountability, deterrence, fair trials and so forth and, on the other hand, because of its relative infancy. My limited view, and hence my unease, is really captured, however, in a more intangible realm; in short, it resides in the question: what is the symbolic importance of the field of modern international criminal law to those who I am incapable of hearing or seeing – let's say, to those beyond the horizon who know the injustice of the real?

I ask this question in full awareness that I might be viewed as occupying an ironic parallel position to that of the International Criminal Court insofar as I seem to be centralizing 'victims' as a justification for my own position and reasoning. I do not feel ethically challenged by foregrounding my concerns with victims (actual or abstract), however.[2] My point is not to try to reconcile international criminal law with justice by speaking of victims (Joyce 2004: 476). It is the very uncertainty of how to speak about the victims/the 'other' of international criminal law/the excluded/the (un)represented or the otherwise invested that underpins my unease.

The chapter, therefore, employs the concept of complicity as a foil for the idea that critique might morally, or academically, free the critical observer from the structures, or structural violence, under scrutiny (Probyn-Rapsey 2007: 69). Complicity, in the legal sense, is not at issue. Complicity is, rather, a methodological tool for understanding an ethical engagement (2007: 65), for want of a better phrase, with speaking about suffering and with the language of rights, the critique of rights, the language of international criminal law and the critique of international criminal law. By complicity, then, I wish to suggest the association – unintended or otherwise – between critique and suffering or harms and wrongs (Kutz 2000: 1; Mandel 2006: 24). In addition, I see complicity as linked to how I might (mis)represent or speak for others.

A critical approach (or multiple critical approaches) to international criminal law necessarily suggests a critique directed towards the institutions, actors, practices, laws and underlying ideologies which form the field of international criminal law. The aim of the inaugural conference on Critical Approaches to International Criminal Law in Liverpool, which provided the basis for this volume, was to engender 'a critique going beyond an effectiveness critique of international criminal law' (Schwöbel *et al.* 2013: 1). In other words, the idea was to move beyond a discussion of the *weaknesses* of the structures, languages and institutions of international criminal law and, rather, to open up (further) for examination, in the sense expressed by Michel Foucault,[3] some of the 'assumptions upon which the field rest' (Schwöbel *et al.* 2013: 1). Potential pitfalls were highlighted: our possible complicity – in strengthening precisely the same structures under scrutiny; and the risk of instrumentalizing – as academics speaking on behalf of 'the other' – the victims of international crimes, for example (2013: 3). The ideas of abandonment of and/or re-engagement with international criminal justice were speculated upon – let's say, these prospective outcomes formed the hazy horizon of our concern about the ends of critique.

The claim of this chapter is, by no means, that there is no need for critiques of international criminal law or that such critiques are prima facie complicit. Moreover, some of the unease discussed here may be answered by contributions elsewhere in this volume. And while I believe that it is not essential to conceptualize a 'generalized practice' of critique (if such a conceptualization is even possible) or to answer perpetually the question of what it might mean to be critical (Butler 2002: 212), my contribution is consumed by the abstract or methodological questions concerning the objective and consequences of critique as well as the problem of representation. In this chapter, therefore, I will speculate on the interrelationship between the critic and the critique, its objectives and consequences. In order to facilitate this speculation, the chapter begins by identifying the critical problem – those challenges to critique posed by complicity, by the difficulty of representation and by the problem of speaking for others. Once I have set out this framework, I will turn to a related discussion – that of the critique of rights and of international human rights law. In particular, I will discuss some of the responses, notably those of Patricia J. Williams and Hilary Charlesworth, which have problematized aspects of the critique of rights. The objective of this discussion is to re-emphasize potentially analogous pitfalls for the critique of international criminal law and to continue the debate – already opened at the conference – as to how these challenges might be confronted.

The critical problem

It could be that there is a simple way to circumvent the problem of speaking for others and the interminable 'crisis in representation' (Said 1989: 205). This might be to think of critique as separated entirely from judgement or from the conclusive evaluation of the object: in our case, an evaluation of the successes or failures of international criminal law. Judith Butler, discussing Foucault's effort at defining critique, notes that in this effort, unable to articulate the meaning of critique with precision, he found only 'a series of approximations'. These approximations, however, are grounded in the idea of critique as a risky, open-ended, uncertain business distinct from judgement:

> Critique will be dependent on its objects, but its objects will in turn define the very meaning of critique … the primary task of critique will not be to evaluate whether its objects – social conditions, practices, forms of knowledge, power and discourse – are good or bad, valued highly or demeaned, but to bring into relief the very framework of evaluation itself. What is the relation of knowledge to power such that our epistemological certainties turn out to support a way of structuring the world that forecloses alternative possibilities of ordering?
>
> (Butler 2002)

In the critique of international criminal law, however, it is difficult to avoid the reality that some kind of evaluation is already in play; judgement has already been cast. The idea that international criminal law might be complicit in injustice, conflict, exclusions and biases already suggests a judgement – 'bad objects' – even if this is not determinate. The very idea that critique is needed and the underpinning sense that international criminal law is 'self-congratulatory, uncritical and overconfident' further imparts the notion that something is already amiss, underexplored, and therefore that a critique is required in order to unmask and explain, with the goal, presumably, of opening up the field to new possibilities for apprehension. This is not an illegitimate starting point. Critique will surely always grow out of an identified problem or a crisis in the field (see Kendall, Chapter 2 in this volume). As Butler, interpreting Foucault, puts it:

> Foucault's contribution to what appears as an impasse within critical and post-critical theory of our time is precisely to ask us to rethink critique as a practice in which we pose the question of the limits of our most sure ways of knowing … One does not drive to the limits for a thrill or experience, or because limits are dangerous and sexy, or because it brings us into a titillating proximity with evil. One asks about the limits of ways of

knowing because one has already *run up against a crisis within the episte-mological field* in which one lives.

(Butler 2002, emphasis added)

Critique naturally emerges where, for instance, the concepts, ideologies and assumptions controlling the discourse are questionable. With respect to international criminal law, problems and contradictions flourish. For example, a permanent international court concerned exclusively with Africa and an uneven prosecutorial strategy that avoids any engagement at variance with the interests of the permanent Security Council member states provide just two easy illustrations of the conceptually and ideologically problematic presumption of *international* justice (Schabas 2013).

How to affect a critique of the authority[4] of international criminal law, however, is less evident. The challenge is *not*, to my mind, due to the rooting out of the injustice, illegitimacy and biases, among other things, of international criminal law in the absence of an orientation as to where this critical clearing of space will lead. Critics are not compelled to answer the question, 'So what?' From my perspective, the challenge is that posed by the relationship between the critic, the object of critique – international criminal law – and the subjects of international criminal law: that is, those somehow connected to or invested in the mechanisms or field of international criminal justice. Within this triad, I am curious, first, about self-critique – that is, the ideological or ontological basis out of which a/(my) critique emerges – and second, about the audibility of the voice(s) of the 'subjects'[5] of international criminal justice. Who is critiquing? Why? Who for? In mapping this challenge, I will attempt to articulate my concerns by engaging the writings of Theodor Adorno, Gayatri Spivak and Edward Said.

Adorno on critique

When Adorno reflected on the meaning of cultural criticism, he highlighted an impasse in its logic:

> The cultural critic is not happy with civilization, to which alone he owes his discontent. He speaks as if he represented either unadulterated nature or a higher historical stage. Yet he is necessarily of the same essence as that to which he fancies himself superior.
>
> (Adorno 2003: 146)

It is, for Adorno, unfeasible either to move outside the object of criticism or to bring the criticism outside: 'Even the implacable rigor with which criticism speaks the truth of an untrue consciousness remains imprisoned within the orbit of that against which it struggles, fixated on its surface manifestations' (2003: 147). Adorno thus raises the difficulty of getting out of the cycle of the relationship between the criticism and the object of criticism (Mandel 2006: 65). Moreover, Adorno emphasizes the reifying nature of this relationship. Cultural criticism, for him, manifests as collaboration.

> The complicity of cultural criticism with culture lies not in the mere mentality of the critic. Far more, it is dictated by his relation to that with which he deals. By making culture his object, he objectifies it once more. Its very meaning, however, is the suspension of objectification.
>
> (Adorno 2003: 149)

Therefore, having determined (outside/independent) transcendent criticism as fictitious and thus obsolete, Adorno advocated for immanent criticism. He did so for the simple reason that he saw it as the inevitable predicament of critical theory (Helmling 2005: 101). The methodology of immanent criticism that Adorno outlines is an anxious one; it is simultaneously critical of the object and of criticism itself.

Adorno's writing, arguably, subsumed a broader context than is at issue with this project. The task of critiquing international criminal law does not fit simply into his account of the traps of cultural criticism. His writings are instructive, however, for the purpose of identifying the limits and the particular complexities of any critical project, whether conceived of as external or internal. Adorno asks the critic some difficult questions: do the ideological tools with which you carve out a critique not stem from the same culture as the object of your critique? In the context of international criminal law, if my critique aims to re-evaluate the discipline – let's say to deconstruct the neo-colonial or the neoliberal tendencies of international criminal law, and, if the critique is reconstructive, from the rubble, to reconstruct a different kind of justice, or to overthrow the institutions or to reform its ends beyond recognition – what is the background presumption or ideology from which I operate and how can my critique escape hegemonic ideology or escape becoming hegemonic ideology? In a reading of Adorno, further questions arise: does my critique risk petrifying the object by applying to it meanings that, in reality, are in continuous flux? Stemming from this question, it is essential to consider how my critique might affect those actors who might appropriate any space opened to them by the field of international criminal law or who might interpret the field for their own ends.

Adorno on the global and the particular

Modern international criminal law, so the familiar story goes, originated in the Allied victory over Germany and the axis powers in the Second World War. The Nuremberg Charter was drawn up by the Allied powers, the International Military Tribunal was composed of judges from the Allied powers, and only the vanquished were prosecuted (Lippmann 2008: 507–14). These features of the post conflict justice model led to the well-known critique of the Tribunal as 'victor's justice' (Luban 2008: 659). This was not, then, *international* justice: rather it was a limited kind of justice; and it was a system of justice in which broader society had little involvement. In other words, this was a top-down system of justice deeply reflective of and entrenched in the hegemonic order that followed the Allied victory. Indeed the injustices of the Allied crimes were concealed within the language of morality and legalism exercised, most notably, against the Nazi regime (Rensmann 2012: 139). Adorno, for his part, doubted the potential for the achievement of justice within the international criminal institutions established in the aftermath of the war (Rensmann 2012: 141). He was opposed to the abstraction of legal and moral principles from the horrors of genocide and atrocity. Such abstraction, as far as Adorno was concerned, ignored the specific inhuman acts and the individual experiences of suffering. Adorno was also adamant that, following Auschwitz, it was imperative to ensure that nothing similar would happen again (Adorno 1973: 365). The imperative 'never again' is difficult to reconcile with his critical reflection that the order required to achieve the imperative was unattainable. As Rensmann puts it:

> Making sure that genocide is prevented, and no similar crimes against humanity are committed, may be all that we can politically achieve for the time being. But it is also the least we can do. However, Adorno also suggests that global societal organization and its laws will ultimately have to be transformed as well, but critical reflection makes us aware of the conditions that prevent this from happening.
>
> (Resmann 2012: 142)

When Adorno is faced with understanding the Holocaust, therefore, he is rendered paralysed in a space between the imperative 'never again' and the burden of critique. In Adorno's critical engagement, his gaze is fixed on the real, on 'perennial suffering' (Adorno 1973: 362). Lars Rensmann and, in a similar vein, Bill Bowring explain how Adorno's thinking is rescued from paralysis because of its 'engagement with the real world' (Bowring 2008: 109). Rensmann argues that in Adorno's writing we can find the idea of a coming cosmopolitanism rooted in the particular – in other words, cosmopolitan ideals might be appropriated at the local level through the vernacularism of universal languages in the dialect of the local struggle (Rensmann 2012: 144).

This idea of the appropriation of universal claims at the sites of struggle leads me to the central source of unease in the critique of international criminal law. The mechanisms of international criminal law pivot, however precariously, on the idea of justice and are founded on abstract moral universalisms and the liberal legal tradition. Adorno would have been opposed to the International Criminal Court as he would likely have seen in the language of justice the potential for injustice, in the language of commonality the potential for exclusion, and in the language of ending impunity the assurance of impunity.

He was well aware of the potential for the subversion of this abstract language (Wolcher 2012a: 545). Yet, with the establishment of an international institution, the objective of which is the prosecution of genocide, crimes against humanity and war crimes, there is a response – contaminated though it is – to the imperative, 'never again'. Mistrust of the institutions of, or the idea of, international criminal law does not negate the possibility that, with their establishment, a space of symbolic importance opened for the excluded and the persecuted. The difficulty with the task of critique of international criminal law is that it has always to be sensitive to the potential for the subaltern to appropriate, perhaps even rewrite, the language of international criminal law. The method of articulating this sensitivity comes with its own challenges.

The voice of the subaltern

Perhaps the response to the anxiety of Adorno simply lies with Foucault who saw the critical attitude as virtue (Foucault 2002: 192). Gayatri Spivak, in considering an exchange between Foucault and Gilles Deleuze, warns, however, of the complexity of critique and of what critique might mean for the (eventual) subject: the other, the represented (even if the critique claims neither to speak for the other nor to represent):

> The participants in this conversation emphasize the most important con-
> tributions of French poststructuralist theory: first, that the networks of
> power/desire/interest are so heterogeneous, that their reduction to a
> coherent narrative is counterproductive – a persistent critique is needed;
> and second, that intellectuals must attempt to disclose and know the dis-
> course of society's Other. Yet the two systematically ignore the question
> of ideology and their implication in intellectual and economic history.
> (Spivak 1988: 271)

In a similar vein to Adorno, Spivak problematizes external or transcendental critique by essentially asking: how have the critics, and thus the critiques, become freed from the ideological bonds which tie their object? Spivak, however, delves deeper than Adorno by insisting with respect to critique not only that the critic must take account of their role in representation but that the critic must face up to their complicity in signifying something through critique and, accordingly, in representing or speaking on behalf of others (1988: 276). Spivak finds, therefore, even in the work of intellectuals who claim not to be speaking on behalf of others – 'the oppressed can know and speak for themselves' – a continuation of the imperialist project (1988: 279). Reading Spivak, it seems impossible to escape this imperialist project.

Readers of Spivak might wonder why I invoke her work in an essay on complicity and critique when her work might seem more obviously useful as a critique of international criminal law. I return here to what might legitimately

be viewed as the naive idea of the International Criminal Court, or other international tribunals, as potentially of symbolic or abstract importance. Spivak does
not call for the study of the subaltern or for the representation of the subaltern
or for the ignoring of the subaltern. On the contrary, she asks that the subaltern
be listened to. 'The subaltern cannot speak' – the infrastructure in an abstract
sense does not exist either for speaking or for being heard; but the subaltern
can be learned from. Moreover, in the subaltern there exists a transformative
potential, a potential for agency to emerge; and, as I read it, with this agency
comes the possibility of making claims to ideals. Spivak's assertion that the
subaltern cannot speak is not a hopeless conclusion. Rather, she translates
the sense that nothing can change for the disenfranchised into the possibility for
transformation (Morton 2003: 56). Spivak's ire with intellectuals who claim
either that they do not represent or that they do not have an effect on representation emerged because she saw in their work the repetition of the colonial
appropriation of the voice of the subaltern. International criminal law and a
critique of international criminal law pose, to my mind, a similar potential to
silence. In the former, however, there is the potential for transformative engagement, if it is viewed as 'not just an imperialist project'. For me, being critical of
the field of international criminal justice is a tricky task because of the unintended potential for appropriation of voices that I have not yet learned from.

I speak

My angst at the ideological and ethical underpinning of the critique I might
produce should be becoming clear. Spivak summed up this angst well when
she noted: 'I confess to a certain unease reading a man's text about a woman.
Yet, when we want to intervene in the heritage of colonialism or the practice of
neo-colonialism, we take our own goodwill for granted' (Spivak 1990: 6). More
recently, Louis Wolcher has articulated what I see as a problem of unintended
consequences due to the background assumptions from which I write:

> But ... it would be well to remember that even the most radical thinkers,
> like all of us, harbor pre-critical orthodoxies of their own. And these
> orthodoxies can prevent them from noticing the inhumane tendencies of
> their own theories – tendencies that always lie concealed like dandelion
> spores in the inevitable cracks of even the most excellent of critiques.
> (Wolcher 2012a: 10)

The critic's work may be politically significant; it is certainly politically,
socially and historically constructed (Said 1989: 211). As Edward Said
observed in *Orientalism*:

> No one has ever devised a method for detaching the scholar from the
> circumstances of life, from the fact of his involvement (conscious or

unconscious) with a class, a set of beliefs, a social position, or from the mere activity of being a member of a society. These continue to bear on what he does professionally, even though naturally enough his research and its fruits do attempt to reach a level of relative freedom from the inhibitions and the restrictions, of brute, everyday reality. For there is such a thing as knowledge that is less, rather than more, partial than the individual ... who produces it. Yet this knowledge is not therefore automatically non-political.

(Said 2003: 10)

That circumstances may bear on the critic's writings is hardly a reason for inactivity. Neither is the fact that the critic's work may have unpredictable, possibly unwanted, consequences. I cannot simply immunize myself from having consequences, from being wrong. As Linda Alcoff writes:

But surely it is both morally and politically objectionable to structure one's actions around the desire to avoid criticism ... In some cases, perhaps the motivation is not so much to avoid criticism as to avoid errors ... However, errors are unavoidable in theoretical inquiry ... and moreover they often make contributions.

(Alcoff 1991–92: 22)

My unease at speaking is not, therefore, a call for silence. It is an expression of disquiet about the role and place of the speaker and the relationship of that speaker to the object (and its underlying preconditions) and to the subjects. International criminal law is a response to the perpetration of war crimes, crimes against humanity and genocide. The critical approaches to international criminal law project is, therefore, one which takes place in a world of human suffering; this amplifies my unease. In the remainder of this chapter, I will try to exemplify the concerns outlined so far with reference to the critique of rights and international human rights law.

Learning from the critique of rights

A well-developed critique has grown up around rights and around the international human rights law movement. The various assessments are by no means homogeneous nor do they emanate from a single discipline. Indeed, the critique covers the entire span of the lives of rights from their uncertain origins through their codification and implementation to their perpetual destruction through violation.

The critique of rights provides a useful foil for thinking through the complexities of being critical in international criminal law. There is, of course, some overlap between the distinct bodies of international criminal law and international human rights law (Schwöbel 2013). This intersection of human rights and international criminal law exists most obviously in the category of crimes against humanity, in fair trial rights and in shared elements of definitions (for example, the definition of torture) and in shared interpretations (for example, of customary international law). The overlap between the two should not be overstated, however. International criminal law has a different entry point from international human rights law – in reality and conceptually – with respect to violence and violations. Very simply stated, international criminal law follows violence. Rights and international human rights law, while certainly concerned with violations and remedies, are conceived of as something *a priori*. International criminal law, in many respects, stems more from and has more in common with international humanitarian law. That said, however, both bodies of law are rooted in liberal legal history and in Western values and ideals. And both bodies of law undoubtedly concern the relationship of the individual or community to the idea of rights and of justice.

Rights and inclusion: Arendt's critique

Hannah Arendt posed one of the greatest challenges to the idea of rights. Arendt captured the paradox of *human* rights in the notion of the 'right to have rights'. She identified in the situation faced by minority and stateless people prior to the Second World War the absence of a *right* to have rights; without this ontological right, these people became non-persons: 'The Rights of Man, supposedly inalienable, proved to be unenforceable – even in countries whose constitutions were based upon them – whenever people appeared who were no longer citizens of any sovereign state' (Arendt 1968: 293). In other words, those who were excluded from state protection and needed to fall back on the protection of their inalienable human rights found themselves without an authority either to recognize these rights or to protect them – loss of national rights, consequently, became synonymous with the loss of human rights. Arendt points out with respect to this loss of rights that 'no one seems to know which rights they lost'. She ultimately concludes that what was lost was, in fact, the 'right to have rights' (Arendt 1968: 296). Her identification of the idea of a *right* to have rights placed the concept of inalienability into unavoidable doubt as a possible source of rights. It became clear, with Arendt, that something else is required prior to attaining rights. For Arendt, the *right* to have rights relied on belonging – a form of 'political membership' (Benhabib 2004: 60; Blus 2013: 432).

In identifying the paradox of the requirement of political membership for the attainment of human rights, Arendt is not throwing out the baby with the bathwater. She does not thrash rights (Fine 2012: 156); indeed, although admittedly it is a rough substitute, in accordance with a reading of Arendt, claims to rights might be ignored but they can still be made. And yet Arendt, like Adorno, was sceptical of any kind of abstract codification of morality and legality. In her analysis of the 'right to have rights', Seyla Benhabib has contended that the Refugee Convention and, indeed, the International Criminal Court are examples of institutional efforts designed to resolve the paradox of rights denial found in Arendt (Benhabib 2004: 67). Arendt, unlike Adorno, would have supported the emergence of an international criminal court (Arendt 1994: 298; Luban 2011: 628). The idea that the International Criminal Court might work as a resolution to the paradox of political inclusion-based rights is not at all obvious. Indeed, I believe Arendt would remain critical and sceptical of international developments and their potential to resolve rightlessness or to promote justice. Beyond speculation, however, it is her emphasis on the prerequisite of political inclusion and on the voice of the excluded which grounds Arendt's critique.

'Things can be better than they are': Tushnet on rights

A robust critique of rights developed, in particular in the United States, during the 1980s. This critique was authored, for the most part, by academics associated with the critical legal studies movement. Mark Tushnet opened his 1984 essay on rights with the provocative announcement: 'The liberal theory of rights forms a major part of the cultural capital that capitalism's culture has given us' (1984: 1363). Tushnet developed four interrelated critiques of rights to bolster his claim that rights discourse is ineffective. These critiques consisted of, first, the inherent instability of rights, due to the fact that rights are ungrounded and contingent on the social setting; second, the indeterminacy of rights which shows rights to be open and elastic to a point of manipulability, perhaps even disutility; third, the charge of reification whereby experiences are filtered through rights language and expressed as such; and fourth, the political disutility of rights in the sense that rights may, in fact, deter activism. Tushnet's critique of rights has an objective, or at least one can read an objective into it. He remarks: 'There is unnecessary suffering in the world we have chosen to create' (1984: 1398). He concludes his essay by advocating the critical perspective starting from the personal:

> It is of course difficult to live one's life believing that the social world is entirely constructed. Every time one thinks about it, the social world dissolves into a set of choices that one has made (what is the meaning of writing this article?). Every decision becomes political. One asks oneself, do I think that this rather than that is, as far as I can tell now, more likely to advance the cause of the party of humanity.
>
> (Tushnet 1984: 1398)

Tushnet encourages this kind of thinking, that is, the continuous making of a choice about what to support, choices grounded in the 'sure and certain knowledge that things can be better than they are' (1984: 1403). For Tushnet, things cannot be better than they are simply by translating lived experiences into abstract rights (1984: 1363).

The double disenfranchisement: Williams' response

Barbara J. Williams' essay responding to the critical legal studies movement's deconstruction of rights, in particular Tushnet's, has stimulated some of the ideas that have percolated throughout this chapter (Williams 1987: 401).[6] Williams saw in the critical legal studies movement's critique of rights a kind of double disenfranchisement for those for who do not necessarily 'have' rights:

> I by no means want to idealize the importance of rights in a legal system in which rights are so often selectively invoked to draw boundaries, to isolate, and to limit. At the same time, it is very hard to watch the idealistic or symbolic importance of rights being diminished with reference to the disenfranchised, who experience and express their disempowerment as nothing more or less than the denial of rights.
>
> (Williams 1987: 405)

Williams' essay suggests the perennial 'crisis in representation'; the inaudibility of the subaltern – that idea articulated so profoundly by Spivak and 'the problem of speaking for others' (Alcoff 1991–92: 5).

Williams wrote her essay in an attempt to outline her discomfort with the critical legal studies movement: specifically, arguments from critical legal studies rejecting or critiquing rights-based theories. Williams' concern primarily was with the juxtaposition between the critique of rights and the struggle for civil rights. Her acute awareness of the truth to some of the claims of the critical legal studies movement about, for example, the contradictory nature of rights or the indeterminacy and instability of rights led her, nonetheless, to the compelling conclusion that rights-assertion remains an experience of rights which ought not to be discredited. The common goal shared between the critical legal studies movement and the victims of rights disenfranchisement was visible to her; however, this overlap could not be seen to signify a common experience of rights: 'while the goals of CLS and of the direct victims of racism may be very much the same, what is too often missing from CLS works is the acknowledgement that our experiences of the same circumstances may be very, very different; the same symbol may mean different things to each of us' (Williams 1987: 409).

In order to bridge this gap in the experience or perception of rights, Williams encouraged a kind of 'double-think' or, at least, 'an attempt to become multilingual in the semantics of each other's rights-valuation'. What Williams is getting at here might be seen as an ethical engagement with the critique of rights, whereby '[b]ridging such gaps requires listening at a very deep level to the uncensored voices of others' (1987: 410, 411). Tushnet and Williams share a common objective – that is, if the alleviation of unnecessary suffering and the empowerment of the disenfranchised can be viewed as somewhat analogous. These aspirations derive, however, as Williams' response tells us, from a completely different perspective of lived reality.

Williams' broad concern is an enduring one. Williams is herself critical of the critical legal studies' movement's advocacy of the language of needs over the language of rights, and in her criticism she gets at something crucial. In the lived experience of the disenfranchised, the absence of rights and the critique of rights look indistinguishable: 'It is this experience of having, for survival, to argue our own invisibility in the passive, unthreatening rhetoric of "no rights" which, juxtaposed with the CLS abandonment of rights theory, is both paradoxical and difficult for minorities to accept' (Williams 1987: 422).

Tushnet's essay was formative for the critique of rights and his concerns about, for example, the indeterminacy of rights, and the abstraction of rights from lived experiences still preoccupy contemporary scholarship and activism related to rights. I do not question the value of Tushnet's insights. I do, however, find Williams' argument to be a persuasive and compelling call for auto-critique and for questioning the background assumptions from which I operate.

'Part of the problem': Kennedy on rights

David Kennedy has, for our purposes, very usefully summarized some of the main critiques of human rights to which he thinks attention should continuously turn. He argues that we need to remain immanently critical of rights for the greater good of understanding the project of human rights as a whole:

> Whatever has been the history of human rights, we do not know its future. Perhaps these difficulties will be overcome, avoided. But we will not avoid them by avoiding their articulation, discussion, assessment – by treating the human rights movement as a frail child, in need of protection from critical assessment or pragmatic calculation.
>
> (Kennedy 2002: 125)

Kennedy embedded his account of rights in a double disclaimer: first, that the human rights movement had undoubtedly done a great deal of good in providing 'an emancipatory vocabulary and institutional machinery for people across the globe', and second, that the critique came in the form of unproven hypotheses (2002: 101). It seems that his efforts at what he hoped was a 'compassionate' critique of rights also stemmed from an awareness of that old adage – 'the road to hell is paved with good intentions':

> The generation that built the human rights movement focused its attention on the ways in which evil people in evil societies could be identified and restrained. More acute now is how good people, well-intentioned

people in good societies can go wrong, can entrench, support, the very things they have learned to denounce.

(Kennedy 2002: 125)

In his critique of rights, he identified and summarized numerous grounds for complaint and contestation. He argued, for example, that human rights have come to dominate the space of 'emancipatory possibility', crowding out alternative approaches. He also discussed the attendant consequences of the particular cultural and legal heritage of the human rights movement, stemming as it does from the Western liberal tradition. He pointed out that rights promise too much but that they are also deceptive insofar as, more often than not, they are used to justify human wrongs. Kennedy also discussed the popularity, professionalization and bureaucratization of the human rights movement which, he noted, crowds out other legal fields and generates a vast problem of representation – that is, people 'working on behalf of' victims. The various concerns identified by Kennedy vary, for him, in their plausibility, although he does not indicate which concerns are more plausible than others (Charlesworth 2002: 127). The purpose of the critique, however, is pragmatic – a call for calculation rather than devotion in the use of the rights discourse.

'Professional performance': Charlesworth's response

In her response to Kennedy's essay on the human rights movement, Hilary Charlesworth identified some of the paradoxes of the critic and the critique. Charlesworth homes in on what she calls 'the self-portrait' painted by Kennedy as a prelude to his assessment. She notes Kennedy's assertion that he is a 'well-meaning internationalist and, I hope, compassionate legal professional'. She asks, pertinently: 'So, what professional performance is going on here?' (2002: 128). Charlesworth suggests that Kennedy is both identifying with and distinguishing himself from the movement he critiques:

> he seems to be seeking affiliation with a cosmopolitan community of international lawyers about which he has long expressed deep ambivalence. At the same time, [he] implies that many members of the human rights movement become seduced by the sense of their own benevolence – you can make a successful jet-setting career, a glamorous but guilt-free and admired livelihood, from ministering to the unfortunate victims of human rights violations. So he is part of this good-hearted world, but in a savvy and ironic way.

(Charlesworth 2002: 128)

Kennedy, as Charlesworth discusses, is concerned overall with how international lawyers participate – let's say, are complicit – in the structures that sustain an unjust legal order. Clearly, for him, the vast humanitarian army of UN workers, NGO practitioners and academics form part of the problem. Kennedy may well be right. The point, however, that we can draw out of his critique of rights is the subjectivity of his own perspective. From Kennedy's perspective, his critique is well-intentioned:

> Kennedy's article ... seems to present its author as squarely occupying a middle ground: the *enfant terrible* who is prepared to voice skepticism about the sacred vocabulary of human rights is at the same time the experienced, urbane international lawyer who can graciously acknowledge the 'enormous achievement' and the 'great deal of good' performed by the international human rights movement.
>
> (Charlesworth 2002: 129)

Conclusion

To me the distinction is not clear-cut between criticism and critique or between criticism/critique of an object for the purposes of making it more effective and criticism/critique of the background conditions of that object. These meanings of critique blur and should not be sieved into distinct parts (Asad 2009: 139). The task of critique becomes increasingly blurry when the wider context is accounted for. That wider context can be viewed through the lens of complicity. Complicity may manifest no matter where one stands on the normative or critical spectrum. An effectiveness critique for the purposes of strengthening institutions may further embed structures that are already 'inherently political' or exclusive (Kearney and Reynolds 2013: 430). A critical perspective, like Tushnet's, which has the improvement of things as its abstract motive, can, as Williams' response demonstrates so keenly, be read as disenfranchising. A critical perspective, which does not admit to any goal or underpinning motive, may have the unintended consequence of appropriating the space of those who cannot speak or who cannot be heard. Or it may abstractly shatter the potential for the formation of infrastructure between disenfranchisement, possibilities and ideals.

The critique of international criminal law is for me a particularly precarious one. That does not mean it is not necessary; rather, I believe it is a critique which, for this author at least, must be undertaken through the lens of auto-critique: who am I critiquing for? Who may be invested in my critique? I do not suggest either the abandonment of the task of critique nor resistance through silence or withdrawal. I do wonder, though, if the most appropriate response is to relentlessly ask – where do I stand in relation to critique? Where do I stand in relation to justice?

Although he is speaking of rights, Wolcher captures the essence of my angst with the project of critical approaches to international criminal law: 'Philosophy and politics know too little about the justice of human rights, but they nonetheless insist on telling us all about it. The real world, on the other hand, knows too much about injustice, and yet it remains sadly tongue-tied and mute' (2012a: 547).

Notes

1 I would like to thank the presenters and participants at the Critical Approaches to International Criminal Law conference for stimulating some of the ideas that are presented in this chapter. Aspects of this chapter were presented at the Irish Centre for Human Rights, National University of Ireland, Galway Annual Doctoral Seminar 2013. I would like to thank the participants for comments and ideas. I would also like to thank Eleanor Drywood, John Reynolds and Christine Schwöbel-Patel for comments on various drafts of this chapter. All misconceptions and errors are of course my own.
2 The word 'victim' is employed reluctantly here. I am aware of the disempowering potential of emphasizing victimhood (Mutua 2001). What I have in mind here is not a 'helpless innocent' but any individual, community or population who might decide to appeal to international criminal law in an effort to achieve their goals (Oré Aguilar 2011).
3 'A critique is not a matter of saying that things are not right as they are. It is a matter of pointing out on what kinds of assumptions, what kinds of familiar, unchallenged, unconsidered modes of thoughts that practices that we accept rest' (Michel Foucault, '"Practicing Criticism," or "Is it really important to think?"', in L. Kritzman, *Foucault, Politics, Philosophy, Culture*, New York: Routledge, 1988, p. 155.
4 I use the word 'authority' here in continuation of the framework of Butler's reading of Foucault.
5 This term is used as short-hand, somewhat tongue in cheek, but also to convey the idea that international criminal law does exert authority and wield power that is, consequently, always a subject of critique in the Foucauldian sense.
6 I would like to thank Professor Louis Wolcher for first alerting me to this article

Bibliography

Adorno, T.W. (1973) *Negative Dialectics*, London: Routledge.
Adorno, T.W. (2003) *Can One Live After Auschwitz: A Philosophical Reader?*, ed. R. Tiedemann, Stanford, CA: Stanford University Press.
Alcoff, L. (1991–92) 'The Problem of Speaking for Others', *Cultural Critique* 20: 5.
Arendt, H. (1968) *The Origins of Totalitarianism*, New York: Harcourt.
Arendt, H. (1994) *Eichmann in Jerusalem: A Report on the Banality of Evil*, London: Penguin.
Asad, T. (2009) 'Reply to Judith Butler', in T. Asad *et al.*, *Is Critique Secular? Blasphemy, Injury and Free Speech*, The Regents of the University of California.
Auckerman, M.J. (2002) 'Extraordinary Evil, Ordinary Crime: A Framework for Understanding Transitional Justice', *Harvard Human Rights Journal* 15: 39.
Benhabib, S. (2004) *The Rights of Others: Aliens, Residents, Citizens*, Cambridge: Cambridge University Press.
Blus, A. (2013) 'Beyond the Walls of Paper: Undocumented Migrants, the Border and Human Rights', *European Journal of Migration and the Law* 15: 413.
Bowring, B. (2008) *The Degradation of International Law*, London: Routledge-Cavendish.

Butler, J. (2002) 'What is Critique: An Essay on Foucault's Virtue', in D. Ingram (ed.) *The Political: Readings in Continental Philosophy*, London: Basil Blackwell.

Charlesworth, H. (2002) 'Author! Author! A Response to David Kennedy', *Harvard Human Rights Journal* 15: 127.

Douzinas, C. (2007) *Human Rights and the End of Empire: The Political Philosophy of Cosmopolitanism*, Abingdon: Routledge-Cavendish.

Fine, R. (2012) 'Debating Human Rights Law and Subjectivity: Arendt, Adorno, and Critical Theory', in L. Rensmann and S. Gandesha (eds) *Arendt and Adorno: Political and Philosophical Investigations*, Stanford, CA: Stanford University Press.

Foucault, M. (2002) 'What is Critique?', in D. Ingram (ed.) *The Political: Readings in Continental Philosophy*, London: Basil Blackwell.

Glasius, M. (2009) 'What is Global Justice and Who Decides? Civil Society and Victim Responses to the International Criminal Court's First Investigations', *Human Rights Quarterly* 31: 496.

Helmling, S. (2005) '"Immanent Critique" and "Dialectical Mimesis" in Adorno and Horkheimer's *Dialectic of Enlightenment*', *Boundary* 32(2): 97.

Joyce, D. (2004) 'The Historical Function of International Criminal Trials: Rethinking International Criminal Law', *Nordic Journal of International Law* 73: 461.

Kearney, M. and Reynolds, J. (2013) 'Palestine and the Politics of International Criminal Justice', in W.A. Schabas, Y. McDermott and N. Hayes (eds) *The Ashgate Research Companion to International Criminal Law: Critical Perspectives*, Aldershot: Ashgate.

Kennedy, D. (2002) 'The International Human Rights Movement: Part of the Problem?', *Harvard Human Rights Journal* 15: 101.

Kutz, C. (2000) *Complicity: Ethics and Law for a Collective Age*, Cambridge: Cambridge University Press.

Lippman, M. (2008) 'Nuremberg: Forty-Five Years Later', in G. Mettraux (ed.) *Perspectives on the Nuremberg Trial*, Oxford: Oxford University Press.

Luban, D. (2008) 'The Legacies of Nuremberg', in G. Mettraux (ed.) *Perspectives on the Nuremberg Trial*, Oxford: Oxford University Press.

Luban, D. (2011) 'Hannah Arendt as a Theorist of International Criminal Law', *International Criminal Law Review* 11: 611.

Mandel, N. (2006) *Against the Unspeakable: Complicity, the Holocaust and Slavery in America*, Charlottesville, VA: University of Virginia Press.

Morton, S. (2003) *Gayatri Chakravorty Spivak*, London: Routledge.

Mutua, M. (2001) 'Savages, Victims and Saviours: The Metaphor of Human Rights', *Harvard International Law Journal* 42: 201.

Oré Aguilar, G. (2011) 'The Local Relevance of Human Rights: A Methodological Approach', in K. de Feyter, S. Parmentier, C. Timmerman and G. Ulrich (eds) *The Local Relevance of Human Rights*, Cambridge: Cambridge University Press.

Probyn-Rapsey, F. (2007) 'Complicity, Critique, and Methodology', *ARIEL: A Review of International English Literature* 38: 65.

Rensmann, L. (2012) 'Grounding Cosmopolitics: Rethinking Crimes Against Humanity and Global Political Theory with Arendt and Adorno', in L. Rensmann and S. Gandesha (eds) *Arendt and Adorno: Political and Philosophial Investigations*, Stanford, CA: Stanford University Press.

Said, E.W. (1989) 'Representing the Colonized: Anthropology's Interlocutors', *Critical Inquiry* 15: 205.

Said, E.W. (2003) *Orientalism*, London: Penguin.

Schabas, W.A., McDermott, Y. and Hayes, N. (eds) (2013) *The Ashgate Research Companion to International Criminal Law: Critical Perspectives*, Aldershot: Ashgate.

Schabas, W.A. (2013) 'The Banality of International Criminal Law', *Journal of International Criminal Justice* 11: 545.

Schwöbel, C. (2013) 'The Comfort of International Criminal Law', *Law and Critique* 24: 23.

Spivak, G.C. (1988) 'Can the Subaltern Speak', in C. Nelson and G. Grossberg (eds) *Marxism and the Interpretation of Culture*, Champaign, IL: University of Illinois Press.

Spivak, G.C. (1990) 'Theory in the Margin: Coetzee's Foe Reading Defoe's Crusoe/ Roxana', *English in Africa* 17: 1.

Tushnet, M. (1984) 'An Essay on Rights', *Texas Law Review* 62: 1363.

Williams, P.J. (1987) 'Alchemical Notes: Reconstructing Ideas from Deconstructed Rights', *Harvard Civil Rights-Civil Liberties Law Review* 22: 401.

Wolcher, L.E. (2012a) 'The Ethics of the Unsaid in the Sphere of Human Rights', *Notre Dame Journal of Law, Ethics and Public Policy* 26: 533.

Wolcher, L.E. (2012b) 'The Critical Imperative', *The Crit: A Critical Legal Studies Journal* 5: 1.

Part II

The politics of international criminal law

Chapter 5

Unveiling (and veiling) politics in international criminal trials

Tor Krever[1]

> *The Court*: This is not a political case as far as I am concerned.
> *Mr Kunstler*: Well, Your Honor, as far as some of the rest of us are concerned, it is quite a political case.
> *The Court*: It is a criminal case. There is an indictment here. I have the indictment right up here. I can't go into politics here in this court.
> (*Chicago Conspiracy* trial transcript, quoted in Lukas 1970: 74)

The indictment of Slobodan Milošević in May 1999 in the midst of a NATO bombing campaign against Yugoslavia invited accusations that the International Criminal Tribunal for the Former Yugoslavia (ICTY) was being used as a political instrument of Western powers. This was precisely how Milošević characterized the indictment and subsequent trial when he eventually appeared before the court two and a half years later. 'I wish to say that the entire world knows that this is a political process,' he announced to the bench; 'we are not here speaking about legal procedures that evolve into political ones. This is a political process to begin with' (*Prosecutor v Milošević*, IT-02-54-T, Transcript, 30 January 2002: 352).

By way of contrast, for the then chief prosecutor at the ICTY, Carla Del Ponte, Milošević's introduction of politics into the legal proceedings tarnished an otherwise apolitical trial. 'This is a criminal trial,' she insisted. 'It is unfortunate that the accused has attempted to use his appearances before this Chamber to make interventions of a political nature' (*Prosecutor v Milošević*, IT-02-54-T, Transcript, 12 February 2002: 6). For the bench, too, political arguments had little place in the proceedings. Responding to the accused's charge that the court was a mere 'political tool', Judge May responded simply: 'You've made all these points, Mr Milošević ... we are not going to listen to these political arguments' (*Prosecutor v Milošević*, IT-02-54-T, Transcript, 30 August 2001: 25).

This rhetorical pattern – recurring attacks on international criminal trials as little more than political show trials and no less persistent refutations that politics has no place in such legal proceedings – is reproduced not only in the courtroom, but also in the international legal literature. Heated debates centre on the political or apolitical nature of international criminal law (ICL) and its institutions. Critics denounce international trials as political tools, while the field's proponents insist they are neutral vehicles for the promotion of international justice and the rule of law. For the latter, in particular, the debate is no mere intellectual argument: fear of the unalloyed trial infected with politics is, perhaps, the central anxiety of the ICL field.

This chapter subjects these debates about the politics of international criminal trials to critical scrutiny. It does so, however, not with a view to pronouncing on one side or the other, but rather in order to analyse the very nature of the debate itself. How do we talk about politics in the context of ICL? What do we mean when we say trials are political? What ideas structure the debate? What is taken for granted and reproduced by both sides? What is lost from sight? And what, ultimately, is at stake?

The chapter approaches these questions by interrogating two dominant conceptions of politics in the context of the international criminal trial. Contemporary debates, it suggests, tend to locate politics first in the instrumentalization of criminal justice. That is, politics lies in the motivation behind a particular prosecution, with the juridical architecture of the trial used for partisan ends – to criminalize and remove a political opponent, for example. Second, debates locate politics in questions of process and procedure. That is, politics is identified with what the chapter calls 'deformed legalism', namely the absence of legalistic process and protections for defendants. Both positions, it is argued here, share a narrow understanding of politics in the context of ICL, as well as a faith that ICL and international criminal trials can be free of politics – that politics is something alien introduced into the trial by the *misuse* of legal proceedings and judicial institutions. While commentators disagree, often fiercely, whether a given trial or court should be characterized as political, they share a faith that ICL *can* and *should* be made apolitical. Such discourses thus, in effect, reproduce the image of the trial itself as an apolitical, neutral institution, masking, and placing beyond scrutiny, the ways in which even the supposedly neutral trial operates politically. These discourses, it will be shown below, function as ideological manoeuvres through which the deeper political meaning of the trial is obfuscated.

Locating politics

What does it mean to say that international criminal law is political? The epithet is invoked with such frequency that one might doubt whether any garden-variety political trial exists. Indeed, few commentators define precisely what they mean by politics or the political.[2] Common, though, to most analyses is a normative position that politics *should* have no place in international criminal law.

This denial of politics in the juridical processes and administration of international justice rehearses a similar insistence on the part of liberal jurists with regard to the municipal rule of law. Proponents of international criminal trials echo Judge Hoffman in the famous US *Chicago Conspiracy* trial (see the epigraph above) in insisting on a clear line between criminal and political trials.[3] The municipal legal academy, too, is characterized by an idealized notion of distinct and independent juridical and political spheres.[4] Concomitant with such a view has been a historic refusal to recognize the existence of political trials in liberal Western jurisdictions. Otto Kirchheimer tracked this position already in 1961:

> many a jurist is likely to deny that there is such a thing as a political trial; to say that the thing exists and often entails consequences of importance is, in the eyes of such men of Law Immaculate, equivalent to questioning the integrity of the courts, the morals of the legal profession.
>
> (Kirchheimer 1961: 47)

Political trials, in the liberal consciousness, are associated with unsavoury historical events: the Dreyfus affair, the execution of anarchists Sacco and Vanzetti, or the Stalinist parody of justice at the Moscow Show Trials. 'To say that a trial is political,' one commentator observes, 'is always to condemn it' (Posner 2005: 88). Indeed, for liberal legalism, the political trial represents an inherent danger as a corrupting influence on the prized rule of law.

In the context of international criminal law, commentators tend to recognize that trials do not exist in a vacuum and often require a political consensus to take place or even establish the international institutions in which a trial might take place. *Political will* on the part of leading international powers is thus necessary to *establish* institutions, but is to be carefully separated from a depoliticized international criminal justice in action. This bright line division was already apparent in Robert Jackson's remarks on the International Military Tribunal (IMT) at Nuremberg, where he was the US chief prosecutor. The decision to establish a tribunal to try German wartime leaders was political, but that decision, Jackson insisted, was quite distinct from the subsequent trial proceedings, what he called 'the legal end of the prosecution' (quoted in Bass 2000). Half a century later, in a leading textbook on international criminal law by Antonio Cassese, a former president of the ICTY, politics again enters into the analysis only in terms of the absence or presence of *political will* on the part of prosecuting powers – again, the Allies at Nuremberg and Tokyo are cited – or in the support, opposition or mere indifference of domestic constituencies (Cassese 2008: 322–3). Similarly, Theodor Meron, current ICTY president, writes of the importance of *political will* for the functioning of criminal justice institutions, distinct from 'a uniform and definite corpus of international humanitarian law' that 'can be applied *apolitically* to internal atrocities everywhere' (1995: 555, emphasis added).

Characteristic of the international justice literature, then, is an implicit juxtaposition between the *political* birth pangs of international criminal tribunals and the subsequent *apolitical* prosecution and trial of alleged war criminals by and within those courts. On this view, as Frédéric Mégret has observed, international criminal justice is 'a phenomenon *anchored* in power yet simultaneously capable of transcending it' (2002: 1264).

On the view of commentators such as Cassese and Meron, politics should ideally be limited to the establishment of international justice institutions alone. But if politics in the context of subsequent trials is necessarily pejorative, in what precisely does a political trial consist? In other words, what makes an otherwise 'ordinary' trial 'political'? Two conceptions of politics in criminal trials predominate in international legal thought. Politics is located first in the instrumentalization of the trial for partisan political ends and second in deformed legal procedures.

Politics as the instrumentalization of criminal justice

In popular usage, the epithet is commonly used to denote those trials in which specific individuals are targeted for their political views. Classic (US) examples, on this definition, include the *Haymarket* trial, its defendants prosecuted for their anarchist affiliations, and the *Chicago Conspiracy* trial, where defendants were tried for their opposition to US government Vietnam-era policy.[5] Under this view of the political trial, prosecutions are used as instruments for partisan political ends, brought often against political opponents for the purpose of eliminating them. Thus, for Donald Hermann, the purpose of the political trial is to 'discredit and obstruct those who pose a threat to the integrity of the state and to those who hold political power' (1972: 571). Hermann contrasts the political trial with ordinary 'non-political' criminal prosecutions that are 'brought to deter, isolate, punish or rehabilitate individuals who threaten the health, safety, and welfare of other citizens and the social community' (1972: 571). In a similar vein, for Noam Chomsky, Paul Lauter and Florence Howe, the political trial represents an instrumentalization of the judicial process by the government 'to ensure obedience to its orders by punishing those who refuse to obey and threatening others who might be tempted to do so' (Chomsky *et al.* 1968). A more recent formulation, suggested by Eric Posner, similarly holds that 'a political trial occurs when the government uses the judicial process against its opponents' (2005: 87). Michal Belknap's definition, if more expansive, likewise points to the use of the trial *vis-à-vis* political opponents. He argues political trials are those:

> intended to affect the structure, personnel, or policies of government … or that results from the efforts of a group within society having control of the machinery of government to use the courts to disadvantage its rivals in a power struggle … or to preserve its own economic or social position.
> (Belknap 1994: xvi)

On a similar note, Judith Shklar famously suggests a political trial is one 'in which the prosecuting party, usually the regime in power aided by a cooperative judiciary, tries to eliminate its political enemies' (1986: 149). Like other authors, Shklar sees such instrumentalization of the trial as injurious to the judicial process. That process, Shklar writes, is designed to deal 'with individual offenders against law, not with the elimination of political groups. To attempt such tasks is to injure the judicial process, because the principle of legality cannot survive them' (1986: 217).

In the international criminal law field, such criticisms are often articulated in the form of accusations of 'victors' justice', the view that victorious powers use *post bellum* trials to criminalize their defeated opponents while their own conduct remains above judicial scrutiny. This was the essence of Milošević's jeremiad against the ICTY, but it is also a common refrain from other defendants before international criminal tribunals. Saddam Hussein, for instance, dismissed the court sentencing him to death as 'servants of the occupiers and their lackeys' and political 'puppets' (quoted in Burns and Semple 2006: A4).

But victors' justice is also central to many scholarly analyses, such as Danilo Zolo's trenchant critique of international criminal justice. In a recent intervention, he indicts the entire project of international criminal law as one long series of instances of victors' justice, from Nuremberg through to the ICTY (Zolo 2009). Victors' justice is also the pivot around which Michael Mandel's polemic proceeds against the ICTY: during the Kosovo war of 1999, NATO also committed war crimes in its campaign against Serbia. The Prosecutor, however, failed to fully investigate NATO's attack on Serbia, let alone prosecute the organisation's leadership (Mandel 2001). Some observers have thus argued that the ICTY, and the trials before it, are deeply political precisely because of the seemingly one-sided approach of prosecutions:

> Of the leaders in the Balkan wars, Clinton, Blair, Izetbegovic and Tudjman have never been indicted by the ICTY, only Milosevic ... This highly politicized justice ... is deeply compromised. And if it is clearly serving a political end and meeting an external political agenda it is almost certain to be biased and fail to bring justice even in dealing with politically eligible targets.
>
> (Herman 2005)

One finds a similar conception of the political in criticisms of other tribunals such as the International Criminal Tribunal for Rwanda (ICTR). Critics argue that ICTR trials of Rwandan *génocidaires* in Arusha have been the subject of selective prosecutions. The ICTR's judicial characterization of the Rwandan genocide has been celebrated by many commentators for memorializing the violence and burying the 'obscene version of history' that would deny 'that what happened in Rwanda in 1994 was neither accidental nor spontaneous' (McGreal 2008). However, the failure to prosecute crimes of the Rwandan

Patriotic Front (RPF, currently the ruling party of Rwanda) has led organizations such as Human Rights Watch to bemoan the politicization of the court (see Human Rights Watch 2009). Former US Attorney General Ramsey Clark has similarly argued that the trials before the ICTR amount to 'a rewriting of history using courts to serve a particular political agenda' (Gehring 2011). Filip Reyntjens, too, suggests that the trials have served as a powerful political tool and an 'ideological weapon allowing the RPF to acquire and maintain victim status' and enjoy 'complete immunity' (2004: 199). He contends that the trials have allowed the Kagame government to shrug off criticisms of authoritarianism, suppression of opposition political activity and outright violence. Makau Mutua, likewise, argues that the Rwanda tribunal serves to legitimize the Kagame regime and 'allows Tutsis a moral plane from which to exact their revenge on the Hutus' (2000: 78).

A slightly different critique of international criminal trials, which nonetheless identifies politics with the (illegitimate) motives behind selective prosecution, can be found in literature on what has become known as 'lawfare'. Subscribers to this school, particularly prominent in the United States, highlight the deployment of international legal norms and judicial processes as strategic weapons, not by victorious Western powers but rather against those powers.[6] 'The enemies of the West … are pursuing a campaign of lawfare that complements terrorism and asymmetric warfare,' warns the US-based Lawfare Project (2012). 'Terrorists and their sympathizers understand that where they cannot win by advocating and exercising violence, they can attempt to undermine the willingness and capacity to fight them using legal means' (Lawfare Project 2012).

Subscribers to this 'lawfare' school see in international criminal law and the institution of the international trial an invitation for the cynical manipulation of the law 'to achieve strategic military or political ends' (Lawfare Project 2012). On this view, international criminal justice takes on a political hue insofar as international criminal tribunals may be politically instrumentalized to *illegitimately* target and prosecute US or allied political and military leaders, a fear not without significant traction in US political culture. The spectre of an unrestrained prosecutor acting willy-nilly in The Hague making frivolous accusations of war crimes against Americans looms large in the US psyche and was central to the Bush administration's opposition to the ICC. In 2002 John Bolton, then US Under Secretary for Arms Control and International Security, famously attacked an 'unaccountable Prosecutor and its unchecked judicial power' as 'clearly inconsistent with American standards of constitutionalism' (Bolton 2002). Another Under Secretary, Marc Grossman (2002), remarked of the Rome Statute that it 'creates a prosecutorial system that is an unchecked power … We believe that the ICC is built on a flawed foundation. These flaws leave it open for exploitation and politically motivated prosecutions.'

Jack Goldsmith and Stephen Krasner, while avoiding the hyperbole of their Lawfare Project and Bush administration compatriots, express a similar fear about politically partisan prosecutions. The ICC, they argue, 'invites questionable and even politically motivated prosecutions. Legal restrictions and definitional limitations are not likely to provide real checks on the ICC's behavior, for the ICC itself is the ultimate interpreter of these norms' (Goldsmith and Krasner 2003: 54).

Perhaps unsurprisingly, defenders of the ICC, and ICL more generally, are at pains to insist that international prosecutions remain purely legal affairs, devoid of political influence. Concern about political influence from either Western powers, or forces opposed to US hegemony, is dismissed as unwarranted (Danner 2003: 1637; Goldstone and Smith 2009: 114). Liberal commentators appeal to 'numerous safeguards' (Kirsch and Robinson 2002: 663; Brubacher 2004: 72; Sadat and Carden 2000: 401) that are 'in place against a politically motivated Prosecutor running off with the bit between his teeth' (Lahiri 2010: 181). The ICC, its former Chief Prosecutor Luis Moreno-Ocampo insists, is a '*judicial* institution' distinct – hermetically sealed, he seems to believe – from the '*political* environment' in which it operates. His own considerations were never political, respecting 'scrupulously my legal limits' (Moreno-Ocampo 2010).

What is important for the argument here is not how convincing either side of this debate is, but rather the ultimate agreement across both critics and boosters of the ICC, and international criminal justice more broadly, that politics resides in the motivation behind the decision to prosecute (or not prosecute) a particular individual or leader – and that politics should have no place in prosecutions and trials. The complaint in each instance is that international criminal law is being *misused* for political ends: the problem is with politics, not the law or trial itself. The implicit corollary is that if only Allied crimes had also been prosecuted at Nuremberg or Tokyo, if only NATO leaders too had been tried in The Hague, if only the RPF had faced justice in Arusha, then all would be well.

Politics as deformed legalism

Not all commentators focus on the motivations behind prosecutions in ascribing or denying politics to or in international criminal trials. Indeed, some commentators have suggested that such an approach is simply vague and analytically unhelpful. Ron Christenson, for example, suggests, 'Most attempts to designate a trial as political become mired in the quicksand of motive.' He concludes simply that we must be satisfied with the assumption that 'we can recognize political trials when we see them' (1999: 2).[7] Many liberal defenders of international criminal trials have tended to focus not on the motivation animating international prosecutions but rather on the degree to which trials accord with certain characteristics of an idealized liberal trial, namely the procedures associated with what has been called 'liberal legalism'.

For Judith Shklar, legalism represents 'the ethical attitude that holds moral conduct to be a matter of rule following, and moral relationships to consist of duties and rights determined by rules' (1986: 1). Shklar is rather critical of this putative equation of morality with rule following and its elevation, especially among jurists, as a 'grand or total ideolog[y]' (1986: 4). As one among many values, Shklar suggests, legalism is to be valued, but in its fetishism of legal process, she sees a dismally narrow view of law abstracted 'from all political, moral and social values and institutions' (1986: 33). Nevertheless, many contemporary advocates of international criminal justice have embraced precisely the process-fetishism of which Shklar was most critical. Paradoxically, legalism's most eager proponents in the international criminal law realm, such as Gary Bass, explicitly invoke their debt to Shklar. For Bass, judicial process in criminal trials is paramount: legalism is 'above all about due process' (2000: 24) – 'international trials must be conducted roughly according to well-established domestic practice' (2000: 20). Social conflicts, dealt with by courts through the architecture of the trial, should be resolved through the application of pre-existing rules to individuals who, in turn, have the opportunity to defend themselves.

For writers like Bass, this position seems to be grounded in a moral philosophical view that values legal process as the embodiment of ideals of fairness and respect for human dignity. But other positions too are possible. Eric Posner takes an instrumental approach to legalism – perhaps reflecting his grounding in the Law and Economics tradition – suggesting that legalism reflects the 'principles and attitudes' embraced by any rational, democratic government seeking to maximize its political support (Posner 2005: 98). If governments relax judicial process – or sidestep the judiciary altogether – they risk undermining their popular legitimacy: 'a government that depends on the consent of the public cannot take the risk of allowing the public to think that the government eliminates political opponents who enjoy the support of at least some of the public' (Posner 2005: 100).

If both approaches to legalism are grounded in different theories – deontological and instrumental – they share the common premise that, again, politics has no place in the legalistic trial; that the political trial is necessarily a departure from liberal legalism. Posner thus argues: 'Political trials cannot occur in a regime of liberal legalism as long as legal institutions uphold this ideal' (2005: 97). The focus on process similarly allows Bass to draw a neat conceptual divide between 'truly legalistic' trials and 'highly politicized trials', of which the show trial provides the leading exemplar (Bass 2000: 16, 310). Thus, on Bass's reading: 'Fair liberal legal arrangements' are 'easily discernible from a Soviet-style show trial' (2000: 24). Following Weber, who emphasized the 'protection of a regular procedure' in modern criminal justice, Bass identifies the leading markers of a 'bona fide trial' as due process, an independent judiciary, the possibility of acquittal, and proportionality in sentencing (2000: 16). Against this benchmark, the show trial stands in sharp relief. For Bass, it represents the 'apotheosis' of political trials and the 'opposite of liberal legalism: the complete subversion of legal norms' (2000: 26). It is characterized by a predetermined outcome ('a show trial has no chance of returning an acquittal') and judges subservient to the prosecution, and 'cares little for procedure' (2000: 16).

In much the same vein, writing during the Milošević trial, Michael Scharf (2003: 915) asked: 'Will history remember Milosevic as ... a scapegoat tried in a show trial before a one-sided court? Or will the Milosevic trial be seen as fair and free of political influence, and its judgment supported by credible evidence?' As with Bass and Posner, the political (show) trial here stands in opposition to the procedurally fair trial; politics is something alien to the latter.

Under this view, the international criminal trial, with its due process guarantees – 'an extension of the rule of law from the domestic sphere to the international sphere' (Bass 2000: 8) – is necessarily an embodiment of legalism *tout court*.[8] Thus for Bass, Nuremberg is to be celebrated as representing the opposite of the show trial sought by the Soviets who 'were piqued when the other three Allies would not let them have it' (2000: 19–20). In a missive to US leaders dispatched from the London Conference, Robert Jackson wrote approvingly of 'provisions which assured to the defendants the fundamentals of procedural "due process of law"' including 'guaranties securing the defendants every reasonable opportunity to make a full and free defense' and rights 'to counsel, to present evidence, and to cross-examine prosecution witnesses' (quoted in Bass 2000: 24). For Bass, Jackson's report, which he cites approvingly, is proof that at Nuremberg defendants faced 'full-blown Western legalism' (2000: 25). For Conway Henderson, too, the question of whether Nuremburg represented justice properly served or the exercise of political power – again, the two stand in antipodal opposition – turns solely 'on due process questions, that is, the rightful procedures of the two tribunals' (Henderson 2010: 276). The question is resolved in the affirmative by Henderson: 'The evidence of their atrocities was massive, yet when doubt arose, several acquittals did result' (2010: 276).

Again it is the '*fairness of the process* that makes [the trial] justice' (Bass 2002b: A33, emphasis added). Moving from Nuremberg to the ICTY, in the face of Milošević's accusations of a politicized victor's justice, Bass merely points to the 'full panoply of United Nations protections' he enjoys:

> Instead of extrajudicial executions, the accused are given the luxury of a full trial, with their crimes laid out in an indictment, with protections of due process and procedure, with the possibility of acquittal and, failing that, a proportionate sentence.
>
> (Bass 2002a: 1040)

This juxtaposition of politics with legalistic procedure (and the association of politics with deformed legalism) implicitly undergirds most contemporary analyses of international criminal tribunals. Moreno-Ocampo defends the

ICC's credibility against claims of politicization with an appeal first to the apolitical nature of his own (then) office – 'my duty is to apply the law without political considerations' – and second to the procedural guarantees provided defendants – 'Full respect for the rights of all the parties involved is the cornerstone of the Court's credibility' (Moreno-Ocampo 2010). A recent intervention by Michael Newton, former advisor to the Iraqi High Tribunal and senior advisor to the US Ambassador-at-Large for War Crimes Issues at the US Department of State, is also symptomatic. Newton recognizes that international trials take place in a deeply political context but, he insists, need not be contaminated thereby. Procedural guarantees including, in particular, on Newton's view, access to competent defence counsel, successfully stand between defendants and 'the raw political whims of powerful states that organize and fund the system of modern international criminal justice' (Newton 2011: 383).

Not all observers are as sanguine in their evaluations of Nuremberg, The Hague, and other seats of international criminal justice. Following the Second World War, Hermann Göring said of the Allied prosecution of German leaders at Nuremberg: 'As far as the trial is concerned, it's just a cut-and-dried political affair.' The final judgment, Göring implied, was already decided before the trial: 'I'm sure the Russian and French judges, at least, already have their instructions … I know what's in store for me' (quoted in Gilbert 1947: 12–13). One former Nuremberg prosecutor, reflecting on the trial, also expresses doubts about how much the trial really embodied conceptions of liberal legalism (Taylor 1992). Even Shklar, while generally positive in her discussion of the IMT at Nuremberg, is compelled to acknowledge that the trial represented 'a genuine moral crisis … for persons of liberal convictions' (1986: 155).

Other commentators, in arguing the trial was *politicized*, have focused on the 'inequality of arms' between prosecution and defendant. Thus, with reference to Nuremberg, Otto Kranzbuhler and Hans Laternser have both emphasized the vast resources at the prosecution's disposal and the huge volume of possibly exculpatory material unavailable to defendants (Kranzbuhler 1965; Laternser 1987). More recently, critics have condemned the 'outrageous departures from proper judicial practice' during Milošević's trial before the ICTY: judges' bias, interference with the defendant's invocation of right to act as his own counsel, failure to declare a mistrial when the presiding judge resigned for health reasons, the use of double hearsay evidence (Falk 2007). The proceedings, critics contend, were little more than a 'lynching' before a 'kangaroo court' (Greenspan 2002; Laughland 2007; Cockburn 2006), with Milošević a 'scapegoat in a show trial with a predestined outcome' (Lopusina and Huzsvai 2002).

While there remains much disagreement between those who would dismiss international criminal trials as egregious departures from the procedural norms of liberal legalism and those who embrace them as exemplars of those norms, there is also, if less apparent, much agreement. The animating concern, for both groups, remains the trial's form: that is, its conformity to the model of liberal legalism. Implicit in the critiques, no less than in the hyperbole of Bass and other defenders of ICL, is the assumption that if the neutrality of the legalistic trial and its formal procedures *could* be safeguarded, the trial would remain free of, and even a suitable check on, politics.

Beyond intrumentalism and liberal legalism

If the instrumentalization of criminal justice for partisan ends and the defor-mation of legal process are markers of the presence of politics in the inter-national criminal trial, are these the only sources of politics in ICL? Might the seemingly neutral, procedurally sound, legalistic application of ICL none-theless also have important political implications? That is, might ICL and international criminal trials in fact be political in ways that are actually hidden and placed beyond scrutiny by a myopic focus on prosecutorial motive or formal legalism? In reproducing the idea of the supposedly apolitical trial – as reality or ideal – might mainstream debates actually blind us to the deeper politics of ICL?

To understand and scrutinize these other political aspects of the trial, one must take a broader optic that takes account of the wider constellation of social relations in which the trial takes place. Mainstream debates, however, focus on politics as the product of the subjective choices of a small universe of specific judicial or political actors. Prosecutors (or the political powers behind them) *choose* to use the trial as a way of removing an opponent. Judges *choose* to allow the deformation of formal processes and erosion of defendants' rights. The two often go hand in hand, of course, as in the classical show trial. But in both cases the source of politics is in the *conscious intent* of actors in or outside the courtroom.

In focusing on judicial (and political) actors' intent and their attendant deci-sions, these mainstream debates recall what Steven Lukes has called the one-dimensional and two-dimensional views of power. In his influential study of power, Lukes critiques these two dominant approaches to the subject and instead offers his own 'radical' three-dimensional view. The one-dimensional approach, he suggests, is preoccupied with 'behaviourism': its focus is on 'behaviour in the making of decisions on issues over which there is an observ-able conflict of (subjective) interests, seen as express policy preferences' (Lukes 2005: 19). The two-dimensional view, by way of contrast, 'allows for consideration of the ways in which decisions are prevented from being taken on potential issues over which there is an observable conflict of (subjective) interests' (2005: 25). However, it is still ultimately focused, Lukes insists, with behaviourism: 'the study of overt, "actual behaviour", of which "concrete deci-sions" in situations of conflict are seen as paradigmatic' (2005: 25). Against these approaches, Lukes argues that 'we need to think about power broadly rather than narrowly – in three dimensions rather than one or two – and that we need to attend to those aspects of power that are least accessible to observation: that, indeed, power is at its most effective when least observable' (2005: 1). Whereas the former approaches focus on the operation of power through 'choices consciously and intentionally made by individuals between alternatives', the three-dimensional view points to the ways in which power also operates to shape and constrain behaviour in ways that are 'neither consciously chosen nor the intended result of particular individuals' choices' (2005: 25). That is, power can 'prevent people … from having grievances by shaping their perceptions, cognitions and preferences in such a way that they accept their role in the existing order of things' (2005: 11).[9]

Might politics in ICL also have a third dimension? Could the international criminal trial have political implications independent of the actions or conscious intent of particular agents? This section considers how the trial – and the discourses, scholarly as well as popular, in which it is embedded – communicate social meaning beyond the immediate actors and events adjudicated in the courtroom. The trial, it is argued, communicates meaning also about social relations and structures more generally. In short, international criminal trials may serve to naturalize and legitimize historically specific social relations and structural sources of crime. Like Lukes' third dimension of power, they contribute to the ways in which people come to accept the existing order of things. As such, even the seemingly neutral, legalistic trial may operate politically, in the sense of politics encompassing broadly the processes, multifaceted and varied, by which social orders and relations of power are sustained or challenged.[10]

Legitimation of social structures

A criminal trial, Kenneth Nunn suggests, 'does more than merely determine the fate of the defendant standing trial' (1995: 746). It also expresses 'fundamental notions about justice and injustice, right and wrong, law-abiding and crime, good and evil' (1995: 746). By labelling particular conduct as deviant, the trial mobilizes censure and social sanction and, at the same time, serves to reinforce the 'internal solidarity of the moral community' (1995: 760). Struggles to criminalize conduct of others are also, however, struggles to validate one's own behaviour. The trial can thus be seen as a 'communicative forum', a 'social practice for producing authoritative judgments of discourses' about society (Hariman 1990: 24). From the interplay of structured meaning arises what Stuart Hall has called a general 'consensus' regarding the accepted parameters of social conduct and institutions – a consensus, in other words, to 'a particular kind of social order' (1982: 63).

The social order affirmed by the trial and reflected in the concomitant 'consensus', however, is one that reflects a 'very definite set of social, economic and political structures' (Hall 1982: 63). It is an order, Peter Gabel and Paul Harris argue, that maintains striking asymmetries in the distribution of material and cultural resources and that is premised on exploitative social relations and the structural violence of private property (Gabel and Harris 1982: 370). While acts of individuals that threaten violence to persons or property are criminalized and censured, other forms of social violence – economic exploitation, say – are not conceived of as crime at all (Kelman 1982: 215). At the same time that it establishes criminal responsibility for some forms of violence, the law seems implicitly to sanction other forms. Moreover, even those individual acts of violence deemed criminal are a manifestation of, or at the very least shaped by, material social conditions – namely, the exploitative social relations that undergird the existence of criminal conduct. Marx, more than one and a half centuries ago, inveighed against those who, like Hegel:

> instead of looking upon the criminal as the mere object, the slave of justice, elevate [...] him to the position of a free and self-determined being. Looking, however, more closely into the matter, we discover that German idealism here ... has but given a transcendental sanction to the rules of existing society. Is it not a delusion to substitute for the individual with his real motives, with multifarious social circumstances pressing upon him, the abstraction of 'free-will' – one among the many qualities of man for man himself!
>
> (Marx 1853)

The criminal trial takes precisely the abstract 'free and self-determined being' as its central subject. This is a 'delusion', Marx suggests, as it ignores the criminal's 'real motives': that is, the complex economic and social forces – the 'multifarious social circumstances pressing upon him' – that shape and animate crime. Others have followed Marx's insights and insisted upon a relationship between social relations and individual criminal behaviour. One interpretation thus holds that 'it is the class struggle both between and among those who own and control the means of production and distribution and those who do not that is the source of all crime in capitalist societies' (Bohm 1982: 570).[11]

We may question whether '*all* crime' should be understood as the direct product of class struggle while still recognizing the more fundamental point that crime is not free-floating, independent of social relations. Much the same can be said of international crimes. The causes of, say, the Iraq war cannot be located solely in the subjective intent of calculating, pious, or evil individuals. As one collective of critical scholars warned in the wake of the war, calls for war crimes trials had perhaps 'privatize[d] and individualize[d] responsibility for that which should rather be seen as public and systemic' (Craven *et al.* 2004: 372). The broader point, here, is that few international crimes occur in isolation. Naomi Klein, for instance, has argued that the human rights abuses in the Southern Cone of Latin America in the 1970s should be understood as rooted in systemic economic transformations. She criticizes, for example, Amnesty International's reporting on human rights violations in Argentina: 'Without an examination of the larger plan to impose "pure" capitalism on Latin America, and the powerful interests behind that project, the acts of sadism documented in the report made no sense at all' (Klein 2008: 119–20). Torture and disappearance cannot be simply abstracted from the context of a violent restructuring of the country's political economy.

If human rights violations or war crimes do not take place in a vacuum, neither do the very conflicts that give rise to them. As a growing body of social science literature has shown, wide-scale violence, be it in the form of internal civil wars or international conflicts, is often – perhaps always – rooted in systemic economic and political forces. Elsewhere, I have argued that the conflict in the former Yugoslavia and the crimes tried at the ICTY cannot be understood independent of the political-economic transformations introduced under World Bank and IMF tutelage in the preceding decades (Krever 2013). The argument has broader application: violent conflict has often followed instances of neoliberal political-economic restructuring. At the core of neoliberal reforms is an emphasis on the opening of countries' political economies to the free movement of goods and financial flows from the North and a transformation of states' domestic social relations. In addition to macro-economic reforms – opening domestic economies to imports, freeing prices from controls, macro-economic stabilization – governments are also instructed to undertake micro-economic reforms such as privatization of state-owned enterprises, financial and labour market liberalization, and deregulation. The role of the state in the economy is to be curtailed and limited to protecting the operation of the free market (Krever 2011; Harvey 2007). The consequence of these reforms, in almost all cases, has been the growth of socioeconomic inequality, insecurity and human misery (Robinson 1996: 339). Such structural violence – 'inequality, exclusion, dispossession, alienation, disempowerment and humiliation' – attendant on Western prescribed economic reforms can be seen in the lead-up to numerous wars, conflicts and genocide (Orford 2003: 106). Christopher Cramer, in his excellent study of violence and economic transformation, argues that 'much of the violence in the world may represent the consequences of and reactions to the failures and choices of government policies, including those policies of wholesale liberalisation and deregulation encouraged by international financial institutions' (2007: 198). Mass violence does not arise from thin air. While particular individuals, acting in a social situation, may well bear responsibility for discrete instances of violence, that responsibility should not be understood in isolation of the social structures in which individuals act and are motivated to act.

The international criminal trial, however, fails to deal with either the material circumstances in which individual acts of crime are rooted or the systemic violence of the contemporary social order. The trial only addresses individual crimes and acts of violence, never the structural whole from which those acts or disputes arise.[12] It punishes international criminals without ever touching on the social relations which throw up particular instances of inter-national crime. That is, while censuring some conduct – war crimes, crimes against humanity, genocide – the trial leaves unscrutinized the social relations and structures out of which that conduct arises. Systemic forces – neoliberalism, imperialism, geopolitical rivalry, or even simply capitalism – are thus lost from sight in the international criminal trial. While trials foreground individual actors, they leave the interventions of international institutions and the systemic inequalities of the status quo unquestioned.

Not only do these trials neglect the role of structural forces and transnational economic processes in exacerbating social conflict and creating environments conducive to violence: they also seemingly absolve them. The trial reproduces the image of a society (or even international society) governed by a neutral rule of law with legalistic proceedings publicly demonstrating the neutral application of legal rules and judicial principles to adjudicate and resolve social conflict. The prosecution's accusation of crime is not taken for granted but must be proved beyond a reasonable doubt; the defendant is afforded an opportunity to contest the charges and provided with 'a panoply of rights that regulate the trial process in a fair manner and protect the defendant from government overreaching' (Nunn 1995: 798). But it is precisely through the apparently neutral application of legal rules and procedures that the 'apparent legitimacy of the existing social order' is reinforced (Gabel and Harris 1982).

Veiling politics

To justify the status quo, with its violence, exploitation and systemic inequali-ties, is, of course, inherently political. But if the international criminal trial operates ideologically to perpetuate 'prevailing constellations of power' (Marks 2007: 208), the debates about the politics of international criminal trials discussed above are also complicit in this same ideological manoeuvre. As already emphasized, the consensus implicit in these debates, regardless of position, is that the neutral, legalistic and apolitical trial does in fact exist.

By directing attention to issues of legalistic procedure or geopolitical calculi, mainstream debates distract from and even blind us to the ideological role of trials in constructing and conveying symbolic forms that sustain often asymmetric and violent international social relations. If particular asymmetri-cal power relations are constituted and reproduced through particular signi-fying practices, we should, if we wish to have a transformative effect on those relations, seek to focus attention on the ideological role of international criminal trials and not retreat into the comfortable but ultimately obfuscatory terrain of a narrowly conceived politics.

And yet contemporary debates about the politics of international criminal trials reproduce and reify the ideal of a trial shorn of politics. Our critical faculties are turned not to the broader ideological operation of the trial, but rather to immediate accusations of politicization in the form of victors' justice or deformed legalism. Efforts to highlight the more subtle ideological moves of international criminal law and to show how trials may in fact contribute to the perpetuation of systemic inequality and injustice are undermined. These dominant discourses on the politics of international criminal trials may thus themselves be understood as *political*, serving once more, like the trials themselves, to deflect attention from systemic and structural concerns to the immediate and contingent.

Conclusion

Mainstream debates about international criminal trials appear hamstrung by the issue of politics. Scholarly analysis tends to oscillate between two poles. On the one hand, critics are quick to dismiss trials as fatally politicized – instantiations of victors' justice and coercive apparatuses deployed to eliminate political enemies. On the other hand, defenders of international criminal law write of such trials in Olympian terms as purified of politics and untarnished by the vagaries of international power relations. But beyond their apparent antagonism, both positions share an idealized notion of an apolitical trial – both insist that war crimes trials *should* and *can* be apolitical. Politics enters in the *misuse* of the legal form for political ends – to eliminate political opponents, as in claims of victor's justice – or in the deformation of procedures and rules or absence altogether of legal process. Common to both positions is a shared view of what the trial *should* represent: the formal, predictable, and equal application of procedures and rules – that together make up the corpus of international criminal law – by a legal body adjudicating the cases presented to it. Where some see a 'sanctimonious … fraud' and 'a political act of the victorious States … dressed up with a false façade of legality' (Mason 1956: 715–16), others see a 'shining example' of 'full-blown Western legalism' (Bass 2003: 84; 2000: 25); but in both cases, politics is something alien and undesired – and something that *can* be eliminated.

This chapter has argued that these debates reproduce a narrow understanding of politics as synonymous with the misuse of legal proceedings and institutions. Politics, on this view, arises from conscious decisions to instrumentalize the judicial architecture of the international criminal trial or to sidestep or undermine liberal legal process. In so doing, these debates elide the ways in which even the neutral, legalistic trial operates to reproduce and legitimate the social structures and forces undergirding international crimes. While charges of overt politicization are not unimportant and need to be addressed by the field's practitioners, they should blind neither critics nor advocates of ICL to the deeper structural limitations – and politics – of the field. Without a clear-sighted analysis of the latter, international criminal trials may at best be a limited, even

Pyrrhic, victory for those seeking to challenge the deeper structural inequalities and violence that contribute to and throw up international crime.

Notes

1 Thanks to Teresa Almeida Cravo, Christine Schwöbel, Rob Knox, Immi Tallgren, Michelle Burgis-Kasthala and Sarah Nouwen for comments on earlier drafts. I have also benefited from discussions with participants at the 2012 Critical Approaches to International Criminal Law Conference in Liverpool where a version of the chapter was presented.
2 A notable exception is Nouwen and Werner (2011). They follow Carl Schmitt in defining politics as the act of distinguishing between friends and enemies (see Schmitt 1996).
3 The *Chicago Conspiracy* trial involved the prosecution of seven defendants (the 'Chicago Seven') for allegedly inciting riots during the 1968 Democratic National Convention in Chicago. See Danelski (1971).
4 A notion fostered and reproduced by legal education. See Kennedy (2004) and Orford (1998).
5 The *Haymarket* defendants were tried following a lethal bombing in Chicago in 1886. While they had advocated violent revolution, no evidence linked them to the bomb thrower. See Avrich (1984).
6 See, for example, United States Department of Defense (2005: 5): 'Our strength as a nation state will continue to be challenged by those who employ a strategy of the weak using international fora, judicial processes, and terrorism.'
7 This is somewhat disingenuous of Christenson, as later he distinguishes 'ordinary' trials from 'political' trials on the basis that the former 'do not involve the dual legal and political agendas that political trials simultaneously address' (Christenson 1999: 8).
8 'Liberal states', Bass (2000: 25) further writes, 'have not been willing to seriously compromise their domestic standards of a fair trial when putting foreign leaders on trial.'
9 Lukes' three-dimensional view of power recalls Gramsci's theory of hegemony, the mode through which the interests of a particular social group take on an appearance of universality, valid for all of society (Gramsci 1971; Thomas 2009). Particular institutions and practices central, and historically specific, to the bourgeois class project come to be seen as both natural and universal. And power, on this view, is exercised through 'subtle mechanisms of ideological integration' rather than direct force (Thomas 2009: 161).
10 This section draws on material and arguments developed in greater detail in Krever (2013).
11 See also Quinney (1978); Groves and Sampson (1986).
12 It may not be only the trial that obscures social structure – Robert Knox suggests this is a feature of the legal form itself (see Knox 2009: 429–33; Knox 2010: 201–11). See also Miéville (2005).

Bibliography

Avrich, P. (1984) *The Haymarket Tragedy*, Princeton, NJ: Princeton University Press.
Bass, G.J. (2000) *Stay the Hand of Vengeance: The Politics of War Crimes Tribunals*, Princeton, NJ: Princeton University Press.

Bass, G.J. (2002a) 'Victor's Justice, Selfish Justice', *Social Research: An International Quarterly* 69: 1035–44.

Bass, G.J. (2002b) 'Why Not Victor's Justice?', *Washington Post*, 15 February: A33.

Bass, G.J. (2003) 'Milosevic in the Hague', *Foreign Affairs*, May/June: 82–96.

Belknap, M.R. (1994) 'Introduction', in M.R. Belknap (ed.) *American Political Trials*, revised edn, Westport, CT: Greenwood Press.

Bohm, R.M. (1982) 'Radical Criminology: An Explication', *Criminology* 19: 565–89.

Bolton, J.R. (2002) 'The United States and the International Criminal Court', Remarks to the Federalist Society, 14 November. Available at: http://2001-2009. state.gov/t/us/rm/15158.htm (accessed 6 July 2013).

Brubacher, M.R. (2004) 'Prosecutorial Discretion within the International Criminal Court', *Journal of International Criminal Justice* 2: 71–95.

Burns, J.F. and Semple, K. (2006) 'Hussein is Sentenced to Death by Hanging', *New York Times*, 6 November: A4.

Cassese, A. (2008) *International Criminal Law*, 2nd edn, Oxford: Oxford University Press.

Chomsky, N., Lauter, P. and Howe, F. (1968) 'Reflections on a Political Trial', *New York Review of Books*, 22 August: 23–30.

Christenson, R. (1999) *Political Trials: Gordian Knots in the Law*, 2nd edn, New Brunswick, NJ: Transaction Publishers.

Cockburn, C. (2006) 'Did Milosevic or his Accusers "Cheat Justice"? The Show Trial that Went Wrong', *The Free Press*, 17 March. Available at: http://freepress.org/columns/ display/2/2006/1332 (accessed 6 July 2013).

Cramer, C. (2007) *Violence in Developing Countries: War, Memory, Progress*, Bloomington: Indiana University Press.

Craven, M., Marks, S., Simpson, G. and Wilde, R. (2004) 'We are Teachers of International Law', *Leiden Journal of International Law* 17: 363–74.

Danelski, D.J. (1971) 'The Chicago Conspiracy Trial', in T.L. Becker (ed.) *Political Trials*, Indianapolis: Bobbs-Merrill.

Danner, A.M. (2003) 'Navigating Law and Politics: The Prosecutor of the International Criminal Court and the Independent Counsel', *Stanford Law Review* 55: 1633–65.

Falk, R. (2007) 'Show Trial or Necessary Proceeding?', *Global Dialogue* 9. Available at: www.worlddialogue.org/content.php?id=421 (accessed 6 July 2013).

Gabel, P. and Harris, P. (1982) 'Building Power and Breaking Images: Critical Legal Theory and the Practice of Law', *NYU Review of Law and Social Change* 11: 369–411.

Gehring, K. (2011) '"War By Another Means": A Conversation with Former US Attorney General Ramsey Clark', *AllAfrica*, 3 April. Available at: http://allafrica. com/stories/200104050180.html (accessed 6 July 2013).

Gilbert, G.M. (1947) *Nuremberg Diary*, New York: Farrar, Straus.

Goldsmith, J. and Krasner, S.D. (2003) 'The Limits of Idealism', *Daedalus* 132: 47–63.

Goldstone, R.J. and Smith, A.M. (2009) *International Judicial Institutions: The Architecture of International Justice at Home and Abroad*, New York: Routledge.

Gramsci, A. (1971) *Selections from the Prison Notebooks*, ed. and trans. Q. Hoare and G.N. Smith, New York: International Publishers.

Greenspan, E.L. (2002) 'This is a Lynching', *National Post*, 13 March: A20.

Grossman, M. (2002) 'American Foreign Policy and the International Criminal Court', Remarks to the Center for Strategic and International Studies, 6 May. Available at: http://2001-2009.state.gov/p/us/rm/9949.htm (accessed 6 July 2013).

Groves, W.B. and Sampson, R.J. (1986) 'Critical Theory and Criminology', *Social Problems* 33: S58–S80.

Hall, S. (1982) 'The Rediscovery of "Ideology": The Return of the Repressed in Media Studies', in M. Gurevitch *et al.* (eds) *Culture, Society and the Media*, London: Methuen.

Hariman, R. (1990) 'Performing the Laws: Popular Trials and Social Knowledge', in R. Hariman (ed.) *Popular Trials: Rhetoric, Mass Media, and the Law*, Tuscaloosa: University of Alabama Press.

Harvey, D. (2007) *A Brief History of Neoliberalism*, Oxford: Oxford University Press.

Henderson, C.W. (2010) *Understanding International Law*, Chichester: Wiley-Blackwell.

Herman, E.S. (2005), 'The Hague Tribunal: The Political Economy of Sham Justice', *Global Research: Centre for Research on Globalization*, 20 November. Available at: www.globalresearch.ca/the-hague-tribunal-the-political-economy-of-sham-justice/1294 (accessed 6 July 2013).

Hermann, D.H.J. (1972) 'Contempt: Sacrilege in the Judicial Temple – the Derivative Political Trial', *Kentucky Law Journal* 60: 565–610.

Human Rights Watch (2009) 'Letter to the Prosecutor of the International Criminal Tribunal for Rwanda Regarding the Prosecution of RPF Crimes', 26 May. Available at: www.hrw.org/node/83536 (accessed 6 July 2013).

Kelman, M. (1982) 'The Origins of Crime and Criminal Violence', in D. Kairys (ed.) *The Politics of Law: A Progressive Critique*, New York: Pantheon.

Kennedy, D. (2004) *Legal Education and the Reproduction of Hierarchy: A Polemic Against the System*, New York: New York University Press.

Kirchheimer, O. (1961) *Political Justice: The Use of Legal Procedure for Political Ends*, Princeton, NJ: Princeton University Press.

Kirsch, P. and Robinson, D. (2002) 'Initiation of Proceedings by the Prosecutor', in A. Cassese *et al.* (eds) *The Rome Statute of the International Criminal Court: A Commentary*, Oxford: Oxford University Press.

Klein, N. (2008) *The Shock Doctrine: The Rise of Disaster Capitalism*, London: Penguin.

Knox, R. (2009) 'Marxism, International Law, and Political Strategy', *Leiden Journal of International Law* 22: 413–36.

Knox, R. (2010) 'Strategy and Tactics', *Finnish Year Book of International Law* 21: 193–229.

Kranzbuhler, O. (1965) 'Nuremberg Eighteen Years Afterwards', *DePaul Law Review* 14: 333–47.

Krever, T. (2011) 'The Legal Turn in Late Development Theory: The Rule of Law and the World Bank's Development Model', *Harvard International Law Journal*, 287–319.

Krever, T. (2013) 'International Criminal Law: An Ideology Critique', *Leiden Journal of International Law* 26: 701–23.

Lahiri, D. (2010) 'The International Criminal Court: Should India Continue to Stay Out?', *Indian Foreign Affairs Journal* 5: 181–8.

Laternser, H. (1987) 'Looking Back at the Nuremberg Trials with Special Consideration of the Processes against Military Leaders', *Whittier Law Review* 8: 557–80.

Laughland, J. (2007) *Travesty: The Trial of Slobodan Milošević and the Corruption of International Justice*, London: Pluto.

Lawfare Project (2012) 'Lawfare: The Use of the Law as a Weapon of War'. Available at: www.thelawfareproject.org/what-is-lawfare.html (accessed 6 July 2013).

Lopusina, M. and Huzsvai, A. (2002) 'Slobodan Milosevic is the Scapegoat in a Show Trial', *LA Times*, 12 February: B13.

Lukas, J.A. (1970) *The Barnyard Epithet and Other Obscenities: Notes on the Chicago Conspiracy Trial*, New York: Harper & Row.

Lukes, S. (2005) *Power: A Radical View*, 2nd edn, New York: Palgrave Macmillan.

Mamdani, M. (2009) *Saviors and Survivors: Darfur, Politics, and the War on Terror*, New York: Pantheon.

Mandel, M. (2001) 'Politics and Human Rights in International Criminal Law: Our Case Against NATO and the Lessons to be Learned from It', *Fordham International Law Journal* 25: 95–128.

Marks, S. (2007) 'International Judicial Activism and the Commodity-Form Theory of International Law', *European Journal of International Law* 18: 199–211.

Marks, S. (2011) 'Human Rights and Root Causes', *Modern Law Review* 74: 57–78.

Marx, K. (1853) 'Capital Punishment – Mr. Cobden's Pamphlet – Regulations of the Bank of England', *New-York Daily Tribune*, 17–18 February. Available at: www. marxists.org/archive/marx/works/1853/02/18.htm (accessed 6 July 2013).

Mason, A.T. (1956) *Harlan Fiske Stone: Pillar of the Law*, New York: Viking Press.

McGreal, C. (2008) 'Rwanda's Himmler: The Man Behind the Genocide', *The Guardian*, 18 December. Available at: www.guardian.co.uk/world/2008/dec/18/ rwanda-genocide-theoneste-bagosora (accessed 6 July 2013).

Mégret, F. (2002), 'The Politics of International Criminal Justice', *European Journal of International Law* 13: 1261–84.

Meron, T. (1995) 'International Criminalization of Atrocities', *American Journal of International Law* 89: 554–77.

Miéville, C. (2005) *Between Equal Rights: A Marxist Theory of International Law*, Leiden: Brill.

Minear, R.H. (1971) *Victors' Justice: The Tokyo War Crimes Trial*, Princeton, NJ: Princeton University Press.

Moreno-Ocampo, L. (2010) 'Keynote Address', Council on Foreign Relations, Washington DC, 4 February.

Mutua, M. (2000) 'From Nuremburg to the Rwanda Tribunal: Justice or Retribution?', *Buffalo Human Rights Law Review* 6: 77–91.

Newton, M.A. (2011) 'Evolving Equality: The Development of the International Defense Bar', *Stanford Journal of International Law* 47: 379–439.

Nouwen, S.M.H. and Werner, W.G. (2011) 'Doing Justice to the Political: The International Criminal Court in Uganda and Sudan', *European Journal of International Law* 21: 941–65.

Nunn, K.B. (1995) 'The Trial as Text: Allegory, Myth and Symbol in the Adversarial Criminal Process – A Critique of the Role of the Public Defender and a Proposal for Reform', *American Criminal Law Review* 32: 743–822.

Orford, A. (1998) 'Embodying Internationalism: The Making of International Lawyers', *Australian Year Book of International Law* 19: 1–34.

Orford, A. (2003) *Reading Humanitarian Intervention*, Cambridge: Cambridge University Press.

Posner, E.A. (2005) 'Political Trials in Domestic and International Law', *Duke Law Journal* 55: 75–152.

Quinney, R. (1978) 'The Production of a Marxist Criminology', *Contemporary Crises* 2: 277–92.

Reyntjens, F. (2004) 'Rwanda, Ten Years On: From Genocide to Dictatorship', *African Affairs* 103: 177–210.

Robinson, W.I. (1996) *Promoting Polyarchy: Globalization, US Intervention, and Hegemony*, Cambridge: Cambridge University Press.

Sadat, L.N. and Carden, S.R. (2000) 'The New International Criminal Court: An Uneasy Revolution', *Georgetown Law Journal* 88: 381–474.

Scharf, M.P. (2003) 'The Legacy of the Milosevic Trial', *New England Law Review* 37: 915–33.

Schmitt, C. (1996) *The Concept of the Political*, trans. G. Schwab, Chicago: University of Chicago Press.

Shklar, J.N. (1986) *Legalism: Law, Morals, and Political Trials*, Cambridge, MA: Harvard University Press.

Taylor, T. (1992) *The Anatomy of the Nuremberg Trial: A Personal Memoir*, New York: Knopf.

Thomas, P. (2009) *The Gramscian Moment: Philosophy, Hegemony and Marxism*, Leiden: Brill.

United States Department of Defense (2005) *The National Defense Strategy of the United States of America*. March. Available at: www.defense.gov/news/Mar2005/d20050318nds1.pdf (accessed 6 July 2013).

Zolo, D. (2009) *Victors' Justice: From Nuremberg to Baghdad*, London: Verso.

Chapter 6

Reading the political

Jurisdiction and legality at the Lebanon tribunal

Heidi Matthews[1]

Introduction

In 2007 the UN Security Council, acting under Chapter VII of the Charter, issued Resolution 1757 establishing a 'tribunal of an international character' to try the 2005 assassination of former Lebanese prime minister Rafiq Hariri as a 'terrorist crime'.[2] The Statute of the resultant Special Tribunal for Lebanon ('the Tribunal') gave the Tribunal jurisdiction over those responsible for the attack that killed Hariri, as well as any other 'connected' attacks of similar 'nature and gravity'.[3] The joint trial *in absentia* of four Hezbollah operatives accused in Hariri's killing, Salim Jamil Ayyash, Mustafa Amine Badreddine, Hussein Hassan Oneissi and Assad Hassan Sabra, began in January 2014. A fifth accused, also associated with Hezbollah, has recently been indicted.[4]

In May 2012, each of the defence teams in *Ayyash et al.* filed preliminary motions challenging the legality and jurisdiction of the Tribunal.[5] They argued *inter alia* that the creation of the Tribunal via Security Council Resolution 1757 constituted an abuse of power on the part of the Council. As such, the Resolution violated the principles and purposes of the UN Charter, and was therefore *ultra vires*. By way of relief, the defence teams asked the Tribunal to declare itself illegally constituted, and therefore without jurisdiction to hear the case. In July of the same year, the Trial Chamber dismissed the motions. In October, the Appeals Chamber upheld the Trial Chamber decision (President Baragwanath partially dissenting), ruling that it was incompetent to judicially review Security Council resolutions. Critically, in explaining their refusal to substantively engage with the defendants' claims, the judges emphasised that the Security Council's decision to create the Tribunal was 'essentially political in nature, and *as such* not amenable to judicial review'.[6]

This refusal to subject Security Council action to judicial oversight can be conceptualized as one technique among many by which international criminal tribunals (ICTs) attempt to formally distance their work from political questions. The Chambers constructed their decisions in *Ayyash* around a conceptual framework in which law and politics were analytically distinct. In so doing, they performed a classic technique of depoliticization that Tor

Krever has identified in this collection: the idea that as a doctrinal matter, a legal firewall must exist between the political will needed to create international tribunals and the subsequent judicial activity of these tribunals (Krever, Chapter 5 in this collection). The *Ayyash* decisions seek to sustain the Tribunal's legitimacy by bifurcating legality (Security Council politics) and jurisdiction (the Tribunal's application of existing law).

Accordingly, the *Ayyash* decisions have been strongly criticized for the way they manage – or rather fail to manage – the relationship between law and politics (Alvarez 2013; Nikolova and Ventura 2013). In avoiding, rather than directly confronting, the political implications of the Security Council's Chapter VII powers, José Alvarez accuses the Appeals Chamber judges of 'bury[ing] their heads in the sand' (2013: 292). This move renders 'an examination of the politics of law itself impossible' (Nouwen and Wouter 2011). The Chambers' decision not to second-guess the unassailable wisdom of the Security Council results in 'a decision that is entirely dictated by politics', and whose impact is to 'empower the powerful while disempowering the rule of law and judges' (Alvarez 2013: 300). In essence, Alvarez argues that *Ayyash* gives the Security Council plenary political power unfettered by legal constraint (Alvarez 2013; Nikolova and Ventura 2013: 641).[7] But such a quest for a political international criminal jurisprudence ultimately proves quixotic: it expresses an already familiar critique in a form that forecloses a nuanced examination of the stakes of depoliticization. Rather than dissolving away in the face of legal interpretive formalism, the depoliticizing moves deployed by ICTs express a politics by other means. Suppressed politics, in hydraulic fashion, often resurface in re-purposed and counter-intuitive ways.

This chapter aims to clarify the stakes of (de)politicization by mapping the concrete impact of the *Ayyash* decisions on the sites of, as well as the participants and modes of participation in, the politics of global governance. The chapter begins with a brief history of the establishment of the Tribunal. It continues on to an exposition of the defence arguments, framing them as objections to a putatively apolitical international criminal justice. The subsequent sections present a close reading of the *Ayyash* decisions. I show how these decisions deprive the defendants of a meaningful space in which to challenge their alleged particular uses of political violence as illegitimate and, therefore, criminal. Throughout, I use Carl Schmitt's legal theory as a lens through which we may begin to articulate what the space 'between impunity and show trials' could look like in international criminal law (Koskenniemi 2002).

Narrating the institutional history of the Tribunal

Legal commentators and the Tribunal itself narrate the dominant account of the Tribunal's creation, wherein both the UN and Lebanon originally preferred a tribunal with a 'hybrid' or 'internationalized' institutional structure. Hybrid tribunals have taken several forms over the last 20 years, ranging from national proceedings with a strong international element (Kosovo, East Timor and Cambodia) to self-contained internationalized institutions (Sierra Leone, Lebanon). All are mandated to apply, to one degree or another, national law, and most are the product of negotiated agreements between the state concerned and UN organs. The host state and the UN also typically share the judicial burden. The closest analogy to the Tribunal was the Special Court for Sierra Leone, which was created by a bilateral treaty concluded between the UN and Sierra Leone. Like the Special Court, the draft Agreement between the UN and Lebanon specified that a minority of the Tribunal's judges would be nominated by the Lebanese government. While the Special Court was entirely funded on the basis of voluntary contributions from the international community, 51 per cent of the Tribunal's funding would come from voluntary contributions, with the remaining 49 per cent to be borne by the government of Lebanon.

In the dominant narrative, this 'intended' bilateral agreement was thwarted when Syrian-allied members of parliament (the 'March 8' alliance) launched a filibuster designed to prevent domestic ratification of the draft Agreement (Wierda *et al.* 2007: 1074).[8] In 2005 Fouad Siniora – then the Lebanese prime minister and acting as part of the pro-Western 'March 14' alliance – requested that the UN Security Council establish an internationalized tribunal to deal with the 'terrorist crime perpetrated against Prime Minister Hariri'.[9] Pursuant to this request, the Security Council passed Resolution 1664, requesting the UN Secretary-General to negotiate an agreement with the Lebanese government to set up such a tribunal. An agreement was negotiated and the Secretary-General approved the draft Agreement and a proposed Statute for the Tribunal in November 2006. Only after the March 8 coalition-allied speaker refused to convene parliament 'to formally ratify the statute of the Tribunal and the bilateral agreement' did the prime minister appeal to the Secretary-General. He requested that the Secretary-General 'help make the Tribunal for Lebanon a reality' by 'put[ting] into effect' the draft Agreement through a 'binding decision' of the Security Council.[10] The Council responded by passing Resolution 1757, according to which, absent domestic constitutional ratification, the 'provisions of the [draft Agreement] on the establishment of [the Tribunal] shall enter into force on 10 June 2007'.[11] In *Ayyash* both the Trial Chamber and the Appeals Chamber held that Chapter VII provided the sole legal authority for the Tribunal.

This conventional narrative posits a moment of domestic failure that both triggers and justifies international intervention. The prime minister's actions are couched in the language of Security Council *assistance* needed to perfect a malfunctioning local constitutional and political system. In eliding the ways in which the draft Agreement process may have violated domestic constitutional requirements even before the alleged stalemate, this narrative presumes the inadequacy of the Lebanese political system. However, as the defence teams point out in their arguments in *Ayyash*, article 52 of the Lebanese constitution mandates that international treaties shall be negotiated by the president in agreement with the prime minister. The president boycotted the extraordinary session of the council of ministers at which the draft Agreement was approved. The Secretary-General was kept apprised of this and other constitutional problems by the president. Rather than complementing, assisting or fixing the domestic system, the Tribunal's creation via Security Council resolution appears more like an imposition of its political and institutional vision in place of allowing Lebanon to conduct its domestic political process – albeit more fractured and contested – on its own constitutional terms.

The Security Council's invocation of Chapter VII's coercive powers, combined with the full story of domestic resistance to the Tribunal's creation, disrupts the official narrative about the cooperative relationship between Lebanon and the UN. The combination of coercive and consensual mechanisms creates a confusing, non-linear narrative about the alignment of domestic politics with the imperative of international justice for Rafiq Hariri (see Burgis-Kasthala, Chapter 11 in this collection). While there is an established history of the Council using Chapter VII to create international tribunals, as was the case with the *ad hoc* tribunals for the former Yugoslavia and Rwanda, Resolution 1757 marked the first time that the Council deployed Chapter VII to resolve an internal political impasse or, stated more strongly, to institute its version of the correct domestic outcome. As Frédéric Mégret has noted, it was non-obvious that the threat to international peace and security that the Security Council alleged the Hariri assassination posed, combined with the non-failed nature of Lebanese domestic institutions, was *a priori* sufficient to legally justify the creation of the Tribunal. Precisely because the 'original intention had very much been that Lebanon would accept the Tribunal' (Mégret 2008: 488), after Resolution 1757 it now appeared that the Council had betrayed the reasonable expectation of a consensus-based tribunal that the UN negotiations had induced in the Lebanese people.

Articulating the political: the defence motions

The defence positions contesting the legality and jurisdiction of the Tribunal consisted of three overarching arguments, each of which contained several sub-arguments. Since the defence teams submitted separate briefs, their arguments did not always track one another. In some instances, the arguments of one team contradicted the arguments of another, or were internally inconsistent. For ease of exposition I have endeavoured to read the arguments more or less as a coherent whole, and in their most favourable light.

Resisting the threat of legibus solutus

The defence argued, first, that the Tribunal possessed the inherent jurisdiction to answer the key question raised by the motions, namely whether the

Tribunal was 'established by law'. Relying on the Appeals Chamber decision on the legality and jurisdiction of the ICTY in *Tadić*, the defence teams argued that all ICTs possess *la compétence de la compétence* as an inherent attribute of their judicial function. Undergirding this position was the structural argument that legality and jurisdiction are interdependent, rather than independent, concepts; in other words, the law-constituting authority – here, the Security Council – could not conceptually be divorced from the law-constituted authority – here, the Tribunal. For the defence, whether an ICT was legitimately empowered to exercise its statutory jurisdiction depended on whether its creation complied with the rule of law and vice versa. As a subsidiary argument, the teams argued that in the absence of a higher body empowered to determine the legality of the Tribunal, Chambers should construe their authority as encompassing the power to rule on their own legality. Having addressed the threshold question of authority to review the Tribunal's legality, the defence teams proceeded to argue that Chambers were authorized to determine whether, in creating the Tribunal through Resolution 1757, the Security Council complied with the UN Charter. The teams submitted that the Council did not enjoy unlimited powers, and that capacity for judicial review is inherent in the notion of creating a tribunal. Finally, they argued that the 'political nature' of Council resolutions 'cannot be relied upon to limit the scope' of judicial review.[12]

The primary concern animating the defence arguments was that if Chambers concluded that they did not have the power to review the legality of the Tribunal's establishment, the Security Council would effectively be accorded plenary power. Counsel for Ayyash argued that the power to review Resolution 1757 becomes a question of the 'principle of legibus solutus'; if the Appeals Chamber refused power to review, the Council would be granted 'full discretionary and legislative powers' unchecked by law.[13] Counsel for Badreddine further argued that this would 'open … an excessive margin for manoeuvre to the [Security Council]'.[14] In essence, lack of judicial oversight of the Council's determinations of what constitutes a threat to international peace and security, as well as of the propriety of its determination of corrective measures under article 41 of the UN Charter, would permit the Council to deploy Chapter VII as a blanket authorization to trump domestic (or, for that matter, all) politics: 'The [Security Council] would thus act as the judge of the internal political situation of States, which would enable it to impose its solutions on them.'[15]

From an international constitutional point of view, the defence was arguing against construing the Security Council as the global sovereign, entitled to decide on the exception: 'The Charter does not grant a supreme authority to the Council … Therefore it is not a sovereign organ.'[16] In other words, were Chambers to recognize their authority to judicially supervise the propriety of Security Council action, this would provide an institutional space in which the defendants could exercise a right of resistance to the international legal order dictated by the Council.

Defining the political

The defence teams struggled to articulate a coherent vision of the proper political role for the Security Council and its relationship to the Tribunal. The teams launched a two-pronged argument against Resolution 1757 based on alleged abuse of the Council's Chapter VII powers. First, they argued that the Council could not have reasonably concluded that, as an isolated internal political assassination, the Hariri killing constituted a threat to international peace and security. Second, they argued that the creation of an ICT to deal with this alleged threat was inappropriate, and constituted an abuse of power. Here, the teams argued that the Resolution violated Lebanese sovereignty in several ways that were inconsistent with the principles and purposes of the Charter. Creating the Tribunal amounted to an attempt to intervene illegitimately in the internal affairs of Lebanon in order to impact the local balance of power. Some teams argued that this intervention was unjustifiably selective and violated the principle of equality before the law. At the oral hearing before the Appeals Chamber, counsel for Ayyash lamented the lack of prosecutions for 'crimes in Guantanamo, and elsewhere', and noted:

> it was totally surprising to see a tribunal established for the sake of trying one category of crimes, even though Lebanon during the civil war … has suffered from thousands of war crimes, crimes against humanity, and these crimes could have been sufficient to establish an international tribunal.[17]

Counsel for Oneissi argued that creating an ICT specifically to try the Hariri murder would be more likely to incite further political violence than to mitigate or deter it, and further submitted that in emphasizing a certain class of 'terrorist' crimes, the statute of the Tribunal both unduly targeted one domestic constituency and prejudged the nature of its acts.

With regard to the Resolution's 'enforcement' of the draft Agreement, counsel for Ayyash argued that the Security Council invoked Chapter VII intentionally to circumvent the ongoing negotiations between the UN and Lebanon. Furthermore, the Resolution contravened key portions of the draft Agreement: namely, that it should only come into force pursuant to the legal requirements contained therein, which included compliance with domestic Lebanese ratification procedures. Counsel for Oneissi also argued that the Tribunal unjustifiably substituted international for domestic jurisdiction, and that Resolution 1757 was passed before all domestic avenues of ratification were exhausted. Related submissions argued that the prime minister did not have authority under the constitution to request that the UN establish an ICT.

At first blush, some of the defence arguments appear to endorse the same apolitical vision of international criminal justice that led Chambers to impose a strict separation of law and politics in *Ayyash*, thereby giving deference to the Security Council's 'political' role. Indeed, some of the defence language borders on suggesting that the political nature of the alleged crimes militates against international jurisdiction. For example, at the appeal hearing, counsel for Badreddine suggested a fundamental incompatibility between the international juridical and the domestic political, arguing that the Hariri murder was 'a political attack, political killing, and in no way an international crime'.[18] In their written submissions, the Badreddine team pressed even harder on this point, arguing that the Tribunal's 'jurisdiction is not therefore characterized by the *legal* nature of the crimes which the judge must deal with – but by the fact that the attack was carried out against the leader of an important *political* faction'.[19]

This approach is subject to several interpretations. On one interpretation, it appears that the defence was arguing against the idea that law and politics should be considered together as mutually constituting spheres of human activity that dialectically produce legitimacy or illegitimacy. This interpretation would fly in the face of the defence teams' cardinal submission that legality and jurisdiction, or law-constituting and law-constituted power, are interrelated questions. A more salutary interpretation, however, would hold that the defence was not arguing for a neutral application of politics at the international level, but was instead claiming that the particular way the Security Council acted with respect to Resolution 1757 undermined open political contestation. In other words, in framing the Hariri attack as requiring adjudication at the international level, the Council effectively neutralized the political role that this decision played within Lebanon. For the defence, in refusing to engage the effects of the Resolution for domestic politics, the *Ayyash* decisions depoliticized the international judicial process and forwent what could have been a productive opportunity to engage with the defendants' political claims.

This interpretation is also more in line with the remainder of the defence arguments, which focus on how the Lebanese polity was misled by the Security Council's decision to forgo continued domestic negotiations in favour of a Chapter VII solution. Counsel for Sabra succinctly summarized this position in its preliminary motion, arguing:

> The Security Council's actions were not consistent with respect for democratic governance, but in fact an affront to it: without the consent of Parliament, and therefore without an expression of citizens' will, the Security Council intervened in the midst of a democratic dispute, *favouring one side.*[20]

Once again, at first blush this argument appears to object to the non-neutral quality of the international justice meted out by the Tribunal. On this reasoning, the creation of a tribunal with the specific purpose of trying *one* act – the Hariri assassination – under the heading of a *single* crime – terrorism – violates a core principle that ICTs have sought to establish over the last

20 years: namely that in order to ensure procedural legitimacy, crimes on all sides of a given conflict should be equally prosecuted (Engle 2005). I argue that this principle, however, is substantively empty. In some cases, there might be good moral reasons to suppose that the substantive political objectives underpinning a defendant's alleged resort to violence may legitimate or even excuse this violence. Alternatively, such objectives may justify its criminalization. Bearing this in mind, one can understand the defence to be claiming that in pre-naming the alleged crime a 'terrorist crime', the Security Council had actually prejudged the question of whether the attack did or did not, in fact, violate the boundaries of legitimate political violence. In so doing, Resolution 1757 depoliticized not only the attack but also the process of its adjudication.

To summarize, the defence did not argue that internal violence can never constitute a threat to international peace and security warranting the establishment of an ICT. Rather, they claimed that in implementing the wishes of one side in the Lebanese political struggle – March 14 – *combined with* the refusal to judicially review Resolution 1757, the Tribunal created a situation wherein the minority – here, March 8 – was structurally excluded from any chance, much less an equal one, of bringing its political position to bear on the international legal adjudication of the alleged crime (Schmitt 1988). Overall, the defence did not object to the role of politics in law. Rather, they called for an expanded role for the political within the ICT adjudication process.

Available primary source documents support the defence claims that the Security Council deliberately and unjustifiably intervened in Lebanon's internal affairs. Chambers arguably could have taken such evidence into account in deciding whether the Council exercised its Chapter VII powers appropriately when creating the Tribunal. While it is well known that France and the United States, two of the five permanent members of the Security Council, were strong supporters of the creation of a tribunal to try the Hariri assassination (Wierda and Triolo 2012), recently leaked US diplomatic cables reveal the full extent of American involvement in the process. Long before the negotiations on the draft Agreement were concluded, the US was working closely with the March 14 coalition to push through a statute for the Tribunal. The cables demonstrate that a Chapter VII 'solution' was on the table at least as early as January 2006.[21] Strikingly, in February 2006, the chief justice of Lebanon's supreme court, Ralph Riachy, lobbied for a Chapter VII-based tribunal. Riachy was one of the key negotiators of the draft Agreement.[22] He would later be appointed to the Tribunal's Appeals Chamber. Leaving aside the question of whether, given his partisan involvement in the Tribunal's creation, Judge Riachy should have recused himself from the *Ayyash* decision, at the very least this shows both that the Security Council knew early in the process that it was unlikely that the Lebanese democratic system would be able to ratify the draft Agreement, and that Chapter VII was not just contemplated as a last resort should local constitutional procedures fail.

In addition, the US saw its interests as aligned with those of March 14, which sought to promote the de-confessionalization and democratization of the Lebanese constitutional system. The Lebanese constitution distributes power in a representative fashion among Lebanon's various religious groups. According to the then-Lebanese minister of justice, Lebanon needed to transition 'to a "real" parliamentary system rather than a confessional system'.[23] The Tribunal was explicitly conceived of as an institution that would facilitate this transition.[24] It was also 'the non-negotiable centerpiece of the [government of Lebanon's] overall strategy to keep Syria out of Lebanon'.[25] Although the Chapter VII option for the Tribunal's creation was understood as a risky option, both by March 14 and the UN – with UN Under-Secretary for Legal Affairs Nicholas Michel worrying that it would dilute Lebanese 'ownership' of the process and reduce the promise of local 'capacity building'[26] – the US assured Siniora that although it was 'not in the business of selecting Lebanon's next president', in case of domestic backlash 'it would not stand idly by and accept another pro-Syria lackey'.[27]

The *Ayyash* decisions on jurisdiction and legality

This section offers a brief overview of the *Ayyash* decisions of the Trial and Appeals Chambers. The most important aspects of the decisions concerning the appropriate ambit of political considerations within international criminal adjudication are recounted.

Trial Chamber decision[28]

In July 2012 the Trial Chamber ruled on the defence motions challenging the jurisdiction and legality of the Tribunal.[29] The Chamber rejected all four motions. Holding that 'legality and jurisdiction are in fact separate legal concepts',[30] the Chamber found that the motions were not challenges to jurisdiction as such, but challenges to legality. Nevertheless, the Chamber ruled that the motions were admissible pursuant to the general right of accused persons to be tried by a court established by law. As such, the Chamber proceeded to investigate whether the Tribunal was indeed established by law.[31]

On this point, the Chamber held that Resolution 1757 was the 'sole legal basis' of the Tribunal, and that the defence arguments that it had violated Lebanese constitutional law were therefore moot.[32] The Chamber held that it was incompetent to decide whether the Council properly determined that the Hariri assassination constituted a threat to international peace and security, and whether the decision to create a tribunal was reasonable in the circumstances. In a legal formalist move, it held that in the absence of explicit authorization to review Security Council action, the Tribunal lacked the competence to judicially pronounce on the manner in which the Council exercised its Chapter VII powers.[33] Holding that the Council had the 'constitutional authority' to create the Tribunal, the Chamber effectively affirmed its legality by default.[34]

Finally, concerning the defence allegation of impermissible selectivity, the Chamber refused to consider whether the domestic situation leading up to Resolution 1757 impacted the reasonableness of the Council's resort to Chapter VII to establish the Tribunal. Focusing instead on the general practice of ICTs, the Chamber held merely that selectivity was 'an inevitable consequence of establishing' an ICT.[35]

Appeals Chamber decision

The Appeals Chamber upheld the decision of the Trial Chamber. It held that preliminary motions challenging jurisdiction do not encompass the foundational charge of illegality. In other words, the primary jurisdiction of the Tribunal – *materiae, temporis* and *personae*[36] – was unassailable. The Chamber distinguished *Ayyash* from its ruling in *El Sayed*, where it held that the concept of inherent jurisdiction permitted it to hear a request for documents launched by an individual formally imprisoned under the authority of the Tribunal.[37] Quoting itself in *El Sayed*, the Chamber noted that inherent jurisdiction 'can be exercised only to the extent that it renders possible the full exercise of the court's primary jurisdiction'.[38] Inherent jurisdiction only applied to 'incidental' issues, and did not extend to the question of the Tribunal's legality. While the defence motions could not fit under the Chamber's narrowly constructed interpretation of 'preliminary motions' under rule 90(A) of the Tribunal's Rules of Procedure and Evidence, the Chamber held that it was nevertheless entitled to address the motions as 'other motions' pursuant to rule 126.

By positing such a sharp distinction between jurisdiction and legality, the Tribunal aligned itself with the legal formalist ideology wherein judges merely apply the law, rather than make it (Kennedy 2006: 63).[39] For the Tribunal, the question of legality was to be contained within the 'political' sphere. By positing 'law' against 'politics', the Tribunal set the stage for its refusal to judicially review Security Council resolutions.

The Appeals Chamber affirmed the Trial Chamber's finding that it was incompetent to review Council resolutions, holding that 'the Security Council's determination as to the existence of a threat to international peace and security is not subject to judicial review'.[40] While acknowledging that the Council is bound to comply with the purposes and principles of the UN Charter, the Chamber held that the Council 'has broad discretion' under Chapter VII, both in its determination of which situations constitute threats to international peace and security, and in the scope of measures that it deems appropriate to address such situations.[41] For the Chamber, this form of judicial oversight was not needed within the UN system. The Chamber stated: 'The composition of the Security Council ... (five permanent members and ten non-permanent members ...) and its voting regime ... ensure an inherent system of internal checks on the Security Council's exercise of its powers.'[42] The Chamber distanced itself from the Appeals Chamber in *Tadić*, which held that 'the so-called "political" or "non-justiciable" nature of jurisdictional challenges going to the legality of Security Council resolutions did not impugn its competence to review such resolutions.[43] On the contrary, the Chamber stated that '[w]hat is important is that' the Council's decision to create the Tribunal was 'essentially political in nature, and *as such* not amenable to judicial review'.[44]

President Baragwanath issued a partial dissent, holding that the inherent power of courts to avoid fundamental injustice meant that the rules governing challenges to jurisdiction should be read to include the fundamental challenge to legality.[45] Stating that '[t]he rule of law requires that the legality of the conduct of any body lacking plenary authority be subject to judicial review',[46] the Chamber's refusal to review Resolution 1757 amounted to according the Security Council illegal plenary authority.[47] While ultimately finding that the defence challenges failed, President Baragwanath suggested a sliding scale of judicial review for Security Council resolutions which would encompass, among other things, the context in which Council decisions are made, including 'important elements of international politics'.[48]

The Security Council, the global sovereign and the exception

The *Ayyash* decisions have been criticized for rolling back the precedent set by the ICTY in *Tadić* in which the Appeals Chamber found that challenges to the legality of ICTs are inherently challenges to jurisdiction.[49] 'The plea based on the invalidity of constitution' of an ICT, wrote the Chamber, 'goes to the very essence of jurisdiction as a power to exercise the judicial function within any ambit.'[50] The ICTY Appeals Chamber considered the question of legality to be especially important to the concept of jurisdiction in the context of international law, which 'does not provide for an integrated judicial system operating an orderly division of labour among a number of tribunals'.[51]

In asserting the coherence of the UN system while abdicating any responsibility to take a decision on the legality of Resolution 1757, the *Ayyash* decisions make a larger statement about the nature of the global constitutional order. In particular, they appear to anoint the Security Council as the global 'sovereign', at once bound by the fundamental law articulated in the principles and purposes of the UN Charter, while also sitting above the Charter in the sense that it enjoys unfettered authority to decide the most fundamental questions of international order outside the shadow of judicial oversight. In the worldview of the Tribunal, judicial institutions are entirely cut off from any kind of dialectical relationship with the law-constituting authority that created them.

We might understand the defence objection to this vision of the Security Council as global sovereign as consistent with an argument not that sovereignty itself is the equivalent of plenary power, but rather that the Council is incapable of sovereignty. Some commentators have arued that 'most UN organs' including the Security Council, which was not originally designed to constitute a legislative body, 'have acted much like parliamentary bodies in their proceedings' (Schachter 1994: 2). However, I argue that the Security Council structurally lacks the power to decide on the exception. In particular, I suggest that the defence arguments are best understood as an attempt to use the Tribunal as a forum for politics in which to actively contest the locus of sovereignty.

Martti Koskenniemi has argued that the 'constitutive paradox' of international criminal law inheres in its duty to both 'convey an unambiguous historical "truth" to its audience' and to conduct a fair trial in which the accused are permitted to speak. In this paradox, the accused's speech will inevitably 'challenge the version of truth represented by the prosecutor and relativise the guilt that is thrust upon him by the powers on whose strength the Tribunal stands. His will be the truth of the revolution and he himself a martyr for the revolutionary cause' (2002: 35).

In *Ayyash*, the defence proposed an account of the Tribunal's creation that was diametrically opposed to the official narrative told by Chambers and the Prosecutor. This alternative history was intended to open space for the accused to argue that the Tribunal was illegally constituted not because it was *too* political, but because it was not political *enough*. In prematurely cutting short the domestic democratic process working to establish a tribunal, and in selectively singling out a single 'terrorist' crime, the defence argued that the Security Council set up an institution bearing an illegitimate relationship to its own political process. Refusal to judicially review this relationship – that of the law-constituting to the legally constituted authority – would, for the defence, simply institutionalize the already objectionable construction of the Council as *legibus solutus* in relation to international criminal law.

But what if, short of declaring the Tribunal illegal, an alternate path to institutional legitimacy was available? President Baragwanath suggests just such a path in his partial dissent when he argues in favour of judicial review. However, his version of judicial review ultimately falls short of providing the more radical space for political speech demanded by the defence. He writes:

> [A] major purpose of judicial review is to ensure that powerful decision-makers comply with the law. *The relevant law is the expression of the will of the member States* who, when adopting the Charter, chose to create the Security Council not as a body having plenary authority but as one limited by law.[52]

While going some way to alleviating defence concerns about the threat of plenary authority, President Baragwanath's account of judicial review is based on a limited understanding of the international system as primarily directed at governing states' duties and obligations to one another. If the Security Council is only accountable to the will of sovereign states, then the individual will of the subjects of international criminal law – the defendants – can play no role.

In *Ayyash*, the defence teams positioned themselves as representing the political minority within Lebanon. As such, they opposed the Security Council's attempt, through Resolution 1757, to promote Lebanese constitutional reform through the creation of an internationalized tribunal; in other words, to declare an exception to the existing domestic constitutional system. Chambers responded by effectively according the Council plenary political authority.

Schmitt's theory of sovereignty is useful in analysing this response because it demonstrates the impoverished nature of the Chambers' understanding of the relationship between legal and political institutions. For Schmitt, sovereignty is intimately bound up with the concrete operation of law. It is constituted in the 'dialectic relation between law constituting power and legally constituted power' (Huysmans 2008: 166); in other words, it inheres not in the identity of political actors or institutions *per se*, but in their relationship to one another. In this system, the sovereign's capacity to declare an exception to a given constitutional structure where its 'formal and rational processes fail' guarantees the authority of both the legal and political structures in place (Huysmans 2008: 168; Agamben 2005; Bates 2006). Schmitt articulates how legitimate political institutions take an inherently juridical form. Political authority itself is premised on more than 'only naked technologies of holding power'; it is intimately bound up with the law, which serves as the vehicle for the expression or representation of a substantive idea (Schmitt 1996: 17). Legal institutions are in turn only politically responsible – that is, capable of facilitating substantive normative governance – to the extent that they go beyond mere legislative formalism or majority rule. For Schmitt, the mechanism of the exception resolves the perennial tension between the supremacy of the formal rule on the one hand, and the principle of majority rule on the other. The former cannot admit of judicial review, since to do so would endanger the 'clear system of legality and render [...] problematical parliament's central position as the source of legality' (Schmitt 2004: 25). The latter, in its persistent 'neutrality toward the difference between justice and injustice', makes the concept of legal abuse of power impossible (2004: 29).

Key to Schmitt's legal theory of the exception is the idea that, although a juridical concept, the exception can never be formally institutionalized: it exists 'neither external nor internal to the law' (Agamben 2005: 54). The moment 'the exception becomes the rule, the machine can no longer function' (2005: 58). This non-institutional ontology of the exception proves fatal to a conception of the Security Council as capable of filling the role of global sovereign – in other words, as capable of declaring the exception. In essence, the Trial and Appeals Chambers' articulation of Council action as not subject to judicial review institutes a contradictory vision of sovereignty that rests on the Council as an institution capable, through its form, of institutionalizing the uninstitutionalizable, the Security Council cannot *declare* the exception because the UN structure attempts to *institutionalize* the exception. First, the permanent five veto means that the identity of the sovereign is fixed. The Council's decisional moments are thus themselves structured such that the capacity to break free from the UN constitutional structure is precluded. Second, the fixity of the permanent five is reproduced at the level of the UN Charter amendment procedure. Amendments to the Charter can only take effect when ratified by two-thirds of the members of the UN '*including all the permanent members of the Security Council*'.[53] As a result, in according the Council unfettered 'political' authority, Chambers make, in Schmitt's words, 'a purely politically motivated claim to subordination, with an equally politically motivated denial of every right to resistance' (2004: 21).

Conclusion

Critical international criminal law scholars often seek to problematize the law/politics distinction, pointing out that law is nothing but politics all the way down. While important, this move is insufficient: it provides neither a theoretical framework for, nor a sense of the stakes of, these politics. Appropriating Schmitt to read the defence arguments in *Ayyash*, I have argued that the political inheres in the sites where the exception is declared. An institutional interpretation of Schmitt demonstrates that defining the exception is thus not about the exercise of individual will but rather the outcome of institutional politics. As a result, I argue not just that the *Ayyash* decisions are 'political', but further that in order to get a sense of their stakes we must trace the sites of institutional political struggle in which the decision to declare the exception takes place. In making the political the exclusive province of the Security Council, the Tribunal elides the incapacity of the Council to decide on the exception. Rather than constituting an institution as a *political* space for the exception, the Council seeks to *institutionalize* the exception itself. That is, the structure of the Security Council – the veto and the Charter's amendment procedure – domesticate the exception, thus precluding its exceptionality.

Scholars and practitioners concerned with the politics of international criminal law should shift their focus and ask how sites of politics are refracted through the global constitutional order away from the Security Council. ICTs can no longer be seen as purely juridical spaces, but as spaces of, and shaped by, global governance. The defence arguments in *Ayyash* sought to contest the locus of global sovereignty and were rebuffed. Nevertheless, when interpreted in light of Schmitt's theory of the exception, they provide a starting point for a new kind of critical engagement with the political. As critical scholars we must understand ICTs as part of a system of institutions that provides many different spaces in which the politics of the exception can be argued. This politics conditions who can participate in the contest over sovereignty and through what means. The defence teams' invitation to reveal the substantive politics of the decision on the exception by integrating it into the Tribunal's adjudicatory process is one example of how this politics could be made explicit and contestable. In short, we must begin to take seriously international criminal law's claim not just to judge, but to *govern.*

Notes

1 Many thanks to Michelle Burgis-Kasthala, Paul Kingsley Clark, Deval Desai, Noah Feldman, Lisa M. Kelly, Duncan Kennedy, Martha Minow, Christine Schwöbel and Richard Tuck for their comments on this chapter. Any errors remain my own.

2 UN Doc. S/RES/1757 (May 30, 2007) In addition, the Tribunal has established jurisdiction over three attacks 'connected' to the Hariri assassination.

3 Statute of the Special Tribunal for Lebanon, art. 1. The Statute was attached to the Agreement between the United Nations and the Lebanese Republic on the establishment of a Special Tribunal for Lebanon, which itself entered into force by mandate of UNSC Resolution.

4 In June 2013, Hassan Habib Merhi was also accused in the Hariri attack.

5 The defence teams did not make identical arguments. I have attempted to summarize them here.

6 *Ayyash et al. v. The Prosecutor,* Special Tribunal for Lebanon, STL-11-01/PT/AC/AR90.1, 24 Oct. 2012, Appeals Chamber, Decision on the Defence Appeals Against the Trial Chamber's 'Decision on the Defence Challenges to the Jurisdiction and Legality of the Tribunal', para. 52 ('AC decision') (emphasis added).

7 See also Separate and Partially Dissenting Opinion of Judge Baragwanath, ibid., para. 71 Partial dissent.

8 See AC decision, op cit., 13 (noting that 'It is undisputed that the Government of Lebanon and the United Nations initially agreed to enter into negotiations for the purpose of establishing a Tribunal of an international character'; citation omitted). Wierda *et al.* explain that 'The imposition of the STL Agreement through a resolution adopted under Chapter VII of the UN Charter was not the original intent of the United Nations but was a consequence of the fact that the Speaker of the Parliament Nabih Berri, leader of the Amal Movement, refused to convene the Parliament in order to ratify the Agreement' (2007: 1074, citation omitted).

9 Annex to the letter dated 13 December 2005 from the Chargé d'affaires a.i. of the Permanent Mission of Lebanon to the United Nations addressed to the Secretary-General, UN Doc. S/2005/783 (Dec. 13, 2005). For an extended discussion of the local political situation, including the split between the March 14 and March 8 coalitions, see Michelle Burgis-Kasthala (Chapter 11 in this volume; and 2013).

10 Letter dated 14 May 2007 from the Prime Minister of Lebanon to the Secretary-General, UN Doc. S/2007/281 (16 May, 2007).

11 UNSC Resolution 1757 op cit., art. 1(a).

12 Appeal Brief of the Oneissi Defence Against the Trial Chamber Decision Relating to the Defence Challenges to the Jurisdiction and Legality of the Tribunal, STL-11-01/PT/AC/AR90.1, 24 Aug. 2012, para. 30.

13 Official Transcript, Appeals Hearing, Special Tribunal for Lebanon, 1 Oct. 2012, 52 Transcript.

14 Preliminary Motion Challenging Jurisdiction of the Special Tribunal for Lebanon Filed by the Defence of Mr Badreddine, STL-11-01/PT/TC, 9 May 2012, para. 41.

15 Ibid.

16 Appellate Brief of the Defence for Mr Badreddine against the 'Decision on the Defence Challenges to the Jurisdiction and Legality of the Tribunal', STL-11-01/PT/AC/AR90.1, 24 Aug. 2012, para. 51.

17 Transcript, op cit., 20.

18 Ibid., 21.

19 Badreddine appeal brief, op cit., para. 56 (emphasis added).

20 Sabra's Preliminary Motion Challenging the Jurisdiction of the Special Tribunal for Lebanon, STL-11-01-PT/TC, 9 May 2012, para. 37 (citation omitted, emphasis added).

21 UN Legal Affairs Chief Briefs P-3 on UNSCR 1644 Follow-Up, 30 Jan. 2006, Wikileaks.

22 Lebanon: GOL Moving Quickly on Special Tribunal, 14 June 2007, Wikileaks, para. 3 ('GOL Moving Quickly').

23 Lebanon: Rizk on GOL Suing Israel, Electoral Law Reform, and the UNIIIC Tribunal, 4 Oct. 2006, Wikileaks.

24 Lebanon: A/S Welch and PM Siniora Coordinate Chapter VII Strategy, 17 May 2007, Wikileaks, para. 10 ('Now that successful resolution of the tribunal issue was within hailing distance, Siniora believed the instrinsic appeal of the pro-reform message has a real chance to succeed, with the result being a president representative of all of Lebanon's communities.') ('Chapter VII Strategy').

25 Ibid., para. 7.

26 GOL Moving Quickly, op. cit., para. 8.

27 Chapter VII Strategy, op. cit., para. 1.

28 For a more detailed recounting of the Trial and Appeals Chamber decisions, see Nikolova and Ventura 2013 and Alvarez 2013.

29 *Ayyash et al. v. The Prosecutor,* Special Tribunal for Lebanon, STL-11-01/PT/TC, 27 July 2012, Trial Chamber, Decision on the Defence Challenges to the Jurisdiction and Legality of the Tribunal.

30 Ibid., para. 28.

31 Ibid., paras 26–41.

32 Ibid., paras 45–50.

33 Ibid., para. 55.

34 Ibid., para. 72.

35 Ibid., para. 87.

36 Rules of Procedure and Evidence, Special Tribunal for Lebanon, STL/BD/2009/01/ Rev. 6 rule 90(A) (as amended Apr. 9, 2013).

37 *In the Matter of El Sayed,* Special Tribunal for Lebanon, CH/AC/2010/02, 10 Nov. 2010, Appeals Chamber, Decision on Appeal of Pre-Trial Judge's Order Regarding Jurisdiction and Standing.

38 AC decision, op. cit., para. 16 (quoting *El Sayed,* ibid., para. 48).

39 Duncan Kennedy describes one of the key elements of 'classical legal thought' as a commitment to 'legal interpretive formalism', whereby legal results are obtained through 'deduction within a system of positive law presupposed to be coherent' (Kennedy 2006: 63). In strictly limiting jurisdiction to the enumerated heads listed in article 90(A) of the Rules of Procedure and Evidence, and distinguishing *Ayyash* from *Tadić* on the grounds that the ICTY's 'broad interpretation of the

term "jurisdiction" was possible because the ICTY Rules of Procedure and Evidence at the time did not define it', the Tribunal performs a distinctly neo-formalist move (AC decision, op. cit., para. 14).

40 AC decision, op. cit., para. 35.
41 Ibid., para. 37.
42 Ibid., para. 38 (citation omitted).
43 Ibid., para. 41 (quoting *Prosecutor v. Tadić*, International Criminal Tribunal for the former Yugoslavia, IT-94-1-AR72, 2 Oct. 1995, Appeals Chamber, Decision on the Defence Motion for Interlocutory Appeal on Jurisdiction, para. 25).
44 Ibid., para. 52 (emphasis added).
45 Partial dissent, op. cit., para. 22.
46 Ibid., at para. 66.
47 Ibid., at para. 71.
48 Ibid., at para. 75.
49 Alvarez 2013 and Nikolova and Ventura 2013.
50 *Tadić*, op. cit., para. 12.
51 Ibid., para. 11.
52 Partial dissent, op. cit., para. 68 (emphasis added).
53 UN Charter, art. 109(2) (emphasis added). I am grateful to Richard Tuck for turning my attention to the Charter amendment procedures as revelatory of the UN's underlying political theory.

Bibliography

Agamben, G. (2005 [2003]) *Stato di eccezione*; trans. K. Attell, *State of Exception*, Chicago: Chicago University Press.
Alvarez, J. (2013) '*Tadić* Revisited: The Ayyash Decisions of the Special Tribunal for Lebanon', *Journal of International Criminal Justice* 11: 291.
Bates, D. (2006) 'Political Theology and the Nazi State: Carl Schmitt's Concept of the Institution', *Modern Intellectual History* 3: 415.
Burgis-Kasthala, M. (2013) 'Defining Justice during Transition? International and Domestic Contestations over the Special Tribunal for Lebanon', *International Journal of Transitional Justice* 7: 497.
Engle, K. (2005) 'Feminism and its Dis(contents): Criminalizing Wartime Rape in Bosnia and Herzegovina', *American Journal of International Law* 99: 778.
Huysmans, J. (2008) 'The Jargon of Exception – On Schmitt, Agamben and the Absence of Political Society', *International Political Sociology* 2: 165.
Kennedy, D. (2006) 'Three Globalizations of Law and Legal Thought: 1850–2000', in D. Trubek and A. Santos (eds) *The New Law and Economic Development: A Critical Appraisal*, London: Cambridge University Press.
Koskenniemi, M. (2002) 'Between Impunity and Show Trials', *Max Planck Yearbook of United Nations Law* 6: 1.
Mégret, F. (2008) 'A Special Tribunal for Lebanon: The UN Security Council and the Emancipation of International Criminal Law', *Leiden Journal of International Law* 21: 485.
Nikolova, M. and Ventura, M.J. (2013) 'The Special Tribunal for Lebanon Declines to Review UN Security Council Action: Retreating from *Tadić*'s Legacy in the *Ayyash* Jurisdiction and Legality Decisions', *Journal of International Criminal Justice* 11: 615.

Nouwen, S.M.H. and Wouter, W.G. (2011) 'Doing Justice to the Political: The International Criminal Court in Uganda and Sudan', *European Journal of International Law* 21: 941.

Schachter, O. (1994) 'United Nations Law', *American Journal of International Law* 88: 1.

Schmitt, C. (1988 [1923]) *Die geistesgeschichtliche Lage des heutigen Parlamentarismus*, trans. E. Kennedy, *The Crisis of Parliamentary Democracy*, Cambridge, MA: MIT Press.

Schmitt, C. (1996 [1923]) *Römischer Katholizismus und politische Form*, trans. G.L. Ulmen, *Roman Catholicism and Political Form*, Westport, CT: Greenwood Press.

Schmitt, C. (2004 [1932]) *Legalität und Legitimität*, trans. J. Seitzer, *Legality and Legitimacy*, Durham, NC: Duke University Press.

Triolo, A. and Wierda, M. (2012) 'Resources', in L. Reydams, J. Wouters and C. Ryngaert (eds) *International Prosecutors*, Oxford: Oxford University Press.

Wierda, M., Nassar, H. and Maalouf, L. (2007) 'Early Reflections on Local Perceptions, Legitimacy and Legacy of the Special Tribunal for Lebanon', *Journal of International Criminal Justice* 5: 1065.

Part III

International criminal legal histories revisited

Chapter 7

Linear law

The history of international criminal law

Gerry Simpson[1]

What is the history of international criminal law?[2] Or, to put it another way, what sort of histories are international criminal tribunals creating?[3] I want to argue here that the histories produced in moments of institutional decision – partly because they occupy a space of authorized history, partly because courts have managed to convince many people that they have access to objective or expert history – are rather important in shaping how we might think of geopolitical trends or national struggle or the very meaning of the 'international'. And I want to say, too, that the tendency has been to produce historical accounts in which certain styles of history-making are preferred over others.

Arthur Koestler once said in a striking phrase: 'But who will be proved right? It will only be known later' (1946: 99).[4] Yet international criminal law is an effort to do a very difficult thing: that is, to fix contemporary history. This is a huge undertaking. And international criminal tribunals have already played a major role in establishing the parameters of official history. Of course, the history of the Holocaust is partly defined by Raul Hilberg and Primo Levi but it also is a product of a peculiar moment of innovation at Nuremberg (Hilberg 2003; Levi 1987; 2001). In a similar vein, the history of the Balkans is part Misha Glenny, part ICTY (Glenny 1999). The genocide in Rwanda, too, is linked ineluctably with the findings of the International Criminal Tribunal for Rwanda. History has been judicialized.

I should say at the outset that I am not so interested here in the debate about whether International Criminal Justice *should* consciously seek to create historical records. That question has been ventilated in Philip Roth's *Operation Shylock* (about the first *Demjanjuk* Trial), in Laurence Douglas's *Memory of Judgment* and in David Hirsh's *Cosmopolitan Justice*.[5] Hannah Arendt, of course, worried in Jerusalem that an excessive attentiveness to historical record produced deformities in legal process, that didactic jurisprudence was a contradiction in terms (Arendt 1994). So, in *Eichmann* there was a sense (and to be fair to the judges, they recognized and tried to limit this tendency) that the trial was the story of the Holocaust, a history lesson for the edification of the Israeli state and the global community (and this recalls Guyora Binder's comment that we must avoid finding war crimes trials edifying). Certainly, we now know that there is a balance to be struck between history and law, between extraneous evidence and best evidence, and between context and act. But that balance is not my subject in this chapter.

The idea essayed here is not whether to make history but rather what sort of histories to make (or, more prosaically, what sorts of histories do international criminal tribunals make?). And why should critical international law be interested in these questions? In particular, are there methodological preferences built into the project of international criminal justice (say, an overvaluing of traditional linear narratives over fragmentary, social histories?) or ideological biases (a preference, say, for histories that reflect well on liberal values of multiculturalism over the regressive tendencies of nation, *ethnie* or religion) or more transparently political biases (a tendency to write histories that somehow accord with the political requirements of the Great Powers). There is a great deal to be said about all of this. For the time being, this chapter will attend to three aspects of the problem of history. First, I want to discuss the 'subjects' of history (through a reading of a moment of institutional crisis at Versailles). Is international criminal justice committed to an idea about individual agency in history? Is this idea defensible? Second, I offer some reflections on the relationship between linear history and chaotic history. Is there a tendency in international criminal tribunals to convert history into narrative? Or to theorize history by producing overdetermined accounts of it? Where do international tribunals stand on the debate between those who believe that history is found or discovered (through archival zealotry, analytical precision, empirical doggedness or judicial exactness) on one hand, and on those who argue instead that history is invented or imagined (through literary device or political decision or methodological preference) in a response to what Hayden White calls the 'inexpungeable relativity' of historical representations (White 1978)? Third, I make some tentative comments on the relationship between history and hegemony. If the victors really do write the histories then are international criminal tribunals simply helping to write the victors' *faux* official histories?[6]

Method: the subjects of history

> The theory of the transference of the collective will of the people to historical persons may perhaps explain much in the domain of jurisprudence and be essential for its purposes, but in its application to history, as soon as revolutions, conquests or civil wars occur – that is, as soon as history begins – that theory explains nothing.
>
> (Tolstoy 1999: 1282)

I want to begin by examining whether Leo Tolstoy's 'domain of jurisprudence' – in the present case, international criminal justice – has a (no doubt sublimated) theory of history at all and whether that theory of history can (or should) explain why or how certain events occur.[7] This problem of history, I argue, returns us to a moment in the institutional development of international criminal law that I have written about previously and that I view as the field's modern origin. I am thinking of the meetings of a commission of legal experts (these included Robert Lansing, Ernest Pollock and James Brown Scott) convened by the delegates to the Versailles Peace Treaty (Simpson 2007). It was here for the first time that lawyer-internationalists had to grapple with the tension sketched by Tolstoy half a century earlier.

In 1919, a committee was established at the Versailles Peace Conference to consider the question of war crimes trials for the defeated German elite (including the Kaiser). This represents the first occasion in international history when there is a somewhat methodical, official statement and interrogation of what were to become some of the central problems in the field.[8] This committee laboured under a curious but revealing title 'The Commission on the Responsibilities of the Authors of the War'. The deliberations turned out to be stormier than the Versailles statesmen might have anticipated. In effect, the Commission began to enact a series of distinctively twentieth-century debates between opposing views of history. The one to which I will give greatest attention involved the nature of historical agency. Here, the Commission began to wrestle with the title it had been given (and the first of its tasks) and the whole idea of 'authorship'. In what sense is history or war authored? And who authors it? Or is 'authorship' the wrong metaphor? And, of course, this was not just a struggle over metaphor. The debate over the authorship of war, or what we now call the crime of aggression, has continued to this day.

Like the Great War, *War and Peace* might be read in a number of different ways. Two distinct interpretations present themselves. One is that it is a book dedicated to reinstating the historical agency of individual human beings in times of geopolitical crisis. It is the story of Prince Andrei, or Napoleon, forging a personal and world history at an extraordinary time. Tolstoy, in his tedious postscript to *War and Peace*, clearly adopts the position that this transference of the collective will to individual persons simply will not do as 'history'.[9] We can perhaps imagine him thinking that individual responsibility operates in only two fictional landscapes: the world of literature and the domain of jurisprudence. Authors or judges take a set of historical materials and, for the sake of moulding an attractive and readable story with compelling characterizations in one case, and forging an image of personal responsibility in the other, they transform these materials into a story with human agency at its heart. Novels and trials, we might say, require characters but history, perhaps, does not.

History, for Tolstoy in his postscript, is the same history endowed with a large H by everyone from Hegel to Fukayama and Bobbitt via Marx. It is history as the motion of forces, or a machine, in which individuals are merely tossed or digested, or a collective will against which individual men and women are powerless. Their stories remain compelling as fiction or biography but in complex historical studies or theories of international relations or historical sociology, they are inadequate. It is an account of history that takes little notice of individual endeavour and imagination: instead, we have – in the materialist camp – the attribution of historical change to geography (Diamond 2005), or technological advances (Bobbitt 2003) or, from an idealist perspective, the working through of history's master plan. Hegel might be taken as an archetype of the latter tendency. As he puts it in *Lectures on the Philosophy of History*, delivered between 1822 and 1831, 'those manifestations of vitality on the part of individuals and peoples ... are, at the same time, the means and instruments of a higher and broader purpose of which they know nothing' (Hegel 1960: 559).

In contrast, international criminal justice must, by definition, be wedded to the idea that men do make history of their own choosing. No theory of individual responsibility could live without it.[10] So, as Article 7 of the ICTY Statute makes clear: 'A person who planned, instigated, ordered, committed or otherwise aided and abetted in the planning, preparation or execution of a crime ... shall be individually responsible for the crime.' And, as the ICTY states in *Tadic*:

> The basic assumption must be that in international law as much as in national systems, the foundation of criminal responsibility is the principle of personal culpability: nobody may be held criminally responsible for acts or transactions in which he has not personally engaged or in some other way participated ...
>
> (*Prosecutor v. Tadic (Judgment)*, 15 July 1999)

Note, for example, the way in which this tension between the two readings of *War and Peace*, or between its postscript and its main text, undergoes a revival every time someone is brought to court. So, the arrest of Ratko Mladic brought in its train the standard posturing about responsibility: Mladic's supporters arguing that Mladic was simply doing Serbian state business in Srebrenica; the ICTY indicting him as an individual, individually responsible for ordering and participating in a crime of genocide.[11] The media obsession with Mladic, Milosevic and Gotovina might lead one to suspect that international criminal law sometimes seems to be in the grip of a Great Man theory of world events.

At the Tribunals, this is offset in two ways: by indicting small fish (the *Tadic* move), and by creating or appropriating doctrines that situate individuals in broader networks of collective responsibility (say, through conspiracy doctrine at Nuremberg or using modes of liability such as joint criminal enterprise or command responsibility at the ICTY) (*Prosecutor v. Dusko Tadic (Judgment)* 15 July 1999: 185 *et seq*; *Prosecutor v. Kordic and Cerkez (Judgment)*, 26 February 2001: 371). Each of these projects is a way of reaching up, down and out to the broader contexts in which crime takes place. The prosecution of minor players demonstrates that crimes against humanity are often opportunistic (*Tadic*) or sadistic (*Jelisic*) or spontaneous (many of the killings on the Eastern Front, as horribly described by Christopher Browning in *Ordinary Men* (1992) or Timothy Snyder in *Bloodlands* (2010); *Prosecutor v. Dusko Tadic (Judgment)*, 7 May 1997; *Prosecutor v. Goran Jelisic (Judgment)*, 14 December 1999).

My hunch, notwithstanding these two complications, is that the ICTY, for example, whether or not it has overemphasized the personal responsibility of leading Serb nationalists, has certainly understated the role of structural or economic forces in creating the conditions for ethnic warfare (there is a passing reference to this in paragraph 70 of the *Tadic* Trial Chamber decision). There has been some work done on the relationship between atrocity and political economy but little of this permeates the work of the tribunals (*Prosecutor v Dusko Tadic (Judgment)*, 7 May 1997: 70).[12] So, for example, some former officials and commentators have remarked upon an apparent relationship between structural adjustment policies that the World Bank insisted that Yugoslavia adopt at the end of the 1990s and the subsequent economic meltdown that may have led to the rise of Milosevic and his clique. Indeed, there may be a whole subfield that needs to develop around genocide and political economy.[13]

The Commission delegates at Versailles faced a different problem: the question as to whether in the case of war – the hard case of criminal liability – there could *ever* be a question of personal responsibility. The politicians who established the Commission adopted the view that the war had been authored by the Kaiser and his associates, and hoped the Commission experts would confirm this through a fairly unproblematic reading or, better, restatement of the legal and historical material. But as Alun Munslow puts it, 'facts never speak for themselves' (Jenkins 1991: xiii). Wars, and especially their causes, have to be interpreted.

The Commission found itself divided. The *Memorandum of Reservations* issued by the Americans took a radically different approach (arguing for sovereign immunity, against command responsibility and against the category of 'crimes against humanity') from that of the majority, but even the Majority Opinion is based around a contradictory reading of the material. The Commission begins by agreeing with the politicians that the Germans (and the Kaiser and his associates in particular) had initiated the war in order to further their loathsome ambitions for territorial expansion.[14]

Later, though, when it comes to assigning legal responsibility, the Commission becomes coy about the stability of historical interpretation, stating that the question of authorship was not a juridical question at all. History, as it were, belonged to the historians; and war to the political or moral philosophers:

> … any inquiry into the authorship of the war must, to be exhaustive, extend over events that have happened during many years in different European countries, and must raise many difficult and complex problems which might be more fitly investigated by historians and statesmen than by a tribunal appropriate to the trial of offenders against the laws

> and customs of war … Any tribunal appropriate to deal with the other offences to which reference is made might hardly be a good court to discuss and deal decisively with such a subject as the authorship of war.[15]

This is a rare moment of diffidence from an international institution willing to deny itself space and prerogatives in a certain field. The most recent contemporary example of this I can think of is Judge Koojimans' separate opinion in *Congo v Uganda*[16] where he regrets international law's inability to come up with a thick description of the war in the Great Lakes (and here again we recall that the applicants wanted a condemnation for Ugandan aggression). 'To explain the intervention of one State into the affairs of another is rarely simple or uncontroversial … Moreover the results are likely to be tentative, partial, and complex. And therefore less than totally satisfying.'[17]

In the era of juridification and inquiry, it is refreshing to witness these denials of expertise. The 1919 Commission's findings hardly represent a full-blown embrace of history as discourse or indeterminacy, but they do manifest an unusually pluralistic approach to history or, at least, the impossibility of law offering definitive accounts of such histories. In a way, the Commission may be conducting its own internal history war anticipating later debates among historians of the Great War.

The Commission both accepts and then implicitly rejects a particular theory of war and political change that overstates the agency of elites (the Great Man theory of history) and has powerful associations with the orthodox concept of history as 'a factual account of the past'. Histories of this type (often in fact historical biographies) are regularly best-sellers. Eagleton dismisses these as a form of human interest story: 'a middle-class alternative to material history, one in which the supreme creation known as the individual may hold sway' (2008: 9). International criminal law seems, at least temperamentally, implicated in this sort of history.

'Millions of people have lived in the past but few of them have appeared in history'; and the same goes for the history of war crimes trials (Jenkins 1991: 9). It is mental states (a deliberate pun) not imperial rivalry or the malfunctioning of the political economy that produce war. When the Versailles experts rejected (in this paragraph at least) the juridical account of authorship and declared the causes of war to be multiple, perhaps even unknowable, certainly structural, they were also rejecting a history that depended on assigning juridical responsibility for war to certain individuals, as in the formula: 'Hitler invaded Poland'. But, still, there is relatively little 'social history' in tribunal accounts of the causes of war or conflict, and this mirrors the way in which – in the study of history generally – over-attention to the behaviour of elites or mandarins has tended to skew history away from the everyday or the social, and the juridification of this over-attention has resulted in histories that favour a particular genus of human action, namely, the deliberate and premeditated over the accidental or unintended.[18] So that what we end up with are histories that are over-determined. The international tribunals are throwbacks or reversions of the old histories of high politics featuring 'morally and politically autonomous individuals, whose decisions reflected in the first place the peculiarities of their own personalities rather than wider forces of any kind' (Evans 1997: 161).

In summary, history can be authored in at least two different, opposing senses.[19] In the first version, there is the Lloyd-George/Clemenceau view developed after the Great War and, to some extent, carried through the modern project of international criminal law, whereby individuals with some sort of criminal intent – and through force of will or malevolent charisma – capture powerful states and transform some political configuration or other. These are what Perry Anderson, discussing the historical novel, called 'costume dramas', featuring a narrative of progress and a melodramatic clash between good and evil played out in over-stylized, simplified terms: this is history in its operatic mode.

In the second version, there is a supreme author of some sort – either God or the working through of some pre-determined Hegelian historical arc (a form of historicism) or the appearance of a revolutionary class capable of acquiring power or an economic form promising happiness for humanity and finality for history. In this history, criminal intent is hardly relevant. In fact, men and women simply find themselves committing errors by ending up on the wrong side of history itself. As Lenin, in his speech at 8th Soviet Congress on 30 December 1920, said of Bukharin: 'he went to one room and found himself in another' (Leites and Bernaut 1954: 153). To conduct criminal trials in the service of extreme versions of such histories is to preside over a show trial. Remember, Merleau-Ponty called the Moscow Show Trials 'dramas of subjective innocence and objective treason' (1969: 202).[20]

Of course, collective responsibility and individual liability both suffer from the same defect. They exonerate a large number of people. If everyone is responsible then perhaps no one is. If individuals are capable of leading a state to disaster – think here of Airey Neave shouting at a tram-load of grim-faced and sullen Germans outside the Palace of Justice in Nuremburg as they survey the devastation wrought by Allied bombing: 'It was Hitler that did this to you' – then perhaps only the (dead) leader is responsible (Neave 1978: 44–5). For many of the leading Nazis at Nuremberg there was only one defence: 'Hitler did it, I was just a cog.' The great order-follower himself, Adolf Eichmann, rested his defence on a variant of this, and his chronicler, Hannah Arendt, gave voice to this idea of Eichmann as a cog but at the same time held him responsible in history and law.[21] Her alternative indictment – an effort to come to terms with history's dual impulse and found towards the end of *Eichmann in Jerusalem* – could be summed up in this way: 'it could have been anyone but it *was* actually you so too bad for you'. Or, as Karl Marx put it (reversing the emphasis but maintaining the duality) men 'make their own history, but they do not make it just as they please in circumstances they choose for themselves; rather they make it in present circumstances, given and inherited' (Carver 1996).

Linear histories

> ... the Russians and French seemed unable to grasp the implications of the concept [of conspiracy]; when they finally did grasp it, they were genuinely shocked ... the Soviets seemed to have shaken their heads in wonderment – a reaction, some cynics may believe, prompted by envy.
> (Bradley Smith 1977, quoted in Danner and Martinez 2006)

Leopold Ranke – at 83 and about to begin his history of the world (he completed 17 volumes by the time he died, aged 91) – wanted to show 'what actually happened' (Evans 1997: 17). Meanwhile, G.R. Elton, the eminent British historian, insisted on objective history and scientific truth. For some time now, though, history's relationship to the past has been obscure. There is greater acceptance that histories are accounts of the past or interpretations of a set of materials about an existing past.[22] Indeed, Carr traced this acceptance back to the Great War and its ending. Just as the Commission on the Responsibility of the Authors of the War was establishing a definitive account of the facts of the war, Carr argued that the facts seemed to smile on us less propitiously than in the years before 1914, and were therefore 'more accessible to a philosophy which sought to diminish their prestige' (1987: 21). With the demise of the single authoritative history, fresh questions have arisen about how to fashion an authentic account from these materials or how to rework the materials altogether. And, of course, there are now serious doubts about whether any sort of non-fictional history is possible.[23] This is what Lyotard, of course, called the 'condition of postmodernity': there is no centre capable of sustaining a single authoritative pronouncement about the past and we are left with a series of 'inscriptions of the past, pretending to be a likeness of it' (Barthes 1977).

Differences in history are then reduced to matters of style and, indeed, new forms have emerged in the wake of these intellectual currents. Orlando Figes (1997) has managed to popularize a history from below: anecdotal but authoritative, recuperative, non-linear, decentralized. Sven Lindqvist (2002) organizes his histories in a way that formally displaces linearity and instead offers the reader a number of ways into and through history.

Yet, international criminal law and its official bodies often are obliged to offer a theory of history that excludes or flattens some of the quirks or anomalies. Indeed, this goes back, again, to 1919 where the Commission,

> ... having examined a number of official documents relating to the origins of the World War ... has determined that the responsibility for it lies *wholly* upon the Powers which declared war in pursuance of a policy of

aggression, the concealment of which gives to the origin of this war the character of a dark conspiracy against the rest of Europe.[24]

I doubt that there is a single historian working today who would find this a complete or even plausible explanation of the origins of the Great War. It is certainly parsimonious. And its great advantages from the perspective of international criminal law is that it offers an account of war that meshes with the juridical requirement that wars be the product of an individual's criminal mind or a small elite's criminal conspiracy.

But A.J.P. Taylor once said, 'States don't commit crimes, they make mistakes.' The Commission's version of the causes of war leaves little room for 'mistakes'. According to the Commission, the conspiracy begins in early 1914, and the assassination of Archduke Ferdinand is a pretext for putting in place an irreversible mobilization for war.

Perhaps we can pause for a moment and consider what is missing from this account. There is nothing about the poisonous and mistrustful nature of nineteenth-century European diplomacy (and this was something that Wilson was agitated about at the time, and sought to supplant with an open system of centralized arrangements based on the League of Nations).[25] There was no reference to the inter-imperial rivalry that had disfigured Anglo-German and Franco-German relations in the late nineteenth century (something that Lenin, of course, had written about at the same time), nor about Germany's fear of encirclement and naval expansion, nor the instability caused by the decline of the Ottoman Empire (and the floating of the Ottoman dreadnought, *Sultan Osman I*), nor the Austrian split with Russia occasioned by the Crimean War. There was nothing about the principle of self-determination and the way it had raised expectations of geopolitical transformation in Central Europe (the proximate cause of the war was Gavril Princip's gesture of nationalist violence). And finally, there was reference neither to an arms race that had led to a very precarious security system in Western Europe, and one which may have encouraged pre-emptive action on the part of Imperial Germany, nor to Taylor's railway timetables, which, he argued, had fixed in advance the need for mobilization and then war at a particular point in time (Taylor 1969). It is not as if these structural explanations exhaust the possibilities either. A number of counter-revisionist histories have begun to re-emphasize the accidental (the timing of Home Rule for Ireland, the particular stage of the Caillaux Affair in France, the wrong turn at Franz-Josef Strasse in 1914) (McMeekin 2013) and the personal (not this time restricting it to German conspiracy but, instead, turning attention to Sasanov's agitations for war, Sir Edward Gray's ambiguous messages to the Germans, and French duplicity and confusion) (McMeekin 2013: 394–405).[26]

At Nuremberg, this tendency continues. Famously, the whole indictment was conditioned by the need to think of the origins of the Second World War as lying in another 'dark conspiracy'; this time one designed and executed by a small cabal of leading Nazis around the figure of Adolf Hitler. This theory of conspiracy – an American idea – permeated and arguably deformed the whole trial.[27] Its sheer and largely undisturbed linearity certainly penetrates the final judgement. At the very least, it fails to reckon with the capricious, improvisational and (sometimes) accidental aspect of the aggression and the accompanying genocides.[28] There was an associated failure to understand the special nature of the Holocaust. Instead, it was viewed as an incidental by-product of the central narrative engine: conspiracy to wage war.[29] The Indictment (based on Bernays' imported theory of conspiracy) states that the Nazi accused had:

> … during a period of years preceding 8 May 1945, participated as leaders, organizers, instigators, or accomplices in the formulation or execution of a common plan or conspiracy to commit … Crimes Against Peace, War Crimes, and Crimes against Humanity … and, in accordance with the provisions of the Charter, are individually responsible for their own acts and for all acts committed by any persons in the execution of such plan or conspiracy.[30]

And the Tribunal took a similar view:

> The seizure of power by the Nazis, the use of terror, the destruction of the trade unions, the attack on Christian teaching and on churches, the persecution of the Jews, the regimentation of youth – all these are said to be steps deliberately taken to carry out the common plan.[31]

Two consequences of this are well documented. Initially, the Jewish victims of the war had to be inserted into this grand narrative as part of national groups (for example, 'Poles') or as enemy populations. The Jewishness of the victims was subordinated to their status as nationals of invaded and occupied states. This meant that the Tribunal had to view events in the East as rationally connected to the aggressive war: 'war crimes were committed when and wherever the Führer and his close associates thought them to be advantageous. They were for the most part the result of cold and criminal calculation.'[32]

But this does not sound at all like the 'bloodlands' described in Timothy Snyder's book of the same name where the killings took place in an atmosphere of irrational savagery and where such killings often were a hindrance to the larger 'war effort' (Snyder 2010). And this meant, in turn and second, that the relationship of the Holocaust to the aggression was poorly understood. The idea that a regime could be so savage as to undertake a genocide in ways that *impeded* the war effort was never properly confronted. The emphasis on a form of personal responsibility conditioned by the rational pursuit of ideological or conscious ends fails to explain something about the special nature of the killing (the role of gender, say, or sex or the unconscious will to violence and so on) and its irreducibility to a single cause or form of behaviour.[33]

Later trials continued in this vein. I have spoken elsewhere of the Trial of Klaus Barbie in Lyon where the prosecution and court went to great lengths to present the war as a single struggle between French resistance and Nazi aggression and torture. This linearity occluded, of course, the recent history of fascism and anti-semitism in France (the *Dreyfus Case*, for example), the Vichy regime's collaboration with the Nazis and the use of torture by French colonial forces in Algeria (Simpson 2007: 90).

In a sense this debate between two ways of thinking about history was at the heart of the half-century-long struggle to find an acceptable framework for the crime of aggression. These problems infected the jurisdictional rules surrounding aggression: who should have authority to decide or determine? Was it a matter for what Judith Shklar (1961) called 'tribunality'? Or should it be a matter of fate the consequences of which could be handled by the Security Council,[34] as well as the effort to draft an acceptable definition of the crime itself.[35]

At first blush aggression is a simple matter: Germany invaded Belgium in 1914, Belgium's neutrality was guaranteed by the Great European powers *ergo* the German state had committed an act of aggression. Philip Bobbitt, though, reminds us that aggressors are not always those who strike first (as in the international law definitions). Again, a nuanced history might produce a different account: 'The move to war is an act of the State and not boys,' Bobbitt concludes enigmatically (2003: 8). Giving him the benefit of the doubt, might it be that the boys are international lawyers feeding off over-simplified narrative histories, and the men are structuralists thinking of war as a form of destiny produced by either the structure of international relations or the proclivities of human nature?

Others may have a better idea of how the ICTY has constructed its histories. It may be that it has made a more self-conscious effort to prepare the historical ground for some of its various decisions than, say, earlier tribunals have done, but that the historical narratives it has produced have a neatness that other historical accounts would resist.

Figes and Lindqvist are examples of what *can* be done with historical materials in order to reflect the often decentralized, ambiguous and obscure causes of historical events as well as the connections between them. But in a way, of course, international tribunals, if one takes into account the defence arguments, *do* produce plural histories. As I have said elsewhere, to read the transcripts of the Milosevic trial, and in particular Milosevic's defence submissions, is to get some sense of how a certain sort of extreme Serbian nationalism became so compelling to a large number of Serbs. This unauthorized or dissident history represents, also, the unauthorized legacy of the Tribunal (Simpson 2007: 79–104).

Hegemonic histories

In the previous two sections I have spoken of the way in which international criminal tribunals might favour histories that emphasize individual agency over structural causation, and linear arrangements of history over those that tend towards ambiguity or fragmentation. A third, and closely associated, possibility is that the histories produced by war crimes trials will, at any particular time, tend to accord with the contemporaneous self-image of the Great Powers. It may be, of course, that this is an attribute of the two deformities traced earlier. By emphasizing individual agency, courts reproduce a dominant account of the international system in which its crimes (hundreds of thousands of preventable deaths every month) are understood as accidents or by-products of international political economy or sovereignty or the free trade in machetes, while its accidents (the system occasionally results in periods of madness (Taylor in Liberia)) or singular political acts (the Hariri assassination in Lebanon) are understood as 'crimes'. International criminal justice then becomes an exercise in displacing, in our attentions, from the profitable but lethal trade in weapons to Naomi Campbell's complaint about the inconvenience of giving evidence in the Taylor case. Privileging the evil intent of a small number of individuals explains away the causes of indecency, atrocity and wrongdoing. Political crises in Rwanda or Yugoslavia are sometimes reduced to the machinations of tiny cabals or the pathology of all-powerful deviant figures.[36] It might be, too, that master-narratives of the sort disparaged by Lyotard (and discussed in the previous section) have a tendency to confirm or sanctify hegemonic accounts of history[37] (Lyotard 1984: xxiii–xxiv).

If the weapons trade was thought of as a crime, this would cause inconvenience (unemployment) and loss of political capital (a drop in support among key constituencies) in large Western states like the United Kingdom. In any event, the intermeshing of military and political elites within most states makes it impossible to contemplate a transformation along these lines. The dominance of the international criminal law model may also allow us to evade responsibilities closer to home. The deaths caused by a particular arrangement of international economic life or a particular consumer desire are screened out of any discussion of legal responsibility or 'fault' in the international system while international tribunals put 'an end to impunity' by insisting that old men are brought to The Hague to face trial.

In a similar vein, international criminal justice tends to produce highly schematic, mono-causal histories in which the antecedents of conflict or genocide are elided. The linear, chronological histories mapped onto events by the tribunals tend to emphasize political event over economic determinant or *longue durée*.[38] If the commission of war crimes has anything to do with the activities of the Great Powers then it is surprising that these activities are so invisible in the reasoning of international tribunals and the writings of international lawyers. Intervention, colonial misadventure or exploitation, economic ruthlessness, the manipulation of local elites, the engagement in proxy wars – the stuff of historical accounts of war – are largely missing from the history produced by international criminal justice. Instead, the focus tends to be on the indigenous cause of violence (the illegitimate seizure of power by local overlords, the abusive projection of that power by 'national-ists' or 'tyrants', the torture and oppression of local populations, the delusions of those local populations and so on) or on providing a Gibbonesque moral (Gibbon 1776–89). Just as the focus on individual agency will sidestep the background influences on political mal-development so, too, will linear history have a tendency to obscure the foreground but antecedent violence of the Great Powers.[39] R.G. Collingwood offered a variation on this claim in *The Idea of History* (1946): 'If we want to abolish war … we must begin by … seeing the problems which our economic or international system succeeds in solving, and how the solution of these is related to the other problems which it fails to solve.'

The histories produced are not self-evidently hegemonic. Indeed, interna-tional criminal justice seems overwhelmingly committed to promoting the rule of law or the idea of humanity *against* hegemonic ambition or sovereign vanity.[40] Nevertheless, the good faith of practitioners and their allegiance to the rule of law hardly disposes of the question of a political project's merit. As E.H. Carr said:

> When modern writers on international politics find the highest moral good in the rule of law, we are equally entitled to ask, What law? And Whose law? The law is not an abstraction. It cannot be understood inde-pendently of the political foundation on which it rests and of the political interests which it serves.
>
> (Carr 2001: 179)

In the abstract, the rule of law, for all its virtues in a stable, liberal democracy, is a form of rule that is likely to favour entrenched elites over resistance groups, vested interests carrying out lawful activity over civil disobedience, official actors over unofficial actors and property owners over protestors. In the international system, where the distribution of power, goods and advantage is so vastly, indefensibly and asymmetrically skewed, where the law is largely written by and on behalf of a powerful minority of states and where institutions are funded by, established at the behest or instigation of (or, at least, with the tacit approval of) and, often, directed by sovereign elites, it is little wonder that the rule of law is regarded either as illusory and distant (in its radical guise) or concrete and violent (in its existing instantiation). China Miéville, in one of the most important sentences ever written about international law, reminds us that the 'death, destruction, poverty, torture: this *is* the rule of law' (2006: 319). International criminal justice might be (self)-regarded as chipping away, imperfectly, and with due regard to its inherent 'politicalness', at all of this injustice or it might be thought of as another example of injustice.

The other idea or rhetoric that energizes international criminal justice, and mobilizes its practitioners and supporters, is the idea of humanity. Certainly, humanity is invoked a great deal in its doctrines ('crimes against humanity'), in its institution's preambular statements and in its rhetorical justifications. People who work in international criminal courts would prefer to see themselves as working for 'humanity' rather than an appendage of the United States Justice Department or the Russian Ministry for Justice. But what if Proudhon – 'he who invokes humanity, cheats' – is right?[41]

Bear in mind here that the perfect system would be one whose norms could be regularly invoked by the Great Powers and whose practitioners were both 'independent' of the Great Powers but also incapable of laying a finger on them or their personnel (because of the structure of international politics or because of the jurisdictional requirements of the relevant court or tribunal). The appearance of neutrality and the good faith of prosecutors, judges and investigators are vital to all of this. It might be possible to be scrupulous and deeply politicized at the same time. This is how international criminal justice begins, after all: with largely decent and often brilliant lawyers like Hartley Shawcross or Francis Biddle or Robert Jackson applying a set of norms that seemed to advance justice and provide a form of retribution for those who had committed ghastly acts. Yet, the history told by the IMT or IMTFE (Justices Pal and Roling are notable exceptions to this general rule) has nothing to say, as far as I can recall, about the fire-bombings of Tokyo, Dresden and countless German medieval towns undamaged by European wars for a millennium but obliterated by Bomber Command in raids that were radically disconnected from the war effort and, in retrospect, seemed almost pathological in their motivation. It had nothing to say about the way in which the Allies had participated in the dismemberment of Czechoslovakia, nothing about Soviet atrocities under Stalin, nothing about the relationship between *Lebensraum* and the model of British colonialism (Mark Mazower's *Hitler's Empire* (2008) is good on this). Nuremberg is by any standard a pretty strange history of the Second World War: a devastating critique of Nazism but also an apologia produced by men with the best intentions who might have been better off heeding the warnings of the Versailles dissenters.

In my view the ICC might be falling into the same trap in its investigations in Libya. The Libyan regime, for which I hold no brief, was a friend of the West for over a decade. During this decade its human rights record was shabby to say the least. A 2008 Human Rights Watch Report describes a state in which there were 'arrests and incarceration of political prisoners, some of them disappeared; the torture of detainees'.[42] Indeed, gross violations of human rights were a regular feature of life in Libya in the 40 years preceding the armed intervention. It was only when it began to defend itself against an armed rebellion that international criminal tribunals became interested.

This, in a system made up of sovereign-states, is a strange moment to accuse a state of crimes against humanity. It might enhance the standing of the ICC greatly if it decided not to respond to a Security Council authorization. The alternative is a risk that at the moment, in some quarters, the ICC looks like NATO's judicial arm.

Robert Cooper, a former adviser to Tony Blair, said:

> The challenge ... is to get used to the idea of double standards. Among ourselves, we operate on the basis of laws ... But when dealing with more old-fashioned kinds of states ... we need to revert to the rougher methods of an earlier era – force, preemptive attack, deception ...
>
> (Cooper 2002)

If this really is the story of the future, then international criminal tribunals are going to have to perform a very delicate series of diplomatic and legal manoeuvres in order to steer a course between complicity and effectiveness on one hand, and marginalization and credibility on the other. International judicial institutions, after all, simply do not have the same status, autonomy or cultural power as their municipal equivalents in the US, UK and Australia.

Again, of course, there is a whole other story to be told about international criminal justice and the way it can be or might be used to unseat these hegemonic histories to which I have referred. Nonetheless, to a visitor from Mars perusing the historical record as set out in international tribunals for the past 60 years, the impression given would be that, with the exception of Bosnian Muslims and Croats tried at the ICTY, war crimes, crimes against humanity and genocide had been carried out only by those states (or rebel groups) that have found themselves opposed to the interests of the North Atlantic elite. Millions have died as the direct consequence of Great Power intervention (Vietnam, Cambodia, Afghanistan, Guatemala, El Salvador) or as an indirect consequence of coups and military action (Iraq, Iran). Not one single national of a permanent Security Council member has been tried before an international criminal court since 1945: 'Every discipline is, I suppose, as Nietzsche saw most clearly, constituted by what it forbids its practitioners to do' (White 1978: 126–7).[43]

International criminal justice is probably best defined by what it cannot do, by what it is prevented from doing and by what it refuses to do. Any heretic histories of the future will have to reckon with and resist the defining methodological and cultural preferences at the heart of the field. We are being perpetually enjoined to 'Never Forget', and yet this injunction is allied to a set of history-making practices that oblige us to remember only in very circumscribed ways. Historians, as Lewis Namier once said, 'remember the future and imagine the past' (Evans 1997: 228). Accepting this might be a useful starting point for our efforts.

Notes

1 Thanks to Catherine Gascoigne for her help with this chapter.
2 Of course, there is now a bit of writing on the history of international criminal law, in the more conventional sense. It now is almost obligatory to trace the development of the discipline back to its roots in 'Tokyoberg' or to the creation of the international criminal tribunals for the former Yugoslavia and Rwanda or to the inception of the ICC or the proposed trial of the Kaiser. For an attempt to redeem or reveal some untold stories of international criminal law see Heller and Simpson (2013). An earlier and shorter version of this chapter appeared as 'International Criminal Law and the Past' in G. Boas, W. Schabas and M. Scharf (eds) *International Criminal Justice: Legitimacy and Coherence*, Cheltenham: Edward Elgar 2012.
3 This is bound to be a contentious idea.
4 This recalls Chou-En Lai's (over)famous comment in 1972 that it was far too early to tell what would be the likely effects of the French Revolution (Schama 1990: 1).
5 See *State of Israel v Demjanjuk* [1988] CrimA (Jer) 347/88 (on 12 May 2011, the Munich District Court found Demjanjuk guilty of 29,000 counts of accessory to murder at Sobibor camp); Roth (2000); Douglas (1996: 100–20; 2001); Hirsh (2003). And, of course, in countless other works: Morgan (1988: 1); Luban (1987); Felman (2001).
6 So, this chapter will hope to tease out some of these problems of history, which turn out also to be problems of law. These dilemmas can be avoided, of course. But the consequences tend to be ideological blindness or doctrinal aridity. I am aligning myself here with the approach of Nicolas Polites and James Brown Scott at Versailles or Justices Pal and Roling in Tokyo.
7 Some of the research for this chapter was undertaken by Monique Cormier, an ARC Research Fellow participating in a larger project tentatively entitled Invoking Humanity: A History of War Crimes Trials. This is a modified version of a chapter of a book entitled *Creating Humanity: A Literary Life of International Law* currently being written as part of this project.
8 Commission on the Responsibilities of the Authors of the War on the Enforcement of Penalties (1920) (hereinafter, Commission Report). The dilemmas faced or identified in 1919 were to repeat themselves throughout modern history of war crimes. The reservations expressed in the Japanese and American dissenting memoranda were to form the basis of the arguments made by the defence at Nuremberg and Tokyo (and by many of Nuremberg's critics). Meanwhile, the American position at Versailles (cautious, sceptical, legalistic, self-interested) was to be repeated in 1998 and subsequently, when the US reverted to its pre-Nuremberg anxiety about international criminal law.
9 Tolstoy's postscriptive essay in *War and Peace* is not widely liked. Discussing *War and Peace* in a paper published in 2011, Perry Anderson adverts to what he calls Tolstoy's 'incoherent philosophical tirades on the nature of history – deplored by virtually all his readers' (2011: 24). The tension between the creative demands of the novel (or narrative history) and philosophical belief about history is repeated in R.G. Collingwood's life. As a number of historians have pointed out, Collingwood's *Oxford History of the Roman Empire* and his *Idea of History* exist in glorious isolation from one another.
10 There may be an association, too, between structural accounts of criminality and the idea that amnesties might be a useful way to reconstruct the peace. At Westphalia, individual responsibility – indeed, any account of the Thirty Year War that found fault with any of the adversaries – was off the table. What replaced it was a commitment of international criminal law's opposite: oblivion: 'That there shall be on the one side and the other a perpetual Oblivion, Amnesty, or

Pardon of all that has been committed since the beginning of these Troubles, in what place, or what manner soever the Hostilitys have been practis'd, in such a manner, that no body, under any pretext whatsoever, shall practice any Acts of Hostility, entertain any Enmity, or cause any Trouble to each other ... but that all that has pass'd on the one side, and the other, as well before as during the War ... shall be bury'd in eternal Oblivion.'

11 'Mladic, who refused to recognize the authority of the war crimes tribunal in The Hague, denied being a killer, adding that all Serbs bore a shared guilt for voting for President Slobodan Milosevic, the architect of the Balkan wars' (Beaumont and Meikle 2011).

12 Of course, it may be that criminal trials – almost by definition – screen out the social. After all, it is hardly incumbent on a magistrate to enquire into the social and economic causes of crime when convicting a serial burglar. But two responses come to mind. One is that international tribunals *do* seem interested in establishing some historical ground for their decisions by, say, tracing the reasons for the disintegration of the Yugoslav Federation. Second, international tribunals – whether they like it or not – are producing pseudo-official histories of international or internal armed conflicts and genocides. It is disingenuous for a person to claim to be simply acting as a judge or a prosecutor when a particular constellation of highly contested political forces has resulted in their appointment.

13 And another sub-field might consider the relationship between theories of corporate liability and individual criminal responsibility. The recent malfeasance of the British banks, for example, suggests a need to redouble efforts to criminalize those responsible for the threat to the British polity posed by bankers' negligence or unlawful activities or banking culture. But, as John Lanchester has pointed out in his recent book and essays on this subject, individual responsibility might be an awkward way to approach the problem of systemic abuse. Lanchester gives the example of Stephen Green, a leading ethicist and priest who also happened to be the CEO of HSBC while it engaged in very serious malpractice. The point is not that Green is guilty of criminal behaviour but that he could do nothing to make himself aware of it; banks might be better viewed as 'loose federations of money-making franchises' or 'nations engaged in perpetual civil war' (quoted in Lanchester 2013: 7).

14 See my discussion below.

15 Commission Report: 119.

16 *Armed Activities in the Congo*, Separate Opinion of Judge Kooijmans.

17 *Armed Activities in the Congo*, Separate Opinion at 1.

18 See discussion of sources in Evans (1997: 137–8).

19 History is written or authored, too, in the strong sense of being subject to the laws of representation: the writer, incapable of transmitting the past, instead writes or 'authors' history. I can't, or don't want to, elaborate on that idea here.

20 The French poet Paul Eluard remarked: 'I am too busy defending the innocent who proclaim their innocence, to have any time left to defend the guilty who proclaim their guilt' (Zizek 2005: 23).

21 Compare, say, the Israeli philosopher Yeshayahu Leibowitz, who argued that Eichmann was 'not responsible for anything ... he is the product of two thousand years of Christianity, whose sole aim was the annihilation of the Jews' (M. Sheshar and Y. Leibowitz, *On an Entire World* (Jerusalem, 1987), quoted in Yablonka 2004: 245).

22 See, for example, Carr (1961), arguing that the writing of history is subject to the workings of ideology, personality, temperament.

23 It is this impossibility that leads Dave Eggers, for example, to describe *What is the What* (2008) as a novel rather than a biography. Though the book is based on the life of a young Sudanese refugee and war victim now based in the US, both

the novelist and the young Sudanese man agreed that this memory of his early life in Sudan was likely to be too faulty to allow for accuracy.

24 Commission Report: 98, my emphasis.

25 See my discussion in Simpson (2012).

26 Of course, there are historians who *do* hold Germany responsible, and think of the Great War has having been provoked by a combination of long-range ambition and short-term pre-emption; see Fromkin (2004).

27 This is not to deny the controversy that surrounded the conspiracy charge nor the limited role it was to play in the findings of the court in relation to specific individuals. Comparatively few conspiracy charges were upheld by the court (only eight of the accused were convicted of conspiracy to wage aggressive war; as a mode of liability it was insignificant in relation to the crimes against humanity and war crimes indictments).

28 I mean here that the relationship of policy to killing could be accidental; I do not mean to suggest here that there was anything accidental about the actual killing.

29 See, too, Arendt (1994: 256).

30 International Military Tribunal (1947: 27, 29).

31 *IMT Judgement* (1946) at 43. Though, the Tribunal, of course, held that the Prosecution had not shown that the pre-1939 deportations, expulsions and persecutions were connected to the conspiracy to wage aggressive war. Did they suddenly become so in 1939?

32 *IMT Judgement* (1946) at 44.

33 Hayden White has spoken of the ways in which history is a refuge for people who 'find the simple in the complex and the familiar in the strange' (1978: 50).

34 In fact, international law played an odd role in the crisis of 1914. It provided a fake *casus belli* on one hand, and plausible source of mediation on the other. International (criminal) law is implicated in all of this in many (relatively underappreciated) ways. The Austrians, on German advice, had proposed an ultimatum with a series of demands that the Serbians, it was felt, could not possibly concede to. In fact, and surprisingly, the Serbians did accept all the demands except one. The single exception now seems strangely legalistic. The Austrians had proposed a judicial inquiry to determine who the guilty parties were. The Serbs agreed to this but insisted that the inclusion of Austrian officials be kept within 'the limits assigned by international law' (Commission Report: 101). Later, on 29 July 1914, Czar Nicholas had suggested to his cousin, the Emperor, that the dispute be submitted to the recently established Permanent Court of Arbitration in The Hague. That request received no reply.

35 See Kampala Conference Agreement (*Resolution RC/Res.6: The Crime of Aggression* (2010).

36 For a debate about Stalin's character and the killings in the Soviet Union see Getty (1985) (for the structural account); and Conquest (1991) and Amis (2002) (for explanations based on Stalin's psychopathic nature).

37 This, of course, is the era of the local or marginal or dissident history (history from below), the history that challenges the linear narratives of the elites.

38 For an account of this three-speed history see Braudel (1972–73) and discussion in Evans (1997: 151–2).

39 Consider the way in which the role of big business or corporate interest is underplayed in trials going all the way back to Nuremberg. For an important debate see Ashby Turner's *Big Business and the Rise of Hitler* (1985) and David Abrahams' *The Collapse of the Weimar Republic* (1981), each concerning the extent to which corporate interests resisted or supported the Nazis.

40 The writings of Cherif Bassiouni are exemplary in this regard (e.g. Bassiouni 1997).

41 This comes from Carl Schmitt quoting Proudhon.

42 See Human Rights Watch (2008), an Amnesty International report describing 'fears that members of the EU and the USA, rather than using the opportunity to encourage reforms, are turning a blind eye to the human rights situation in order to further their national interests, which include cooperation in counter-terrorism, the control of irregular migration, trade and other economic benefits'. According to this report, fighting in eastern Libya in the late 1990s had been accompanied by large-scale, deliberate and indiscriminate attacks on civilians (2008: 9).

43 Certain specific crimes remain 'forbidden', as it were. We cannot, for example, seem to think of certain consumption patterns as possible crimes. And, to take two other examples from recent literature, there is Anne Manne's horrifying essay (2010) on gendercide (the systematic or widespread and state-tolerated killing of female children) and Mike Davis's book about man-made famine (2002). So many people die preventable deaths and yet international criminal law has nothing much to say about this. Indeed, the relationship between international criminal law and capitalism remains relatively under-rehearsed, to say the least.

Bibliography

Abrahams, D. (1981) *The Collapse of the Weimar Republic*, Princeton, NJ: Princeton University Press.

Amis, M. (2002) *Koba the Dread: Laughter and the Twenty Million*, New York: Jonathan Cape.

Anderson, P. (2011) 'From Progress to Catastrophe', *London Review of Books* 33(15): 24–8.

Arendt, H. (1994) *Eichmann in Jerusalem: A Report on the Banality of Evil*, London: Penguin.

Barthes, R. (1977) *Image, Music, Text*, London: Fontana.

Bassiouni, C. (1997) 'From Versailles to Rwanda in Seventy-five Years: The Need to Establish a Permanent International Criminal Court', *Harvard Human Rights Journal* 10: 11–62.

Beardsley, M. (ed.) (1960) *The European Philosophers*, New York: Modern Library.

Beaumont, P. and Meikle, J. (2011) 'Ratko Mladic denies ordering Srebrenica massacre, says his son', *The Guardian*, 30 May.

Bobbitt, P. (2003) *The Shield of Achilles: War, Peace and the Course of History*, London: Penguin.

Braudel, F. (1972–73) *The Mediterranean and the Mediterranean World in the Age of Philip II*, London: Collins.

Browning, C. (1992) *Ordinary Men: Reserve Police Battalion 101 and the Final Solution in Poland*, New York: Aaron Asher.

Carr, E.H. (1961) *What is History?* New York: Random House.

Carr, E.H. (2001) *The Twenty Years' Crisis*, Basingstoke: Palgrave Macmillan.

Carver, T. (ed.) (1996) *Marx: Later Political Writings*, Cambridge: Cambridge University Press.

Collingwood, R.G. (1946) *The Idea of History*, Oxford: Oxford University Press.

Commission on the Responsibility of the Authors of the War (1920) *American Journal of International Law* 14(1/2): 95–154.

Conquest, R. (1991) *Stalin, Breaker of Nations*, London: Weidenfeld and Nicolson.

Cooper, R. (2002) 'The Postmodern State' in M. Leonard (ed.) *Reordering the World*, London: Foreign Policy Centre.

Danner, A. and Martinez, J. (2006) 'Guilty Associations: Joint Criminal Enterprise, Command Responsibility and the Development of International Criminal Law', *Public Law and Legal Theory Working Papers Series*, 87, Stanford Law School.

Davis, M. (2002) *Late-Victorian Holocausts*, London: Verso.

Diamond, J. (2005) *Guns, Germs and Steel: The Fates of Human Societies*, 2nd edn, New York: W.W. Norton.

Douglas, L. (1996) 'The Memory of Judgement: The Law, Holocaust and Denial', *History and Memory* 7: 100–20.

Douglas, L. (2001) *The Memory of Judgment: Making Law and History in the Trials of the Holocaust*, New Haven, CT: Yale University Press.

Eagleton, T. (2008) 'Determinacy Kills', *London Review of Books* 30(12), 19 June.

Eggers, D. (2008) *What is the What*, London: Penguin.

Evans, R. (1997) *In Defence of History*, London: Granta.

Felman, S. (2001) 'Theaters of Justice: Arendt in Jerusalem, the Eichmann Trial, and the Redefinition of Legal Meaning in the Wake of the Holocaust', *Critical Inquiry* 27 (Winter): 201–38.

Figes, O. (1997) *A People's Tragedy*, London: Pimlico.

Fromkin, D. (2004) *Europe's Last Summer: Who Started the Great War?* New York: Knopf.

Getty, J.A. (1985) *Origins of the Great Purges: The Soviet Communist Party Reconsidered, 1933–1938*, Cambridge: Cambridge University Press.

Gibbon, E. (1776–89) *The History of the Decline and Fall of the Roman Empire*, London: Penguin.

Glenny, M. (1999) *The Balkans, 1804–1999: Nationalism, War and the Great Powers*, London: Penguin.

Hegel, G.W. (1960) *Lectures on the Philosophy of History*, trans. J. Sibree (1881), in *The European Philosophers*, ed. M. Beardsley, New York: Modern Library.

Heller, K. and Simpson, G. (2013) *Hidden Histories of War Crimes Trials*, Oxford: Oxford University Press.

Hilberg, R. (2003) *The Destruction of the European Jews*, 3rd edn, New Haven, CT: Yale University Press.

Hirsh, D. (2003) *Cosmopolitan Trials*, London: Glasshouse Press.

Human Rights Watch (2008) *Libya: Rights at Risk*, Amnesty International Report, *Libya of Tomorrow: What Hope for Human Rights*.

International Military Tribunal (1947) 'Indictment', in *Trial of the Major War Criminals* Reports.

Jenkins, K. (1991) *Rethinking History*, London: Routledge.

Koestler, A. (1946) *Darkness at Noon*, New York: Scribner.

Lanchester, J. (2013) 'Let's Consider Kate', *London Review of Books* 35(14): 3–8.

Leites, N. and Bernaut, E. (1954) *Rituals of Liquidation*, Glencoe: Free Press.

Leonard, M. (ed.) (2002) *Reordering the World*, London: Foreign Policy Centre.

Levi, P. (1987) *If This is a Man; and The Truce*, trans. S. Woolf, London: Abacus.

Levi, P. (2000) *The Voice of Memory: Interviews 1961–1987*, ed. M. Belpoliti and R. Gordon, Cambridge: Polity Press.

Lindqvist, S. (2002) *A History of Bombing*, London: Granta.

Luban, D. (1987) 'The Legacies of Nuremberg', *Social Research* 54(4): 779–829.

Lyotard, J. (1984) *The Postmodern Condition: A Report on Knowledge*, Minneapolis: University of Minnesota.

Manne, A. (2010) 'Gendercide', *The Monthly* 57, June.

Mazower, M. (2008) *Hitler's Empire: How the Nazis Ruled Europe*, New York: Penguin.

McMeekin, S. (2013) *1914: Countdown to War*, London: Icon.

Merleau-Ponty, M. (1969) *Humanism and Terror: An Essay on the Communist Problem*, trans. J. O'Neill, Boston, MA: Beacon Press.

Miéville, C. (2006) *Between Equal Rights*, London: Haymarket.

Morgan, E. (1988) 'Retributory Theater', *American University Journal of International Law and Policy* 3(1).

Neave, A. (1978) *Nuremberg: A Personal Record of the Trial*, London: Hodder & Stoughton.

Roth, P. (2000) *Operation Shylock: A Confession*, London: Vintage.

Schama, S. (1990) *Citizens: A Chronicle of the French Revolution*, London: Random House.

Shklar, J. (1961) *Legalism: Law, Morals, and Political Trials*, Cambridge, MA: Harvard University Press.

Simpson, G. (2007) *Law, War and Crime*, Cambridge: Polity Press.

Simpson, G. (2012) 'International Law in Diplomatic History', in J. Crawford and M. Koskenniemi (eds) *Cambridge Companion to International Law*, Cambridge: Cambridge University Press.

Snyder, T. (2010) *Bloodlands: Europe Between Hitler and Stalin*, New York: Penguin.

Taylor, A.J.P. (1969) *War by Timetable*, New York: American Heritage.

Tolstoy, L. (1999 [1865–69]) *War and Peace*, Oxford: Oxford University Press.

Turner, A. (1985) *German Big Business and the Rise of Hitler*, Oxford: Oxford University Press.

White, H. (1978) *Tropics of Discourse: Essays in Cultural Criticism*, Baltimore: Johns Hopkins University Press.

Yablonka, H. (2004) *The State of Israel vs Adolf Eichmann*, New York: Schocken.

Zizek, S. (2005) 'The Empty Wheelbarrow', *The Guardian*, 19 February.

Chapter 8

Silences in international criminal legal histories and the construction of the victim subject of international criminal law

The nineteenth-century slave trading trial of Joseph Peters

Emily Haslam[1]

Introduction

On 11 June 1812, Joseph Peters was tried and convicted of the felony of slave trading before the Vice Admiralty Court at Sierra Leone, a conviction based almost entirely on the testimony of Africans, including some individuals he had enslaved (*Trials of the Slave Traders* 1813). This case, the British Slave Trade Felony Act 1811 on which it was based, and the extensive litigation in the early part of the nineteenth century dealing with the abolition of the slave trade more generally (slave trade abolition litigation) have gone largely unremarked in international criminal law commentaries.[2] Typically international criminal legal histories locate the origins of international criminal law in the principles established by the Nuremberg and Tokyo trials (Cassese 2002; Fatumura 2008; Heller 2011; McGoldrick 2004), with the result that political and legal developments that took place prior to these tribunals are less remarked upon and discussed. The near exclusive focus in scholarly accounts of the origins of modern international criminal law on Nuremberg and Tokyo gives rise to institutionally linear accounts which gloss over questions concerning African agency in the development of international criminal law and, with some exceptions, the relationship between European colonialism and international criminal law.[3] In the present context with the controversial focus of the International Criminal Court (ICC) on Africa this has done little to enhance the legitimacy of the international criminal justice project.

This contribution asks how returning to slave trade abolition litigation might reframe current international criminal legal histories and with what effect for contemporary debates. In particular, it questions whether the centrality of African testimony in the trial of Peters might suggest the possibility of – and need to develop – a more inclusive account of the development of international criminal law. What impact might such a history have on the framing of contemporary debates concerning the relationship between Africa and international criminal law, specifically the ICC? How might such a history cast light on, and challenge, the ways in which the figure of the African victim is constructed in contemporary international criminal law?

This chapter begins by locating abolition within the development of international criminal law more generally before turning to explore the trial of Joseph Peters. This trial was included in an account of a handful of trials written in a pamphlet by a 'gentleman resident at Sierra Leone to an advocate for abolition, in London' (*Trials of the Slave Traders* 1813). African testimony was central to establishing the charges against Peters. However, the record is silent about key aspects of African participation both in the trial and in the events which led up to it which formed the factual basis of the case. This lack of detail is all the more noticeable for the way in which it contrasts with descriptions given about the witnesses' swearing-in. These silences are mirrored by the more general silence about abolition and African agency therein in international criminal legal histories which, it is suggested, is paralleled by a more general marginalization of the contribution of Africans, including victims of international crime, to the development of international criminal law, to say nothing of the marginalization of crimes committed by the West (Jones 2004). Interrogating cases such as that against Peters constitutes a step in the process of constructing a more multifaceted international criminal legal history. Among their significance is their demonstration of the existence within the legal record of alternative narratives about the relationships between African subjects and the development of international criminal law than is evident from the more general focus on post-Second World War trials. Such narratives also demonstrate a complex and multifaceted subjectivity on the part of victims of international crime. As such they offer the potential to challenge facets of the normalization of the trope of the African subject victim in international criminal justice which remains a central challenge that arises from the focus of the ICC on situations in Africa in its formative years.

Abolition and international criminal legal history

The origins of modern international criminal law are overwhelmingly traced to the legal principles established in the Nuremberg and Tokyo trials that took place after the Second World War, with even the Rome Statute's Preamble focusing on victims of the twentieth century. This results in contemporary international legal developments taking place without much looking back to longer-term histories. International criminal law does not easily lend itself to acknowledging longer-term continuities because it characteristically proceeds from progressive narratives,[4] where progress is all too often measured in institutional terms. Moreover, transitional justice and international criminal law are premised on a fundamental break with the past.[5] These tendencies result in the glossing over of slavery, abolition and colonialism in the foundational narratives of international criminal law. Arguably, slavery and abolition constitute a central part of international criminal law's development.

While it would be overstated to claim that international criminal law began with the slave trade, the importance of abolition to the development of international criminal law is undeniable. First, over the nineteenth century slave-trading developed as a crime in international law.[6] Second, abolition gave rise to controversial international legal questions and institutional innovations. Many of these controversies were provoked by British attempts to enforce slave trade abolition at the international level. Having played a leading role in the slave trade, Britain took a series of controversial – and at times illegal – actions against suspected slave traders on the international plane. Many of these activities, including the policing activities of the Royal Navy, gave rise to a plethora of thorny international legal issues. These included the limits of intervention against suspected foreign slave ships and the extent of criminal jurisdiction over suspected traders. Many of these issues were litigated in British and colonial courts, in particular the Vice Admiralty Court at Sierra Leone. Eventually, these controversies led to, among other developments, the establishment of the institutionally innovative Mixed Commission Courts, which were established by treaty between Britain and Spain, Britain and Portugal and Britain and Brazil amongst other states to adjudicate captured slave ships (Bethell 1966; Martinez 2012). Although much of this litigation has gone unexplored in international criminal legal histories, there is evidence that Mixed Commission Courts were not entirely forgotten when the Nuremberg Charter was drafted in 1944 (Martinez 2012: 152–3). Third, abolition more generally proved strategically and rhetorically foundational for subsequent international criminal justice and human rights campaigns.[7] The campaigning techniques, including petitions, boycotts and lobbying, played a central role in nineteenth-century activism (Keck and Sikkink 1998: 45). These techniques continue to exert significant sway in contemporary civil society campaigns. In these respects abolition was seminal.

Finally, with the controversial contemporary focus of the ICC on situations in Africa it is timely to return to slave trade abolition litigation to put these debates into a broader historical context. At one level, and rather simplistically, the focus of the ICC on Africa is explicable because regionally Africa has generated the largest number of ratifications to the Rome Statute (ICC 2013). More fundamentally, Ann Sagan has argued that the ICC's sense of self is discursively bound to its construction of African subjects (Sagan 2010: 4). This focus has given rise to challenges to the court's impartiality and legitimacy. The emphasis of the court on African situations coupled with the referral to the ICC of situations by the United Nations Security Council, constituted by permanent member states some of whom are not party to the Rome Statute (SC Res 1593, 31 March 2005; SC Res 1970, 26 February, 2011), has given rise to claims of double standards. Michael Mandel has pointed to the danger of conflating the fight against impunity with the punishment of enemies of the US,[8] suggesting that international criminal law looks set to operate as a manifestation of power (Mandel 2003: 132). But even if the critique of imperialism in international criminal law is not accepted, the focus of the ICC on Africa in its developmental period gives rise to significant questions about the representation of Africans in and through international criminal processes (Sagan 2010).

Arguably, the figure of the victim as beneficiary of international criminal law has become a central part of international criminal law's claims to legitimacy (Sagan 2010: 12). With the ICC's focus during its formative years on African situations, there is a danger that the figure of the African subject victim has become normalized in international criminal law. This can be seen as part of a more general phenomenon. Writing in the context of the violence against women movement, Ratna Kapur demonstrates how 'the Third World victim' has come to signify the true victim (Kapur 2002: 2). This is problematic because all too often this discursive framing positions the victim as recipient of, rather than agent in, international criminal justice. Writing in the context of debates about the Responsibility to Protect doctrine, Mahmood Mamdani has described a dualistic framing of victims, first as 'citizen', second as 'ward', with citizens unlike wards retaining 'agency' (Mamdani 2009b: 471). His observations resonate with Makau Mutua's masterful critique of human rights more generally (Mutua 2002). Despite commendable efforts to transform the position of victims in international criminal law, most notably through the institution of victim participation at the ICC (Jorda and de Hemptinne 2002: 1389), concerns about the construction of victims as subjects with limited agency persist, as explored further in later sections of this chapter. This chapter questions whether, and how, the writing of international criminal legal histories might respond to the imperative to recognize survivors' agency or, to adopt Mamdani's classification, citizenship in international criminal law and with what effect.

Historical accounts of abolition and emancipation have increasingly come to acknowledge and emphasize the contribution of Africans, including those who were, or had been, enslaved (Williams 1964; James 2001; Gates 1987). This literature challenges so-called imperial histories of abolition,[9] which emphasized the professed humanitarian aspects of British abolitionism (Oldfield 2007: 171). However, the implications of this body of literature have gone largely unexplored in international (criminal) legal scholarship. The final reason then for writing slavery and abolition more firmly into international criminal legal histories is to ask if, and how, narratives that emerge about the role of Africans in slave trade abolition litigation disrupt assumptions underlying the prevailing constructions of African victims in international criminal law today. Using the case against Peters as a springboard, this contribution asks whether abolition litigation might reveal the presence within law and the legal record of alternative accounts of the relationships between African subjects, in this case victims of international crime, and international criminal law, than is evident in its mainstream histories.

The Slave Trade Felony Act and the trial of Joseph Peters

Britain was one of the major slave-trading nations during the eighteenth century. In the nineteenth century Britain became the leading state advocating abolition (Nadelmann 1990: 491–2), although Denmark was the first Western state to declare the trade illegal in 1792 (Redman 1995: 768). This, formally at least, ended a trade that had caused immeasurable misery to millions, although slave trade abolition legislation was not always effectively enforced; Marika Sherwood persuasively argues that Britain's involvement in the slave trade continued after abolition (Sherwood 2007). The interplay between economic and humanitarian causes in abolition is debated vigorously (Williams 1964; Ashworth 1987; Haskell 1987). Historians have also emphasized the role of civil society (Drescher 1991; 1994) and criticisms have been rightly directed against the marginalization of the contribution of Africans, including those enslaved, in more traditional accounts of abolition and emancipation (Williams 1964). Slave rebellions in European colonies from the end of the late eighteenth century contributed to abolition.[10] Whatever complex motivations lay behind abolition on the international plane, it has been persuasively argued that abolition was deployed as a justification for British imperial enlargement (Rieff 2002: 64; Miers 1975; Hamilton and Salmon 2009). The coupling of humanitarianism, militarism and empire is a recurrent theme in international (criminal) law (Rieff 2002: 61; Nesiah 2004).

The 1807 Abolition Act, which set out to abolish the British slave trade, relied on a system of fines for its enforcement.[11] These financial penalties proved inadequate to prevent the trade with the result that the Slave Trade Felony Act was passed in 1811.[12] This made the removal or assisting in the removal, transportation and shipment of slaves by British subjects, or in British territory, a felony with punishment of imprisonment and hard labour for between three and five years or transportation for 14 years and brought the slave trade firmly within the realm of criminal law. Litigation under the Slave Trade Felony Act forms part of the broader body of slave trade abolition litigation, which as argued above is instructive for the development of international criminal law.

The case against Peters was one of the first, but not the only, prosecution for slave trading in which Africans testified at Sierra Leone and elsewhere. Sierra Leone was a central site in British abolition. It was the location of Vice Admiralty and then the most active of the Mixed Commission Courts. It was also symbolically important for British abolitionists who had been active in the attempts to establish it as a colony (Lambert 2007: 105–6).

Among the other cases reported in the pamphlet, Samo's case, which had taken place two months previous to the trial of Peters generated the most legal debate and interest. This was primarily because Samuel Samo, a prominent slave trader based on the Iles de Los, challenged the applicability of the Slave Trade Felony Act to the area outside British jurisdiction where he had been apprehended. This question of the jurisdictional reach of the Slave Trade Felony Act gave rise to bitter and damaging contestation in a pamphlet debate between Chief Justice Thorpe and the African Institution (Haslam 2012; Mouser 2013). When Sierra Leone became a colony in 1807 the directors of the former Sierra Leone Company established the African Institution. Ostensibly advisory, the African Institution was able to exert considerable power over government policy (Helfman 2005–06: 1130–1). The pamphlet in which the trial of Peters is described is not an official report. The author is not identified. However, in the disputes between Thorpe and the African Institution dealing with among other matters the jurisdictional reach of the Slave Trade Felony Act, the African Institution suggests that the pamphlet was published either by Chief Justice Thorpe or by his friends (African Institution 1815: 93). There are clearly limitations to the account as a historical record. It is incomplete. At the end of the account of the trial against Peters, the author recounts that Thorpe made 'several brief and appropriate remarks' (*Trials of the Slave Traders* 1813: 48): these are not recorded. Nor is there any indication that the African witnesses spoke more than was written down. The account of their testimony is a summary rather than a verbatim record. The trial of Peters is reported in only nine pages. This contrasts with the admittedly more legally complicated account of Samo's case, covered in 31 pages. In Samo's case the Chief Justice's comments and those of the Attorney General are reported in much more detail. This might reflect in part the relative importance of the defendants, but it might also suggest that less importance was attributed to proceedings where the principal witnesses were African. Moreover, what was actually spoken, how it was uttered, and the effect it had on the courtroom, is lost. However, in the absence of an official report, it is from this report that the following account of the case is drawn.

Joseph Peters was accused of selling or bartering five or six Africans from Tasso Island; of removing 'nearly forty unfortunate Africans' to be treated as slaves and of receiving the 'benefits of their unrewarded labour' (*Trials of the Slave Traders* 1813: 41). Peters was convicted almost solely on the testimony of Africans, including those he had enslaved. Testimony was translated and each witness was sworn 'according to the custom of his country and the religions he possesses' (1813: 42). Chief Justice Thorpe said:

> We cannot by any other mode so securely affect the conscience of these poor people, they all believe in a Supreme Being, and acknowledge he is an avenger of falsehood, and a rewarder of truth, but they have no generally established form of worship.
>
> (1813: 41)

Witnesses testified that Peters had rewarded individuals including Dallamoodoo and King Murra Brimer for having helped him recapture fugitive slaves.[13] Of these only Dallamoodoo gave evidence. He presented a letter in which Peters requested his help. Dallamoodoo explained how he had helped recapture 28 slaves and was given three women, one man and a child as slaves in return. Dallamoodoo affirmed that without his and Murra Brimer's help the escaped slaves would not have been recaptured (1813: 42).

Others testified about Peters' slave trading activities. Among them, Yangyarra, the head man on Tasso, testified that Peters sent away 30 slaves who did not return (1813: 44). Foosingbag explained how Peters 'sold her to Dallamoodoo', and 'her mother and two children to Murra Brimer' (1813: 47). Katta spoke of how she had been sold along with her mother (1813: 47). Witnesses gave evidence about the currency used for slave trading transactions. Quiepa explained that Peters sold a slave in exchange for 'three goats, three sheep, one bull, and a ton of salt' (1813: 45),[14] and Saree gave evidence of slaves being exchanged for 'bullocks, sheep, and goats' (1813: 46).

A number of witnesses testified to their mistreatment at the hands of Peters. Bondoo testified that he was beaten by Peters and that Peters sold him, his wife and two children (1813: 45). Borega had been sold by Peters to Dallamoodoo. He testified that he had toiled industriously for Peters and that Peters had flogged him. Irons placed around his wrists and ankles made him bleed (1813: 47). Banta testified that slaves were transported from Tasso in a canoe and beaten (1813: 42). Boree explained that Peters had first given him a wife, who had then been removed from him and sold (1813: 47–8).

Peters called no witnesses in his defence. He challenged the veracity of the witnesses' accounts and denied responsibility for activities at Bance Island and Tasso. However, the jury found him guilty after hearing witnesses' descriptions of, in the words of the Attorney General, 'scenes of oppression and cruelty' (1813: 48), and Peters was sentenced to the penalty of transportation for seven years, although he received the Governor's pardon on condition that he did not return to Africa (African Institution 1814: 15). The next day the court tried a black partner of Peters, William Tufft, who had received his education in England. The identical witnesses testified. Tufft argued that he had been acting under orders, a defence that was not backed up with sufficient evidence, and he was sentenced to three years' hard labour (1813: 48–9).

Silences and African testimony

African testimony was central to the trial and conviction of Peters. And yet the account of the case is silent about critical aspects of African participation in the legal process and in the events that led up to it. Notable are silences surrounding the attempts on the part of the slaves to liberate themselves. This contrasts with the detail given about the witnesses in Samo's case and the swearing-in of witnesses in the case against Peters.

Overall very little information is given about the Africans who testified, and there is none about how they came into contact with the court and the legal process. For example, the reader learns that Banta was a Timmany man, but very little else about him. In Samo's case more detailed explanations were given about how the court obtained the evidence of slave traders and how Attorney General Biggs was able to persuade some of them to testify. One individual Biggs was apparently able to convince of the evil and horrors of the trade was Skelton, who had been clerk to Samo. Biggs distinguished Skelton's conduct in being willing to testify from that of other slave traders, whom he listed by name, who had refused to give up the trade (*Trials of the Slave Traders* 1813: 24; Haslam 2012: 17). Biggs further explained how David James Lawrence died before testifying against Samo, putting his death down somewhat dramatically in part to the impact of the treatment Lawrence received from other slave traders who were angry at his willingness to testify against Samo (1813: 24–5). In the account of the case against Peters, however, there is a marked absence of comparable information about the witnesses, including those, such as Dallamoodoo, who testified to aiding Peters.

While the self-liberation of slaves and the assistance given by other Africans in their recapture was key to the factual circumstances, little was recorded (and perhaps asked) about those slaves who escaped, the circumstances in which they ran away and were caught. Mention of any assistance that was given to fugitive slaves is also absent. For example, the account of Katta's testimony explains in a few words that she ran away after being sold with her mother and that she was handed over to Dallamoodoo on her recapture (1813: 47). Similarly, the account of Bondoo's testimony mentions only that 'he made his escape' (1813: 45). Perhaps the details of the running away were not considered relevant to the courtroom story, or perhaps they did not seem relevant to the correspondent. This might also be explained by the structures and strictures of the legal process, which necessarily focused on the question of the defendant's culpability and slave trading as the legal event. Silence might also be a result of witnesses' possible or even likely reluctance to testify about the details of their escape. These silences are striking, however, when set against descriptions given about the same witnesses' swearing-in. Take what the pamphlet tells us about Banta:

> He was sworn according to the custom of the Timmany nation; he swore by his mother, and wished she might die if he did not speak the truth, and he hoped that God might strike him dead as the earth (on which he rubbed his two forefingers and applied the dust to his tongue) if he did not relate the whole truth.
>
> (1813: 42)

The reader also learns that Yangyarra 'was sworn in a very solemn manner, according to his nation, by praying that God would cause the earth to open and receive him, if he told not the whole truth' (1813: 44). Monday 'was sworn on the New Testament, and on the earth', Bondoo on the Old Testament (1813: 45). Quiepa 'knelt down and kissed the earth, and was thus sworn to tell the truth' (1813: 45). Saree was 'sworn by his mother and the earth' (1813: 46) and Boree 'was sworn by God, his mother, and the earth' (1813: 47). At first glance these details may be regarded as simply reflecting the court's need to prove veracity – and perhaps the reporter's concern for authenticity – and they can be read as supporting a narrative of inclusion, with Attorney General Biggs observing that although the witnesses were not Christian they believed in 'the existence of an infinite Providence' and possessed 'a solemn sense of moral responsibility' (1813: 41). At the same time, however, this emphasis on the exotic reflects and supports assumptions about civilizational differences between Christian and non-Christian witnesses which underpinned the broader colonial project. Noteworthy in this respect is the apparently more respectful description given of the monotheistic Dallamoodoo, who had lent aid to Peters, described by the pamphlet writer as 'an intelligent chief' who 'spoke English well' and 'was sworn on the Koran, with great solemnity' (1813: 42).

The trial against Peters is shot through with multiple possible stories about agency, including the role of African resistance to, and participation in, the slave trade. And yet this aspect of the case is surrounded by silence. Such silence finds its parallel in more general silence about abolition in international criminal legal histories, and more specifically in questions about African agency in abolition. This is reflected in a more general marginalization in international criminal legal histories of the contribution of victims, and more specifically African victims, of international crime to the development of contemporary international criminal law.[15]

Victims and international criminal legal histories

Characteristically, narratives about the treatment of victims in international criminal proceedings start with the observation that Nuremberg and Tokyo provided survivors with few opportunities to participate. So too, the International Criminal Tribunals for Rwanda and Yugoslavia were not empowered to provide compensation and did not permit victims to participate other than as prosecution or defence witnesses. Accounts emphasize the difference in the treatment of victims at the ICC, which can offer both compensation and victim participation (Karstedt 2010; Jorda and de Hemptinne 2002). At first sight victim participation promises expansive prospects for survivors to participate, from investigation to reparation stages, but it has also generated significant practical challenges for the court, not least because of the numbers of potential victim participants (Haslam and Edmunds 2012). Moreover, there are significant limitations on the ways in which the victim is constructed as a legal subject through the institution of victim participation. In general, the participation of victims in international criminal processes has often been seen as curative, even if international criminal processes are not well placed overall to fulfil a therapeutic function (Dembour and Haslam 2004). More specifically, according to the interview findings of Jo-Anne Wemmers, victim participation at the ICC is principally seen as 'expressive' in practice (2010: 642).

What is being suggested in this chapter is that this positioning might also be considered reflective of the ways in which international criminal legal histories have typically glossed over the contributions to the development of international criminal law of survivors' struggles. Take the anti-apartheid movement. This is barely referred to in international criminal legal histories, which generally depict the Cold War as a period in which the opportunities presented by Nuremberg and Tokyo were squandered through superpower rivalries. However, the anti-apartheid movement, in which the national liberation movement was recognized to have played the critical role (Reddy 1999; Shepherd 1977: 10),[16] in cooperation with the United Nations General Assembly has been credited with having contributed to shifts in fundamental norms of international law (Klotz 2002 62–4; Gassama 1996; Klotz 1995). Eventually apartheid was established as a crime against humanity (The International Convention on the Suppression and Punishment of the Crime of Apartheid 1973). Similarly, institutional accounts of the International Criminal Tribunal for Rwanda rarely mention Rwandan survivor group protests, despite the impact they had on the practice of the court (Haslam 2007). The glossing over of the part played by African survivors of international crime in the development of international criminal law, including in some cases by challenging it, may well have contributed to the ICC's failure to predict the opposition among some parts of Ugandan civil society to ICC arrest warrants against the leaders of the Lords Resistance Army in October 2005 (Haslam 2011: 231).[17]

There is a striking continuity in the marginalization of the resistance of survivors of international crime in accounts of the development of international criminal law, and victims' rights more specifically, and the glossing over of abolition and African agency therein in international criminal legal histories. In the trial of Peters there is sufficient evidence to suggest even from the brief pamphlet report that the victims of Peters' crimes were not objects of intervention only. Key to the factual circumstances of the case, if not the legal issues, was their self-liberation. Moreover, it seems likely that Peters would not have been prosecuted without their testimony and perhaps also without the actions of other Africans outside the courtroom. It is, of course, impossible to know now how witnesses perceived their participation in the trial against Peters. At the very least, however, what emerges is the possibility of an additional account of the relationships between African victims of international crime and the development of international criminal law. It follows that the glossing over of slavery and abolition in international criminal law is problematic because it erases a complex set of narratives about the agency of the victims of slavery that emerge from (or in fact in spite of) the legal encounter.[18] Such encounters challenge the progressive institutional framing of accounts of the development of victims' rights in international criminal law. They also offer the potential to challenge the ways in which the figure of the victim, specifically the African subject victim, is typically constructed in international criminal law.

Conclusion

This chapter is concerned with silences in international criminal legal histories. Establishing a historical record is central to the practice of international criminal law. However, within the discipline there is less systematic reflection as to the identity of its own memory keepers. It is clear that the trial of Peters cannot be read definitively, not least at this distance, and that understanding the participation of Africans in abolition litigation presents profoundly difficult and insurmountable methodological challenges. At most, fragments of individuals emerge from the legal record: from the heavily mediated accounts of witness testimony to descriptions of those who can only be referred to in their absence whether by name or status, such as Boree's wife mentioned above. In a context where concerns have been expressed about the normalization of the figure of the African victim in international criminal law, cases such as Peters can invite critical reflection about the relationship between international criminal legal history and the construction of international criminal law's subjects. To the extent that the construction of international criminal law's subjects is linked to a particular version of international criminal legal history, a retelling, or broadening, of that history can contribute to re-positioning the ways in which international criminal law's subjects are framed. The case against Peters suggests that alternative narratives about the role of African victims of international crime subsist within the legal historical record. At one level these both rest on, and offer the potential to acknowledge, specific acts of resistance on the part of victims of international crime. More broadly, this disconnect between what can be read from the legal historical record on the one hand, and the conventional historical narratives of international criminal law on the other, suggests that an alternative history of international criminal law might be told – one in which the existence of contesting accounts of the legal subjectivity of victims, specifically here African victims of international crime, might operate as a central narrative theme. This is a theme that could take its place alongside those narrative frameworks to which the important, but inevitably incomplete, institutional accounts stemming from the focus on Nuremberg and Tokyo give rise.

For sure, further research is needed to determine the extent and nature of African involvement in abolition litigation more generally.[19] There are limits to what can be drawn from one case. Yet the trial of Joseph Peters provides a lens to examine the relationship between the past, present and future of international criminal law through reflection of the discipline's silences. International criminal legal histories are typically silent about abolition and about the role of Africans in it, including in litigation. Revisiting this history has the potential to offer much in the contemporary context where the focus of the ICC on Africa has given rise to concerns about the normalization of the trope of the African subject victim.

Notes

1 Earlier drafts of this chapter were presented to the Transitional Justice Research Network, University of Oxford; the Centre for Law, Gender and Sexuality, University of Kent; Critical Approaches to International Criminal Law Conference, University of Liverpool and the 31st annual Australian and New Zealand Law and History Society Conference, UTS Sydney. I am grateful to participants for their insightful comments. My thanks also go to Rod Edmunds.
2 With the most notable recent exception being the discussion of Mixed Commissions by Martinez (2012).
3 On the colonial legacy of the exclusion of non-Europeans from the laws of war, see further Mégret (2006).
4 On the impact of 'evolutionary narratives' in international law more generally see further Johns *et al.* (2011: 2). For a critique of the idea of progress in international legal discourse see Skouteris (2010).
5 Even if the precise balance between looking backwards and looking forwards is contested, see further Teitel (2000). For a masterful critique of the idea of breaking with the past see Meister (2010).
6 Although the High Court of Admiralty held emphatically that slave trading was not piracy under the Law of Nations in *Le Louis* (1817) 165 Eng. Rep. 1464, slave-trading was declared an act of piracy in the first half of the nineteenth century by a number of states in their domestic law and in bilateral and multilateral treaties, for example the Treaty of London between Austria, Britain, Prussia, Russia and France in 1841. For the argument that the slave trade was also a crime against humanity see Muhammad (2004).
7 This rhetorical function was not without its problems. See further De Vries (2005: 45).
8 For an extended discussion of friends and foes in international criminal law see Nouwen and Werner (2010).
9 On imperial and multicultural histories of abolition and the dilemmas of negotiating them see Oldfield (2007: 173–4).
10 See further Ishay (2004: 157) and James (2001).
11 An Act for the Abolition of the Slave Trade 47 Geo. III c 3, 25 March 1807.
12 An Act for Rendering More Effectual an Act made in the Forty Seventh Year of His Majesty's Reign, entitled An Act for the Abolition of the Slave Trade, 51 Geo III C 23, 14 May 1811 (hereafter Slave Trade Felony Act).
13 See for example testimony of Adam, Yangyarra, Kenneth Macauley and Samuel Scott in *Trials of the Slave Traders* (1813: 44–7). According to Samuel Scott, Peters also rewarded Murra Sery.
14 See also testimony of Duboo, *Trials of the Slave Traders* (1813: 46).
15 On the marginalization of third world resistance and the imperative to bring it firmly within international law see Rajagopal (2003).
16 On the influence of national liberation movements on human rights more generally, see Bowring (2008: 77).

17 On the ICC's reaction to Ugandan civil society opposition see Allen (2006).
18 There are of course dangers and challenges in emphasizing agency and resistance given the extreme degradation that surrounded and constituted the slave trade. Elizabeth Kowaleski Wallace's masterful summary of the difficulties of writing about the horrors of the slave trade while acknowledging the agency of Africans might also be said about the dilemmas of writing about, and responding to, victims of international crime more generally (Wallace 2006: 35–6).
19 This is the subject of a broader project. See Haslam, *British Slave Trade Abolition Litigation and the Development of International Criminal Law* (in progress). Cf., however, Martinez (2012: 150), who argues that enslaved Africans did not play a major part in the operation of Mixed Commission Courts.

Bibliography

African Institution (1814) *Eight Report of the Directors of the African Institution*, London: Ellerton and Henderson.

African Institution (1815) *Special Report of the Directors of the African Institution Made at the Annual General Meeting on the 12 of April 1815 Respecting the Allegations Contained in A Pamphlet Entitled 'A Letter to William Wilberforce'*, London: Ellerton and Henderson.

Allen, T. (2006) *Trial Justice: The International Criminal Court and the Lord's Resistance Army*, London: Zed Books.

Ashworth, J. (1987) 'The Relationship between Capitalism and Humanitarianism', *The American Historical Review* 92: 813–28.

Bethell, L. (1966) 'The Mixed Commissions for the Suppression of the Transatlantic Slave Trade in the Nineteenth Century', *Journal of African History* 7: 79–93.

Bowring, B. (2008) *The Degradation of the International Legal Order: The Rehabilitation of Law and the Possibility of Politics*, Abingdon: Routledge-Cavendish.

Cassese, A. (2002) 'From Nuremberg to Rome: International Military Tribunals to the International Criminal Court', in A. Cassese, P. Gaeta and J.R.W.D. Jones (eds) *The Rome Statute of the International Criminal Court: A Commentary Vol. I*, Oxford: Oxford University Press.

Dembour, M.-B. and Haslam, E. (2004) 'Silencing Hearings? Victim-Witnesses at the ICTY', *European Journal of International Law* 15(1): 151–77.

De Vries, P. (2005) '"White Slaves" in a Colonial Nation: The Dutch Campaign Against the Traffic in Women in the Early Twentieth Century', *Social and Legal Studies* 14(1): 39–60.

Drescher, S. (1991) 'British Way, French Way: Opinion Building and Revolution in the Second French Slave Emancipation', *The American Historical Review* 96: 709–34.

Drescher, S. (1994) 'Whose Abolition? Popular Pressure and the Ending of the British Slave Trade', *Past and Present* 143: 136–66.

Fatumura, M. (2008) *War Crimes Tribunals and Transitional Justice: The Tokyo Trial and the Nuremberg Legacy*, Abingdon: Routledge.

Gassama, I. (1996) 'Reaffirming Faith in the Dignity of Each Human Being: The United Nations, NGOs, and Apartheid', *Fordham International Law Journal* 19: 1464–541.

Gates, H.L. Jr (ed.) (1987) *The Classic Slave Narratives*, New York: NAL.

Hamilton, K. and Salmon, P. (2009) *Slavery, Diplomacy and Empire: Britain and the Suppression of the Slave Trade, 1807–1975*, Brighton: University of Sussex Press.

Haskell, T.L. (1987) 'Convention and Hegemonic Interest in the Debate over Anti-Slavery: A Reply to Davis and Ashworth', *American Historical Review* 92: 829–78.

Haslam, E. (2007) 'Law Civil Society and Contested Justice at the International Criminal Tribunal for Rwanda', in M.-B. Dembour and T. Kelly (eds) *Paths to International Justice*, Cambridge: Cambridge University Press.

Haslam, E. (2011) 'Subjects and Objects: International Criminal law and the Institutionalization of Civil Society', *International Journal of Transitional Justice* 5(2): 221–40.

Haslam, E. (2012) 'Redemption, Colonialism and International Criminal Law: The Nineteenth Century Slave-Trading Trials of Samo and Peters', in D. Kirkby (ed.) *Past Law Present Histories: From Settler Colonies to International Justice*, Canberra: ANU e-press.

Haslam, E. and Edmunds, R. (2012) 'Common Legal Representation at the International Criminal Court: More Symbolic than Real?', *International Criminal Law Review* 12: 871–903.

Helfman, T. (2006) 'The Vice Admiralty Court at Sierra Leone and the Abolition of the West African Slave Trade', *Yale Journal of International Law* 115: 1122–56.

Heller, K.J. (2011) *The Nuremberg Military Tribunals and the Origins of International Criminal Law*, Oxford: Oxford University Press.

ICC (2013) *The States Parties to the Rome Statute*. Available at: www.icc-cpi.int/en_menus/asp/states%20parties/Pages/the%20states%20parties%20to%20the%20rome%20statute.aspx.

Ishay, M. (2004) *The History of Human Rights from Ancient Times to the Globalization Era*, London: University of California Press.

James, C.L.R. (2001) *The Black Jacobins*, London: Penguin.

Johns, F., Joyce, R. and Pahuja, S. (2011) *Events: The Force of International Law*, Abingdon: GlassHouse.

Jorda, C. and de Hemptinne, J. (2002) 'The Status and Role of the Victim', in A. Cassese, P. Gaeta and J. Jones (eds) *The Rome Statute of the International Criminal Court: A Commentary*, Oxford: Oxford University Press.

Jones, A. (2004) *Genocide, War Crimes and the West: History and Complicity*, London: Zed Books.

Kapur, R. (2002) 'The Tragedy of Victimization Rhetoric: Resurrecting the "Native" Subject in International/Post-Colonial Feminist Legal Politics', *Harvard Human Rights Journal* 15: 1.

Karstedt, S. (2010) 'From Absence to Presence, from Silence to Voice: Victims in Transitional Justice Since the Nuremberg Trials', *International Review of Victimology* 17(1): 9–30.

Keck, M. and Sikkink, K. (1998) *Activists Beyond Borders*, Ithaca, NY and London: Cornell University Press.

Klotz, A. (1995) *Norms in International Relations: The Struggle Against Apartheid*, Ithaca, NY: Cornell University Press.

Klotz, A. (2002) 'Transnational Activism and Global Transformations: The Anti-Apartheid and Abolitionist Experiences', *European Journal of International Relations* 8: 49–76.

Lambert, D. (2007) 'Sierra Leone and Other Sites in the War of Representation over Slavery', *History Workshop Journal* 64: 103–32.

Mamdani, M. (2009a) *Saviors and Survivors: Darfur, Politics and the War on Terror*, New York: Verso.

Mamdani, M. (2009b) 'Response', *International Journal of Transitional Justice* 3: 470–3.

Mandel, M. (2003) 'Opinion: Illegal Wars and International Criminal Law', in A. Anghie, B. Chimni, K. Mickelson and O. Okafor (eds) *The Third World and International Order: Law, Politics and Globalization*, Leiden: Martinus Nijhoff.

Martinez, J. (2012) *The Slave Trade and the Origins of International Human Rights Law*, Oxford: Oxford University Press.

McGoldrick, D. (2004) 'Criminal Trials Before International Tribunals: Legality and Legitimacy', in D. McGoldrick, P. Rowe and E. Donnelly (eds) *The Permanent International Criminal Court: Legal and Policy Issues*, Oxford: Hart.

Mégret, F. (2006) 'From "Savages" to "Unlawful Combatants": A Postcolonial Look at International Humanitarian Law's "Other"', in A. Orford (ed.) *International Law and its Others*, Cambridge: Cambridge University Press.

Meister, R. (2010) *After Evil: A Politics of Human Rights*, New York: Columbia University Press.

Miers, S. (1975) *Britain and the Ending of the Slave Trade*, London: Longman.

Mouser, B. (2013) *American Colony on the Rio Pongo: The War of 1812, the Slave Trade and the Proposed Settlement of African Americans, 1810–1830*, Trenton, NJ: Africa World Press.

Muhammad, P. (2004) 'The Trans-Atlantic Slave Trade: A Forgotten Crime Against Humanity as Defined by International Law', *American University International Law Review* 19: 883.

Mutua, M. (2002) *Human Rights: A Political and Cultural Critique*, Philadelphia: University of Pennsylvannia Press.

Nadelmann, E. (1990) 'Global Prohibition Regimes: The Evolution of Norms in International Society', *International Organization* 44: 479–526.

Nesiah, V. (2004) 'From Berlin to Bonn to Baghdad: A Space for Infinite Justice', *Harvard Human Rights Journal* 17: 75–99.

Nouwen, S. and Werner, W. (2010) 'Doing Justice to the Political: The International Criminal Court in Uganda and Sudan', *European Journal of International Law* 21: 941–65.

Oldfield, J. (2007) *'Chords of Freedom': Commemoration, Ritual and British Transatlantic Slavery*, Manchester: Manchester University Press.

Rajagopal, B. (2003) *International Law from Below: Development, Social Movements and Third World Resistance*, Cambridge: Cambridge University Press.

Reddy, E.S. (1999) 'AAM and the United Nations', symposium paper, The Anti-Apartheid Movement: A 40 Year Perspective, London. Available at: www.anc.org.za/centenary/show.php?id=6851.

Redman, R.C. (1995), 'The League of Nations and the Right to be Free from Enslavement: The First Human Right to be Recognized as Customary International Law', *Chicago-Kent Law Review* 70: 759–802.

Rieff, D. (2002) *A Bed for the Night: Humanitarianism in Crisis*, London: Vintage.

Sagan, A. (2010) 'African Criminals/African Victims: The Institutionalized Production of Cultural Narratives in International Criminal Law', *Millennium Journal of International Studies* 39(1): 3–21.

Shepherd, G.W. (1977) *Anti-Apartheid: Transnational Conflict and Western Policy in the Liberation of South Africa*, Westport, CT: Greenwood Press.

Sherwood, M. (2007) *After Abolition: Britain and the Slave Trade since 1807*, London: I.B. Tauris.

Simpson, G. (2007) *Law, War and Crime*, Cambridge: Polity Press.

Skouteris, T. (2010) *The Notion of Progress in International Legal Discourse*, The Hague: TMC Asser Press.

The Trials of the Slave Traders, Samuel Samo, Joseph Peters and William Tufft Before the Hon. Robert Thorpe, L.L.D. with Two Letters on the Slave Trade From a Gentleman Resident at Sierra Leone to an Advocate for the Abolition in London (1813), London: Sherwood, Neeley and Jones.

Teitel, R. (2000) *Transitional Justice*, Oxford: Oxford University Press.

Treaty of London (1841) *Treaty for the Suppression of the African Slave Trade*, British and Foreign State Papers 30: 269.

Wallace, E.K. (2006) *The British Slave Trade and Public Memory*, Chichester: Columbia University Press.

Wemmers, J.-A. (2010) 'Victims' Rights and the ICC Perceptions within the Court Regarding Victims' Rights to Participate', *Leiden Journal of International Law*, 23(3): 629–43.

Williams, E. (1964) *Capitalism and Slavery*, London: André Deutsch.

Chapter 9

Making ICL history

On the need to move beyond pre-fab critiques of ICL

Grietje Baars[1]

Introduction

Since Schwarzenberger's provocative statement in 1950 that there is 'no such thing as an international criminal law' and nor ought there to be (Schwarzenberger 1950), international criminal law (ICL) has been given a relatively easy ride by critics. According to Schwarzenberger, most of what others called ICL was in fact internationally prescribed or authorized municipal criminal law. He queried the need for an 'international' criminal law *per se.* This he illustrated by discussing the then newly created Genocide Convention, and quoting Hartley Shawcross: 'murder remains murder whether committed against one or a million' (1950: 292).[2] Schwarzenberger adds, 'in either case a criminal can only be hanged once' (1950: 292). The crimes covered by what others might call ICL were covered by domestic law in most cases, and a horizontal extension of jurisdiction, plus international cooperation on extradition, and evidence gathering, for example, could be used to cover crimes committed by citizens abroad. This therefore begged the question (although Schwarzenberger did not explicitly pose it himself), that if ICL was not needed for the purpose it was said to have been created – the accountability of the Nazi leadership – what *was* it really, and what was it *for*?

Today, the ontological question is no longer asked and critics are mostly concerned with how we can improve and *complete* ICL. In recent years the phrases 'war crimes' and 'crimes against humanity' have become ubiquitous, in the media, on the streets, in legal practice and also in the academy. There are high expectations that ICL will be deployed to remedy many ills in the world, and these have, in the first ten years of 'mature' ICL practice, only been 'realistically tempered'. For example, a mood of only marginally cautious celebration pervades the ICC's tenth birthday issue of the *Journal of International Criminal Justice* (e.g. Akhavan 2013; Schabas 2013; Roht-Arriaza 2013). Elsewhere I have argued that law, and lawyers' role in capitalism, amounts to a 'congealing' of capitalism (Baars 2011; 2012). Law, by virtue of its very form, which approximates the commodity form (Pashukanis 1978: 38), is a *sine qua non* of the capitalist mode of production (see also Miéville 2005;

Knox 2009). Lawyers (as part of a global class of administrators or global governance bureaucrats) are important agents in the construction of law, the (continually evolving) frame or skeleton around which capitalism congeals. I am interested in the dialectical relationship between the material world in which certain ideas arise, how these ideas are translated by lawyers into legal terms of art, which then gain a function within sets of processes, rules and institutions, that become part of and in turn affect, material reality. In this chapter I focus on one of the important ways lawyers congeal capitalism, namely through shaping the idea, or what I will call the 'knowledge' of ICL. The core argument is that ICL lawyers' congealing of capitalism works through this ICL knowledge by creating its own critique, which in turn serves to strengthen and legitimize ICL as a legal regime, and as an essential part of capitalist international law. I return to Schwarzenberger's ontological question, describe how 'the idea of ICL' was constructed, how ICL became the accountability tool of choice and why it is seemingly so critique-proof. My aim is, through reopening the ontological question, to provide impetus and pointers to a radical critique of ICL.

What immediately becomes apparent when attempting to describe ICL knowledge is that it is not homogenous but exists in a slightly different configuration in different interpreters' minds and texts. In a typology of mainstream scholarship constructing the foundational narrative ('dominant knowledge') of ICL four main strands are distinguished: the humanitarian, the institutional, the positivist and the pragmatist perspective. The four strands implicitly connect with different legal traditions and cultures, consequently respond to different expectations of what 'makes' an area of law, set (slightly) different parameters, and employ different markers. Yet I argue that together these four form the mutually reinforcing building blocks of dominant 'ICL knowledge'.

The descriptive exercise – making us see that which is so close to us that we normally do not see it (Orford 2012: 618) – of the making of ICL knowledge evinces the 'productive character' of ICL knowledge. Each of the four approaches I identify produces, within scholarship and what we could call the 'policy-world', their own critique. Each such 'pre-fab' critique serves to resolve the 'problematic' suggested by the approach itself. This insight reveals that *current ICL critique*, such as it is, is produced by, and remains within the parameters of, hegemonic ICL knowledge. Moreover, as I will show, critiques that reach beyond are foreclosed. Later in the chapter I comment further on how this productive character of ICL relates to the specific function of ICL in neoliberal governance and the capitalist mode of production.

That this global status quo warrants changing is a matter of broad agreement and need not be elaborated here (e.g. Marks *et al.* 2013: 2). It is hoped that the description of ICL knowledge construction and its pre-fab and foreclosed critiques, in other words, the work of law(yers) congealing capitalism through ICL, brings into view the contradictions where space to drive a wedge of 'critical knowledge' exists (Orford 2012: 622; Baars 2012; Marks 2003: ch. 6).

Such critical knowledge (or immanent, transformative, or radical critique: Marx 1976; Horkheimer 1972) should then aid in 'dissolving' ICL knowledge, and form part of a broader effort to resist neoliberal hegemony.

The chapter proceeds as follows: I first describe the construction of ICL's knowledge, or the making of ICL, which occurred after the Second World War trials at Nuremberg. I then discuss the ICL knowledge and 'pre-fab' critiques produced by the four approaches within dominant ICL knowledge and show which critiques are foreclosed by the dominant narrative. In the final section I offer a more detailed example of one such foreclosed, or radical, critique – what I call 'commodified morality'.

The (re-)making of ICL: constructing ICL's foundational narrative

In this section I show the process of law(yers) congealing capitalism in the 'making of ICL'. ICL as we know it today, was largely (re-)constructed, while building on the post-Second World War experience, by lawyers, state representatives, and other members of the same class post-Cold War. Here, I focus on academic[3] lawyers' role in constructing ICL's foundational narrative: the knowledge that contains (constructs) its history, meaning and purpose. At Nuremberg (and Tokyo) what became known as ICL was employed and generally understood as a political intervention (e.g. Taylor 1992). ICL was criticized predominantly by lawyers and on *legal* terms – it was said, for instance, that it had been applied retrospectively (Kelsen 1947: 153; Schwarzenberger 1946– 47: 351; Jescheck 2008 [1957]: 408). Some also argued that by virtue of their selectivity (failure to try Allied crimes), Nuremberg and Tokyo had amounted to victors' justice (Minear 1971; Koskenniemi 2002). Overwhelmingly, however, legal scholars took up the task of turning the political tool of ICL into a (respectable, neutral) legal regime. In this process, during the 1940s and 1950s, but mostly in the past two decades, from the *partial*, particular geopolitical circumstance of the application of ICL post-Second World War, a *universal* ICL was fashioned.

It is legal scholars' task (habit, or even compulsion) to take legal events (such as Nuremberg and Tokyo) and make doctrinal sense of them. ICL in this mode is treated as a found object, or an unreturnable gift left to us by a previous generation. It needs to be studied, analysed, its parts named and explained. In particular, we need to figure out how it fits into our pre-designated categories (or whether it requires new categories?) and how it fits into our broader system of law, that abstracted, artificial 'whole'. Academic lawyers perform a *post-hoc* legal rationalization of an event, attach to it a history and a logic and send it forward into 'progressive development'.[4] Lawyers' explaining, legitimating and rationalization may or may not be consciously 'ideological devices' (see Marks 2003: 18–25) – but they inevitably become so. These are then employed by state negotiators (and the official law-makers, e.g. parliaments), civil society groups, business people and others (potentially members of different classes) to negotiate over, and struggle for. Lawyers are thus not the 'myopic handmaidens' of this world order, but active 'chefs' (Scott 1994: 435), members of the 'invisible college' (Schachter 1977: 223), 'ruling' elite, congealing capitalism (Baars 2012).

Academic lawyers' provision of a foundational narrative of ICL, providing it with a history, a sense of 'where it came from', can be contrasted with the way history has been written out of the mainstream international law texts. This is because international law is considered mature and settled in its identity (Koskenniemi 2004), as opposed to ICL, which to some extent is still fluid. Yet while ICL is acknowledged to be new (e.g. Boas 2010: 501), there is also a felt need to historicize it, for it to gain venerability.[5] Although lawyers' construction of ICL knowledge serves partly to congeal ICL's fluidity, it has resulted in different views on the related questions of the meaning of 'international criminal law', what constitutes an 'international crime', and subsequently what ICL's purpose is. This construction is where one can see structural dynamics and individual agency at work, dialectically.

The parameters and markers delimiting ICL now range from the humanitarian approach of Cassese, to the strict doctrinal (positivist) approach adopted by Werle and others, and the very narrow approach (one could call this an institutional approach) adopted by Cryer *et al.* These first three approaches I discuss here are variants of what Kress in the *Max Planck Encyclopedia of International Law* calls ICL '*stricto sensu*' (Kress 2009); a fourth is the 'omnibus' approach espoused by policy-oriented[6] authors (Cryer 2005:1; Ratner *et al.* 2009: 12). In the penultimate section of this essay I show how each of these four approaches contributes to the overall making of ICL.

Against all atrocities: a distinction based on morality

The ICL narrative with by far the strongest appeal, including outside of legal academia, is the 'humanitarian' school of thought, of which the late Antonio Cassese was a major proponent. With clear echoes of Jackson's Nuremberg orations, Cassese described the *telos* of international criminal law (in line with the ICC Statute Preamble) 'protecting society against the *most harmful transgressions* of legal standards of behaviour perpetrated by individuals' (Cassese 2008: 20, emphasis added). In this perspective, international crimes are something qualitatively different from 'ordinary' crimes, and should have their own, exclusive, 'area' of law. Calling ICL a new branch of international law, Cassese explicitly excludes piracy, as in his view the concept has not only become obsolete, but it 'does not meet the requirements of *international crimes proper*' (2008: 12). Piracy was not punished for the purpose of protecting a *community value*, and not thought so *abhorrent* as to amount to an international crime. Cassese further stated: 'the notion of international crimes does not include illicit traffic in narcotic drugs and psychotropic substances, the unlawful arms trade, smuggling of nuclear and other potentially deadly materials, or money laundering, slave trade or traffic in women' (2008: 13). This is because these are normally perpetrated by private individuals or criminal organizations, 'states usually fight against them, often by joint action … as a rule these offences are committed against states' (2008: 13). Apartheid is also excluded, as according to Cassese the prohibition has not yet reached the status of a customary international law (CIL) norm (2008: 13). Cassese restricts ICL to offences occurring predominantly in the 'public sphere', and perpetrated mostly by public actors for political motives. He includes as international crimes, war crimes, crimes against humanity, genocide, torture, aggression and terrorism (2008: 3). Comparison with the next two approaches will show that even among the authors who limit their understanding of ICL to 'core crimes', crimes *stricto sensu* or 'international crimes proper', there is disagreement over what those are.

Optimists and sceptics: a distinction based on enforcement mechanisms

The next most prominent perspective is one that builds on historical ICL enforcement attempts. It anchors ICL's foundational narrative in international legal institutional development. Cryer and his colleagues, in *An Introduction to International Criminal Law* (the 'first authoritative' (O'Keefe 2009: 485) and now 'market-leading' (Cryer *et al.* 2010: back cover) textbook on the subject) define ICL as the law of the crimes over which international courts and tribunals have been granted jurisdiction in general international law (Cryer *et al.* 2007: 2; 2010: 4). This covers what the book lists as 'core crimes', namely genocide, war crimes, crimes against humanity and aggression but *not* terrorism or torture. Those that delineate ICL in relation to international enforcement mechanisms (but also other *stricto sensu* proponents) normally commence any discussion of substantive ICL with a historical progress narrative which traces ICL's origin to the legendary trial of Peter von Hagenbach in 1474 (Cryer *et al.* 2007: 91) or the Allies' attempts at prosecuting the German Kaiser Wilhelm II, and ends at the present-day ICC (see Cassese 2008: 30–1; Werle 2007: 1–30; Bassiouni 1987: 414; Schabas 2007: 1; Ratner *et al.* 2009: 3–9). The narrative suggested by the lawyers at Nuremberg as a putative justification for the IMT trial – which emphasized that international law would only make sense with a working enforcement mechanism (Taylor 1992: 37) – is here taken and naturalized. This narrative would list certain key moments in the development of the ICL enforcement regime, starting just before Versailles. Following the First World War, seemingly unwilling to allow the Kaiser's self-imposed exile in the Netherlands to secure his immunity from prosecution for the heinous acts committed in Germany, the victorious Allies created a commission to look into the question of responsibility of the 'authors of the war'. The Commission reported to the 1919 Preliminary Peace Conference, that the Central Powers (the losing side in the First World War) had committed numerous acts in violation of established laws and customs of war and the elementary laws of humanity (WWI Commission Report 1920). This led to the inclusion in the 1919 Treaty of Versailles of three clauses in which the states party ordered the prosecution of the Kaiser and almost 900 others by an international tribunal (Versailles Treaty). Versailles marks the first time the concept of individual criminal responsibility was explicitly mentioned in an international treaty. Thus, in this narrative, the ICL notions of war crimes and an emerging concept of crimes against the laws of humanity had been introduced at this point (Schabas 2007: 4; Werle 2007: 8; Ratner *et al.* 2009: 6).[7] Histories of this kind then narrate the very tentative 1920 proposals for an ICC (Draft Statute 1927; Phillimore 1922–23), and following this the concrete proposal (which was supported by only 13 member states (Werle 2009: 18) by the League of Nations following the assassination of King Alexander of Yugoslavia in 1934 (ICC Convention 1937; Cryer *et al.* 2007: 92). Eventually, the determination of the Second World War Allies led to the conclusion in 1945 of the 'London Agreement', with annexed to it the Nuremberg Charter, and the establishment of the two international military tribunals (IMTs) at Nuremberg and Tokyo (IMT Charter 1945; IMTFE Charter 1946, and on the latter, see especially Boister and Cryer 2008). While the Allied post-Second World War trials are thus construed as laying the foundation for contemporary *global* ICL, its further development was taken over by the UN system. The United Nations General Assembly tasked its International Law Commission in 1947 to draft a 'Code of Offences Against the Peace and Security of Mankind' based on the IMT Charter principles and judgment (UNGARes. 177; and see ILC Nuremberg Principles 1950; *ICL Nuremberg Principles* Commentary 1950; Ratner *et al.* 2009: 8). After formulating the draft code in 1954 (ILC Draft Code 1954), the ILC suspended its work until it neared the end of the Cold War impasse in 1983.

Such histories invariably describe the development of international criminal law gaining momentum after the end of the Cold War with the establishment of the International Criminal Tribunal for the former Yugoslavia (ICTY) and the International Criminal Tribunal for Rwanda (ICTR). These momentous events were followed by the completion in 1996 of a new Draft Code, which then formed a basis for the negotiations over the International Criminal Court (ICC) Statute. Thus, the history of ICL culminates in the establishment of the ICC (Schabas 2007: 1–21; De Than and Shorts 2003: 271–341; Schwarzenberger 1950: 263; Ambos 2004 uses the term '*gipfelt*', which translates as 'culminates'). In this narrative, the ICC Statute forms the embodiment of a maturing system of ICL (Werle 2007: V; see also Van Sliedregt 2003: 3; Werle 2009: 4, 18; Ambos 2004). Strikingly, all cast their histories back before Nuremberg, not accepting that as its moment of origin – as Werle does, by calling the London Charter the 'birth certificate of ICL' (Werle 2007: 14), but rather considering Nuremberg just one step in a logical sequence. This has the effect of rendering the flaws many saw in Nuremberg (retrospectivity, selectivity) as specific to Nuremberg rather than innate to ICL.

German positivists: a distinction based on doctrine

The third narrative is internal to law: the 'legal scientist's perspective'. It is the positivist's task to explain law and 'legal happenings' resulting from legal processes, as part of, and in terms of, a coherent, autonomous system of law. This perspective is dominant in German-speaking legal academia, where *Völkerstrafrecht* (equivalent terms exist in Portuguese, Spanish, French and Italian but not in English – Kress diplomatically suggests 'international criminal law *stricto sensu*': Kress 2009; Vitzthum 2010: 19) is defined as 'all norms of PIL, that directly create, exclude, or in another way regulate criminal liability' (Werle 2007: 34, fn 153). In their narrative, *Völkerstrafrecht* must be distinguished from *Internationales Strafrecht* (Werle 2007: 35). In the French literature the same distinction is made between *droit international pénal* on the one hand, and *droit pénal international* on the other.[8] Thus, the international crimes within this definition are what authors such as Cryer identify as 'core crimes'. The subtle difference with the enforcement narrative above is that core crimes here additionally include CIL crimes that do not fall under the jurisdiction of the ICC or the international tribunals, such as certain specific crimes in internal armed conflicts (Werle 2007: 942), and single occurrences of war crimes and crimes against humanity and the CIL norms on crimes in civil war (some of) which are included in the jurisdiction of the ICTR and ICTY. The core crimes covered in *Völkerstrafrecht* are as a category included in the ICC jurisdiction and defined there; however, *Völkerstrafrecht* generally includes custom and other sources, where these crimes are also regulated (Ferdinandusse 2006: 11). Implicitly, Article 22(3) of the ICC Statute itself evidences that there exist other international law (IL) crimes than those listed in the Statute. The bigger difference with the enforcement approach is the motivation for the distinction, in that the 'German' approach includes as *Völkerrechtsverbrechen* all those crimes the substantive content of which is found in IL, regardless of where (or even whether) these crimes may be prosecuted. It is thus a distinction that finds its source in doctrine *per se*. The substantive content of the *Völkerrechtsverbrechen* should be found *directly* in IL itself. Additionally, whether a domestic constitution does or does not permit the direct application of the international norm containing the crime in domestic law does not affect the validity of the norm in IL (Werle 2007: 111). Crimes such as torture (in the Convention Against Torture sense)[9] or certain crimes against air traffic are thus not ICL *stricto sensu*, but 'international criminal law in the meaning of internationally prescribed/authorized municipal criminal law' (Schwarzenberger 1950: 266; Werle 2007: 111).

In the German understanding, when *Völkerrechtsverbrechen* occur in the context of a systematic or massive attack or use of force, for which a collective, normally a state, is responsible, the collective deed is the sum of all individual deeds (Werle 2007: 4). *Völkerstrafrecht* thus forms part of a gapless system of IL, and borders the law on state responsibility. *Völkerstrafrecht* forms part of *Internationales Strafrecht* (literally, international criminal law), which encompasses all areas of criminal law that have international aspects (2007: 52). This includes supranational criminal law (criminal law made by supranational organizations, which thus far does not exist), the law on the international cooperation in matters of criminal law (which includes, for example, extradition treaties), and national choice of law and jurisdiction norms (2007: 54).[10]

A key aspect of the German approach is the *Individualisierung* of responsibility provided by ICL. Werle, moving outside of the perspective internal to law, explains how (or that) this view of ICL correctly and appropriately mirrors our material experience:

> The individual allocation shows that international crimes are committed not by abstract entities such as states, but always require the cooperation of individuals. This individualization is important for the victims and their families because they have a right to the whole truth. The individualization of the perpetrators provides an opportunity to process their personal stake in the system crimes. Finally, it is important for society, because it rejects a theory of collective guilt.
>
> (Werle 2007: 43)

No distinction: the catch-all 'omnibus' approach

Alternative narratives of ICL compared to the three discussed above *do* start their account of ICL's origins with the international norms applicable to piracy (e.g. Bantekas and Nash 2007: 1). According to these, since the time of the Phoenicians and the Vikings piracy has been condemned as a crime against the law of nations (e.g. Ferencz 1995: 1123). In this view, the activities of pirates, committing acts on the open seas that under most national jurisdictions would amount to crimes, led to the development and application of international rules (such as ATCA in the US; see also, for example, *In re Piracy*). These histories also include early regulation of the slave trade, the opium trade, and other phenomena, in addition to the events and developments described above (Ferencz 1995: 1126; Cryer 2005: 57; Schabas 2007: 10). In this narrative, slave trade and piracy were both crimes in CIL before treaties were adopted which included crimes with a similar content. Neither offences had (or have) specific international enforcement mechanisms attached to them, but 'every state may seize a pirate ship ... and arrest the persons and seize the property on board' (*In re Piracy*) according to treaty law the capturing state, and according to CIL, applying universal jurisdiction, any state may prosecute the pirate (see generally Guilfoyle 2008). The prohibitions, violations of which amount to crimes in this approach, constitute *erga omnes* obligations, meaning that every state in the world has an interest in their observance. As the enforcement of the norms on piracy occurred only in national courts, *stricto sensu* authors argue that the CIL rule on piracy is merely jurisdictional (Cassese 2008: 28). Counter to this stands the 'omnibus' view that the crime of piracy is defined in IL (both the content of the crime and the fact that it is a crime), regardless of where that norm may be enforceable. Crimes like piracy are thus considered 'international crimes' in this perspective regardless of enforcement, or even whether they are explicitly designated as 'crimes' or indeed 'international crimes' in international law (Bantekas and Nash 2007: 6). Whether the ICL norm can be directly applied in a domestic court or needs the intermediation of a piece of domestic legislation does not detract from the 'international' nature of the crime (2007: 6). This approach is the most catholic (Ratner *et al.* 2009: 12), pragmatic, problem-solving-oriented approach.

As opposed to the German positivist approach which is to explain doctrinal inconsistencies or lacunae as deliberate exceptions or distinctions, the policy approach deals with a 'messy' reality by overriding inconsistencies in the name of a desired policy outcome. Such inconsistencies and lacunae exist, for example, where IL instruments do not clearly specify whether a crime in question is an 'international' crime (e.g. Art. 1, Genocide Convention 1949), or whether a crime is subject to international jurisdiction, to universal jurisdiction in national or international fora, or whether the treaty only obligates or authorizes states to criminalize a certain event in domestic law (e.g. Art. 5, Organized Crime Convention) and/or to prosecute or extradite a suspect (e.g. Art. 4, Convention Against Torture). In the omnibus approach, this situation is dealt with on a case-by-case basis, with authors coming to occasionally different conclusions (compare the lists of crimes considered ICL crimes in Van den Wijngaert and Dugard 1996; Steiner and Alston 2007: 1136). Generally the crimes that Werle would designate as 'international crimes' are included.

ICL knowledge, pre-fab critiques and foreclosed knowledges

Soederberg, in Gramscian vein, has noted that neoliberal hegemony is not static and must continually renegotiate and re-establish itself 'through complex social struggles and contradictions that emerge within, are shaped by, and shape, the structures and processes of capital accumulation' (Soederberg 2010: 16–17). For ICL, as an aspect of this neoliberal hegemony, this renegotiation becomes apparent in the description of the production of 'pre-fab critiques' and 'foreclosed knowledges' by ICL's dominant knowledge.

ICL knowledge

Each of the four narratives described above contributes one of the vital elements of ICL knowledge. What we see is that the apparent disparities between the approaches, in fact serve to support a more or less coherent dominant knowledge. Each of the approaches fit into each other, complement each other. This linkage becomes apparent when authors acknowledge the validity of others' narratives implicitly and occasionally explicitly.

First, Cassese's approach provides ICL with the key element of the ideological justification, almost the emotional need, for intervention in 'foreign' jurisdiction 'for the protection of higher values' (2008: 11). This at once universalizes ICL, purports to serve us, our community interest and represent us, our collectively held values. It does not seem to matter that Cassese does not further explain what those values are and how we may discover them. Instead, in an attempt to defend and legitimate his position, he uncomfortably moves into positivist territory: 'The values at issue are not propounded by scholars or thought up by starry-eyed philosophers. Rather, they are laid down in a string of international instruments, which, however, do not necessarily spell them out in so many words' (2008: 11).

Likewise moving outside of their comfort-zone, positivists would recognize that broad aspirational statements of 'values' are regularly found in preambles to treaties. Triffterer, for example, notes that those declarations found in the Preamble to the ICC Statute 'echo, in the arena of international affairs, the loftiest aspirations of an ever advancing society' (Triffterer 2008: 6). The 'humanitarian' here shines through for positivists as both an explanatory (this is why we have ICL) as well as a legitimating factor.

Aside from such departures, the 'German' variant seems to approach law from a purely analytical, scientific perspective. It thus appears to be technical, value neutral. The differences and distinctions found by adherents to this school of thought may appear of limited value other than from the intellectual pursuit of studying law as a system. For example, Kress's remark that the ICC Statute contains crimes that are not in fact 'international crimes' (Kress 2009) is likely to find resonance with only the smallest circle of specialists and would not likely concern even the ICC itself – something Kress must realize. Yet, precisely such debates serve to give ICL doctrinal credibility.

Proponents of the 'omnibus approach', presumably like the ICC itself, display a more 'relaxed' attitude to such questions, preferring to be more practice-oriented. Bantekas and Nash, for example, conceptualize ICL as a 'fusion of IL and domestic criminal law' and include in their textbook on ICL discussion of IOs' and NGOs' efforts on issues such as human trafficking (Bantekas and Nash 2007: 1). Grant and Barker's *Deskbook of International Criminal Law* (a documents bundle, aimed at the ICL practitioner) contains conventions ranging from the 1926 Slavery Convention to the European Convention on Cybercrime (Grant and Barker 2006). Van den Wijngaert and

Dugard (1996: 1) see ICL as a means for states to help each other in the application of their respective domestic criminal laws, necessitated by the internationalisation of crime – and thus come closest to interpreting ICL in the practical sense permitted in Schwarzenberger's critique. Ramasastry (2002), possibly at the pragmatic extreme of this group of scholars, expresses no view on the doctrinal nature of ICL, but asks only 'what it can do for us'.

Within the narrative focused on the enforcement mechanisms and possibilities of ICL, two strands can be detected: those that consider the court half full (Roht-Arriaza 2013) and those that consider it half empty (Schabas 2013). Both provide us with a history of how ICL was built up brick by brick, how this logical development culminated in an overarching ICC. What binds the two together, then, is that the ultimate desire, objective and mark of success is a full court,[11] something they share first and foremost with the pragmatists. That ICL is a good thing, and should be improved, implemented and promoted, is not called into question by anyone within the four approaches.

Viewing these approaches as key 'ingredients' of today's ICL, we can see that ICL is a mixture (in varying quantities) of emotions, rationality, pragmatics and 'legal soundness' – altogether, an irresistible combination to lawyers, policy-makers and the general public. The pragmatic element gives it flexibility, for example, to develop new rules/policies in the 'war on terror' context, the positivist foundational narrative gives it 'academic kudos', while the enforcement focus supports efforts to strengthen institutions. Moreover, as ICL symbolizes 'justice' in IL (Mégret 2010: 210, 220, 224; Tallgren 2002: 580), it has become something to believe in: it 'carries a religious exercise of hope that is stronger than the desire to face everyday life' (Tallgren 2002: 593). Its crimes have become reasons (or rather, justifications) to invade other countries. *This* is why ICL is in fashion. It is something to propose as a remedy to a perceived problem (such as 'business in conflict': see Stewart 2012, for example), and, something to rally around, to continually work to improve. Most of all, ICL communicates to us, reassuringly, its *exceptionality* (e.g. Cassese's effort to exclude certain 'less grave' crimes), while also confirming to us that these select international crimes are the ills of international society. All other problems pale in comparison or even disappear altogether.

The seeming contradictions between the four approaches described above do not pull apart, but rather serve to strengthen the cohesion of the dominant knowledge. They do so by implicitly accepting the main parameters of the knowledge, being silent as to the ontology of the knowledge, and also by keeping much of the critical debate within the parameters of the knowledge itself.

Pre-fab critiques and foreclosed and subjugated knowledges

Above it was noted that ICL is seemingly 'critique-proof'. It would be more precise to say that critique rarely sticks, or is rarely radical. This is not to say that there is no ICL critique – on the contrary, each of the four narratives outlined above generates its own specific set of critiques,[12] and a lively academic debate around them (e.g. Van Sliedregt 2013). In this section the types of critiques produced by each approach are briefly outlined. As opposed to such 'constructive' critiques, the critical scholar must generate critical knowledge (Marks 2003: ch. 6) or radical, transformative critique (Horkheimer 1972), thereby ultimately contributing to radical, systemic change. Here I offer some pointers towards such radical, transformative critiques.

The most commonly aired critique today is of ICL's selectivity when it comes to situations and defendants (e.g. Cryer 2005, esp. ch. 5; Heller 2010). This critique, and more generally questions regarding effectiveness and how to improve the workings of ICL institutions, is produced by the enforcement approach. Other critiques produced regard the inadequate representation or protection by one or another group in the judicial process (witnesses, victims, women) or the focus on some crimes but not on others (e.g. Charlesworth 1999 on sexual crimes). In regard to these latter two points, rather than arguing for an improved regime of inclusion, a more intricate, transcendental or radical critique could be made, for example regarding the way women are constructed as victims (and thus denied agency and responsibility in conflict) in trials relating to sexual offences (e.g. Engle 2005).

Implicit in the pre-fab enforcement critiques is that all of ICL's problems will be resolved when we have strong, professional international institutions that apply the rules equally to all. The latter is also a concern for the German positivists. Both, however, assume that it is a structural possibility for this to become reality: these approaches therefore enable a 'progressive' debate and practical activity on improving and expanding ICL's institutions. Curiously, at the same time, it also allows for the argument *not* to expand ICL enforcement: we must not grow too fast. Crawford has suggested that the current limitation of the ICC's jurisdiction is quite simply motivated by the risk of the court being 'swamped' otherwise (Crawford 2002: 122).

Both enforcement and pragmatic approaches favour the question of 'How can we …?' over 'Why are we not …?'. This becomes clear when examining Crawford's argument more closely. The 'size' of the court merely depends on the funding governments make available. An argument analogous to Crawford's on the domestic level is almost inconceivable. At the same time, restrictions impeding ICL's effectiveness are often considered to be financial. For example, in his monograph, Cryer lays the cause of selectivity at the dependence of courts on states' contributions – although he expects this situation to change with time. Finance appears as an external 'fact of life' to ICL. Any more fundamental critique, such as that which asks why governments are generally outwardly very supportive of ICL but leave the courts to struggle with very limited funds, would be unconstructive, and almost unsportsmanlike. Already, Cryer states that the ICC 'represents a quantum leap beyond what went before' (2005: 231). Radical critiques could start from the bureaucratic and political decision-making processes behind the budgeting of the ICL institutions or even the drafting of budgetary provisions pre-adoption. It is interesting for a start – something rarely mentioned in the literature – that the ICC and the other tribunals are expected to, and in fact do, actively seek private, including corporate, funding for their activities (ICC Statute; Del Ponte 2005; PICT Report). In the manner suggested by Orford (2012), a descriptive study of, for example, the independent auditor's recommendations as to the reinforcement and clarification of the roles of the Prosecutors and the Registrar of the ICC (ICC Financial Statement 2012: 9–10) could reveal budgetary constraints on the prosecutor's independence.

Rather than expressing disappointment with the achievements of the ICC ten years after it opened its doors, most authors of the *JICJ* special anniversary issue urged readers to display pragmatic realism: for example, 'the hangover after the euphoria [of 1992] should be used to correct the sky-high expectations' (Roht-Arriaza 2013: 537). Yet, our faith in ICL is sustained (at most, pending another 'Pinochet moment': Schabas 2013) by the fantasy that one day, the likes of George W. Bush and Tony Blair, or their equivalents in a different time, will face justice.

What Cryer and others overlook is the fact that the impunity gap which exists as a result of selectivity is itself also created through ICL. The makers of ICL create its inclusions as well as its exclusions. By analogy to Marks' 'planned misery' in relation to poverty, we could term this 'planned impunity' (Marks 2011). The recognition of the planned nature of such impunity is also a recognition that selectivity cannot simply be 'corrected'. Why, by whom and how such impunity is planned and what mechanisms are in place to cause us to believe it can be overcome are questions ripe for a radical critique.

Similarly, the almost anti-intellectualist pragmatist perspective forecloses fundamental theoretical questions in favour of constructive critiques aimed at achieving maximum effectiveness in the face of immediate, urgent and 'real' problems ('while babies are dying'). In a particularly apposite example, Stewart offers an in his view urgent, pragmatic corrective to theories of corporate liability that are 'not sensitive to the complexities of reality' (Stewart 2012: 38). Yet, the theories he discusses are themselves reflective, and reconstitutive of that very same reality that produces the corporate exploitation Stewart wishes to eradicate. Such eradication requires instead a radical critique of the corporation itself (Spicer and Baars 2015 forthcoming).

A further often heard critique relates to doctrinal issues. The positivist approach invites debate over whether this rule or that concept is properly interpreted, or within the purview of ICL. Much of this debate surrounds the proper interpretation by the three main international tribunals of their constituent instruments. For example, debates abound about the ICC Prosecutor's actions in relation to former Sudanese President Omar Al-Bashir (e.g. Luban 2013). Here, problems are often seen to be due to the inexperience of the courts' officials and critiques can also be *ad hominem*. Others surround the progressive development in the courts of ICL doctrine where such matters are not covered by the instruments – and where problems are thus thrown up by ICL being a 'new' and as yet not fully developed discipline. One example here is the debate over the correctness or otherwise of the joint criminal enterprise (JCE) doctrine (e.g. JICJ Symposium 2007). Lost in doctrinal detail, the critiques produced by the doctrinal approach guarantees bigger questions will not be asked. Most importantly, they set the 'legal scientist' – who rightly only concerns herself with questions of legal doctrine – apart from the politician and thus denies lawyers' role in, among others, congealing capitalism.

Schwarzenberger's critique (as set out at the start of this chapter) pulls the rug from under the preceding justifications of ICL. If domestic and transnational criminal law worked, we would not need ICL. If ICL, and new ICL norms and institutions, are not in fact needed to try 'murderers' and 'torturers', then why do we call for them? Designating certain behaviour as an international crime to be tried in an international forum implies another motivation and purpose than immediate practical necessity. What ICL allows for, and what cannot be 'done' in any way fitting law's configuration as it stands, is to intervene in other states to criminalize through supranational law acts that are not criminal in the relevant domestic law (or not prosecuted domestically), and to allow for their prosecution externally (or post-regime). In other words, by 'lifting' certain behaviour, events and individuals into international law, ICL creates the option of centralizing the administration and management of this regime according to the interests (or disinterest) of the global ruling class directly. When stripped of the practical justifications, what remains is the violence of ICL, made possible by its ideology – namely, the way that ICL designates certain behaviour as 'international crimes which form an attack on the fundamental values of the international community' (ICC Statute). This ideological element has very real practical uses: one is (through ICL prosecutions) to create specific explanations of conflicts that exempt/exonerate the economic/capitalism (e.g. Baars 2013), often, in the process of what Klein has called the post-intervention 'human rights clean-up operation' (Klein 2007: 126). Another is to form the diversion or Trojan horse for the intervention in states that goes much further than ICL, for the purpose of 'regime change', 'civilization', or indeed 'capitalization'. Both we have seen in Nuremberg and Tokyo, and also in the contemporary context in e.g. the former Yugoslavia (Baars 2013b; 2012). ICL thus forms an important function in legitimating other parts of, and actions under, international law.

This function appears to be beyond enquiry. Cassese's refusal to engage in the question where ICL's universal values come from – insisting instead they must thus be self-evident to us, forecloses, most importantly, the *why* question – and with that, any ontological critique of ICL knowledge. As noted,

Schwarzenberger's reservations regarding the need for an ICL still stand today. Yet, the question is no longer posed (Cryer 2005: 2). ICL continues to be constructed, and 'believed in' (Tallgren 2002: 593; also generally, Koskenniemi 2007; *JICJ* 2013).

Ultimately the designation 'more harmful' used by Cassese appears to be Cassese's own, to reflect his moral indignation. Yet, aside from the harm caused, a transcendental critique might note that Cassese also seems to imply that the emotive reaction to his 'international crimes proper' ('so abhorrent as to offend the international community as a whole': ICC Statute Preamble) is universally felt and absent (or less) in the case of other crimes, or, for example, in the face of mass starvation, or tens of thousands of children dying preventable deaths each day (Beckett 2012).

Schmitt famously quoted Proudhon: 'Whoever invokes humanity wants to cheat' (Schmitt 1996: 54). The humanitarian narrative was reconstructed, reinvented, re-emphasized after Nuremberg (and Tokyo). Importantly, it allows assertion of the moral high ground, a positioning of us (good) v. them (bad). Ferdinandusse recognizes such normative claims in ICL 'as techniques in a hegemonic struggle for greater control between different actors in international law' (2006: 158). As a starter for a transcendental critique, therefore, ICL can be said to play an instrumental role in the distribution of power among global actors.

A critique of the 'humanitarian' narrative of ICL may be made analogously to Marks' critique of the concept of 'humanitarian intervention' (Marks 2006). Presenting ICL as a necessity for the benefit of humanity, against atrocities, works as a rhetorical move, the function of which is to justify inaction of the political field *vis-à-vis* certain situations of suffering, and to ignore the root causes (Marks 2006: 344; 2011). This critique can be made in both a constructive way (Miller 2008: 'if only global political focus was less selectively pointed towards hot conflict/away from structural problems') and transgressively through interrogating why the global leadership's finger is pointed in that direction and not another (e.g. Franzki and Olarte 2013).

The essential contradiction between the factual and normative in Miller's critique is visible in a slightly different way also in Ambos: 'the worldwide impunity for grave human rights violations leads to a factual accountability gap, the closure, or at least the narrowing, of which ICL has made as its highest priority task'. The author adds in a footnote: 'It concerns a *factual*, not a *normative* accountability gap, because the impunity can be traced back not to a lack of norms on international crimes, but on a lack of States' political will to prosecute' (Ambos 2000: 39). Why, one might ask (Ambos does not), would state leaders create a body of norms to do something that they do not in fact *want* to do? It only makes sense, if (a) that body of law is not, in fact, designed to do this thing; (b) it is so designed, but only in relation to specific others, or exceptional, acceptable situations; or (c) if it is done in response to a felt need (or public call) to be 'doing something' and the creation of these norms alone, with the promise of enforcement satisfies this need. ICL gives us faith that 'something is being done'. In a realist/transcendental critique, Akhavan posits:

> In contrast to the prevention of ongoing atrocities through military intervention or peacekeeping, and substantial post-conflict economic assistance and social rehabilitation, resort to international tribunals incurs a rather modest financial and political cost. However, the attractive spectacle of courtroom drama, which pits darkness against the forces of light and reduces the world to a manageable narrative, could lead international criminal justice to become an exercise in moral self-affirmation and a substitute for genuine commitment and resolve
>
> (Akhavan 2001: 30).

Or, indeed, a cloak for the systemic root causes of 'crimes', which may be endemic to the current mode of production (Baars 2013b).

A popular demand for justice for certain occurrences in certain places is thus produced based on criminal law's visceral appeal (Tallgren 2002a: 591), and deployed, with Cassese's emotive discourse providing the legitimizing element. Critique following an historical materialist methodology should serve to elucidate exactly how ICL 'works' in this regard. As Tallgren suggests:

> Perhaps [ICL's] task is to naturalize, to exclude from the political battle, certain phenomena which are in fact the preconditions for the maintenance of the existing governance; by the North, by wealthy states, by wealthy individuals, by strong states, by strong individuals, by men, especially white men, and so forth.
>
> (Tallgren 2002a: 595)

Commodified morality

By way of offering an example of how a further radical critique of ICL could be made I now propose the concept of 'commodified morality' as a Marxist critique based on Pashukanis' commodity form theory of law (see further Pashukanis 1978; Baars 2012). Pashukanis analysed the particular element that makes criminal law (CL) so attractive, and seem so necessary, and as something we cannot do without. Applying the commodity form theory to criminal law on the domestic level, he notes that criminal procedure 'contains particular features which are not fully dealt with by clear and simple considerations of social purpose, but represent an irrational, mystified, absurd element. We wish … to demonstrate that it is precisely this which is the specifically legal element' (Pashukanis 1978: 177). The practical social purpose he refers to is the compensation of victims (which is often absent in CL in any case), the protection of society (which could be achieved better in other ways) or the treatment and rehabilitation of the offender (which is likewise not normally a priority) (Pashukanis 1978: 176–8). The value in CL according to Pashukanis lies in its 'morality' – which is present both in its demonstrative function and in the 'compulsory atonement' it demands of the convicted criminal (Pashukanis 1978: 185–7). Criminal law functions as the 'remoralization' of society after the imposition of the cash nexus in the transition to capitalism (Marx and Engels 1848) and analogous to the 'humanitarian makeover' of IL in the mid twentieth century (Baars 2012). Once law has replaced human relationships with legal relationships, law is – or law-makers are – there to inform us what is right. 'Law creates right by creating crime' (Pashukanis 1978: 167). This commodified morality[13] tells us when to feel revulsion, or when to ignore or forgive; it is 'canned morality', served up in the 'bourgeois theatre' (Orzeck 2012) of international criminal trials. It can be fostered and instrumentalized – and develop on its own according to the logic of the market. What 'commodified morality' does, then, is shape our response to certain instances of suffering and not others (e.g. Libya v. Syria, Palestine, Bangladesh) as part of a broader liberal-capitalist hegemony.

Commodified morality thus produces 'accountability' in the Weberian sense – meaning that by means of 'calculable law' costs, benefits and risks of political actions can be calculated, managed, and even optimized (Weber 1982: 277). In other words, commodified morality can be deployed to control and optimize public sentiment in this or that situation. As the independence of the ICC Prosecutor and thus the supposed unpredictability of the court's activity is a major factor in ICL's legitimacy, in particular a study of the financial and other constraints on the Prosecutor could reveal the actual power relations behind the scenes of ICL. Akhavan has noted that ICL produces spectator's justice (2013: 530). The public become passive consumers of spectacle (cf. 'opium for the masses') and simultaneously producers and reproducers of commodified morality – and reproducers of ICL, when baying for ICL blood. Despite, and at the same time because of, ICL's individualizing function, it unites us (significantly, in this pluralist time) *with* the state/elite against the accused, and *away* from structural questions. It is this move, which is being resisted sporadically, that legal scholars, through radical critique, must work to subvert.

Conclusion

I have tried to show in this chapter how lawyers and legal scholars have played an important role in the construction of the knowledge known as ICL. They have created an almost critique-proof system through its four building blocks, of which the most important is the humanitarian. The 'epidermic' humanitarian aspect contains the values that 'ennoble ICL' (Tallgren, Chapter 3 in this volume) and cause an overwhelming 'oceanic feeling' (Schabas 2013: 549) that we could not possibly resist, or definitely not politely refuse. I have argued that each of the four approaches within ICL knowledge creates its own 'constructive critique' which serves to strengthen ICL and perpetuate both ICL's and implicitly, as part of IL, capitalism's status quo. In certain instances also, the ready-made constructive critique silences other critiques. While this descriptive process in itself should create its own knowledge, I have also pointed to various different ways in which our critique can transcend problem-solving and create critical knowledge.

In conclusion, I have argued that a comprehensive, transcending, emancipatory critique of ICL must start by again posing Schwarzenberger's ontological question, and challenging ICL's hegemonic knowledge through 'retelling' the story of ICL, what ICL *is* and what it is *for*. Rather than playing a part in congealing capitalism, we should work towards dissolving it.

Notes

1 I am grateful to Ioannis Kalpouzos, Isobel Roele, Immi Tallgren, Vanja Hamzić, Alessandra Asteriti, Hannah Franzki, Christian Garland and Christine Schwöbel for their insightful comments on earlier drafts of this essay. All errors and omissions are mine alone.
2 Hartley Shawcross was the head of the British prosecution team at Nuremberg.
3 As, especially in ICL, there is no clear separation between academic and practising lawyers, it would be more accurate to say, lawyers acting in their academic capacity.
4 The fact that ICL was taken up as a project for (re-)construction suggests that similar material circumstances existed to the latter half of the 1940s that – in the dominant ideology – required some manner of intervention. From within the discourse of IL, the 'need' for an ICL can be deduced from its role as the missing piece of the IL project (as perceived pre-Nuremberg – Baars 2012).
5 On this term, see Marks (2003: 19–20).
6 I use 'policy-oriented' here in the ordinary sense of the words rather than to refer to the New Haven policy-oriented school of thought.
7 No individuals were in fact prosecuted under these provisions, although some were tried by domestic German tribunals in the 'Leipzig Trials'.
8 The distinction on the same basis also exists in the Portuguese, Italian and Spanish legal tradition (Cassese 2003: 15). See also Hollán (2000); Schwarzenberger (1950).
9 For the view that these and other crimes attracting universal jurisdiction should be counted as *Völkerrechtsverbrechen* see also Dahm *et al.* (2002: 999).
10 In Werle's view, the source of the universal jurisdiction principle for *Völkerrechtsverbrechen* is domestic law (Werle 2007: 54).
11 For Roht-Arriaza (2013) this is a full domestic court enforcing ICL rather than a full ICC.
12 In Marx's and Horkheimer's terms these ought rightly to be called 'criticisms' rather than critiques (Marx 1972; Horkheimer 1972).
13 Or what Shamir (2008) calls 'market-embedded morality'; see also Baars (2011).

Bibliography

Primary sources

ATCA/ATS: Alien Tort Statute (28 U.S.C. 1350).
Convention Against Torture: Convention Against Torture and Other Cruel, Inhuman and Degrading Treatment and Punishment 1984, 1465 UNTS 85.

Draft Code 1996: Draft Code of Offences Against the Peace and Security of Mankind 1996, UN Doc A/48/10 (1996).

Draft Statute 1927: Draft Statute for an International Criminal Court, International Law Association, Report of the 34th Conference, 1927.

ICC Convention 1937: 1937 Convention for the Creation of an International Criminal Court (1938) League of Nations Official Journal Special Supplement 156.

ICC Financial Statement 2012: Financial statements for the period 1 January to 31 December 2012, ICC-ASP/12/12. Available at: www.icc-cpi.int/iccdocs/asp_docs/ASP12/ICC-ASP-12-12-ENG.pdf.

ILC Draft Code 1954: Draft Code of Offences Against the Peace and Security of Mankind 1954, UN Doc A/2693 (1954).

ILC Nuremberg Principles: Principles of International Law Recognized in the Charter of the Nuremberg Tribunal and in the Judgment of the Tribunal 1950, UN Doc A/CN.4/SER.A/1950/Add.1.

ICL Nuremberg Principles Commentary: Commentary, *International Law Commission Yearbook*, Vol. II, (1950) 374.

IMT Charter: London Agreement Establishing the Nuremberg Tribunal, 82 UNTS 279 (no. 251), 1945.

IMTFE Charter: Charter of the (Tokyo) International Military Tribunal for the Far East 1946, TIAS No. 1589.

In re Piracy Jure Gentium [1934] A.C. 586.

Transnational Crime Convention: United Nations Convention Against Transnational Organized Crime, 2000, UNTS 2225, 209.

UNGARes. 177: United Nations General Assembly Resolution 177 (II) of 21 November 1947.

WCCLR: Law Reports of Trials of War Criminals, Selected and prepared by the United Nations War Crimes Commission, 1947–49.

WWI Commission Report: Commission on the Responsibility of the Authors of the War and on Enforcement of Penalties, Report Presented to the Preliminary Peace Conference, 29 March 1919, reprinted in 14 AJIL 95 (1920).

Secondary sources

Akhavan, P. (2001) 'Beyond Impunity: Can International Criminal Justice Prevent Future Atrocities?' *American Journal of International Law* 95(7).

Akhavan, P. (2013) 'The Rise, and Fall, and Rise, of International Criminal Justice', *Journal of International Criminal Justice* 11(3): 527–36.

Alston, P. (1997) 'The Myopia of the Handmaidens: International Lawyers and Globalization', *European Journal of International Law* 3: 435.

Ambos, K. (2000) 'Individual Criminal Responsibility in International Criminal Law: A Jurisprudential Analysis – From Nuremberg to The Hague', in G. McDonald and O. Swaak (eds) *Substantive and Procedural Aspects of International Criminal Law*, Vol. 1, Netherlands: Kluwer Law International.

Ambos, K. (2004) *Der Allgemeine Teil des Völkerstrafrechts: Ansätze einer Dogmatisierung*, Duncker u. Humblot GmbH.

Anghie, A. (2007) *Imperialism, Sovereignty and the Making of International Law*, Cambridge: Cambridge University Press.

Baars, G. (2011) 'Reform or Revolution: Marxian vs Polanyian Approaches to the Regulation of "the Economic"', *Northern Ireland Legal Quarterly* 17(4): 415.

Baars, G. (2012) Law(yers) Congealing Capitalism: On the (im)possibility of restraining business in conflict through international criminal law, UCL PhD thesis.

Baars, G. (2013a) 'Capital, Corporate Personhood and Legitimacy: The Ideological Force of "Corporate Crime" in International Law', paper presented at the IGLP Conference New Directions in Global Thought: 5 Years of Heterodoxy, Harvard Law School, 3 June.

Baars, G. (2013b) 'Capitalism's Victor's Justice? The Hidden Story of the Prosecution of Industrialists Post-WWII', in G. Simpson and K. Heller (eds) *Untold Stories: Hidden Histories of War Crimes Trials*, Oxford: Oxford University Press.

Bantekas, I. and Nash, S. (2007) *International Criminal Law*, London: Routledge-Cavendish.

Barker, C. and Grant, J. (2005) *Deskbook of International Criminal Law*, London: Routledge-Cavendish.

Bassiouni, M. (1987) *A Draft International Criminal Code and Draft Statute for an International Criminal Tribunal*, Netherlands: Kluwer Law International.

Beckett, J. (2012) 'Critical Legal Thought in Public International Law', in C. Douzinas, M. Stone and I. Wall (eds) *New Critical Legal Thinking: Law and the Political*, London: Routledge.

Boas, G. (2010) 'The Difficulty with Individual Criminal Responsibility in International Criminal Law', in C. Stahn and L.J. van den Herik (eds) *Future Perspectives on International Criminal Justice*, The Hague: TMC Asser Press.

Boister, N. and Cryer, R. (2008) *The Tokyo International Military Tribunal: A Reappraisal*, Oxford: Oxford University Press.

Cassese, A. (2003) *International Criminal Law*, Oxford: Oxford University Press.

Cassese, A. (2008) *International Criminal Law*, Oxford: Oxford University Press.

Cassese, A. (ed.) (2009) *The Oxford Companion to International Criminal Justice*, Oxford: Oxford University Press.

Charlesworth, H. (1999) 'Feminist Methods in International Law', *American Journal of International Law* 93: 379–94.

Cox, R.W. (1981) 'Social Forces, States and World Orders: Beyond International Relations Theory', *Millennium Journal of International Studies* 10(2): 126–55.

Crawford, J. (2002) *The International Law Commission's Articles on State Responsibility: Introduction, Text and Commentaries*, Oxford: Oxford University Press.

Cryer, R. (2005) *Prosecuting International Crimes: Selectivity and the International Criminal Law Regime*, Cambridge: Cambridge University Press.

Cryer, R., Friman, H., Robinson, D. and Wilmshurst, E. (2007) *An Introduction to International Criminal Law and Procedure*, Cambridge: Cambridge University Press.

Cryer, R., Friman, H., Robinson, D. and Wilmshurst, E. (2010) *An Introduction to International Criminal Law and Procedure*, Cambridge: Cambridge University Press.

Dahm, G. *et al.* (2002) *Völkerrecht*, Band I/3, Berlin: De Gruyter Verlag.

De Than, C. and Shorts, E. (2003) *International Criminal Law and Human Rights*, London: Sweet & Maxwell, 2003.

Del Ponte, C. (2005) 'The Dividends of International Criminal Justice', Goldman Sachs, London 6 October. Available at: www.icty.org/x/file/Press/PR_attachments/cdp-goldmansachs-050610-e.htm.

Dugard, J. and Van den Wijngaert, C. (eds) (1996) *International Criminal Law and Procedure*, Aldershot: Ashgate.

Engle, K. (2005) 'Feminism and Its (Dis)Contents: Criminalizing Wartime Rape in Bosnia and Herzegovina', *American Journal of International Law* 99: 778

Ferdinandusse, W.N. (2006) *Direct Application of International Criminal Law in National Courts*, The Hague: Asser Press.

Ferencz, B. (1995) 'International Criminal Court', in R. Bernhardt (ed.) *Encyclopedia of Public International Law*, Vol. 2, Amsterdam: Elsevier.

Franzki, H. and Olarte, M.C. (2013) 'Understanding the Political Economy of Transitional Justice: A Critical Theory Perspective', in S. Buckley-Zistel *et al.* (eds) *Transitional Justice Theories*, London: Routledge.

Grant, J. and Barker, C. (2006) *International Criminal Law Deskbook*, Sydney: Cavendish.

Guilfoyle, D. (2008) 'Piracy off Somalia: UN Security Council Resolution 1816 and IMO Regional Counter-piracy Efforts', *International and Comparative Law Quarterly* 57(3): 690.

Heller, K. (2010) 'Situational Gravity under the Rome Statute', in C. Stahn and L.J. van den Herik (eds) *Future Perspectives on International Criminal Justice*, The Hague: TMC Asser Press.

Hollán, M. (2000) 'Globalization and Conceptualization in the Sphere of International Criminal Law', *Acta Juridica Hungarica* 41(3): 225.

Horkheimer, M. (1972) 'Traditional and Critical Theory', in *Critical Theory: Selected Essays*, New York: Continuum.

Jescheck, H.-H. (1995) 'International Crimes', in R. Bernhardt (ed.) *Encyclopedia of Public International Law*, Vol. 2, Amsterdam: Elsevier.

Jescheck, H.-H. (2008 [1957]) 'The Development of International Criminal Law after Nuremberg', in G. Mettraux (ed.) *Perspectives on the Nuremberg Trials*, Oxford: Oxford University Press.

Journal of International Criminal Justice (2007) Symposium on Joint Criminal Enterprise, 5(1): 67–226.

Kelsen, H. (1947) 'Will the Judgment in the Nuremberg Trial Constitute a Precedent in International Law?', *International and Comparative Law Quarterly* 1(2): 153.

Klein, N. (2007) *The Shock Doctrine: The Rise of Disaster Capitalism*, London: Allen Lane.

Knox, R. (2009) 'Marxism, International Law and Political Strategy', *Leiden Journal of International Law* 22: 413.

Koskenniemi, M. (2002) 'Between Impunity and Show Trials', *Max Planck Yearbook of United Nations Law* 6: 1.

Koskenniemi, M. (2007) 'The Fate of Public International Law: Between Technique and Politics', *Modern Law Review* 70(1): 1.

Koskenniemi, M. (2004) 'Why History of International Law Today?' *Rechtsgeschichte* 4.

Kress, C. (2009) 'International Criminal Law', *Max Planck Encyclopedia of Public International Law*, online edition.

Luban, D. (2013) 'After the Honeymoon: Reflections on the Current State of International Criminal Justice', *Journal of International Criminal Justice* 11(3): 505–15.

Marks, S. (2003) *The Riddle of All Constitutions: International Law, Democracy, and the Critique of Ideology*, Oxford: Oxford University Press.

Marks, S. (2006) 'State-Centrism, International Law, and the Anxieties of Influence', *Leiden Journal of International Law* 19(2): 339.

Marks, S. (2011) 'Human Rights and Root Causes', *Modern Law Review* 74(1): 57.

Marks, S., Craven, M. *et al.* (2013) 'The London Review of International Law begins', Editorial, *London Review of International Law* (June): 1–5.

Marx, K. (1976) *Capital: Critique of Political Economy*, Vol. 1, London: Penguin Classics.

Marx, K. and F. Engels (1848) *The Communist Manifesto.*

Mégret, F. (2010) 'In Search of the "Vertical": An Exploration of What Makes International Criminal Tribunals Different (and Why)', in C. Stahn and L.J. van den Herik (eds) *Future Perspectives on International Criminal Justice*, The Hague: TMC Asser Press.

Miéville, C. (2005) *Between Equal Rights: A Marxist Theory of International Law*, London: Pluto.

Miller, Z. (2008) 'Effects of Invisibility: In Search of the "Economic" in Transitional Justice', *International Journal of Transitional Justice* 2(3): 266–91.

Minear, R. (1971) *Victor's Justice: The Tokyo War Crimes Trial*, Princeton, NJ: Princeton University Press.

O'Keefe, R. (2009) Review of R. Cryer *et al.* (eds) *International Criminal Law* (2007), *International and Comparative Law Quarterly* 58(2): 485.

Orford, A. (2012) 'In Praise of Description', *Leiden Journal of International Law* 25: 609–25.

Orzeck, R. (2012) 'International Criminal Trials as Bourgeois Theatre', paper presented at the Workshop on New Marxist Writing in International Law, City University, London.

Pashukanis, E. (1978 [1924]) *Law and Marxism: A General Theory*, London: Ink Links.

Phillimore, Lord (1922–23) 'An International Criminal Court and the Resolutions of the Committee of Jurists', *British Yearbook of International Law* 3: 79.

PICT Report (Project on International Courts and Tribunals) (n.d.) 'The Financing of the International Criminal Court – A discussion paper'. Available at: www.pict-pcti.org/publications/ICC_paprs/FinancingICC.pdf.

Ramasastry, A. (2002) 'Corporate Complicity: From Nuremberg to Rangoon – An Examination of Forced Labour Cases and their Impact on the Liability of Multinational Corporations', *Berkeley Journal of International Law* 20: 91.

Ratner, S., Abrams, J. and Bischoff, J. (2009) *Accountability for Human Rights Atrocities in International Law: Beyond the Nuremberg Legacy*, 3rd edn, Oxford: Oxford University Press.

Roht-Arriaza, N. (2013) 'Just a "Bubble"? Perspectives on the Enforcement of International Criminal Law by National Courts', *Journal of International Criminal Justice* 11(3): 537–43.

Schabas, W. (2007) *An Introduction to the International Criminal Court*, Cambridge: Cambridge University Press.

Schabas, W. (2013) 'The Banality of International Justice', *Journal of International Criminal Justice* 11(3): 545–51.

Schachter, O. (1977) 'The Invisible College of International Lawyers', *Northwestern University Law Review* 72: 217.

Schmitt, C. (2007) *The Concept of the Political*, expanded edn, University of Chicago Press.

Schwarzenberger, G. (1946–47) 'The Judgment of Nuremberg', *Tulane Law Review* 21: 351.

Schwarzenberger, G. (1950) 'The Problem of an International Criminal Law', *Current Legal Problems* 3: 263.

Scott, S. (1994) 'International Law as Ideology: Theorizing the Relationship between International Law and International Politics', *European Journal of International Law* 5: 1.

Shamir, R. (2008) 'The Age of Responsibilization: On Market-Embedded Morality', *Economy and Society* 37(1): 1.

Soederberg, S. (2010) *Corporate Power and Ownership in Contemporary Capitalism: The Politics of Resistance and Domination*, London: Routledge.

Spicer, A. and G. Baars (eds) (2015 forthcoming) *The Corporation: A Critical, Interdisciplinary Handbook*, Cambridge: Cambridge University Press.

Steiner, H.J. and Alston, P. (2007) *International Human Rights in Context*, 3rd edn, Oxford: Oxford University Press.

Stewart, J. (2012) 'A Pragmatic Critique of Corporate Criminal Theory: Lessons from the Extremity', NYU School of Law, Public Law Research Paper No. 12–54.

Tallgren, I. (2002) 'The Sensibility and Sense of International Criminal Law', *European Journal of International Law* 13(3) 561.

Taylor, T. (1992) *The Anatomy of the Nuremberg Trials*, London: Bloomsbury.

Triffterer, O. (2008) *Commentary on the Rome Statute of the International Criminal Court*, Nomos Verlagsgesellschaft.

Van Sliedregt, E. (2003) *The Criminal Liability of Individuals for Violations of International Humanitarian Law*, The Hague: TMC Asser Press.

Vitzthum, W. (2010) 'Begriff, Geschichte und Rechtsquellen des Völkerrechts', in W. Vitzthum (ed.) *Völkerrecht*, Berlin: Gruyter Recht.

Weber, M. (1982) *General Economic History*, New York: Transaction.

Werle, G. (2007) *Völkerstrafrecht*, Mohr Siebeck Gmbh & Co.

Werle, G. (2009) *Principles of International Criminal Law*, The Hague: TMC Asser Press.

Part IV

The visible and the invisible in international criminal law

Chapter 10

International criminal law and individualism

An African perspective

Christopher Gevers

Introduction

This chapter considers the prevalence within the international criminal law project and surrounding discourse of 'individualism' – in terms of its *methodology* (the 'construction of the individual as the central unit of action': Drumbl 2007: 5), its *narrative* and the *ends* it seeks to achieve – and the consequences of this for concerns raised by African states in relation to the project. It will do so by exploring the influence that this 'individualism' (broadly construed) has on three aspects of the field – its histories, the question of purpose, and its 'performance'.

First, when one considers ICL's relationship with history – both in terms of its own history and the histories it 'produces' – the individual is at its centre. The mainstream history of the field is very much the history of the individual: both a history of individuals and a history of the rise of *the individual* within international law. This individualized account of ICL's history has a number of significant consequences. From an African perspective, these include side-lining or downplaying the historical failure of ICL to address colonial crimes, as well as the misrepresentation of the complex relationship between ICL and sovereignty in a manner that conceals both its hegemonic tendencies and emancipatory potential (Mégret 2002: 1279). Similarly, when international courts and tribunals produce histories they are often reductionist, linear and *individualistic*, displaying a tendency to 'emphasize individual agency over structural causation' (Simpson, Chapter 7 in this volume).

Second, individualism is also at the centre of the dominant discourses on why 'we' punish international crimes – by 'we' I mean we the 'faithful', not we the 'dangerous heretics' (Tallgren, Chapter 3 in this volume) – which Drumbl terms the 'quest for purpose' (2007: 149). The two main schools of thought with regard to ICL's purpose – retribution and deterrence – are predicated on the assumption of the individual as an autonomous moral agent, despite ample evidence that atrocities might require a more complex conception of agency. The problems with these purposes are well known, but here I would like to further explore these problems in light of concerns raised by African states specifically.

Third, given this focus on the individual in the field's history and 'quest for purpose', it is not surprising that when it comes to measuring (and calibrating) the 'performance' of international criminal courts there is a tendency to prefer the field's individual objectives over the broader ones that are often ascribed to it (such as promoting peace and human rights), while at the same time eschewing broader concerns regarding the ICL project.

Before going further it is important to qualify the aims of this chapter, and the claims it is making (and not making). In broad terms, the aim is to demonstrate some of the ways in which that what we might call the 'politics of individualism' blunts, misrepresents, distorts or dismisses concerns about international criminal law that have been raised by African states, or that are particularly relevant from an African perspective. The term 'politics' is used very cautiously here. The claim that ICL is political is no longer the heresy it was a decade ago – on the contrary, it is now an article of faith among many 'critical' international criminal lawyers. However, this acknowledgement of the political nature of ICL works in different ways and at different levels, and its effects on our understandings of the field still have to be worked through and systematized. This chapter is not about this important endeavour (for a beginning of this see Krever, Chapter 5 in this volume).

So, while individualism might be appropriately considered as the 'dominant metanarrative of international criminal law' (Drumbl 2005b: 103), no attempt is made here to set out the 'meta-politics' of the field. Liberalism (of some variant: liberal-legalism, or liberal-cosmopolitanism) is the generally accepted front-runner, but it is possible to give liberalism too much credit for the project. In all likelihood the 'field' is an amalgam of a number of different political projects – both high and low: it is a broad church. No single political project can arguably take credit for ICL, although that does not stop liberalism from trying (Mégret 2002: 1271). Nor is it clear that a single, meta-politics for the field is required, or desired. As Simpson notes, 'a fully coherent theory of politics or a maximally or comprehensively legitimate form of politics will tend towards totalitarianism' (Simpson 2012: 125).

Perhaps it is better, then, to describe this chapter *minimally* as a set of concerns, or even inclinations, about international criminal law from an African perspective arranged around the theme of individualism; where individualism might have been replaced by a number of other themes, such as progress, identity, hegemony.[1]

The histories of international criminal law

Histories are at the heart of the international criminal law project. Since their establishment, international courts and tribunals have been implicated in the creation of official histories, and have been the sites for the explication (and defence) of unofficial ones. Similarly, although they tend not to acknowledge it, international lawyers themselves 'do history' (Skouteris 2012), and international criminal lawyers are no different.

There is of course more than one way in which 'the relationship between international law and "history" … [can be] conceived' (Craven 2006: 6). Applying Craven's three categories to international criminal law, one might (a) write a *history of criminal international law* which will take the form of 'a history mapped out in terms of its trajectory or teleology; a history written in narrative form that provides a story about its origins, development, progress or renewal'. Alternatively (b), one might address the question of *history in criminal international law*, concerning 'the place that historical events or persona occupy within substantive discussions of law, and of the role they play in arguments about law itself'. Finally (c), there is the broader question of *international criminal law in history*, which considers 'how international law, or international lawyers have been engaged, or involved themselves, in the creation of a history that … stands outside the history of international [criminal] law itself' (2006: 6).[2] The argument made below is that individualism shapes all the named classifications of the ICL-history dynamic: both the histories of the 'field', and the broader history it 'produces' are individualistic (and this has consequences for African concerns in particular).

History I: histories of international criminal law

Concerns about the histories *of* international criminal law relate to the manner in which international criminal lawyers and academics record or represent the history of ICL as a 'discipline'. It is worth pointing out at the outset that international criminal lawyers enjoy considerable flexibility in this endeavour: when 'we' recount or represent our history we are free to choose what to remember and what to forget, and how we do so (what is emphasized, and sublimated); we can even rely on *passé* 'grand narratives'. A brief survey of the mainstream histories of international criminal law reveal them to be, among other things, rooted in individualism. That is to say that the 'official history' of the field is very much the history of the individual. It is both a history of 'individuals' (Eichmann, Barbie, Milosevic), and a history of *the individual* within international law (Simpson 2007: 55). Within this narrative, the coming of age of international criminal law is nothing less than a moment of triumph: of individuals (human rights) over the collective (sovereignty); of (international) law over politics. It may even represent a moment of redemption, if not completion, of international law as it 'anticipates the future enforceability of … [its] norms' (2007: 55).

International criminal law's association with the other 'individualist' projects of international law (chiefly, human rights law) is represented differently within these histories. Sometimes it is incidental, as part of international law's broader progressivist trajectory: its 'inbuilt moral direction to make human rights, justice and peace universal' (Koskenniemi 2012: 4). At other times it is instrumental, where ICL is *part of* the larger human rights discourse (Robertson 1999). For others, ICL emerges out of usefully less normative 'laws of war' – which themselves have ostensibly undergone an 'individualization' of sorts, at least rhetorically (Meron 2000).

A key feature of this individualist narrative is the purging (perhaps once and for all) of sovereignty: the '*bête-noire* of the international criminal lawyer' (Cryer 2005: 980). In this struggle the stakes could not be higher, Mégret characterizes these histories thus: 'Global justice is a struggle that pits human rights, overwhelmingly associated with justice, against the hypocrisy of sovereignty, "the traditional enemy of the human rights movement"' (Mégret 2002: 1266). Notably, histories of this sort often rely an unstated enthusiasm for a cosmopolitan legal order, 'or at least, significantly, on the categorical imperative to act as if a cosmopolis were realizable' (Mégret 2001: 259).

There is much to suggest that these individualistic histories of international criminal law are significantly foreshortened. Notwithstanding the 'individualism that lies at the heart of much international justice rhetoric' (Simpson 2007: 58), its past is littered with collective moments and projects. Simpson has sketched out the 'hidden' collective moments of the field's history (2007: 58). These include the recurring question of collective punishment, which emerges at Versailles in 1919, where the failed attempt at individual punishment (Articles 228–30, Treaty of Versailles) was overshadowed by the collective financial, military and political punishment imposed on the German state (and the German people). While Nuremberg – the 'birth certificate' of international criminal law proper – represented the successful individual punishment of the Nazi leadership, the spectre of collective punishment remained through the punishment of the German people once again at Potsdam (Simpson 2007). Since then the idea of collective punishment has been a recurring, inconvenient contradiction to the pursuit of individual justice, through, *inter alia*, debates regarding 'state crimes', spearheaded by the International Law Commission (ILC). While this formal notion of collective punishment was recently purged (it seems) with the abandonment of the notion of state crimes by the ILC, as discussed below it may well survive in other forms (Simpson 2007; Mégret 2001).

What is more, the trials that did take place were not just about punishing individuals; there were broader projects at play. Nuremberg, for example, in addition to discrediting the Nazis as individuals, was designed to 'discredit their particular philosophy of racial supremacy' (Matua 1997: 170–1), and arguably to exculpate the German people as a whole so that they may participate in the reconstruction of Europe – a task that would have been complicated if 'the trials satanized the German people as a whole and painted the evils they committed as symptomatic of a national, genetic pathology' (Ibid.). Such concerns were also implicated in who was *not* tried, as Koskenniemi notes: 'The failure of the Allied powers to agree on a "trial of industrialists" may have reflected emerging concern in the West about the appearance of a new enemy – the Soviet Union – and the need to enlist a democratic Germany on their side' (2002: 14). Finally, Nuremberg was (for the few remaining idealists at least) also about the pursuit of peace. These collective projects re-emerge in the project in the interceding half-decade that separates 'Tokyoberg' from Rome; not just at an international level, but also at a domestic level as well in the trials of Eichmann in Jerusalem and Barbie in France, among others. Even the establishment of the International Criminal Court – perhaps the final victory of the *individual* Nuremberg model over the *collective* Versailles model of punishment (Simpson 2007) – did not purge the collective instincts from the field. The principle of complementarity – whereby states are afforded 'primacy' over the ICC when it comes to prosecuting international crimes on certain conditions (Article 17, Rome Statute) – has been applied (both formally and rhetorically) as a trial of a state's capacity to dispense justice (a key function of a modern, democratic state it seems). The two states that have invoked complementarity to date (Kenya and Libya) have certainly seen it this way.

There is, of course, a lot to be said regarding the individualization of the history of ICL, and the suppression of its collective moments and projects, some of which is discussed elsewhere in this collection (see Simpson, Chapter 7). I wish to focus on two sets of consequences or concerns of particular relevance to Africa and African states. First, the individualist narrative downplays (or in its extreme form displaces) the historical failings of ICL, both specific and structural. International criminal lawyers fall prey to 'the seductive tendency to sprinkle the past with some revisionism to make the past conform to contemporary understandings of how it ought to look' (Drumbl 2005b: 105). Individualism is a key part of this narrative; it gives the field a simple yet powerful teleology – punishing evil individuals – that downplays aspects of the field's past that fall outside of this. One of the 'victims' of these hagiographic histories is a frank engagement with ICL's failure to address the countless atrocities committed under colonialism and during the decolonization process.

These dissident colonial histories begin with Justice Radhabinod Pal's fierce dissent at the International Military Tribunal for the Far East (IMTFE). Among other things, Justice Pal was concerned about the 'history of colonial domination by the Western powers' (Wei 2007: 220). In this vein, Justice Pal questioned the 'moral authority of Great Britain, a colonial power, to pass judgement on the defeated colonial policies of Japan' (Maga 2001: 66). He also took issue with the purpose of the post-war trials, which were designed to 'ensure that the frontiers created by the original sin of colonial misdistribution would remain fixed by the legitimating force of an international rule of law' (Simpson 2007: 147).[3] For Pal, the 'problem of colonialism' went to the very heart of what the nascent international criminal justice system was trying to achieve. Justice Pal's anti-colonial tome was formally hidden from the offical history of the project for a number of years by virtue of General MacArthur's ban on reading dissenting judgments in court, let alone released for public consumption. However, as it was then outside of the formal jurisdiction of the IMTFE, it remains now outside the individualist imagination of the mainstream histories of the field.

The *unwritten* dissent at Nuremberg was not as much about the colonial past as about the colonial present. As Matua notes:

> The irony of Nuremberg, and the White men who created it, was that the adjudicating states either condoned (or practiced as official policy) their own versions of racial mythologies: Britain and France violently put down demands for independence in 'their' colonies in Africa and Asia while the United States denied its citizens of African descent basic human rights.
>
> (Matua 1997: 170–1)

The uncomfortable question of 'colonial crimes' again emerged during the trials of Second World War crimes in France four decades later. The Barbie trial, at the instigation of the defence, became about 'colonialism and France's moral standing' (Kaplan 1992: 79). Recently, the 'cognitive dissonance' among international criminal lawyers regarding the field's relation to colonialism resulted in yet another reminder of colonial crimes – this time at the insistence of fate – going relatively unnoticed. In October 2012, the very same week that six Kenyans were making their first appearance in The Hague on charges of crimes against humanity, another group of Kenyans were appearing in the High Court in London seeking some measure of justice for the crimes committed against them by British forces during the brutal suppression of the Mau Mau uprising over half a decade ago (see generally Elkins 2005). Their justice was consigned to a claim for collective reparation and therefore not the business of ICL, and not part of its history; it passed quietly without remark.

One might consider – in a somewhat circular manner – the failure to comprehend colonial crimes as part of the history of ICL as a failure not just of law, but also of 'history'. To my mind at least, while the crimes committed under colonialism are widely known, they are seldom represented as crimes of *individuals*. If, then, ICL produces histories that stand outside of itself – and histories of atrocities are (to paraphrase Simpson) part-historian, part-tribunal (Simpson, Chapter 7 in this volume) – then ICL is both the cause and the effect of the failure to conceive of colonial crimes as individual crimes.

Be that as it may, for now colonialism remains a collective sin, for which many are and nobody is responsible, for which law has offered very little expiation, and ICL nothing. Leaving aside the more challenging question of why ICL has not addressed colonial crimes, the continued failure to acknowledge this within mainstream histories is in part a result of the individualist narrative outlined above.

A footnote to this is the issue of apartheid – which is ineluctably linked to colonialism – where the failure to subject crimes (quite literally defined as crimes against humanity) to the rigours of ICL, far from being glossed over, is celebrated both within South Africa's rainbow nation rhetoric (although not without challenge: see the South African Constitutional Court case of *AZAPO v The President of South Africa* 1996 (4) SA 672), and the broader 'transitional justice' field. The reasons for this relatively recent exception to the 'no peace without justice' refrain, and its broad acceptance, are beyond the scope of this chapter, but one gets the sense that they are not flattering for ICL and its supporters when considered in light of the above critique.

A second concern arising from the individualization of the history of ICL is the manner in which it downplays or misrepresents the role that sovereignty has played in constituting the field (and *vice versa*). As noted above, the mainstream history of ICL often characterizes its development as a gradual triumph of individualism over sovereignty. In this narrative sovereignty is maligned, if not caricatured. As Cryer notes:

> When sovereignty appears in international criminal law scholarship, it commonly comes clothed in hat and cape. A whiff of sulphur permeates the air. Generally, international criminal law scholars see sovereignty as the enemy. It is seen as the sibling of *realpolitik*, thwarting international criminal justice at every turn.
>
> (Cryer 2005: 980–1)

At the extremes of this view, sovereignty (in the guise of sovereign immunity) functions simply to afford 'protection to rulers who loot or otherwise misappropriate vast sums of public money'.

Histories of this sort share a disturbingly 'unsophisticated concept of sovereignty' (Mégret 2002: 1279). In fact, the relationship between sovereignty and ICL is far more complex than this narrative suggests. As a starting point, ICL owes much to sovereignty for its historical development and continued operation. At an institutional level, '[w]ithout sovereignty there are no courts, and without courts there are no prosecutions' (Cryer 2005: 987). Substantively, 'international criminal law is not a body of law that has fallen from on high fully formed, but is the outcome of political contestation', and the exercise of sovereignty (2005: 989). Specific crimes, like aggression, far from representing the abrogation of sovereignty, punish its violation. The casual relationship between international crimes and sovereignty is equally complex; as Cryer has pointed out: 'An excess of sovereignty and state power can lead to international crimes, as in the Holocaust, but so can a lack of sovereign authority, as in Somalia or Sierra Leone' (2005: 1000). In one sense at least ICL plays a redeeming role in relation to sovereignty – by condemning the incorrect exercise thereof. As Mégret notes:

> [I]f it is indeed *individuals* who commit international crimes (and, for all Nuremberg's premonition, that fact has only become more clear both legally and as a matter of our world view in recent years), this also means that it is not, at least in any useful way, *abstract entities* that go on committing them simultaneously.
>
> (Mégret 2001: 263)

At best, then, a more considered history of sovereignty reveals that it has played an 'ambivalent' and 'multifaceted' role in the development of ICL, and continues to do so (Cryer 2005: 1000). At worst, this 'unsophisticated' version of sovereignty is not just incomplete; it sublimates both its historical relationship to hegemony (and colonialism, see Anghie 2005), as well as its 'emancipatory potential' (Mégret 2002: 1279). It relies on a construction of sovereignty as a stable, universal concept – all states are equally affected by its gradual demise or dilution by ICL. However, if one adopts a broader view of ICL's history – one that reintroduces its collective moments – and a more sophisticated construction of sovereignty, the history of ICL's relationship to sovereignty looks vastly different.

According to one version, ICL has historically played an important part in the creation and maintenance of hierarchy in the international order. According to Simpson, this hierarchy is created and maintained through 'juridical sovereignty', which is 'constructed around an interaction between sovereign equality and two legal forms in which distinctions between states are mandated and authorized': anti-pluralism and legalized hegemony (Simpson 2004: 6). Both are implicated in the broader history of international criminal law.

International criminal law has (both formally and rhetorically) been instrumental in the designation of 'outlaw states'. The formal designation of outlaw states in ICL takes the form of collective criminalization, beginning at Versailles, re-emerging at Potsdam and then institutionalized in the protracted and divisive discussion regarding the notion of 'state crimes'. While the notion has been formally abandoned, the criminalization of states survives in other forms (for example, the *de facto* criminalization of Iraq and Libya by the Security Council), and within much of the rhetoric surrounding ICL. The designation of 'outlaw states' in ICL has also taken place more subtly – but to equal effect – through 'anti-pluralism' (Simpson 2004: 6). Historically, this has been done through the use of human rights as the proverbial 'standard of civilization', in terms of which states that do not meet a set of ostensibly objective criteria are not afforded (or forfeit) certain privileges associated with sovereignty (2004: 6). Increasingly, the enforcement of international criminal law has become the yardstick against which states are measured and sovereign privilege is granted or revoked (see, for one, complementarity). One might suggest that increasingly international crimes are doing the rhetorical work that the notions of human rights and development can no longer undertake as effectively after years of sustained critique.

Equally, international criminal law has been (and still is) implicated in the perpetuation of the 'legalized hegemony' of the Great Powers. Consider the role that the UN Security Council has played in the project (the creation and delimitation of the *ad hoc* Tribunals for the former Yugoslavia and Rwanda) and continues to play (the role the Security Council plays in the ICC: Articles 13 and 16, Rome Statute). Within the contemporary practice of the Great Powers (both inside and if needs be outside the Security Council), international criminal law is one part of a set of tools that includes the 'mere exercise of military and economic power' (Tallgren 2002: 590). The latest example of this is Libya (see Security Council Resolutions 1970 and 1973), where the 'ICC intervention helped transform the outcome in Libya by contributing to the delegitimisation of the Gaddafi regime' (Sands 2011).

African states have been increasingly aware (and critical) of both these anti-pluralistic and hegemonic potentials of the ICC, and the international criminal justice project generally. For example, Kenya's 2011 complementarity-based admissibility challenges before the ICC were directed as much, if not more, at defending the Kenyan state and its new Constitution as they were at the legally relevant question of what steps Kenya had taken towards pursuing justice for 2007 post-electoral violence;[4] as were the statements made in support of Kenya's efforts by the African Union. Similarly, the African Union's complaints regarding the referral of Sudan and Libya to the ICC by the Security Council have been equally about the 'injustice' of the P5 prerogative, and the resultant immunity they and their allies enjoy, as they were about the specifics of those situations. In addition to complaints regarding direct targeting of African countries by the Security Council, questions have been raised about the manner in which 'the loose criteria for picking defendants ("gravity") invariably appear to be in the eyes of the beholder and take international criminal justice's gaze away from the West and onto Africa' (Mégret 2013: 24). Beyond the ICC, concerns have been raised about the perceived abuse of ICL by states acting independently and in particular the manner in which 'transnational judicial flows typically follow a North South route, often one strangely reminiscent of former colonial paths' (2013: 23). The African Union has been voicing concerns since 2008, on a regular basis, regarding the perceived abuse of the 'Principle of Universal Jurisdiction' by states generally and European states in particular. African states' indignation peaked in 2011 when the AU adopted a decision requesting its member states to 'apply the principle of reciprocity' in respect of countries that had instituted proceedings against African State officials (i.e. France, Belgium and Spain) and – with the assistance of other African states – institute criminal proceedings against the officials of such states in response (see *Decision on the*

Abuse of the Principle of Universal Jurisdiction, January 2011, AU Doc. EX. CL/640(XVIII)).[5]

Arguments about the ICL-sovereignty dynamic also move in the other direction. Sovereignty is not just at the disposal of the powerful; it has 'emancipatory potential' as both 'a framework for the polity's organization' and 'a bulwark against imperialism' (Mégret 2002: 1279). Notably, African states have utilized (or attempted to utilize) international criminal law to trigger both sovereignty's anti-imperialist and constitutive potentials.

African states have tried to employ ICL to protect sovereignty's potential as a 'bulwark against imperialism' through their persistent attempts to include aggression in the jurisdiction of the ICC (Du Plessis and Gevers 2010a). When it came to defining aggression in Kampala in 2010, the common African position was to get rid of the proposed hegemonic prerogative of the UN Security Council to determine when an act of aggression had taken place (Du Plessis and Gevers 2010a). They have also tried to purge the ICC of one of its existing hegemonic prerogatives through an amendment to the Rome Statute that would dilute the power of the Security Council to defer matters under Article 16, by granting the General Assembly a residual power to do so (Du Plessis and Gevers 2010b). The relationship goes both ways; recent discussions to establish an 'African Criminal Court' might be viewed as an attempt to employ sovereignty to protect the ICL project generally (and African states) from its own imperialistic tendencies or potential, or at least the ICC's.

African states (as well as others) have also attempted to utilize ICL as a (if not *the*) constitutive element of sovereignty. For example, in its admissibility challenge before the ICC, the new Libyan government noted: 'The NTC emerged from a liberation struggle against the tyranny of the Muammar Gaddafi regime ... Its *raison d'être* is to ensure justice for the victims of State-sponsored human rights abuses and to usher in a new era of democracy and prosperity for the Libyan people.' In extolling the virtues of the revolution and its political progeny – the new Libyan state – the applicants were creating and sustaining a broader narrative about legitimacy of that state. ICL, then, is a site of both the 'destruction' and 'reconstruction' of sovereignty.

The relationship between sovereignty and ICL is and will remain highly contested and certainly 'not easily reducible to shibboleths on either side' (Cryer 2005: 1000). At the very least the above examples reveal a far more complicated picture of the ICL-sovereignty dynamic than the mainstream individualist histories of the field suggest. That picture is further complicated by recent studies on the historical relationship between sovereignty and colonialism, and its continuing effects (see Anghie 2005). What is clear is that, for African states, sovereignty remains central to the ICJ project. The historical narrative of the triumph of the individual over some highly caricatured version of sovereignty misses all of this, with significant consequences for African complaints. Concerns regarding sovereignty's role in ICL, and ICL's role in the perpetuation of geopolitical hierarchy, are seen as outmoded or retrogressive when set against this history. Worse still, invocations of sovereignty are seen as political – understood to be nothing less than summoning the devil himself or herself (Cryer 2005: 1000).

History II: doing 'justice' to history

International courts and tribunals have been implicated in the production of histories from the project's outset. Oftentimes these histories share the characteristics of international law histories generally in that they are linear, progressive, totalizing, positivist and hegemonic – with a humanizing/civilizing *telos* (see Skouteris 2012; Koskenniemi 2012). Here the distinction between Craven's second and third categorizations of the law/history dynamic becomes more blurred. In adjudicating international crimes generally courts are required to delve into some form of historicizing – often in terms of establishing the contextual elements of the crime, which 'calls for a broader optic in which individual conduct must be assessed in the light of activity carried out by organizations or groups in specific settings, sometimes over extended periods of time' (Damaska 2008: 336). This is most appropriately located in Craven's 'history in international criminal law' category as it concerns 'the place that historical events or persona occupy within substantive discussions of law'. However, these contextual enquiries can easily descend (or ascend – depending on one's perspective) into broader enquiries. As Damaska notes: 'Judges are thus driven to engage in broad fact findings that easily shade into historical inquiries' (2008: 336). To the extent that these are attempts to construct histories that 'stand outside the history of international law itself' they belong in Craven's third category: 'international law in history'. That said, both of these historical accounts are implicated in individualism and – in particular – the tendency to 'emphasize individual agency over structural causation' (Simpson, Chapter 7 in this volume).

Before considering this in more detail, it is worth pointing out that as long as they have been doing so, international courts and tribunals have been criticized for their historicizing, on both principled and methodological grounds. The liberal legalist critique of this is that courts should not do history because it is not their job; history is not 'legally relevant'. The most famous critic of this variety is Hannah Arendt, who insisted: 'Justice demands that the accused be prosecuted, defended and judged, and that all other questions of seemingly greater import … be left in abeyance' (Arendt 1963: 5). For others, international criminal law generally is simply 'bad' at history-telling – whether thick or thin – an accusation which has been levelled by both lawyers and historians. For example, Wilson (2011), writing from the perspective of the historian, 'finds much evidence to support a critical view of law's ability to write history'. The ability of historians to produce 'good' history is left unscathed by Wilson's critique. Similarly, Damaska (a lawyer) puts forward a number of more forgiving, predominantly institutional, reasons why international criminal courts produce poor histories; these include time constraints, legal doctrine, burdens of proof and the adversarial nature of (some) criminal trials (2008: 335–8). A hidden assumption of both these sets of concerns is that 'good' history is not just possible, but desirable. In this regard Skouteris notes that 'concerns about poor quality history are only meaningful against the backdrop of the claim that historiography, if done well, yields knowledge the accretion of which incrementally improves our collective skills in social engineering or our approximation to truth' (2012: 101).

These criticisms and questions, while important, need not detain us here. We are less concerned with whether international criminal law *ought* 'do history', and more with 'what sorts of histories are international criminal tribunals creating?' (Simpson, Chapter 7 in this volume).[6] As Simpson discusses in his contribution to this collection, the question of 'how to do history' emerged at length at the project's inception, when historiographical disputes emerged among the members of the Commission on the Responsibilities of the Authors of the War. Among other things, the representatives at Versailles grappled with the problem of 'individual agency in history', with some raising questions as to 'whether in the case of war – the hard case of criminal liability – there could *ever* be a question of personal responsibility' (Simpson 2012: 132). The Commission ultimately adopted a diffident position on the question of 'individual agency in history' (2012: 132). Since Versailles, this circumspection has long since yielded to zealous embrace of 'individual agency in history' by courts and within the surrounding discourse, with few exceptions (see however, Simpson 2012: 132–3). This methodological bias continues to dominate and define the histories produced by the project.

Some level of individualism might be inevitable. As Simpson notes: 'international criminal justice must, by definition, be wedded to the idea that men make their own history of their own choosing … No theory of individual criminal responsibility could live without it' (Simpson, Chapter 7 in this volume). However, while this might be true of the 'thin' histories that are required for establishing criminal responsibility, the same cannot be said of the broader (or 'thick') histories produced by courts and tribunals. Should courts choose to stray into areas of historical enquiry that are not strictly necessary for the purposes of establishing individual responsibility, they are arguably free to adopt a more pluralistic approach that is not so wedded to individualism, and takes into account structural accounts of history. Nor does this explain the persistence of the 'Great Man theory' identified by Simpson, in terms of which history is not just made by individuals, but by particular individuals (Simpson 2012: 133).[7]

Whatever its etiology, this individualism has significant consequences, three of which will be discussed briefly. First, individualization renders incomplete accounts of conflicts, that not only emphasize the role of individuals but, by implication, de-emphasize the role of other causes of conflict. As Koskenniemi notes, 'individualization is not neutral in its effects. Use of terms such as "Hitlerism" or "Stalinism" leaves intact the political, moral and organizational structures that are the necessary condition of the crime' (2002: 14). In doing so it misrepresents, and possibly even sublimates, the role of structural forces such as economic reforms (and disparities), geographical factors, political instability, social marginalization and, more pertinently, colonial borders and institutions. This notwithstanding plenty of evidence that these factors play an important, if not determinative, role in modern conflicts. In this regard, African states have for some time complained about the under-inclusiveness of the crimes currently prosecuted in ICL. Notably, the draft statute for a proposed 'African International Criminal Court' includes crimes of a commercial nature (corruption, money laundering, financing mercenarism, and the illicit exploitation of natural resources) among its provisions (see *Draft Protocol on Amendments to the Protocol on the Statute of the African Court of Justice and Human Rights* (May 2012), EXP/Min/IV/Rev. 7). Furthermore, African civil society representatives recently called for more attention to be paid to 'economic actors and economic crimes', noting that '[n]on-state actors, including corporate and commercial actors, in Africa have been complicit in mass atrocities', and calling on states to 'promote reform of mechanisms of accountability for mass atrocities to ensure that such entities are held accountable' ('Promoting Accountability for International Crimes in Africa' 2013).

This bias has serious implications for the questions of ICL's purposes; it exculpates – as a matter of both legal and historical record – these other drivers of conflict. What is more, as in Africa many of these structural conditions can be linked back to colonialism and its remnants, it puts further distance between ICL and its colonial reckoning. As Drumbl notes:

> The ICTR's judicial reductionism absolves the role of international agencies, transnational economic processes, the foreign policies of influential states, *and colonial policies*, each of which exacerbated ethnic conflict by creating an environment conducive to violence in Rwanda.
>
> (Drumbl 2005b: 119)

This, in turn, raises questions about legitimacy; the failure to address colonialism is not just a matter of historical record, it is causal. Furthermore, if the history of the Rwandan genocide is 'linked ineluctably with the findings of the [ICTR]' (Simpson, Chapter 7 in this volume), then the failure to consider its broader causes lets colonialism 'off the hook' not only legally but historically as well.

Second, to the extent that ICL aims to create a broader history outside of itself – a historical account of modern mass atrocities – these other histories and atrocities are not just sidelined; they are hidden. ICL's universal pretences lead to a totalizing history: atrocities that weren't prosecuted didn't happen. Similarly, other forms of suffering that are structurally excluded from ICL's focus are 'displaced'. For example, hundreds of thousands of preventable deaths that are the result of lack of access to lifesaving medicine or famine are 'understood as accidents', not crimes (Simpson, Chapter 7 in this volume).

Finally, as Simpson states in his chapter, mainstream ICL histories may reveal a 'tendency to write histories that somehow accord with the political requirements of the Great Powers' (Simpson, Chapter 7). In so doing, they sideline concerns about the international system – 'where the distribution of power, goods and advantage is so vastly, indefensibly and asymmetrically skewed, where the law is largely written by and on behalf of a powerful minority of states' (Simpson, Chapter 7) – and about international law. In this regard these histories work against the projects of reform of both the international system and international law that African states have been pursuing since their independence.

Individualism and the 'quest for purpose'

Individualism also permeates international criminal law's (still ongoing) 'quest for purpose': on which international criminal lawyers have arguably spent scandalously little time (Drumbl 2007). Over the years a number of 'purposes' have been thrown out, almost casually, not all of which are compatible (Damaska 2008). These range from the classic domestic criminal law goals of retribution, deterrence (general and specific), incapacitation and rehabilitation, to new, more ambitious ones, such as the creation of 'a reliable historical record of the context of international crime', 'giving voice to international crime's many victims', 'promoting human rights values', and 'stopping an ongoing conflict' (Damaska 2008: 331).

However, the two most oft-cited purposes of ICL – and those formally focused on by courts and in texts – remain the classic domestic purposes of retribution ('to punish because the criminal deserves it') and deterrence ('to punish to prevent future crime'); which are employed both as self-standing justifications and in concert (Drumbl 2007: 149). Notably, both of these putative purposes of ICL are premised on an individualized account of agency: 'on a construction of the individual as the central unit of action'; ICL aims to punish *individuals* for agency-based crimes, or *deter* other individuals from committed similar crimes. As Drumbl notes: 'This means that a number of selected guilty individuals squarely are to be blamed for systemic levels of group violence' (Drumbl 2005a: 542). This is so despite evidence that atrocities might require a more complex conception of agency (Drumbl 2005a; Tallgren 2002; Koskenniemi 2002). Aside from the general assumption of individual agency, scholars have identified a number of more specific difficulties with both the dominant 'retributive' and 'deterrent' aspirations of international criminal law.

First, there is the recurring problem of *selectivity* – both in terms of perpetrators and the causes of conflict that are prosecuted. In respect of those targeted for prosecution, 'prosecuting only a small number of individuals in cases of massive levels of violence leads to a very partial print of justice' (Drumbl 2007: 153), whatever the causes thereof. Then, as far as the causes of conflict are concerned, with no attention being paid to structural factors – such as 'deeply globalized forces, including acts and omissions of international agents and foreign governments' (2007: 153) – the result will be that 'only some evil gets punished, whereas much escapes its grasp, often for political reasons anathema to Kantian deontology' (2007: 151).

As far as 'purposes' go, retribution is also problematic for reasons of *proportionality*. In this regard Drumbl notes: 'If the retributive value of punishing extraordinary international criminals truly were to be engaged, perhaps punishment would have to exceed anything ordinary' (2007: 157). As a result, 'proportionate sentences then might involve torture or reciprocal group elimination' (2007: 157). It is almost impossible to imagine a punishment that fits certain international crimes and still remains within the bounds of (liberal) human rights standards, which 'cabin the parameters of sanction' (Drumbl 2007). Here the individualist projects of modern international law – ICL and human rights – collide: it is impossible to truly hold individuals responsible (in a proportionate sense) without violating the very principles upon which ICL is based, and possibly from whence it springs forth (see Robinson 2010).

Finally, retribution raises the question of *moral authority*. If retribution 'emanates from morals' (Tallgren 2002: 591), then the question becomes what morals (or whose) are being enforced and in whose name? Where do international courts and tribunals receive the moral authority to punish from: sovereignty, cosmopolis, humanity?

The deterrent aspirations of ICL run into similar difficulties. At first blush, deterrence appears to move away from the excessive focus on the individual to collective gains in the form of utility (for the lawyer, a welcome move away from the moral and religious undertones of retribution). However, empirical and conceptual problems soon emerge. For one there is little evidence to suggest that ICL deters in practice, or deters more effectively than other less cost-intensive exercises. While this might be put down to problems of 'application' – to be remedied by a better (uniform, definite, apolitical, universal, credible) system of ICL (Meron 1995) – the conceptual difficulties are more problematic. These problems are addressed more fully elsewhere (Tallgren 2002; Drumbl 2007); suffice it to point out a few challenges related specifically to the problem of individualism.

First, there is the assumption of *perpetrator rationality*, 'grounded in liberalism's treatment of the ordinary common criminal', which appears misplaced 'in the context of the chaos of massive violence, incendiary propaganda, and upended social order that contours atrocity' (Drumbl 2007: 171). As Mégret (2002) notes: 'It beggars belief to suggest that the average crazed nationalist purifier or abused child soldier ... will be deterred by the prospect of facing trial.' Second, if ICL's deterrent effect hinges on a prospective perpetrator refraining from acting out of fear of the negative consequences of his or her action, then the problems of *proportionality* and *selectivity* outlined above both undermine the likelihood of effective deterrence (Tallgren 2002: 575–6). Furthermore, to the extent that prevention relies on the perpetrator 'internalizing the moral values behind the punishment' (2002: 570), international crimes do not typically take place under the same conditions as 'ordinary' crimes; rather, 'the offender is likely to belong to a collective, sharing group values, possibly the same nationalistic ideology' (2002: 573). As a result, he or she 'may be less likely to break the group values than the criminal norms' (2002: 573). Here too, the failure of ICL to take into account the unique contexts and shared collective values at play in many international crimes renders it far less likely to achieve its stated deterrent effect in respect of such crimes. Finally, and once again, there is an assumption of individual agency on the part of the rational perpetrator who – either out of fear or punishment or having internalized the values – adjusts his or her behaviour accordingly. The multiple problems with the deterrent aspirations of ICL led Tallgren to conclude that 'the manner in which the "international criminal justice system" works now or could ever work in the future, measured in utilitarian terms, does not have much relevance for the *why* question' (2002: 590–1).

However, notwithstanding these difficulties, international criminal law (for the most part) remains wedded to retribution and deterrence as its dominant 'purposes'. This commitment, serious misgivings notwithstanding, has consequences relevant to concerns expressed by African states regarding ICL – a few of which I will briefly sketch out. First, the general absence of a broader more considered consensus on the purpose(s) of ICL curtails the possibilities for critique. It allows those wishing to defend ICL, or an instantiation thereof, to shift between the different purposes as they please. In this regard it is notable that while ICL is often 'sold' or 'marketed' with reference to multiple purposes, it is mostly defended in relation to individual ends of retribution (ending impunity or 'justice' for victims), not its collective end (truth-seeking, peace). Supporting and promoting ICL on the basis of a 'sensibility' (it just feels right) (Tallgren 2002) is far easier when its effects are far removed than when it has social and political costs (as it does for Africa).

Second, as far as the retributive aspirations are concerned, the three problems outlined above (selectivity, proportionality and moral basis) have particular relevance in light of African concerns about ICL. As far as *selectivity* is concerned, the 'retributive shortfall' of international criminal law squares with concerns raised consistently by African states. Under the current international criminal justice system, African states have consistently voiced concerns about the issue of selectivity of situations (all the current cases before the ICC are from Africa) and defendants (the failure to target a broader range of actors involved in the conflict). Even if these concerns can (partly) be explained (not justified) by structural reasons or tactical choices (Heller 2010), the fact remains that the retributive shortfall does not fall evenly across regions. What is more, it is worth pointing out that many of those who have been structurally excluded from this retributive net in respect of crimes committed in Africa (such as those who provided weapons or funded civil unrest in exchange for access to illicit resources) have done so from Western locales. However, the 'retributive shortfall' means that 'only a few people receive their just deserts while many powerful states and organizations avoid accountability' (Drumbl 2005b: 119). In light of this, to the extent that this concern leaves the retributive aspirations open to valid criticism, those criticisms are heightened in the case of Africa.

Notably, the current individualistic focus of ICL's retributive aspirations also sidelines other alternatives that might address this shortfall. In this regard Drumbl notes:

> Although it may seem counterintuitive, restorative justice modalities and institutions that push reintegrative shaming could in fact augment overall retribution by capturing a far greater number of individuals and organizations in the accountability process, albeit not to the severity of depth characteristic of the criminal conviction.
>
> (Drumbl 2007: 153)

Finally, questions about the moral basis of retribution are particularly important set against centuries of intervention in Africa in which morality (and law) has played no small part. Since the formal abandonment of the 'civilizing mission', noble ends such as ending slavery, then colonialism, then discrimination (and FGM) have all been employed as the basis for intervening in the affairs of African states. This is particular concerning given that manner in which 'transnational judicial flows typically follow a North–South route, often one strangely reminiscent of former colonial paths' (Mégret 2013: 23). What is more, it's worth remembering that the hidden 'anti-colonial' histories discussed above (Justice Pal, Barbie) specifically raised questions regarding the moral authority of the particular tribunal.

Given the preponderance of conflicts in Africa, the promise of international criminal law having a *deterrent* effect is not easily dismissed. However, the difficulty with consequentialist justifications for international criminal law is that they must actually achieve the results they aspire to – and as noted above there is some doubt that they do in fact do so (in part because of their excessive individualism), especially if there is a political, economic and social cost involved. This focus also sidelines – both indirectly and at times directly – other interventions aimed at addressing conflict. In addition, even if there is some effect to deterrence, the 'good' achieved must be greater than what might be achieved through other available means.

What is more, to the extent that the individualistic focus of ICL downplays other structural causes of conflict, its effects might well be the opposite to those desired (and advertised): it might exacerbate conflict. It leaves more structural causes of conflict intact, but assuages conscience of the international community that they have done all they can to address it. The Rwandan Security Council delegate alluded to this 'comforting' purpose when, in casting the only vote against the establishment of the ICTR, he noted: 'a tribunal as ineffective as this would only appease the conscience of the international community rather than respond to the expectations of the Rwandese people' (Goodman 2004).

Finally, it is worth briefly considering whether the purposes – slavishly taken from domestic criminal law and maintained despite significant questions – might serve as a distraction for another, more devious, end. Tallgren has previously suggested that 'the "rational and utilitarian" purposes of international criminal law could partly lie elsewhere than in the prevention and suppression of criminality' (Tallgren 2002: 566). These purposes – Tallgren suggests – may be 'to establish a system of symbols, analogous to domestic criminal law, that gives reason to believe that the "international community", the world, can be submitted to a similar kind of rational governance as that of a national state' (2002: 595).

If these ill-suited but oft-repeated purposes are intended to have a distracting effect, then building on Tallgren's insight one might argue that they play this role in respect of the continuation of the hegemonic and anti-pluralistic geopolitics that are part of the field's history. As Mégret notes, historically 'international criminal responsibility always seems to be about "others"' (2001: 262), and possibly even *othering*. Arguably international criminal justice remains an important part of the 'othering' of states, or is at the very least perceived to do so. The traces of these tendencies within the International Criminal Court's structure, and its 'serendipitous' (at least for the Great Powers) exclusive focus on Africa to date, do little to contradict this.

Individualism and performance

This leads us to the third and closely related set of concerns relating to 'performance'. International criminal law is increasingly about performance, in the functional not theatrical sense of the word (although the latter may well have application). It is no longer the case that the mere 'existence' of international tribunals is to be celebrated (Meron 1995), they must *perform*. In recent times both academics and civil society organizations have begun to lament the poor performance of ICL, and the ICC in particular. (For example, see Schabas (2013: 546): 'The ICC's Disappointing Performance'; and Posner (2012): 'even by the low standards of international tribunals [the ICC's] performance should raise an eyebrow'.) One could argue that performance has been institutionalized in the Rome Statute 'system' through the principle of complementarity. It is the ability of states to 'perform' that allows them to displace the jurisdiction of the ICC (although formally the emphasis lies the other way around). Performance is not just *ex post facto* consideration, it conditions the strategies adopted by actors in the ICL field (such as the ICC Prosecutor) prospectively.

The notion of performance, along with the associated language of efficacy, efficiency, delivery and so on raises a number of interesting questions. For these purposes I wish to make some tentative observations regarding the manner in which the performance of international criminal tribunals (chiefly the ICC) is measured by different actors and the effect of individualism on this process. As with the discussions regarding its history and purpose, this will be done with an eye to concerns raised by African states with regard to ICL.

At the outset it must be mentioned that any conversation about performance is likely to be conditioned by two preliminary difficulties (which are far from easily overcome). The first is the recurring question of purpose. As noted above, determining the purpose or purposes of ICL is an ongoing and fraught process. Not only are ICL's potential purposes numerous, not all of them are harmonious and they may even sometimes conflict (Damaska 2008). One way around this question might be to argue that ICL's performance ought to be measured in terms of the number of convictions, nothing more. However, it is not simply a 'numbers game' and clearly not all convictions are the same. This is particularly true of consequentialist justifications for ICL where the conviction of an accused is not an end in itself; rather it is a means to another end (such as deterrence). Incidentally, the ICC's Office of the Prosecutor (OTP) appears to have accepted this broader view of performance in the latest strategy which notes: 'In working on *performance measurement*, the Office will pay special attention to mandate [sic] of securing convictions *while pursuing the truth*' (OTP, Strategic Plan June 2012–2015, para. 97). Therefore 'measuring' performance – at least measuring it *holistically* – requires first selecting one (or more) of the purposes that are meant to be achieved. In this regard, despite the difficulties raised above, the front-runners remain retribution and deterrence.

Second, measuring performance is likely to be an abstract or highly speculative exercise; at least insofar as the consequentialist purposes of ICL are concerned, as they are not subject to empirical evaluation (deterrence, reconciliation, peace, truth-telling). There have been some attempts to measure the deterrent value of ICL – but they have not been very convincing, neither have the results been very encouraging. These challenges are reflected in the latest OTP Strategic Plan, which notes:

> To evaluate the (cost-)effectiveness of the Office requires first determining what outcome the Office is supposed to produce: prevention of crimes, complementarity achieved, justice (seen to be) done, etc. Then one needs to determine how to measure the impact of the Office on the outcome which comes with challenges of isolating its impact from that of many other actors and factors and with the challenge of organizing a reliable measurement. To evaluate the productivity, quality and efficiency of the Office also poses conceptual challenges when one is dealing with a limited number of cases which are furthermore different in nature and investigated under different conditions. While the Office has been commended in the past for the quality of its performance indicators, it intends to evaluate whether a refocused and limited set of indicators might be more

suitable for the Office (e.g. using the confirmation or conviction rate of persons and charges).

(OTP Strategic Plan June 2012–2015, paras 94–5)

Incidentally, this passage is also an instructive example of just how casually the question of purpose is often addressed. The strategy refers blithely to various 'outcome[s] the Office is supposed to produce: prevention of crimes, complementarity achieved, justice (seen to be) done, etc.' These difficulties aside, the more immediate point is that the existing discourse around performance mirrors the individualistic instincts of the field.

First and foremost, in addressing performance there is a tendency to focus on the individualistic objectives of ICL or by prefacing these over its broader ones. Although ICL is 'sold' or 'marketed' with reference to a number of aims – such as retribution, general deterrence, incapacitation and rehabilitation, truth-telling, victim participation, promoting human rights and the rule of law, and 'stopping an ongoing conflict' (Damaska 2012: 331) – it is measured largely (if not wholly) in terms of its ability to pursue individual responsibility. While this can be justified insofar as the field's retributive aspirations are concerned, punishment alone is not, in and of itself, sufficient for the broader purposes espoused by ICL. In fact, generally speaking, questions are raised far less often regarding whether or not ICL is 'performing' in relation to these broader purposes at all.

What is more, the pursuit of individual responsibility, often clothed in emotive language of ending impunity or securing 'justice' for victims, generally takes precedence over all other ends (even if they themselves are one of the stated 'purposes' of ICL) and concerns.

Tentatively, one might reconsider the well-rehearsed peace versus justice debate in this light. Leaving aside the question of whether there can be peace without justice (a supposition that is 'impossible to verify by any empirical means' (Tallgren 2002: 592), and therefore the point beyond which most discussions on the topic cannot usefully proceed), in this debate 'justice' is generally shorthand for ICL, while 'peace' is often portrayed as shorthand for 'politics' or 'amnesty' or 'impunity'. However, if 'peace' *itself* is one of the objectives of ICL (as it is at least for some), then this debate is one that takes place *within* ICL – between its own purposes – rather than one of ICL (or law) versus politics. More importantly, those who are on the side of 'peace' in one of the many rehearsals of this debate are not (necessarily) on the side of the political, or worse still on the side of sovereignty.

If this is correct, then it is significant for a number of concerns raised by African states regarding the ICL project that are currently characterized as 'political', and then dismissed on this basis. However, these concerns – which include the effect of the arrest warrant issued by the ICC for Sudanese President al-Bashir on Sudan's fragile peace process, and the violation of international law immunities by domestic courts and judicial officers – are not that far removed from the purposes of ICL. In fact, a broader view of the purposes of ICL, or the rehabilitation of sovereignty's place with the field, casts African concerns in a different light.

A broader view of the functions of ICL, and how it should 'perform' them, also opens up space for renewed, more appropriate, discussions regarding its purpose(s). However, should ICL scholars and courts wish to continue to embrace the field's individualist instincts, then they ought to accept the retributive aspirations of the field – uncomfortable moral and religious undertones notwithstanding – and refrain from 'marketing' ICL with reference to its non-retributive, rational, utilitarian ends.

Second, focusing exclusively on the narrow purposes of ICL (punishing individuals) also occludes discussions on the broader concerns about the field and its flagship, the ICC. As Mégret notes:

> The language of the efficacy of 'enforcement' and 'compliance' has tended to displace discussions about the justice or even the conceivability of interference … In encouraging this trend, often uncritically, human rights lawyers have arguably furbished the tools of the hegemon …
>
> (Mégret 2013: 23)

African states have raised a number of concerns in this regard, many of which are discussed above. It is worth noting that these are not solely concerns of African states. At the height of the recent kerfuffle regarding the African Union's Extraordinary Summit regarding the ICC, a number of members of African civil society released a communiqué which, in addition to making recommendations to all the relevant actors, raised a number of broader concerns about the ICL project and the ICC. These included the need to be 'conscious of the fact that international justice takes place within a political, socio-economic and cultural context'; that the ICC should 'acknowledge its own shortcomings and be receptive to constructive criticism'; and that the P5 should ratify the Rome Statute as it is 'impossible for states to effectively call for an end to impunity while attempting to make themselves immune from international justice processes'. However, as Tallgren notes, as things stand, the 'sacred cow' of criminal justice leaves little space for 'critical questions, not to even mention transformative agendas' (Tallgren, Chapter 3 in this volume).

Conclusion

The aim of this chapter has been to use the theme of 'individualism' to highlight some of the hidden assumptions, preferences and/or biases within international criminal law and its associated discourse and, having done so, consider these in light of concerns raised about the project by African states. To some extent, the chapter's focus on individualism (even broadly construed) leaves it open to the criticisms that it is both under-inclusive and oversimplified. Individualism was not the only contributing factor to the concerns raised above in respect of the histories, purposes and performance of ICL – and perhaps at times is more accurately described as an outcome than a cause thereof. As noted above, these concerns might have been organized around 'progress', 'identity' or 'hegemony'.

What is more, throughout the chapter 'colonialism' has asserted itself as a possible additional theme around which to organize a critical discussion of ICL. 'The colonial moment will not go away' for international law (Mégret 2013: 9); it has and continues to shape international law's past, present and futures in ways that are still being articulated today. This is equally true of international *criminal* law, where colonialism and the discipline's failure to come to terms with it not only haunts its past, but threatens its future. Consider, for one, the current 'appetite' among the ICC and its supporters for African crimes (and victims) of modern-day mass atrocities against the backdrop of the continued failure to address crimes committed against Africans – but by Europeans and those of European descent – in fairly recent times (slavery, colonialism, apartheid) and on an unprecedented scale.

That said, individualism certainly has had a marked effect on the field, and continues to do so. If this assertion holds true, then the reasons for this commitment to individualism on the part of international criminal law and international criminal lawyers remain to be explored in the future. Tentatively, it may betray a commitment to a certain 'form' of politics, a professional bent shared by lawyers, or a personal commitment born of vanity – if 'great men' and international law make history, international lawyers are themselves not insignificant – or despair: 'at least something can be done' (Tallgren 2002: 594).

Ultimately, whatever device one uses to highlight these hidden assumptions, preferences, biases or *commitments* within ICL and its discourse, the point is that they are not given or inevitable. Their adoption, maintenance and concealment are arguably acts of 'politics', not 'law'. Furthermore, the failure to acknowledge these aspects of the field (and their politics) results in undermining, distorting and dismissing – often somewhat ironically as 'political' – the legitimate concerns raised by African states in respect of ICL. It also prolongs the life of the illegitimate ones. This undermines any reconstructive attempts for the ICL project, a project that holds considerable promise. To crudely paraphrase Drumbl, a fuller picture of the problems facing ICL will only emerge to the extent that 'we' resist simple, and comforting, explanations and reach deeper to a more embarrassing place (Drumbl 2007: 173).

Notes

1 Similarly, the aim here is not to make sweeping claims about African politics either. However, for the most part, the 'concerns' discussed herein emanate from decisions taken by consensus by all African states through the African Union.

2 These are not exacting distinctions, and there is of course some overlap between them. In this regard Craven notes that 'any particular text will tend not to distinguish these three types of historical account, and in most cases will seek to conjoin two or more within the framework of a single project' (Craven 2006: 7). This is certainly the case in respect of the second and third categories insofar as international criminal law is concerned.

3 Justice Pal was also concerned about the racist undertones of the trial, which he himself experienced when he arrived in Japan and was initally accommodated separately from the other judges (Maga 2001: 66). At the time, a Japanese court clerk, having had sight of Pal's dissent, described it as 'a courageous shout of the colored races against the white race!'

4 See Pre-Trial Chamber II, *Situation in the Republic Of Kenya, In the Cases of Prosecutor v. William Samoei Ruto, Henry Kiprono Kosgey, Joshua Arap Sang And Prosecutor v. Francis Kirimi Muthaura, Uhuru Muigai Kenyatta And Mohammed Hussein Ali* ICC-01/09-01/11-19.

5 At its recent Ordinary Summit in May 2013, the African Union Assembly noted 'the need for international justice to be conducted in a transparent and fair manner, in order to avoid any perception of double standard, in conformity with the principles of international law'. See *Decision on International Jurisdiction, Justice and The International Criminal Court (ICC)*, AU Doc. Assembly/AU/13(XXI).

6 The *ought* question cannot be completely separated from the *how* as, for some critics, the nature of the histories produced by ICL are the reason they ought not do so.

7 As Simpson points out, there are antinomies to the 'great man' theory within ICL, such as the indictment of lower level offenders (*Tadic*) and the development and use of modes of responsibility that 'situate individuals in broader networks of collective responsibility' (Simpson, Chapter 7 in this volume).

Bibliography

Anghie, A. (2005) *Imperialism, Sovereignty and the Making of International Law*, Cambridge: Cambridge University Press.

Arendt, H. (1963) *Eichmann in Jerusalem: A Report on the Banality of Evil*, New York: Viking Press.

Craven, M. (2006) 'International Law and its Histories', in M. Craven, M. Fitzmaurice and M. Vogiatzi (eds) *Time, History and International Law*, Leiden: Martinus Nijhoff.

Cryer, R. (2005) 'International Criminal Law vs State Sovereignty: Another Round?', *European Journal of International Law* 16(5): 980.

Damaska, M. (2008) 'What is the Point of International Criminal Justice?', *Chicago-Kent Law Review* 83: 329.

Drumbl, M. (2005a) 'Collective Violence and Individual Punishment: The Criminality of Mass Atrocity', *Northwestern University Law Review* 99: 539.

Drumbl, M. (2005b) 'Pluralizing International Criminal Justice', *Michigan Law Review* 111.

Drumbl, M. (2007) *Atrocity, Punishment, and International Law*, New York: Cambridge University Press.

Du Plessis, A. and Gevers, C. (2010a) 'Africa and the Codification of Aggression: A Pyrrhic Victory?', *African Legal Aid Quarterly* 2.

Du Plessis, M. and Gevers, C. (2010b) 'Making Amend(ment)s: South Africa and the International Criminal Court from 2009 to 2010', *South African Yearbook of International Law* 34: 1.

Elkins, C. (2005) *Imperial Reckoning: The Untold Story of Britain's Gulag in Kenya*, New York: Owl Books.

Goodman, A. (2004) 'UN Establishes Rwanda Genocide Tribunal', *Reuters* (8 November 1994).

Heller, K.J. (2010) 'Situational Gravity under the Rome Statute', in K. Stahn and L. van den Herik (eds) *Future Directions in International Criminal Justice*, The Hague: TMC Asser Press.

Kaplan, A. (1992) 'On Alain Finkielkraut's "Remembering in Vain": The Klaus Barbie Trial and Crimes against Humanity', *Critical Inquiry* 19(1): 70.

Koskenniemi, M. (2002) 'Between Impunity and Show Trials', *Max Planck Yearbook of United Nations Law* 6: 1.

Koskenniemi, M. (2012) 'Law, Teleology and International Relations: An Essay on Counterdisciplinarity', *International Relations* 26: 3.

Maga, T. (2001) *Judgment at Maga: The Japanese War Crimes Trials*, Kentucky: University Press of Kentucky.

Matua, M. (1997) 'Never Again: Questioning the Yugoslav and Rwanda Tribunals', *Temple International & Comparative Law Journal* 11: 167.

Mégret, F. (2001) 'Epilogue to an Endless Debate: The International Criminal Court's Third Party Jurisdiction', *European Journal of International Law* 12(2): 247.

Mégret, F. (2002) 'The Politics of International Criminal Justice', *European Journal of International Law* 13(5): 1261.

Mégret, F. (2013) 'Where Does the Critique of International Human Rights Stand? An Exploration in 18 Vignettes', in J. Beneyto and D. Kennedy (eds) *New Approaches to International Law: The European and American Experiences*, The Hague: TMC Asser Press.

Meron, T. (1995) 'International Criminalization of Internal Atrocities', *American Journal of International Law* 89: 554.

Meron, T. (2000) 'The Humanization of Humanitarian Law', *American Journal of International Law* 94(2): 239.

'Promoting Accountability for International Crimes in Africa' (2013) Communiqué adopted at meeting convened in Arusha, Tanzania by the Pan-African Lawyers Union, International Refugee Rights Initiative and the Eastern Africa Center for Constitutional Development, October.

Posner, E. (2012) 'The Absurd International Criminal Court', WSJ. Available at: http://online.wsj.com/article/SB10001424052702303753904577452122153205162.html (10 June).

Robertson, G. (1999) *Crimes Against Humanity: The Struggle for Global Justice*, New York: New Press.

Robinson, D.(2010) 'The Two Liberalisms of International Criminal Law' in C. Stahn, C. and L. van den Herik (eds) *Future Perspectives on International Criminal Justice*, The Hague: TMC Asser Press.

Sands, P. (2011) 'Where Should Saif Gaddafi be Put on Trial?', *The Guardian*, 20 November.

Schabas, W. (1997) 'Sentencing by International Tribunals: A Human Rights Approach', *Duke Journal of Comparative Law* 61.

Schabas, W. (2013) 'The Banality of International Justice', *Journal of International Criminal Justice* 11(3): 545.

Simpson, G. (2004) *Great Powers and Outlaw States: Unequal Sovereigns in the International Legal Order*, Cambridge: Cambridge University Press.

Simpson, G. (2007) *Law, War and Crime*, Cambridge: Polity Press.

Simpson, G. (2012) 'International Criminal Justice and the Past', in G. Boas, W.A. Schabas and M.P. Scharf (eds) *International Criminal Justice: Legitimacy and Coherence*, Cheltenham: Edward Elgar.

Skouteris, T. (2012) 'Engaging History in International Law', in J. Beneyton and D. Kennedy (eds) *New Approaches to International Law: The European and American Experiences*, The Hague: TMC Asser Press.

Tallgren, I. (2002) 'The Sense and Sensibility of International Criminal Law', *European Journal of International Law* 13(3): 561.

Wei, U. (2007) 'Pal's "Dissentient Judgment" Reconsidered: Some Notes on Postwar Japan's Responses to the Opinion', *Japan Review* 19: 215.

Wilson, R.A. (2011) *Writing History in International Criminal Trials*, Cambridge: Cambridge University Press.

Chapter 11

An arresting event

Assassination within the purview of international criminal law

Michelle Burgis-Kasthala[1]

Introduction

On 14 February 2005 Lebanon's former Prime Minster, Rafiq Hariri, along with a number of bystanders, was killed by a massive and extremely sophisticated bomb that exploded as his high-security motorcade proceeded along Beirut's shore. Video footage from passing spectators captured the death and destruction and served as the first source of the crime's documentation. Beamed around Lebanon and the world, this footage not only prompted local and regional unrest, but it was also the impetus for investigations sponsored by the United Nations (UN). After a number of reports recommending further international oversight, the Special Tribunal for Lebanon (STL) was established in The Hague in 2007 and began its work two years later. The Tribunal's supporters alleged that Lebanon's weak and politically divided crime agencies and judiciary were unwilling and unable to address the crime impartially. In contrast, the Tribunal would be able to blind itself to the local political unrest, which continued to escalate after its creation. The Tribunal's purview would necessarily be limited yet focused on the 'legal' dimensions of this instance of political violence turned 'terrorist' crime. This would be the first instance where an international criminal tribunal (ICT) would prosecute crimes not carried out in war, but rather, domestic 'terrorist' acts occurring during peacetime. Thus, the STL was the first dedicated international 'terrorist court'.

This chapter uses the case of Hariri's killing and subsequent international reactions to explore how the professional field of international criminal law (ICL) disciplines and directs the gaze of its scholars and practitioners. I argue that one of the most important disciplinary devices is the instruction of what to see and what not to see in a given situation. When presented with graphic depictions of the Hariri assassination,[2] why is it that ICL scholars and practitioners were willing to support political lobbying efforts for the creation of a new tribunal that purported to transform politics into ICL? How does an intimate, voyeuristic and perhaps even guilty moment on the part of ICL practitioners transpire into a collective turn to support internationalization and tribunalization? In transforming a political assassination into an international – indeed, 'terrorist' – crime, what incompatible realities or alternate interpretations are taken out of view? As scholars and practitioners of ICL, how are we trained to limit our gaze? What aspects of the case are deemed to be beyond the competence of our expert observation?

Within international law generally, and ICL specifically, scholars and practitioners alike make sense of political complexity by deploying dominant narratives and frames. The narrative of domestic incompetence made good through the progressive promise of international legal intervention is a familiar one to international lawyers and is particularly pronounced in the case of ICL, with its selective attention to certain parts of the globe. As a purportedly perpetually unstable state, Lebanon was an ideal site in which to construct such a narrative of redemption through ICL, and Hariri's killing served as the perfect trigger. This chapter interrogates how the framing of this event by Hariri supporters in Lebanon domestically and internationally allowed for very particular 'reconstructive' ICL responses that coalesced into the establishment of the STL.

Thus, this chapter reveals what is typically *seen* as well as *not seen* within the ICL field when political events such as assassinations are transformed through the standard international law narrative devices of *internationalization, depoliticization* and *naturalization.* After setting up a rationale for critique I move on to provide background to the assassination and its domestic and international fallout, before examining the production of ICL narratives in the work of the STL as showcased in its two decisions on the scope of its jurisdiction. I conclude by suggesting that there are multiple lenses through which the assassination can be viewed, and that the STL's narrow construction of the Hariri assassination can be critiqued and retold by those of us working within the field of ICL. Moves to destabilize ICL's progressive but narrow narrative about the need for the STL are vital for critique within the field. This kind of scholarship can also demonstrate the significant role that international lawyers play in contributing to the (in)stability already witnessed in Lebanon in the wake of the STL's work.

'Making visible those things that are already visible': interrogating the narrative architecture of ICL

In this chapter, I am interested in exploring the ICL professional community, understood as composed of scholars and practitioners who share a common intellectual and professional identity. This identity centres on their shared endeavour of working towards a world governed by international law, especially ICL. Professional communities are established and sustained in large measure through the narratives that construct the origins of the profession, its future trajectory, and identify its purpose. Later in the chapter is an illustration of how dominant ICL narratives underpin the rationale and work of the STL.

This section begins by highlighting the constitution of a community of international law professionals through disciplinary techniques including the production of international law narratives. It then moves on to consider some specific ICL narrative devices. Finally, the section explores how to engage with such narrative structures by considering the role of critique for the field of ICL through a turn to description of what Anne Orford characterizes as that which is 'already visible' (2012: 617).

The construction of professional communities is a mutually constitutive relationship of identity consolidation. For Michael Barnett, an 'identity is the understanding of oneself in relation to others. Identities … are not personal or psychological, they are fundamentally social and relational, defined by the actor's interaction with and relationship to others' (1999: 9). Where actors share a narrative vision, they also possess a common identity (1999: 13). Such narratives simplify the complexity of daily life and provide a framework for common action.[3] Narratives then are crucial in understanding how groups sustain an identity distinct from others. As argued by Robert Cover:

> The intelligibility of normative behavior inheres in the communal character of the narratives that provide the context of that behavior. Any person who lived in an entirely idiosyncratic normative life would be quite mad. The part that you or I choose to play may be singular, but the fact that we can locate it in a common 'script' renders it 'sane' – a warrant that we share a *nomos*.
>
> (Cover 1983–84: 10)

Narratives shape the conduct of professional community members, but they also contribute to the reproduction of the discipline's foundational narratives, thereby sustaining the discipline itself. To be disciplined into a scholarly field, such as international law,

> is to learn to embody, to perform, and to enact on a daily basis … not only the academic genres that constitute the theories and practices of the discipline, but also the genres of social relations and embodied subjectivity that constructs the discipline as 'a body' of knowledge … To succeed in the discipline means to be able to perform its genres, and be able to speak and write and embody its favourite discourses, myths, and *narratives.*
>
> (Threadgold, quoted in Orford 1998: 3, emphasis added)

For an international lawyer, then, it is not enough to demonstrate doctrinal proficiency; she must be able to frame her arguments within dominant narratives and through accepted professional postures. In turn, these narrative frames will also shape the core work of the international lawyer – legal interpretation. Furthermore, as David Koller argues, to 'define oneself as an international lawyer and to partake in international legal argument is to accept the existence and unified structure of a thing called international law' (2012: 109). This is more specifically the case for the international criminal lawyer who sees the world through the prism of crimes and their remedy or prevention through ICL. As members of a scholarly community, international lawyers 'cannot read concepts, ideas or words apart from the larger content in which they appear, or apart from the function they perform in that context' (Burgess 2012: 306). Competence to speak the language of international law is thus often manifested in the subtle art of narrating or storytelling, where a faith in the progress of international law ensures its centrality to the plot.

The international lawyer as storyteller participates in the (re)production of particular renderings of international law's past, present and future trajectories. These storylines tend to converge around a (liberal) progress narrative that assures those in the international law fold of the discipline's unceasing development and improvement (Mégret 2002; Skouteris 2010; Krever 2013). By contributing to these 'reconstructive' narratives, international lawyers shore up their field and its core aims of realising a world governed through law. Crises – or narrative climaxes – can thus be read as moments of law's absence (Charlesworth 2002), requiring the assistance of international lawyers who can 'do something' (Orford 1998: 11) while still remaining aloof from the dirty world of politics. Even when unsavoury aspects of the past cannot be denied, rupture rather than repetition (Kennedy 1999–2000) is emphasized so that, for example, post-colonial, 'benevolent' ICL interventions can appear far removed from colonial policies dependent on the distinction between civilized and barbaric peoples (Orford 1998: 22, 29). This 'image of international lawyers as humane, professional, elite advisers to real decision-makers is seductive, promising access to power while denying responsibility for its exercise' (1998: 11).

The power of the international lawyer is perhaps most palpable in the context of international criminal trials where international law is transformed into a hard power tool of punishment for perpetrators and redemption for victims. As was the case for Hariri's killing, living in a media-saturated context, the international criminal lawyer can learn of mass atrocity seconds after it occurs, often thousands of kilometres away. Viewing such spectacles of suffering may elicit feelings of guilt in these moments of violent voyeurism; 'doing something' through ICL (Tallgren 2002: 594) presents an active alternative to the passive condition of a frustrated sideline spectator, and can soothe the conscience of the international criminal lawyer dedicated to the progressive promise of ICL (Koller 2008: 1059). For Sarah Nouwen, the 'project of international criminal justice assuages the moral hunger for a response to visible and yet unimaginable human suffering, reassures the idealist of her own identity … and nurtures a sense of belonging to an "international community"' (2012: 330). Working in ICTs will often be the ideal way of embodying an active ICL response.

ICL narratives are thus part of a collective endeavour that provides the international criminal lawyer with an identity and a purpose. Koller argues that despite a lack of evidence affirming many of ICL's purported aims, the international criminal lawyer can nevertheless continue to act as its advocate through her shared faith in its promise of ending impunity (Koller 2008).[4] Crucially, as for narratives *per se*, this faith is not only an individual attribute, but is dependent on a group so that collective ICL identity and faith are 'mutually reinforcing' (2008: 1023).

The production of faith, identity and narratives takes place within specific institutional settings. For the international criminal lawyer, the burgeoning professional opportunities offered through work in ICTs sustain the ICL enterprise. An understanding of ICL narratives produced by an ICT such as the STL is only possible then through an examination of both ideational and institutional factors. According to Barnett: 'To concentrate on the ideational to the neglect of the institutional is to ignore the political context in which actors strategize and are potentially organized across a political space and toward a policy outcome' (1999: 16).

Thus we can understand ICL as an institution of professional postures, shared narratives and identities that are supported by, and in turn (re)constitute, the sites of ICL production: ICTs, the headquarters of intergovernmental organizations and non-governmental organizations as well as universities as centres of research and teaching. In particular, ICL is understood as a practice that occurs within and about the ICTs (Mégret 2013). This perspective is supported by the disproportionate volume of ICL books and articles written by lawyers based in these tribunals, relative to public international scholarship in general. Such ICL scholarship shores up the legitimacy of the tribunals. Even when criticism is offered, it is usually in the vein of reconstruction: namely, to perfect ICL faults.[5] This is particularly pronounced in relation to scholarly writings on the STL that are overwhelmingly written by those who have worked at the STL or some other ICT.

One way of grounding this interrelationship between ICL institutions and ideas is to explore the narrative production of ICL geographies, which enable certain places to discipline others constructed as being comparatively more violent and chaotic. As Koller reminds us, 'international law is punctuated by a series of geographical placeholders … [that] do substantial conceptual work, dividing and segmenting international law and together establishing a geography of the field' (2012: 98). Reference to particular places, such as New York or Geneva, provides international law with a 'normative direction' that, as we saw above, converges towards a journey of 'progressive development' (2012: 98). In these narratives, global cities are the core of international law production and evolution and it is from these hegemonic sites that particular, peripheral spaces can be disciplined and governed. As a quest for the universal, international law institutions in these global cities can thus help obscure particular practices and politics, suggesting that such spaces are more neutral and less political than their (third world) counterparts (Pearson 2008: 498–505). Such moves underscore one of the three key ICL narrative devices explored here – depoliticization (Krever 2013). In his work on securitization, Shapiro argues that how 'we have the world is a matter of the shape we impose on it, given the ideational commitments and institutional practices through which spatio-temporal models of identity-difference are created' (2007: 294). Just as the security analyst creates 'architectures of enmity' in their practice of 'violent cartographies' (2007: 294), so too do international lawyers (re)construct particular narratives about spaces of violence in contrast to spaces able to tame such violence. When we peruse the docket of the ICC, for example, it is easy to see a world radically fractured into spaces in need of ICL and those willing and able to dispense it. As we will see, Lebanon too has availed itself of the need for ICL intervention through this narrative device, necessitating The Hague's civilizing force over Lebanon's unruly and politicized legal system.

This brief consideration of ICL's reliance on particular geographical narratives points more broadly to the core narrative devices that sustain the ICL enterprise as scholarship and as practice today: internationalization, depoliticization and naturalization. First, by its very nature, international criminal law must demonstrate why a given national legal system is either procedurally or normatively deficient. This, in fact, was one of the crucial steps required in transforming Hariri's murder into an international terrorist investigation, as it was alleged that Lebanese institutions were politically compromised and weak. Here, then, a binary emerges between the merits of international forms of justice over national or local variants. For Clarke, 'what is critical in the way that [international] justice is made real is its concealment of other justice narratives or its monopoly of symbolic and enforced power to exercise the authorial meaning of justice – the fiction of justice' (2009: 13). Local variations of justice practices are trumped and silenced through this turn to 'international' criminal justice, where the 'international' can remain suspended above the politics of everyday life. As we saw in relation to global cities, resorting to the 'global' or 'international' nature of a crime removes it from the practices of particular politics so that the international can be seen as the more neutral (Pearson 2008: 502), even the more 'natural' choice.

Both ICL and international law in general frame their mandates as unique through the construction of law as distinct from non-law (Koller 2012: 109), particularly politics. As is the case with any assassination, the Lebanese context of Hariri's killing is replete with politics, but to be able to justify a role for ICL, first a scenario must be constructed that can insulate ICL from politics, so that it can distinguish itself from (rival) domestic and regional responses. Partly, this insulation occurs through the process of internationalization and neutralization described above. Depoliticization more simply relies on the construction of narratives that tend to overemphasize particular narratives about these local politics, while obscuring the politics practised at the international level, especially those global cities mentioned above, such as The Hague (the STL, the ICC) or New York (the UN). Thus, politics can simply be written out of ICL's narrative altogether (Mégret 2002: 1280). We will see below how the STL has sustained its work through such narrative tropes.

These practices of internationalization and depoliticization culminate in the most fundamental move for ICL: naturalization. According to Susan Marks in her consideration of Karl Marx as applied to international law, we can understand the process of naturalization occurring when particular social arrangements appear as obvious and self-evident. Discursively, binaries (national/international, and law/politics) sustain the notion of reality as simply given, and susceptible to either/or solutions – such as ICL or (domestic) impunity. The flux of politics stalls into a static form of knowledge that no longer needs interrogation. Crucially, within this framework of naturalness, certain objects and practices are seeable or capable of speaking, while others remain unseeble and silenced in the shadows (Marks 2003: 22). This is precisely what occurs in the production of ICL narratives that simplify complexity and direct our gaze into only certain corners of the world, suggesting select (ICL-based) solutions.

I end this section by returning to Orford's use of Foucault and the role that scholars can play in making 'us see what we see' (Foucault, quoted in Orford 2012: 617). Through processes such as naturalization that shape both disciplinary and quotidian realities, we often overlook those practices that enable us to glance over and miss daily details. As one method to overcome this, Orford suggests the 'practice of cartography or mapping':

> When we make a map, we always have to decide what details to leave in and what to leave out. We have to think of our audience and the purposes for which they will use the map. We have to think about how to design the map so that the information in it can be absorbed – a map cannot simply reproduce the world if it is to take a useful form.
>
> (Orford 2012: 625)

We have already seen how the international criminal lawyer sustains her identity as a member of the ICL fold through certain progressivist ICL narratives and maps or 'architectures of enmity' (Shapiro 2007) whose naturalness must be interrogated. The remainder of the chapter explores the STL's founding narratives in order to offer alternative maps that can reveal what the discipline of ICL would prefer we overlook.

The killing of one man: assassination as cause for international criminal tribunalization

The spectacle created by Hariri's killing, outside a popular hotel at midday, meant that the crime would be seen by many eye-witnesses along with millions more once recordings went viral online. Of interest, however, is not the fact that this event was so visible but what has since been emphasized or obscured in the push to criminalize and internationalize it, especially in the STL's discourse. This section provides context to the killing before exploring its local, regional and international ramifications.

Backdrop to the assassination

Lebanon's modern history is littered with trauma resulting from civil war, foreign interventions and occupations, as well as ongoing political sectarianism and violence. From such experiences, it is only a very small narrative step to portray Lebanon as a weak or even 'failed' state in need of 'international' redemption, and this has indeed occurred numerous times, especially during its 15-year civil war. In trying to 'do justice' to Lebanon's past, it is important then that we remain mindful of the palpable suffering caused through domestic and foreign forces, while being careful that such events do not suggest certain policies and responses as 'natural' or inevitable. Hariri's killing was only one of many moments in Lebanon's past that scar the landscape. Why did it elicit an ICL response in the form of the STL when so many other crimes remain overlooked? To answer this question, we must situate this particular event in its domestic, regional and international context.

The particular sectarian and confessional make-up of the Lebanese political system has weakened the state since independence from France in 1943 and has also allowed for foreign intervention in the name of protecting particular groups[6] – a practice that had been prevalent for centuries (Traboulsi 2007). The influx of Palestinian refugees (many of whom were armed guerrillas, or *fedā'yeen*) after their retreat from Jordan in the early 1970s disturbed the fragile sectarian balance and culminated in the outbreak of Lebanon's civil war between 1975 and 1990 (Sayigh 1997: 28). This conflict resulted in around 150,000 mainly civilian casualties, whose killing was often the result of confessional affiliation. Assassination of prominent political figures was also rife during this period. Throughout the conflict, Syria had been the main foreign actor, and this predominance was sanctified in the post-war Ta'if Agreement of 1990 or *Pax Syriana* (Wierda *et al.* 2007: 1069). This meeting in Ta'if, Saudi Arabia, brought together the main wartime parties (aside from Israel) and endorsed Syria's *de facto* control over much of Lebanon through its extensive military and secret police (*mukhābarāt*) presence.

Along with Israel's control of the south until 2000, these foreign occupations precluded the possibility of concerted post-war reconciliation. While various civil society initiatives ensured that Lebanon would not forget its victims (Knudsen 2012), the state remained blind to such refrains, preferring 'social amnesia' (Jaquemet 2009) or 'whitewash' (Mugraby 2008: 176), most of the time mixed with amnesty for Lebanon's most prominent figures, who often had blood on their hands. The weakened post-war state thus displayed a general lack of regard for bringing perpetrators from the past to account, and such a stance has continued into the twenty-first century (Mugraby 2008).

Within this context, then, it was very easy to construct a narrative about the desirability of ICL action in the face of domestic impunity.[7] What was more surprising, however, was ICL's purview in Lebanon – not thousands of civilian wartime casualties, as we see with other tribunals, but one prominent individual. Such selectivity of the STL continues to undermine its legitimacy and calls for finely tuned legal arguments from the Tribunal and its supporters to justify its mandate.

Although Syria had intended to retain its predominance over Lebanon, the US invasion of Iraq in 2003 fractured the regional order and called on both state and non-state actors to state their positions as supporters or opponents of the war. As one of the most powerful politicians from Lebanon's Sunni sect and the key patron of Beirut's reconstruction, billionaire property developer Rafiq Hariri found himself increasingly reluctant to align himself with Syria. By the summer of 2004, tensions continued to rise. First, and in breach of the constitution, Syria extended the presidential term of a key ally, President Émile Lahoud. Second, the United Nations Security Council (UNSC) passed the American and French sponsored Resolution 1559, which requested Syria's withdrawal from the country, the disarming of militias – including Syria's ally, Shi'ite Hizbollah, as well as the holding of free and fair elections.[8] Despite being ignored at the time, the Resolution polarized an already fractured political field. Hariri seemed damned if he backed Syria (Iran and Hizbollah) and damned if he supported the US-Arab Gulf opposition. Increasing tensions were also manifested in a spate of high-profile assassination attempts,[9] which began with the abortive attempt against Finance Minister Marwan Hamadeh on 10 October 2004.[10] More 'successful' was the attempt on Hariri's life on 14 February 2005, which also claimed 22 bystanders. Irrespective of whether Hariri had supported Resolution 1559, the fallout from his killing radically altered the domestic and regional power balance. Hariri's supporters accused Syria of the murder and Syria swiftly complied with the earlier UNSC Chapter VI Resolution of 1559 by withdrawing its troops two months after the blast.

Domestic unrest arising from the bombing precipitated the resignation of pro-Syrian Prime Minister Omar Karami, as well as the so-called Cedar Revolution – mass demonstrations supporting Hariri which sought Syria's withdrawal. Conversely, pro-Syrian anti-Hariri groups massed, on 8 March 2005, less than a month after his killing, and took the date as the name for their bloc. The March 8 bloc continues to act as one of Lebanon's two main political factions. Its counterpart, March 14, is also named after a mass rally commemorating the one-month anniversary of Hariri's assassination. March 14 called on its international allies, such as France and the US, for an international investigation into Hariri's murder. Equally strident was March 8's categorical refusal of any foreign intervention over the killing. These divisions continue to plague the STL's work, as examined below.

Internationalizing the assassination: from fact-finding to investigation to tribunal

Within the context described, any international response to the murder would have been interpreted in diametrically opposed terms by Lebanon's two key political groups, March 8 and March 14. As a penetrated and 'weak' state, foreign intervention continues to mar Lebanon's landscape, but what was new after 2005 was the way in which this assassination became internationally criminalized and then tribunalized. Although certain Hariri supporters had sought a tribunal from the very beginning, the STL was preceded by a number of preparatory internationalizing moves, all of which fuelled a narrative about the necessity, or naturalness, of an ICT.

Perhaps part of the reason for the response elicited was Hariri's stature, not simply as head of Lebanon's Sunnis and its post-war reconstruction billionaire, but also as a friend and ally to powerful international friends. Hariri had amassed his fortune in Saudi Arabia, which remains a strident opponent of Syria, Iran and Hizbollah. French colonial ties are still pronounced in Lebanon, and Jacques Chirac made sure to attend Hariri's funeral. Thus if we consider Hariri's prominence within the Lebanese and regional order at the time, strong French and US reactions were not at all surprising. Only the day after his death, the UNSC met to condemn this 'terrorist bombing' and called on the Secretary-General to act.[11] He did so with alacrity, establishing a fact-finding commission under Peter Fitzgerald on 18 February, only four days after the bombing. This initial taskforce interviewed numerous Lebanese officials to draw up general findings and recommendations only a month later. The report implicated Syria in the tensions leading up to the assassination, as Syria had been in overall control of the country's (in)security. It concluded by calling for an international independent investigative commission due to 'the Lebanese investigation process … [suffering] from serious flaws'.[12] Here we see the domestic versus international binary ensuring the need for (depoliticized) international action.

The UNSC duly responded by passing Resolution 1595, which established the United Nations International Independent Investigation Commission (UNIIIC)[13] with the support of the Lebanese government at the time.[14] The Commission was assigned a three-month investigative period, but its mandate was repeatedly extended until it relinquished its role in February 2009 on the eve of the STL's opening.[15] The work of the UNIIIC took place in a context of growing polarization over the internationalization of Hariri's killing. While the UNSC spoke of purportedly 'unanimous demand of the Lebanese people that those responsible be identified and held accountable',[16] this desire did not translate into unified Lebanese support for the UNIIIC's work or for the creation of the STL. This is most clearly illustrated by the way in which the STL's birth was ultimately induced (Cockayne 2007).

The UNSC had intended the STL to be the product of agreement between itself and the Lebanese government. Such a hybrid ICT model would follow on from examples such as the Special Court for Sierra Leone and the Extraordinary Chambers in the Court of Cambodia. These hybrid courts differ from the first two ICTs for Yugoslavia and Rwanda, which were created through UNSC Chapter VII Resolutions (Raub 2008–09). Although March 14 leader and Prime Minister Saniora pushed for his government's agreement on the STL in 2006, opposition to the move led to the resignation of a number of March 8 parliamentarians, blocking the possibility of a UN-Lebanon treaty establishing the Tribunal. The resulting text of Resolution 1757 ultimately passed under Chapter VII, but it also reflects earlier aims of gaining Lebanese agreement.[17] Thus, like the ICTs for Rwanda and the former Yugoslavia (the ICTR and the ICTY), the STL would be a UNSC creature rather than the hybrid form initially envisaged.

Framing one man's killing: exploring the narrative structures of STL discourse

Since Hariri's killing in 2005, numerous actors have been accused of the crime along with associated assassinations that took place before and afterwards.[18] Initially, attention focused on Syria in light of the new regional dynamics discussed above and the Syrian *mukhābarāt*s overweening presence across most of the country before its withdrawal in mid-2005. Increasingly, however, international attention shifted from Syria (Wierda *et al.* 2007: 1076) whose agents could not be compelled to appear before The Hague (Wetzel and Mitri 2008: 92; Korecki 2009) to Hizbollah, the Shi'ite Lebanese armed resistance group which is closely allied to both the Syrian and Iranian regimes. Given Hizbollah's place in various Lebanese cabinets over this period, any hint of possible prosecution fuelled political unrest, particularly once four of its mid-ranking members were indicted by the Tribunal in mid-2011 (Burgis-Kasthala 2013: 511–512). Although defendants in the *Al-Ayyash* case (Al-Ayyash, Badreddine, Oneissi and Sabra) remain at large and will probably be tried *in absentia*, defence lawyers have challenged the nature of the indictment on a number of grounds.[19] Aside from a large number of minor procedural hearings, the most significant ICL contribution to emerge from four years' work by the STL centres on jurisdictional decisions in the cases of *Al-Ayyash* and *El-Sayed*,[20] as well as the Appeals Chamber's Interlocutory Decision on the Applicable Law.[21] This section considers ICL narrative devices through an examination of the ways in which the Tribunal has managed to deflect challenges to its authority in the *Al-Ayyash* jurisdiction cases. In doing so, what emerges is a highly selective story spun by the Tribunal's judges about the necessarily progressive role that ICL must play in ending impunity within Lebanon.

Rhetoric suggesting the international response to a domestic crime is often challenged by STL opponents, and this argument also figured in various Defence briefs before the Trial Chamber and Appeals Chamber in the *Decision on the Defence Challenges to the Jurisdiction and Legality of the Tribunal.*[22] The Trial Chamber summarized the key Defence arguments as follows:

(i)   the legal basis of their challenges (which goes to the issue of the admissibility of the motions as challenges to jurisdiction);
(ii) the alleged unconstitutionality of the establishment of the Tribunal under Lebanese law;
(iii) the power and scope of the Trial Chamber [or STL as a whole] to review Security Council Resolution 1757;
(iv) Resolution 1757's alleged violation of Lebanese sovereignty; and
(v)   the alleged violation of the fundamental rights of the Accused by the Tribunal's establishment, e.g., in breaching international law and the United Nations Charter.[23]

Perhaps of greatest interest to international lawyers will be point (iii) and how the STL has characterized its inherent jurisdiction to hold that it possesses no review power over the UNSC, a debate beyond the scope of discussion here.[24] More specifically in relation to point (i), both the Trial and Appeals Chambers responded in a highly technical and narrow reading of the Tribunal's Rules to argue that (*contra Tadić* on appeal)[25] questions of legality were distinct from jurisdiction and that various procedural requirements had not been met to allow a hearing on jurisdiction.[26] Despite such barriers and in response to Defence point (v) on the STL not being 'established by law', the Trial Chamber agreed to 'deal with this fundamental question of international human rights law' through a consideration of its jurisdiction.[27] For the purposes of this chapter, points (ii)–(iv) best illustrate the STL's responses through internationalization and depoliticization, and are examined below.

Points (ii) and (iv) concern the shift from Lebanese authority to international oversight. A 'major theme of the Defence submissions was that at May 2007 there was no "threat to international peace" but only serious political trouble of a national scope'.[28] Although Judge Baragwanath agrees with the Defence in his partial dissent from the Appeals Chamber that this is the first tribunal constituted under Chapter VII in the wake of an assassination occurring within a domestic setting, its internationalization is not exceptional if read within the context of earlier UNSC actions relating to terrorism.[29] According to the Appeals Chamber, domestic terrorist acts can be of such gravity as to constitute threats to international peace and security. Thus, *any* domestic crime of a terrorist nature can be *internationalized* by the UNSC, thus enabling the STL to deflect a key aspect of the Defence's brief.[30] The pre-eminence of UNSC action emerges not only from the UN Charter itself, but also the Lebanese Constitution, the Preamble of which the Trial Chamber referenced to demonstrate the binding nature of Chapter VII Resolutions.[31] Once international law trumps Lebanese law, then any arguments raised about the violation of Lebanese legal standards become irrelevant.[32] The STL took a similar move in its 2011 Interlocutory Decision on the Applicable Law,[33] which tried wherever possible to ensure that customary international law could filter down and override Lebanese law (Burgis-Kasthala 2013: 508–510). This judgment was therefore seminal in providing a normative justification for the STL's work as the first international 'terrorist court'.

We see in the Tribunal's jurisprudence, then, that the domestic is first silenced through the process of internationalization and then seemingly revived through the Tribunal's schooling of Lebanese institutions in international best practice. Thus, after a strong defence for the international criminal tribunalization of Hariri's murder, Judge Baragwanath re-domesticates the matter when he assures us that the 'Statute does no more than try to bring Lebanese criminal law to bear in an effective manner to ensure due investigation and fair trial of persons alleged to have committed the attacks over which the Tribunal has jurisdiction'.[34] Here we see the way in which domestic incompetence necessitates international criminal legal action, or complementarity. Once the case is seen in such terms, Defence arguments about threatened Lebanese sovereignty fade from (pur)view as this mode of legal interpretation falls outside the dominant ICL narrative subscribed to by the STL.

The STL also limits our vision of the assassination's context through a variety of depoliticizing techniques that rely on a law/politics binary between the Tribunal itself as the exemplar of judicial values and the UNSC embodying political action. Such a construction is vital for the Tribunal's robust refusal to exercise any judicial review power over the UNSC under point (iii). In characterizing the UNSC's creation of the STL under Articles 41 and 42 of the Charter, the Appeals Chamber concludes: 'What is important is that this decision is essentially political in nature, and as such not amenable to judicial review.'[35] The law/politics binary is developed further by Judge Baragwanath in his partial dissent when considering Defence allegations of unfairness and partiality. Echoing an interview given on Lebanese television a month later,[36] Judge Baragwanath assures us that the 'Tribunal has no interest in Lebanese or any other politics. It is concerned solely with the law and any evidence that tends to prove or disprove the commission of crimes within its jurisdiction.'[37] Characterizing the STL as apolitical and lacking in review power over the UNSC also allows the Tribunal to deflect Defence arguments about the highly selective purview of the STL's jurisdiction. It was solely for the UNSC to determine the scope of the Tribunal's work. Furthermore and reflecting narrative techniques of naturalization, the Trial Chamber reminds us that '"selectivity" is part of the history of international criminal jurisdictions, and an *inevitable* consequence of establishing an international criminal court or tribunal'.[38] At this point, it becomes difficult to make an argument against the naturalness of the Tribunal's creation, especially if wishing to operate within the dominant progressivist ICL narrative of ending domestic impunity as exemplified by the STL.

Conclusion

Amid the complexity of the Lebanese domestic and regional system, most members of the ICL professional community have retreated to the sturdy narrative bulwark of decontextualization and 'judicial reductionism' (Krever 2013: 720–2) as perfected by the STL in its recent jurisprudence. Here, a compelling narrative emerges about domestic impunity, international neutrality and the desirability or even inevitability of resort to ICL as embodied in the STL's mandate. Yet within this narrative frame, cracks soon emerge as to the scope of the STL's exceptionally narrow purview and its failure to recognize the very palpable politics as well as political effects of its work. Although perhaps valuable to international criminal lawyers for its engagement with certain legal technicalities, we need to question the significant resources[39] already invested in the STL and the particular interests – within and beyond the STL – that it sustains.

In this chapter I have identified the narrative devices of internationalization, depoliticization and naturalization as central in sustaining the progressive trajectory of the ICL field generally as well as the work of the STL in particular. When trying to make sense of our role in the world, international lawyers not only participate in esoteric exercises explicable to the elect; they (re)construct the world through particular linguistic devices that then enable members of their community to see only certain aspects of a given event. In the case of Hariri's murder, the polarization it has precipitated in Lebanon and beyond attests to the impossibility of agreeing on one story of assassination. Yet, this has not been my point. Instead, I have sought to use the case of the STL to remind international criminal lawyers of our own responsibility in the stories we construct through law and the many ways we can shape the purview of ICL.

Notes

1 Many thanks to Sarath Burgis-Kasthala, Heidi Matthews and Christine Schwöbel for their feedback on this chapter.
2 For example, the first photo on the STL website's section about its creation: www.stl-tsl.org/en/about-the-stl/creation-of-the-stl (accessed 4 September 2013).
3 'In order for actors to have a sense of how to proceed, they must have some understanding of where they have been, and those narrative understandings constitute the cultural stock that individuals use to reason, calculate probabilities and estimate the consequences of their actions for the future' (Barnett 1999: 14). Immi Tallgren also makes this point specifically in relation to ICL regarding the way it simplifies complexity for the international criminal lawyer (2002: 593).
4 Also see Krever (2013); and Stahn (2012: 260).
5 A good example of this is the special section of *Journal of International Criminal Justice* (11(3), 2013), assessing the work of the ICC ten years on, where faults are acknowledged, but the general tone is still one of optimism in ICL's development along the current trajectory.
6 Thus, for Khalaf, 'much of the *displaced* and *protracted* character of the collective strife that has beleaguered Lebanon at various interludes could well be a reflection of two other constant features of its fractious political history; namely the radicalization of

communal solidarities and the unsettling, often insidious, character of foreign intervention' (2002: 273, emphasis in original).

7 For example, see presentation by President Baragwanath, 'How can the STL Contribute to the Rule of Law in Lebanon?', 1 March 2012. Available at: www.youtube.com/watch?v=6b6LDbmqsbU&feature=share&list=UUV30kCf1LRRw KFgY8QYCe_g (accessed 4 September 2013).

8 UNSC Resolution 1559 (2004), 2 September.

9 For a tabulation of political assassinations, see Knudsen (2010).

10 Hamade's guard was killed in the attack: Volk (2010).

11 Statement by the Security Council, S/PRST/2005/4, 15 February 2005. Available at: http://domino.un.org/unispal.nsf/5ba47a5c6cef541b802563e000493b8c/13e7 27b26544f7b085256faa0054fee3?OpenDocument.

12 Letter dated 24 March 2005 from the Secretary-General to the President of the Security Council, S/2005/203, 24 March 2005, at para. 62. Available at: http:// unispal.un.org/UNISPAL.NSF/0/79CD8AAA858FDD2D85256FD500536047.

13 UNSC Resolution 1595 (2005), 7 April. For a useful chronology of the events discussed here, see *Prosecutor v. Al-Ayyash et al., Decision on the Defence Challenges to the Jurisdiction and Legality of the Tribunal*, 27 July 2012, Trial Chamber, Special Tribunal for Lebanon (hereinafter 27 July 2012 Trial Chamber Decision), at paras 5–14.

14 Letter of 29 March 2005 from the Chargé d'affaires a.i. of Lebanon to the United Nations to the Secretary-General (S/2005/208).

15 Namely in UNSC Resolutions 1636 (2005), 31 October; 1644 (2005), 15 December; 1686 (2006), 15 June; 1748 (2007), 27 March.

16 UNSC Resolution 1595.

17 UNSC Resolutions 1757 (2007), 30 May.

18 This is reflected in the jurisdiction of the STL, which is concerned with Hariri's killing as well as associated crimes as per Article 1 of the Tribunal's Statute: 'The Special Tribunal shall have jurisdiction over persons responsible for the attack of 14 February 2005 resulting in the death of former Lebanese Prime Minister Rafiq Hariri and in the death or injury of other persons. If the Tribunal finds that other attacks that occurred in Lebanon between 1 October 2004 and 12 December 2005, or any later date decided by the Parties and with the consent of the Security Council, are connected in accordance with the principles of criminal justice and are of a nature and gravity similar to the attack of 14 February 2005, it shall also have jurisdiction over persons responsible for such attacks.'

19 For a full list of the hearings in the *Al-Ayyash* case, see www.stl-tsl.org/en/the-cases/ stl-11-01 (last accessed 3 September 2013).

20 STL, *In the Matter of El Sayed*, Case No. CH/AC/2010/02, Decision on Appeal of Pre-Trial Judge's Order Regarding Jurisdiction and Standing, 10 November 2010 (*El-Sayed Appeal Decision*)

21 STL, *Prosecutor v. Ayyash et al.*, Case No. STL-11-01, Interlocutory Decision on the Applicable Law: Terrorism, Conspiracy, Homicide, Perpetration, Cumulative Charging, 16 February 2011 (Interlocutory Decision on the Applicable Law).

22 27 July 2012 Trial Chamber Decision; and *Prosecutor v. Al-Ayyash et al., Decision on the Defence Appeals against the Trial Chamber's Decision on the Defence Challenges to the Jurisdiction and Legality of the Tribunal*, 24 October 2012, Appeals Chamber, Special Tribunal for Lebanon (hereinafter 24 October Appeals Chamber Decision).

23 27 July 2012 Trial Chamber Decision, at para. 16 (footnotes omitted).

24 See Nikolova and Ventura (2013). For a more detailed discussion of the STL's inherent jurisdiction than that developed in the *Al-Ayyash* case, see *El-Sayed Appeal Decision*, paras 38–57.

25 ICTY, *Prosecutor v Tadic*, IT-94-1-AR72, Decision on the Defence Motion for Interlocutory Appeal on Jurisdiction, 2 October 1995.

26 Ibid., para. 29; also see Riachy J (sep. op.), 24 October Appeals Chamber Decision, para. 10.
27 27 July 2012 Trial Chamber Decision, para. 40. See dissenting opinion of Baragwanath J in general as well: 24 October Appeals Chamber Decision.
28 Baragwanath J, 24 October Appeals Chamber Decision, para. 84.
29 24 October Appeals Chamber Decision, para. 28; Baragwanath J, 24 October Appeals Chamber Decision para. 86.
30 This point is made by the Prosecution in 27 July 2012 Trial Chamber Decision, para. 52.
31 Namely, 'Lebanon is also a founding and active member of the United Nations Organization and abides by its covenants and by the Universal Declaration of Human Rights. The Government shall embody these principles in all fields and areas without exception.' Part B of the Preamble, quoted in 27 July 2012 Trial Chamber Decision, footnote 63. See also 24 October Appeals Chamber Decision, para. 30.
32 27 July 2012 Trial Chamber Decision, paras 74–78.
33 Interlocutory Decision on the Applicable Law.
34 Baragwanath J, 24 October Appeals Chamber Decision, para. 94.
35 27 July 2012 Trial Chamber Decision, para. 52.
36 Interview on LBCI's *Kalaam An-Naas*, link no longer available. Some extracts available at: www.naharnet.com/stories/en/62817 (last accessed 3 September 2013).
37 Baragwanath J, 24 October Appeals Chamber Decision, para. 94.
38 27 July 2012 Trial Chamber Decision, para. 87, emphasis added.
39 For example, in 2011, the STL's budget was $US66 million, half of which was borne by Lebanon, a huge sum for such a small country and tantamount to around half of Lebanon's entire justice outlay: Mugraby (2008) and Knudsen (2012).

Bibliography

Barnett, M. (1999) 'Culture, Strategy and Foreign Policy Change: Israel's Road to Oslo', *European Journal of International Relations* 5.

Burgess, S. (2012) 'Review Essay: Foucault's Rhetorical Challenge to Law', *International Journal of Law in Context* 8: 297.

Burgis-Kasthala, M. (2013) 'Defining Justice During Transition? International and Domestic Contestations over the Special Tribunal for Lebanon', *International Journal of Transitional Justice* 7: 497).

Charlesworth, H. (2002) 'International Law: A Discipline in Crisis', *Modern Law Review* 65: 377.

Clarke, K. M. (2009) *Fictions of Justice: The International Criminal Court and the Challenge of Legal Pluralism in Sub-Saharan Africa*, Cambridge: Cambridge University Press.

Cockayne, J. (2007) 'The Special Tribunal for Lebanon – A Cripple from Birth?', *Journal of International Criminal Justice* 5: 1061.

Cover, R. (1983–84) 'Nomos and Narrative', *Harvard Law Review* 97: 4.

Jaquemet, I. (2009) 'Fighting Amnesia: Ways to Uncover the Truth about Lebanon's Missing', *International Journal of Transitional Justice* 3: 69.

Kennedy, D. (1999–2000) 'When Renewal Repeats: Thinking against the Box', *New York University Journal of International Law and Politics* 32: 335.

Khalaf, S. (2002) *Civil and Uncivil Violence in Lebanon: A History of Internationalization of Communal Conflict*, New York: Columbia University Press.

Knudsen, A. (2010) 'Acquiescence to Assassinations in Post-Civil War Lebanon?', *Mediterranean Politics* 15: 1.

Knudsen, A. (2012) 'Special Tribunal for Lebanon: Homage to Hariri?', in A. Knudsen and M. Kerr (eds) *Lebanon after the Cedar Revolution*, London: Hurst.

Koller, D.S. (2008) 'The Faith of the International Criminal Lawyer', *New York University Journal of International Law and Politics* 40: 1019.

Koller, D.S. (2012) '… and New York and The Hague and Tokyo and Geneva and Nuremberg and …: The Geographies of International Law', *European Journal of International Law* 23: 97.

Korecki, L. (2009) 'Procedural Tools for Ensuring Cooperation of States with the Special Tribunal for Lebanon', *Journal of International Criminal Justice* 7: 927.

Krever, T. (2013) 'International Criminal Law: An Ideology Critique', *Leiden Journal of International Law* 26: 701.

Marks, S. (2003) *The Riddle of all Constitutions: International Law, Democracy and the Critique of Ideology*, Oxford: Oxford University Press.

Mégret, F. (2002) 'The Politics of International Criminal Justice', *European Journal of International Law* 13: 1261.

Mégret, F. (2013) 'Logics of Practicality and the Construction of the Field of International Criminal Justice', European Society of International Law Research Forum, Amsterdam, 24 May.

Mugraby, M. (2008) 'The Syndrome of One-Time Exceptions and the Drive to Establish the Proposed Hariri Court', *Mediterranean Politics* 13: 171.

Nikolova, M. and Ventura, M.J. (2013) 'The Special Tribunal for Lebanon Declines to Review UN Security Council Action: Retreating from *Tadi*'s Legacy in the *Ayyash* Jurisdiction and Legality Decisions', *Journal of International Criminal Justice* 11: 615.

Nouwen, S.M.H. (2012) 'Justifying Justice', in J. Crawford and M. Koskenniemi (eds) *The Cambridge Companion to International Law*, Cambridge: Cambridge University Press.

Orford, A. (1998) 'Embodying Internationalism: The Making of International Lawyers', *Australian Year Book of International Law* 19: 1.

Orford, A. (2012) 'In Praise of Description', *Leiden Journal of International Law* 25: 609.

Pearson, Z. (2008) 'Spaces of International Law', *Griffith Law Review* 17: 489.

Raub, L. (2008–09) 'Positioning Hybrid Tribunals in International Criminal Justice', *New York University Journal of International Law and Politics* 41: 1013.

Sayigh, Y. (1997) 'Armed Struggle and State Formation', *Journal of Palestine Studies* 26: 17.

Shapiro, M.J. (2007) 'The New Violent Cartography', *Security Dialogue* 38: 291.

Skouteris, T. (2010) *The Notion of Progress in International Law Discourse*, The Hague: Asser Press.

Stahn, C. (2012) 'Between "Faith" and "Facts": By What Standards Should We Assess International Criminal Justice?', *Leiden Journal of International Law* 25: 251.

Tallgren, I. (2002) 'The Sensibility and Sense of International Criminal Law', *European Journal of International Law* 13: 561.

Traboulsi, F. (2007) *A History of Modern Lebanon*, London: Pluto.

Volk, L. (2010) *Memorials and Martyrs in Modern Lebanon*, Bloomington, IN: Indiana University Press.

Wetzel, J.E. and Mitri, Y. (2008) 'The Special Tribunal for Lebanon: A Court "Off the Shelf" for a Divided Country', *The Law and Practice of International Courts and Tribunals* 7: 81.

Wierda, M., Nassar, H. and Maalouf, L. (2007) 'Early Reflections on Local Perceptions, Legitimacy and Legacy of the Special Tribunal for Lebanon', *Journal of International Criminal Justice* 5: 1065.

Zahar, M.-J. (2012) 'Foreign Interventions, Power Sharing, and the Dynamics of Conflict and Coexistence in Lebanon', in A. Knudsen and M. Kerr (eds) *Lebanon after the Cedar Revolution*, London: Hurst.

Chapter 12

The market and marketing culture of international criminal law

Christine Schwöbel[1]

A visit to the Hague

Imagine yourself in The Hague. You have just alighted from the train at the central station. The train to The Hague has taken you directly from the futuristic Schiphol airport to Den Haag Centraal. It is raining. You are here to attend one of the city's numerous conferences, events, seminars, or receptions relating to international criminal law. You enter a large imposing building, maybe the modern white enormity of the International Criminal Court (ICC) itself, or one of the older buildings in the centre of the city. A cluster of people have gathered near the entrance, greeting each other amicably. We are all friends here. There's Judge Soandso, how wonderful that he could find the time to come! The language is English, the suits are grey, the faces freshly shaved. Sophisticated small-talk: the latest book by one of the attendees published with one of the big presses, the latest weekend trip to New York, the new restaurant near the Plein. Coffee is served. After the talk, there will be wine, maybe even canapés. Backs are straight, oozing confidence. The area is decked out with banners bearing the blue logo of the ICC (two scales surrounded by two interlocking branches) and the blue logo of the UN (a world map surrounded by the same interlocking branches). There is a bullish sense of success in the air. Loud laughter fills the room. It is time to enter the lecture theatre. Seating is according to hierarchy: those in important positions sit at the front (judges first, then academics), the less important (students, and other researchers), sit at the back. The speaker straightens his suit, neatens the hair at his temples, which is showing the first signs of grey, zips on the blue PowerPoint slide and begins to speak about ... well, about mass atrocities of global concern.

In the following I aim to provide some initial thoughts on the parallel between the central paradigms of neoliberalism and the central paradigms of international criminal law (ICL). I explore whether ICL's tenacity and relative success are due to its commitments to *growth* (its market culture) and *branding* (its marketing culture).

In terms of its market culture, I argue that ICL is a greedy discipline. It moves from norm to norm, from the crime of genocide to the crime of terrorism, claiming each as its own. Moreover, it claims to have responses to the major threats of the twenty-first century, expanding its reach from the fight against impunity to a general idea of global justice. Such growth is justified by means of reference to its investment proposition: ICL makes a claim to maximizing on investments more efficiently than its competitors, namely other disciplines and other actors of international law or political theory. In my critique of ICL's greed for growth, I draw analogies between David Harvey's critique of the flow of capital in the *Enigma of Capital* and the 'flow' of ICL. Significant likenesses between the impetus for 'flow' and expansion are discovered between capitalism and ICL.

The marketing culture of ICL has boosted the discipline's success. Despite its many 'product' flaws, it is recognized – certainly in the Western world – as the primary discipline dealing with rogue political leaders. The branding of ICL is one of a discipline fighting impunity, a beacon of global justice, the heroic few internationalists who dare to fight big power-players. For understanding ICL as a successful brand and its critique, I refer to Naomi Klein's *No Logo*. Klein's central thesis is that branding places undue emphasis on image at the expense of content, symbolism at the expense of substance. I show how ICL, as a relatively new discipline coming into its own at the height of branding successes in the 1990s, not only employs branding as a way of disseminating information, but has branding at its very core, its logic.

Understanding ICL as inextricably bound up in the logic of neoliberalism – as evidenced in its market and marketing culture – provides a previously largely unexplored insight into the 'why?' of ICL's rise. In addition, I explore the question of who benefits and who loses out in a neoliberal model of ICL. I argue that ICL, by operating within the parameters of neoliberalism, is in fact strengthening the big power-players (rather than fighting them), maintaining and reproducing an international elite. At the same time, the very group in whose interest the fight is supposedly being fought – the victims – lose out through mechanisms which fix their identities, racialize, feminize, and infantilize them.

The opening lines are intended to literally 'set the scene' for the following theoretical discussions. The scene evokes several possible pertinent critiques: gender critique, hegemony, remoteness from the *real* atrocity, a centre/periphery critique, and a class critique, among others. Not all can be dealt with in the detailed analysis they deserve. What the following focuses on (while attempting to take the aforementioned sites into account) is an understanding of the 'bullish sense of success' which is in the air when one attends an ICL function in The Hague.

The market culture

In this section, the reasoning for and the method of ICL's growth will be exposed as being in line with the reasoning and method in which capital is made to grow according to neoliberal principles.[2] Neoliberalism relates to the idea of putting capital (money and other assets) to use. Capital is, according to David Harvey, 'not a thing but a process in which money is perpetually sent in search of more money' (2010: 40). Similarly, ICL can be regarded as a process which is perpetually sent in search of new markets. This is facilitated through a normative growth narrative: one which tracks the development of ICL (its growth) through its norms, say, the criminalization of genocide or crimes against humanity.

Neoliberalism is today largely employed as a term of critique. It is commonly used by those who are concerned about the prioritization of private property, the declining appreciation and understanding of ideas of community and commonality, the preoccupation with markets, with the individual (and individual freedoms), and the domination of a small class of ruling elite who have gained and maintained their wealth at the expense of the poor. It is a term commonly used by a left-leaning group of intellectuals. My points of departure for neoliberalism are both the workings of the market and the workings of marketing.

Growth narratives

The purpose of the neoliberal market is development through growth (Harvey 2007: 7–8). ICL's growth is inextricably tied to a historical narrative of progress, particularly institutional progress which has enabled the criminalization of gross rights violations. Thus, one of the key growth markers for the discipline has been the number of crimes which have been internationalized (a normative growth narrative). The *accepted* history, as Sarah Nouwen wisely calls it (2012: 328), is one which (with a few detours to piracy and slavery) begins with the Nuremberg and Tokyo tribunals. Then, so the accepted history continues, there was a period of stagnation prompted by the Cold War. And, finally, in the 1990s and the 2000s the discipline 'came into its own'. The tribunals and the permanent court were established and so it is now a discipline in its own right with a bright future of fighting impunity ahead. The history of the discipline is one associated with growth, development, and a coming-of-age story: from its infancy in Nuremberg, and its flaws, to the growing pains of its adolescence in the 1990s, to the establishment of the mature ICC as a beacon of justice.[3]

The normative growth narrative is particularly interesting in view of the fact that the catalogue of crimes is rather short. The Rome Statute, the treaty establishing the ICC, references only four international crimes: genocide, war crimes, crimes against humanity, and the crime of aggression (Art. 5 I, Rome Statute). This is contrary to developments in other international law disciplines in which the growth of the discipline has gone hand in hand with proliferation in the number of rules; most notably this is the case in human rights law. In ICL, the preferred strategy for growth so far has been to subsume new international crimes under the already existing crimes by means of wide interpretations. For this purpose, 'crimes against humanity' and 'war crimes' have seemingly been employed as catch-all crimes. Illustrative is Article 7 of the Rome Statute (crimes against humanity), which not only acts as the provision to include crimes committed within the borders of states (precluding the previous requirement of 'inter-national' crimes), it also includes the provision of 'other inhumane acts' as acts which 'intentionally [cause] great suffering, or serious injury to body or health'. The judges at the ICC and at the *ad hoc* tribunals have been inclined to interpret such provisions widely (Kress 2010). Such normative growth through interpretation has at times been referred to (with a possibly negative connotation) as 'judicial activism' (Schabas 2008), at other times as (the much more pleasant-sounding) 'judicial creativity'. Joseph Powderly states that 'it is far from an exaggeration to claim that judicial creativity, the sculpting of the relatively featureless granite of existing law in order to give it form, effect, and reason, is the life blood of international criminal law' (2011: 18).

International criminal lawyers employ interpretation as a tool for growth even if '*direct* criminalization [is] impossible', as Larissa van den Herik notes in a recent contribution (2013). Van den Herik proposes that ICL's 'blind spot' on socio-economic abuses should be addressed through the criminalization of the infringement of socio-economic rights (2013: 7). She argues that ICL's mandate should be understood as stretching beyond the strict lens of criminal law to include broader reflections on post-conflict justice and peace management (2013: 19). These are areas which were previously served by the field of transitional justice. Transitional justice is commonly defined as the 'conception of justice associated with periods of political change, characterized by legal responses to confront the wrongdoings of repressive predecessor regimes' (Teitel 2003: 69). In Teitel's understanding, ICL is merely a component of the wider idea of transitional justice, which will also include questions on truth commissions, reparations, and institutional reform. Yet, ICL has appropriated these mechanisms, understanding itself (its experts, statutes, vocabulary) as the primary discipline for such questions, therefore arguably swallowing the entire discipline of transitional justice.

Mergers and acquisitions

These examples of growth narratives are noteworthy since growth is not occurring into previously uncharted territories. Indeed, there is significant overlap between ICL and other disciplines – international human rights law, international humanitarian law, transnational justice research, post-conflict studies, development studies, and not to forget domestic criminal law. The fact that accountability questions are already addressed in other disciplines, organizations and theories leads one to question the need for expansion. There appears to have emerged a 'discipline creep' in which ICL, and with it individual responsibility of the 'big fish', has become the primary mechanism for accountability. One could even argue that this is more than a 'creep', that in fact we are dealing with one of neoliberalism's more truculent policies – an aggressive mergers and acquisition (M&A) strategy. One speaks of an aggressive M&A strategy if the chosen mechanism for growth is *inorganic*. Inorganic growth is pursued when particularly fast growth is sought through the exploitation of a series of new markets and/or the purchasing of access to new customers.

Harvey's work on capitalism is instructive in regard to understanding the preoccupation with (inorganic) growth and its creation of inequalities. In *The Enigma of Capital*, Harvey follows the journey of capitalism through the past decades. He is particularly interested in the 'flow' of capital. Capital has, according to Harvey (2010), the ability to flow into the tiniest crevices – even appearing to be immune to disruptions such as the global financial crisis. He begins his enquiry into the flow of capital with the history of the housing market as the market which prompted the financial crisis in 2008 (2010: 17). In the 1980s and 1990s, the suppression of labour earnings meant the beginnings of a credit society – consumer spending is crucial for growth, especially in the US where it is the main single contributor to GDP. The credit market was initially restricted to the steadily employed population; but this market was exhausted by the 1990s. The issue was that (debt-financed) property developers were still building properties. Thus, a demand problem became apparent. Growth of the market was prompted by extending debt-financing to people with no steady income; a policy which occurred through exercising political pressure on financial institutions. These sub-prime loans were to be the locality of the uncovering of the fragility of the system.

> The demand problem was temporarily bridged with respect to housing by debt-financing the developers as well as the buyers. The financial institutions collectively controlled both the supply of, and demand for, housing!
>
> (Harvey 2010: 17)

The need for growth, even at the expense of the low-income population, was the overriding interest of the few who were running the financial institutions. Growth was facilitated through artificially created demand and supply. Capital accumulation in this form created new class inequalities and deepened existing ones (2010: 240–1).

Arguably, similar patterns can be found in ICL. Growth narratives are initiated from the centres of international law (the UN, the Hague tribunals), and are brought to bear on the periphery (those states and actors which are not allied with the international hegemons) through calls for criminal responsibility. The proponents of ICL seek to exploit new markets when they claim jurisdiction over a new geography or a new crime. The establishment of the Special Tribunal for Lebanon (STL) may serve as an example: The 2005 assassination of Lebanon's former Prime Minister Rafiq Hariri was internationalized through dubbing his killing 'an act of terrorism' and granting jurisdiction to an international tribunal set up through Security Council resolution (Burgis-Kasthala, Chapter 11 in this volume). Both domestic criminal law and the Lebanese institutions were deemed inadequate to deal with the crime. Given that the STL is part-funded by voluntary contributions, a new group of consumers (donor states) was accessed.

The first situation before the ICC, in the form of the self-referral of the Ugandan government, is a further interesting example of growth from the centre (despite it being a *self*-referral). It was apparent after the fanfare-accompanied establishment of the ICC that the court needed its first case. The supply had been established, but there was no demand. When the Ugandan government approached the Office of the Prosecutor (OTP) regarding the possibility of a self-referral in regard to crimes allegedly committed by the Lord's Resistance Army, a militant movement which was challenging and resisting the power of the government forces, the Prosecutor took on the situation in northern Uganda lock, stock and barrel. The need for creating demand for the supplied services was so great that the possible crimes committed by the Ugandan government forces themselves were ignored in the investigations. Seemingly, the Prosecutor was happy for the ICC to be used as a military strategy for delegitimizing the political opposition. The ICC provided the Ugandan government with a world stage and allowed them to entrench their narrative of the conflict in history (Nouwen and Werner 2011). One cannot help but be suspicious that the ICC was willing to compromise on its ideas of fighting impunity, fighting the big power-players, in favour of growth.

The Ugandan self-referral led to a whole string of self-referrals – self-referrals by the Democratic Republic of Congo and the Central African Republic followed quick on the heels of Uganda's self-referral. That the impetus came from the states themselves, no less, highlights the point of the neoliberal-like flow of ICL. The expansion of big brands is often facilitated by the creation of demand with the help of the *manufactured consent* of the local population. Indeed, manufactured consent can be traced back to the Prosecutor actively inviting voluntary referrals – and giving these cases preference – stating that this 'increases the likelihood of important cooperation and support on the ground' (ICC 2006). The expansion of, say, Coca-Cola has operated in much the same way, prompting critics to refer to this form of cultural neo-imperialism as 'Coca-colonisation' (Pendergast 1993).

According to Harvey, the exportation of capital and cultivation of new markets around the world is systematic; a truly effective mechanism could be established only with the construction of a globally interlinked system (2010: 18). Therefore, a substantive *legal* principle is necessary to construct and enable the uninhibited flow of ICL. The search for such a principle leads us to an unlikely and possibly counter-intuitive candidate: the principle of complementarity. The principle of complementarity, as set out in the Rome Statute, dictates that the ICC only has jurisdiction over a situation if the domestic judiciary is 'unwilling or unable' to investigate or prosecute the case (Art. 17, Rome Statute).

This principle purports to enable the decentralization of international criminal justice, and stresses the priority of domestic courts. Could this really be the hegemonic principle at the core of the interlinked system? The ICC is the most likely institutional candidate since it is, as opposed to the other institutions of ICL, a permanent court. Crucially, one has to ask *whose* standards are applied when the Rome Statute speaks of 'unwilling or unable'? Who determines whether the criteria have been met? Without doubt, international criminal justice has followed Western ideas of criminal justice. The crimes, procedure, prioritization of consequentialist and punitive means of criminal justice, and courts and detention facilities, are modelled on Western criminal justice. How could non-Western countries ever meet these standards? The standards and requirements of the centre's ideas of international criminal justice are presented as achievable yet remain unattainable for peripheral states.

This section has explored the narratives and policies pursued by the proponents of ICL to further the growth of the discipline, referred to here as the market culture of ICL. It has been suggested that the rhetoric of addressing impunity and fighting for global justice may be a screen – a narrative adopted which veils the purpose of growth and ultimately empire-building. The advocates of ICL appear to be artificially creating gaps, declaring the given norms, institutions and experts inadequate to address injustices. They then present the world with the necessary solution – that is, the norms, institutions and experts of international criminal law. ICL, according to these findings, is a means of creating, maintaining and justifying the perpetuation of power with certain elites. ICL should thus be understood as a driver for deepening inequalities rather than as a mechanism of addressing questions of global injustice.

Marketing culture

This section considers the branding and marketing success of ICL, particularly of its flagship institution the ICC. The enquiry focuses on how the 'flow' of ICL is, through clever branding strategies, enabled and legitimized. The consumers of ICL, the most important group being donor states, are sold a story of how the principles, institutions and experts of ICL can have certain political benefits. Security, governance and development can be pursued through the paradigms of ICL.

A distinction must be made first. Branding and marketing are often employed synonymously; however, a difference is worth noting in that branding and marketing are mostly part of a two-step process. A product is branded and brand-managed first. Branding involves the creation of a unique name and image for a particular product. This is about the attributes of a product, the promise: *ICL has the ability to fight impunity in order to achieve global justice.* Marketing regards the selling of the product: *If recognized as the tool for fighting impunity and pursuing global justice, ICL will bring certain (political) benefits.* The two are interdependent. Branding a product will be with a view to marketing it; marketing without branding is almost impossible (Kotler and Keller 2011, Ch. 9).

Branding

In this order, then, let us take a closer look at the branding of ICL: that is, its promise of fighting impunity in order to attain global justice. I argue that the logos, slogans, promotional clips and documentaries do not merely represent information and communication; rather, they are reminiscent of the way a superbrand like Google goes about its self-promotion. In the public sphere, this type of promotion is mostly referred to as propaganda, but more on that later.

In a neoliberal society the search for more money is facilitated through branding. Branding involves the creation of a unique name and image for a particular product. Global brands which come to mind are Coca-Cola, Nike, or Levi's. Branding is, of course, not only employed by manufacturers; it is also employed by service corporations: Google, eBay, Yahoo. Branding has become so prominent, so ubiquitous in everyday life, that it is not confined to the private sector, it has also taken on the public space. Exemplifying this, Naomi Klein refers to President Obama of the United States as the first political Megabrand (Klein 2010: xix–xxxi). International organizations also employ branding in order to market their services. The UN, with its blue logo of the globe, employs branding.

In her book *No Logo* Naomi Klein explores how management theorists in the 1980s developed the 'seemingly innocuous idea … that successful brands must primarily produce brands, as opposed to products' (2010: 3). One corporation she followed in this change from product to brand is Nike. 'Nike isn't a running shoe company, it is about *the idea of transcendence through sports*' (2010: xvii, original emphasis). In the wake of this change in strategy, Nike closed its original factories. Production was outsourced to an intricate web of contractors and subcontractors, preferably abroad. This, according to Klein, allows corporations to pour resources into the design and marketing required to fully project the big idea (2010: xvii). 'Creating meaning was the new act of production' (2010: xviii). What is left at the centre of the corporation is a shell – the workers and the factories have been replaced by a small group of brand managers.

The operation of ICL appears to bear some resemblance with this. The idea behind ICL is no less ambitious than *global justice* – a 'big idea', and those who promote its principles have arguably taken on the role of brand managers. Whether it is the easily understandable four international crimes or the clarity which comes with a guilty/not guilty verdict, much of the appeal of ICL lies in its simple message. Elsewhere, I have described this as the 'comfort' of ICL (Schwöbel 2013). Such stripping down of a complex relationship of accountability, negotiation, culpability, punishment and deterrence to a simple message seems to bear much resemblance with the branding of contemporary superbrands. Both superbrands and ICL have a distinct preference for symbolism over substance.

The ICC offers itself as a particularly apt example of symbolism over substance with the clever workings of brand managers. Preference for symbolism over substance can, somewhat crudely, be demonstrated through the very few cases which have, in the past 11 years, come to trial (at the time of writing, 18 cases in eight situations). This can be contrasted with the many press statements, documentaries, meetings and photo opportunities in the same period.

The symbolism is particularly strong when one regards the ICC building. Whenever the ICC is mentioned in the mainstream media, the same image of the building is depicted. The ICC is modern, white and imposing, set against a blue sky. Interestingly, most photos are taken from below, causing the onlooker to understand themselves as *looking up* to this edifice of global justice. Entering 'International Criminal Court' in a search engine such as Google Images leads one to several variations of this same picture. Interspersed with pictures of the modern white architecture is the image of Thomas Lubanga, the first defendant whose case came to sentencing in the trial chamber. Only a headshot is shown, reminiscent of a mug shot. He is black, smiling wryly. Notwithstanding the long-standing promise that the court will move into a different building, as well as the fact that the current Prosecutor is herself black, one is fed imagery that speaks to the stereotypes of white-equals-good, black(man)-equals-bad.

The role of brand manager was taken particularly seriously by the former Prosecutor of the ICC, Luis Moreno-Ocampo, who has previously stated ambitiously that the ICC is not only an institution which addresses impunity but one which addresses the 'threats and challenges of the twenty-first century' (Moreno-Ocampo 2008: 215). In April 2012, Moreno-Ocampo attended a Hollywood dinner with film directors, producers and actors to further the cause of Invisible Children, the NGO which launched the Kony 2012 campaign – a social media movement which itself suffered credibility issues due to its preference of symbolism over substance. At this dinner, he declared: 'It's a new world. All over the world, the new generation says, "Stop ignoring crimes by our leaders." We cannot live in such a world. And that is my mission, too' (Reuters 2012). Without doubt, this is the brand manager of a *big idea* speaking, using evocative yet simple language to explain his promise.

The stereotypes of black-man-equals-bad as well as black-child/woman-equals-victim are used in the documentaries about the ICC and about its former Prosecutor. In the trailer for the 2010 film *Prosecutor*, which follows Moreno-Ocampo ('the man in the white suit') through the first trials of the ICC, a soft voice opens: 'A war was fought on these hills [*lush green countryside is shown*], and war crimes were committed [*a young black man carrying a big gun*], that's why the man in the white suit has come to this Congolese village [*a white helicopter is landing, from which Ocampo jumps, wearing a white suit, the camera sweeps to African villagers assembled outside, it rests too close on the face of a young villager, the camera sweeps back to Ocampo*], his name [*pause*]: Luis Moreno-Ocampo.' The trailer goes on to describe Moreno-Ocampo as taking on the role of salesman for 'a new idea [*pause*] global justice'. Other documentaries, including *The Reckoning* from 2010 and *The Court*, released in 2013, make use of the same narrative of heroes, victims and perpetrators (Werner 2014). All are narrated from the perspective of the Office of the Prosecutor, with the Prosecutor undoubtedly inhabiting the role of the hero – and in addition to this, the role of brand manager of ICL.

The ICC employs a highly evocative language, making abundant use of superlative adjectives – a strategy also favoured by branding experts. One glance at the Preamble of the Rome Statute is indicative of the extent of this language. 'Mindful that during this century millions of children, women and men have been victims of *unimaginable* atrocities that *deeply* shock the conscience of humanity' (emphases added) is one case in point. The story is one beginning with desperation and ending with salvation.

Such a feel-good image of global justice is particularly appealing in light of economically difficult times and daily reports on conflicts and casualties across the world. According to Klein, the market research of corporations in the 1990s 'had found a longing in people for something more than shopping – for social change, for public space, for greater equality and diversity' (Klein 2010: xxxi). In her tenth anniversary issue, Klein bravely explores this feel-good factor in regard to the superbrand of the current President of the US, Barack Obama: 'As a brand, the Obama White House's identity is probably closest to Starbucks: hip, progressive, approachable – a small luxury you can feel good about even during tough economic times' (2010: xxv). Grand symbolic gestures are favoured above deep structural change. While considering Obama, it should be noted that the fact that the US is not a signatory to the Rome Statute has not seemingly weakened ICL's *global* justice image. Indeed, ICL has incorporated the self-exclusion (or exceptionalism) of the US into its branding message: The US, the big power-player among nations, is the Goliath among the world's Davids who are fighting for justice.

One has to ask whether the imagery is simply a case of (harmless) information – informing potential victims and the international community on the mechanisms of ICL –; or can it be regarded as (the more sinister) propaganda? Arguably, the branding exercise is manufacturing the consent by which to mobilize support for the special interests that dominate activities of the elite. In their book *Manufacturing Consent* Edward S. Herman and Noam Chomsky argued that the US media is operating in conformity with elite priorities (Herman and Chomsky 1994). The mass media has, according to them, coalesced in processing news in a way that fails to place US policy into meaningful context and systematically suppresses evidence of US violence and aggression. Although the democratic postulate is that the media are independent and committed to reporting the truth, they operate in a way which furthers the interests of state and private activity. This is an outcome of the workings of market forces. The promise of global justice through ICL operates in a similar way. The context of crimes is omitted and evidence of the involvement and complicity of the big power-players in violence and aggression is suppressed. Although the postulate of ICL is ideological neutrality and universality, it operates in a way to further the interests of the world's hegemons. We are dealing with propaganda, not information.

There are further examples of the preference for symbolism over substance in ICL; the images of the ICC, the documentaries, and the wording of the Preamble of the Rome Statute have been selected as particularly appropriate to provide a sense of the branding which has placed ICL as the primary institution for global justice. In this, a simple black-and-white (often literally) message is employed.

In this section I have argued that the inorganic growth – the aggressive search for new markets and consumers – is facilitated through branding. By using examples of the ICC, the symbolism employed by ICL was explored. This symbolism is employed to, in Naomi Klein's words, create meaning over production. The promise of global justice (the brand) is created, tended and prioritized over the actual fight against impunity.

Marketing

How, then, is this brand of global justice marketed across the world? In other words, how and to whom is the product, or the grand idea, sold? In *Marketing Management*, a widely used textbook on marketing, Kotler and Keller (2011) stress the importance in marketing of 'identifying unfulfilled needs and desires'. Conflict, poverty, terrorism, torture provoke unfulfilled needs for peace, equality and punishment of those responsible. ICL claims to have an answer in the form of fighting impunity of those responsible for heinous crimes. Where international humanitarian law, human rights law, the social sciences, and sometimes domestic criminal law, fall short is in regard to enforcement mechanisms. ICL, however, with its ability to punish and even imprison those who have violated international crimes, offers a solution to this unfulfilled need. Yet, the responses ICL can provide to global injustice are also *managed*. Efficiency plays a major role in the assessment of what is encompassed in responses to global injustices. The proponents of ICL not only expand its mandate, they also limit it when failure looks like a possibility. One provocative example of such management lies in the lack of investigations into international crimes committed by Western leaders.

According to Kotler and Keller, marketing 'defines, measures and quantifies the size of the identified market and the profit potential'. Without question, the market of ICL is global. But whom is the marketing directed at? Who 'buys' ICL? Arguably, there are a number of different potential consumer groups, with some having greater buying power than others. First, there are the potential victims. ICL is 'sold' to victims, and civil society organizations representing their interests, as the solution to their problems. However, the victims of international crimes and their representatives have little buying power. Then, there are the possible donors to international criminal justice; these may be states or private sector donors, who have considerably more buying power. The Special Court for Sierra Leone, as well as the tribunals for Cambodia (ECCC) and Lebanon (STL) are financed entirely through voluntary state contributions. Such 'donor-driven justice', as Barbara Oomen (2005) calls it, is not motivated by altruism. Rather, certain political ends may be met by the sponsorship of an international criminal tribunal. 'Politically, donor states may regard international criminal courts as vehicles for their own foreign-policy objectives, including security, governance, and development' (Kendall 2011: 587). Carla del Ponte, then Prosecutor of the ICTY, famously gave a speech at Goldman Sachs in which she spoke of the 'dividends' of ICL; in particular she stated that the 'profits' of ICL lie in its ability to stabilize war-torn countries so that private actors may then invest in the state (Del Ponte 2005). Fighting impunity is not the only unfulfilled need for donors – political power struggles can be settled with the help of ICL. These particular donors, those who can afford it, make attractive consumers of ICL. The third target market is no less than the international community itself. The more the international community, in the form of the media, the public demand, bloggers and tweeters, refer to ICL and its institutions as providing solutions in times of crisis, the more the institutions gain in legitimacy (and funding). In public debate, it has become commonplace for despot leaders to be labelled 'war criminals', and their accountability before an international tribunal to be demanded.

   ICL therefore is branded as a means by which to achieve global justice, and is then marketed to its consumers as a political tool, predominantly to donor states who wish to pursue security, governance and development ends through it.

The context

In this section, I aim to sketch out some of the conditions which have led ICL to enjoy this extent of tenacity. I am interested in the question why ICL and its central paradigms – its market and marketing culture – have been so successful. To begin with a somewhat vapid turn of phrase: ICL does not exist in a vacuum. Context must be taken seriously. Taking context seriously, according to China Miéville, means reaching beyond the idealist constructivism, which is the limitation of most contemporary critique (Miéville 2008: 95). In order to attempt to reach beyond idealist constructivism, this section aims to privilege the specific historical context in which the paradigms of ICL take hold, and how; rather than viewing ICL as a set of abstract concepts – such as accountability, complementarity (as would be the idealist constuctivist approach). Certainly, one can speak of the judicialization of international law, juridified diplomacy, or similar phrases, when considering the historical context. But, this is an attempt to go further than even that. In order to unearth the systematic structural constraints and dynamics operating in and on ICL, Miéville's commodity-form theory could be an appropriate point of departure.

Miéville's premise is that it does not go far enough to claim that the neoliberalist leaning of international law is due to domestic analogies. The world is not simply composed of a number of individual states subscribing to the ideology of neoliberalism. The international and transnational are *themselves* spaces of neoliberalism: 'The logic of modern inter-state relations is defined by the same logic that regulates individuals in capitalism, because since the system's birth – and in the underlying precepts of international law – states, like individuals, interact as property owners' (Miéville 2008: 96). Relying on the work of Bolshevik legal theorist Yevgeny Pashukanis, Miéville notes that the legal form itself functions as a commodity. Individuals are regarded as legal personalities, the bearers of rights. The punishment of the infringement of these rights must be understood as the ultimate enforcement of capitalism. Coercion (violence) is, as Miéville notes, 'at the heart of the commodity form. For a commodity meaningfully to be "mine-not-yours" – which is, after all, central to the fact that it is a commodity that will be exchanged – some forceful capabilities must be implied' (2008: 113). This 'mine-not-yours' attribute and the coercion which comes with it can be mapped onto an understanding of ICL in its claiming the freedom of those found guilty.

Whether one follows the commodity-form theory, which admittedly paints a rather dismal picture for any progressive potential of ICL, or not, one must certainly agree that political economy and the law are inextricably intertwined. David Kennedy has recently argued that elements of economic life – capital, labour, credit, money, liquidity – are creatures of the law; meaning they are *created* by law. This is also the case with elements of political life – power and right (Kennedy 2013: 8). I would like to add that the same applies vice-versa: law is itself determined by economic and political life. In applying this thinking to ICL, one must conclude that it operates through neoliberal paradigms, not necessarily due to the states, organizations or individuals who further its cause, but because neoliberalism pervades its core, its logic.

At first blush, this realization may not seem particularly profound; yet, it does become worthy of attention if legitimation of an area of law is awarded through seemingly ideology-neutral tropes and slogans. 'Global justice' in today's world, and therefore in today's ICL, is not a neutral term, but one which is aligned with the features of neoliberalism (see Krever, Chapter 5 in this volume). Given that the discipline is regarded as only fully 'coming into its own' at a time when the clash between the two predominant ideologies was decided in favour of liberalism, such a synergy was arguably inescapable. This explains the attitudes of the international criminal lawyers from the opening scene. They fit perfectly with the predominant ideology. ICL is hip, smart and bourgeois, just like the world in which its advocates live. Yet, what of those who have none of these traits, the so-called 'bottom billion', and *their* 'global justice'?

Who wins, who loses?

So far, some of the stakes have been briefly highlighted; although it cannot be explored fully here, this final section brings the question of who wins and who loses sharper into focus. Essentially, the big power-players benefit from ICL. This is significant given that ICL is branded as *fighting* the big power-players in the name of global justice. Who loses out then? The very group in whose interest the fight is supposedly being fought: the victims – and this term must be understood as a strategic rather than definable or definitive label.

Let us investigate the situation of the victims of serious international crimes a little closer. The neoliberal mechanism for centralizing supply and demand for the purpose of growth can arguably lead to the depoliticization of victims. What does this mean? If institutions are defining certain crimes (controlling demand) and are at the same time offering the exclusive mechanism for addressing these crimes (controlling supply), this limits the possibilities for victims to achieve redress. ICL is creating a single mechanism of redress which victims of crimes must match themselves and their concerns up to. ICL undoubtedly privileges punishment over reconciliation. Individual responsibility of those carrying the greatest responsibility is established as the only mechanism of redress, while *all others are obscured.* Prompted by this area of law becoming technicalized with definitions, legal hoops to jump through, processes to observe, the victims' interests are depoliticized. Even at the ICC, where victims' interests may be represented through victim participation, 'ICC intervention tends to lead to a *depoliticization* of those victims by promoting among them a political dependency mediated by international law. This depoliticization hinders the realization of justice for those subject to violence,' states Adam Branch (2007: 180). He is concerned that the ICC may be silencing and disciplining victims as it claims to empower them (Branch 2011: 193). Such technicalization and depoliticization puts victimhood at risk of becoming a fixed identity (Kendall and Nouwen 2013). Kendall and Nouwen argue that the legal categorization of what is a broad base of victims, 'juridified victimhood', results in a narrowing of the victims considered 'legally relevant'; only those victims who are legally recognized as such, because their suffering is recognized as an international crime or because they have registered for participation in ICC proceedings, may seek redress. The fixed identity of victims allows for their control as well as the management of the promise of ICL.

A further theme which has been alluded to in the above is the racializing property of ICL. The focus of international criminal justice on Africa in conjunction with the simplifying features of ICL has led to a stereotyping of African roles. The black man is the perpetrator; the black child and woman are the victims; the white Western intervener is the hero. Such reduction demonizes and exceptionalizes perpetrators, infantilizes and feminizes victims, and celebrates Western interveners while exonerating them from any complicity in the crimes. The masculine, bullish atmosphere in the opening paragraph is one of triumph: we are building empires, ruling the world from the epicentre of ICL, is what these figures say. Anne Orford (1999) has labelled such endeavours 'muscular humanitarianism'. In stark contrast to the Other (here the victims of international crimes), mainstream international lawyers view themselves as the masculine, strong heroes who speak in the name of justice. Thus, a narrative of a binary is created between the strong, interventionist, active, masculine on the one hand and its polar opposite, the weak, subjugated, passive, feminine on the other hand. The logic behind it is empire-building; the reasoning is reducing costs through efficiency of scale.

Arguably, ICL campaigns and suppressions, the shading of some issues and emphasizing of others, the selection of context, premises, and the general agenda of 'global' justice are particularly functional for established power. The support, framing, and financing of international criminal tribunals goes at the behest of those states which have the largest economic and military capabilities (the world's hegemons). Supporters, framers and financers are conveniently never subjected to the jurisdiction of these tribunals – they are the heroes, rarely the victims, and never the perpetrators. So while claiming to fight big power-players, ICL is in fact privileging their interests at the expense of the vulnerable in society. It turns out that those who lose out are precisely those in whose name the market and marketing policies are promoted.

Conclusion

In his book titled *Neoliberalism*, Harvey surmises:

> Neoliberalism has, in short, become hegemonic as a mode of discourse. It has pervasive effects on ways of thought to the point where it has become incorporated into the common-sense way many of us interpret, live in, and understand the world.
>
> (Harvey 2007: 3)

The above has tried to show how, by means of a market and a marketing culture, ICL has not been spared these pervasive effects of neoliberalism. Indeed, neoliberalism's pervasiveness is what explains the stellar rise and appeal of the discipline. ICL has adopted a market culture in that it is fore-grounding growth: ICL is arguably employing an aggressive merger and acquisition strategy in order to eliminate its competitors, while employing the argument of a gap in accountability, and a need for global justice, as its reasoning. This is happening at the expense of victims of conflict and at the expense of alternative justice mechanisms. Further, ICL has adopted a marketing culture with the use of branding strategies: ICL, particularly the ICC as its most important institution, are promoted as the exclusive mechanisms for attaining global justice. This image is sold to victims of conflict, donor states and the international community. Such strategies are privileging elites in the international community – the states, organizations and individuals who have the greatest political and economic power – at the expense of those whom ICL is supposedly assisting: the victims of conflict, the poor, minorities, the socially disadvantaged.

While the neoliberal context explains some of ICL's parameters, it is no exoneration of the complicity of ICL and its proponents in the neoliberal ideology. Possibly, it is also not a final explanation of ICL's biases; there may yet be a progressive potential in the discipline. However, that may be for others to explore. This has merely been the examination of a threshold issue, namely unveiling the neoliberal ideology which lies at ICL's core.

Notes

1 My thanks to Michelle Burgis-Kasthala, Ioannis Kalpouzos, Rob Knox, Tor Krever, Sarah Nouwen, James O'Connor, and Immi Tallgren for very helpful comments on earlier drafts. All errors are my own.
2 Tor Krever explores the political economy of ICL in his interrogation of the ideological character of ICL discourse (see Krever 2013); see also Grietje Baars, Chapter 9 in this volume.
3 See Part III (chapters by Simpson, Haslam, and Baars) for suggestions to unsettle this accepted history.

Bibliography

Branch, A. (2007) 'Uganda's Civil War and the Politics of ICC Intervention', *Ethics and International Affairs* 21: 179–98.

Branch, A. (2011) *Displacing Human Rights: War and Intervention in Northern Uganda*, Oxford: Oxford University Press.

Del Ponte, C. (2005) 'The Dividends of International Criminal Justice', Goldman Sachs, London, 6 October. Available at: www.icty.org/x/file/Press/PR_attachments/cdp-goldmansachs-050610-e.htm (accessed 19 June 2013).

Harvey, D. (2007) *Neoliberalism*, Oxford: Oxford University Press.

Harvey, D. (2010) *The Enigma of Capital*, London: Profile Books.

Herman, E.S. and Chomsky, N. (1994) *Manufacturing Consent*, London: Vintage Books.

ICC (2006) OTP Report, 'On the Activities Performed During the First Three Years' (June 2003–June 2006), at www.icc-cpi.int/NR/rdonlyres/D76A5D89-FB64-47A9-9821-725747378AB2/143680/OTP_3yearreport20060914_English.pdf (accessed 31 July 2013).

Kendall, S. (2011) 'Donors' Justice: Recasting International Criminal Accountability', *Leiden Journal of International Law* 24: 585–606.

Kendall, S. and Nouwen, S. (2013) 'Representational Practices: The Victim as the Sovereign of the International Criminal Court?', *Law and Contemporary Problems*, 76.

Kennedy, D. (2013) 'Law and Political Economy of the World', *Leiden Journal of International Law*, 26: 7–48.

Klein, N. (2010) *No Logo*, 10th anniversary edn, London: Fourth Estate.

Kotler, P. and Keller, K. (2011) *Marketing Management*, New Jersey: Prentice Hall.

Kress, C. (2010) 'On the Outer Limits of Crimes against Humanity: The Concept of Organization within the Policy Requirement: Some Reflections on the March 2010 ICC *Kenya* Decision', *Leiden Journal of International Law* 23: 855–73.

Krever, T. (2013) 'International Criminal Law: An Ideology Critique', *Leiden Journal of International Law* 26: 701–23.

Miéville, C. (2008) 'Commodity-Form Theory of International Law', in S. Marks (ed.) *International Law on the Left: Reexamining Marxist Legacies*, Cambridge: Cambridge University Press.

Moreno-Ocampo, L. (2008) 'The International Criminal Court: Seeking Global Justice', *Case Western Reserve Journal of International Law*, 40: 215–25.

Nouwen, S. (2012) 'Justifying Justice', in J. Crawford and M. Koskenniemi (eds) *The Cambridge Companion to International Law*, Cambridge: Cambridge University Press.

Nouwen, S. and Werner, W. (2011) 'Doing Justice to the Political', *European Journal of International Law* 21: 941–65.

Oomen, B. (2005) 'Donor-driven Justice and its Discontents: The Case of Rwanda', *Development and Change* 36: 887–910.

Orford, A. (1999) 'Muscular Humanitarianism: Reading the Narratives of the New Interventionism', *European Journal of International Law* 10: 679–711.

Pendergast, M. (1993) 'Viewpoints; A Brief History of Coca-Colonization', *New York Times*. Available at: www.nytimes.com/1993/08/15/business/viewpoints-a-brief-history-of-coca-colonization.html (accessed 21 June 2013).

Powderly, J. (2011) 'Judicial Interpretation at the *Ad Hoc* Tribunals: Method from Chaos?', in S. Darcy and J. Powderly (eds) *Judicial Creativity at the International Criminal Tribunals*, Oxford: Oxford University Press.

Reuters (2012) 'ICC Prosecutor Courts Hollywood with Invisible Children', *Reuters*. Available at: www.reuters.com/article/2012/04/01/us-kony-campaign-hollywood-idUSBRE8300JZ20120401 (accessed 25 June 2013).

Schabas, W. (2008) 'Prosecutorial Discretion v. Judicial Activism at the International Criminal Court', *Journal of International Criminal Justice* 6: 731–61.

Schwöbel, C. (2013) 'The Comfort of International Criminal Law', *Law and Critique* 24: 169–91.

Teitel, R. (2003) 'Transitional Justice Geneology', *Harvard Human Rights Journal* 16: 69–94.

Van den Herik, L. (2013) 'Economic, Social and Cultural Rights – International Criminal Law's Blind Spot?', in E. Riedel, C. Golay and G. Mahon (eds) *Economic, Social and Cultural Rights: Contemporary Issues and Challenges*, Oxford: Oxford University Press. Available online at: http://papers.ssrn.com/sol3/papers.cfm?abstract_id=2274653 (accessed 19 June 2013).

Werner, W. (2014) 'Showing Trials: ICC Documentaries and the Crafting of Humanity' (forthcoming), on file with the author.

Bella. A love song for war

Johannes C.S. Frank

I
bella, my darling, you're usually so interruptive
can't you see that our platonic parenthesis
has entertained us far too long?

our subclauses have become so complex
in their simplicity that i'm sorry to say you've lost
your sex appeal. absolute reality – that was your promise

say, bella, have you forgotten your alphabet of triumphs?
baghdad, beirut, bombay, busan, belfast, borodino, buchenwald
i love your bs, your bs, your *b-b-b-beats*

and remember how you danced to your own hymn
hips a'shakin', men a'groanin', lips a'roarin', men a'groanin'
oh, how we all joined in with our aspirations: hail, hosiannah, hurrah!

but hush, my dear, and lift your snout
from your tranquility trough
it seems you've become quite dumb
or tell me, have you merely moved your *b-b-b-beats*
beneath the boards where they sound so muffled
between *treatments*

 or have you joined the troops of affluence
 are you, too, to be found on casual thursdays
 snorting ticker tape shrapnel?

 bella, baby, you and gardening
 don't you remember what old winston said?
 why hide behind the lotus leaves?

 i tell myself: mutatis mutandis
 so come now, bella, sweet sweet bella,
 shake your hips once more
 and rise again for your divine digestion

II

let us dream together, bella, just for a moment
and imagine your utility were not that of a deterrent
but that of a relentlessly rampant raging realization

and if progress is measured along the path of your
                                        persistent pace
then why have you become – to others, darling – so
                                        repellently repugnant?

the old fogeys racked their brains on how to make
                                        something of nothing
let us give them a refreshing answer by making
                                        nothing of something

herodotus, theucydides, xenophon, polibius, tacitus
let me add a verse with my apologia pro poemate meo

just a minute, bella, then i'll be ready
let me just lather my face
with the foam of other poets' thoughts
where the past is revealed in anecdotes
through which I can see fuck all but *beauty*

but bella, darling, why get bogged down in aesthetics
when we can still go out with a *b-b-b-bang*
so pass me your old chum's scythe
so I can shave my head to suit your style

III

masks are handed out and wander through
                                        trembling fingers
to start the flow of oxygen, pull the mask towards you,
place it firmly over your nose and mouth,
secure elastic band and breathe normally.
your valentine's gift: an identity surplus for your ballo, bella,
as all join in in your one-two-three-one-two-three
countering their counter-response:
                        push, advance, push, advance
and the sky erupts with the shower of your sparkler bombs
that *b-b-b-bubbles* so nicely down the horizon's throat

Quick, boys! someone cries
in the tone of *Daddy's coming!*
but bella, darling, if they only knew
they've got their gender ascriptions all wrong
the father of us all? no bella, not you
the mother of us all, perhaps?

come now, don't be coy, boys
you whisper with your wonderful wisp of
oleoresin capsicum
the lover in your heart of hearts,
your brothel of brothels
a taste inherent, not acquired

i tell myself: mutatis mutandis
as you come now, bella, sweet sweet bella,
and shake your hips once more
and rise again for your divine digestion

(c) 2012, Johannes C.S. Frank

Index

In at the De

A comedy

Derek Benfield

Samuel French — London
New York - Toronto - Hollywood

Please see page iv for further copyright information

In at the Deep End

Characters
(in order of appearance)

Gerald, a middle-aged builder in search of peace and
  tranquility
Rodney, a young window-cleaner with an eye for the girls
Potter, a highly moral manager obsessed with decency
  and decorum
Linda, a romantic young lady in pursuit of love
Sandra, an amorous secretary in pursuit of her employer
Marion, a formidable wife whose acceptance of truth is
  found wanting

It all takes place in various parts of a health farm during the
summer

ACT I   A Friday afternoon
ACT II   A few minutes later

Time - the present

Based on the author's earlier play
A Toe in the Water

Other plays by Derek Benfield published by Samuel French Ltd

ACT I

A health farm in a delightful part of the country

The audience are, so to speak, sitting in the swimming-pool, and in the downstage area there is a sun lounger C *with a low coffee table beside it. A colourful padded seat and a light garden table are* DR, *and a wicker chair is* DL

An archway DL *leads to the bedrooms and the deep end of the swimming-pool. A swing door* DR *leads into the steam baths and sauna and* UR *there is a way out to the main entrance and garden, and an archway through which you go to the massage parlour and various offices. Beyond the poolside area is a bedroom with a door* UL *to the corridor, another* UC *to the bathroom and a practical sash window. In the bedroom is a divan bed with a bedside table on which is a lamp and the telephone, and a small armchair to the* R *with a table beside it. The bedroom is on the first floor and should be raised slightly above the level of the pool area. In Act II the bedroom will serve as two different bedrooms on different occasions, differentiated by a change of number on the outside of the door which must be clearly visible to the audience*

The Lights come up in the pool area. Gentle, soothing music is playing. An altogether peaceful, relaxing scene

A figure wrapped in a large towel is lying motionless on the sun lounger, its face hidden from view. Dead to the world

Rodney comes in from the main entrance, looking about, uncertainly. He is young, good-looking, normally a perky lad with an eye for the girls, but at the moment lacking confidence in the strange surroundings in which he finds himself. He carries a weekend bag

Rodney does not notice the figure wrapped in towelling and wanders down to look around. He notices the door to the steam baths and goes to it, puzzled, wondering to where it leads. He reaches out and is about to push the door open when a voice startles him

Gerald Aren't you going to take your trousers off?

Rodney jumps, nervously, and turns to look about for the source of the voice.
The music stops

Rodney Sorry?

A head thrusts out from the towel like a tortoise from its shell. Gerald Corby
is a pleasant, middle-aged man, a builder by trade and a little bit of a snob

Gerald Not *many* people go into the steam bath fully clothed.
Rodney (*appalled*) Is that what it is?
Gerald Steam bath and sauna.
Rodney Blimey…!
Gerald Isn't that what you came for? The treatment?
Rodney No fear!
Gerald (*abruptly*) Ah!
Rodney (*jumping again*) What?

Gerald stares at him, suspiciously

Gerald You're here for something else!
Rodney Yes… (*He grins, sheepishly*)
Gerald About time, too! Where the hell have you been?

Rodney consults his wrist-watch

Rodney I'm only two hours late.
Gerald Two *days* more like! People could be dropping dead in there.
Rodney What?!
Gerald So you can forget what I said about taking your clothes off. Plumbers
    are exempt.
Rodney Plumbers?

Gerald rises like Lazarus in his mound of towelling

Gerald That steam bath has developed a mind of its own. The pipes are
    practically bursting. If it gets any hotter, we'll end up in orbit. So roll up
    your sleeves and get to work!
Rodney But *I*'m not a plumber!
Gerald Well, if you're not a plumber and you're not here for the treatment
    what the hell *are* you here for?
Rodney I'm meeting someone.
Gerald An assignation? In *this* place?
Rodney Yes, *I* thought it was a bit odd, too…

Gerald So why did you book it?
Rodney I didn't. *She* did.
Gerald Who?
Rodney My girlfriend.
Gerald You're meeting a girl? *Here*?
Rodney Yes…

Gerald laughs

Gerald Perhaps you'd *better* take your clothes off, then! (*He opens the door to the steam bath and groans*) Ugh…!
Rodney (*horrified*) You're not going *in* there, are you?
Gerald Well, I've paid for it, haven't I? And if I've paid for it, it must be good for me.

Gerald goes into the steam bath and lets the door swing to after him

Potter comes in, busily. He is a respectable, highly moral man, suffering under the burden of responsibility. He is wearing tracksuit trousers and a T-shirt that bears the health farm logo. He carries the register

He sees Rodney standing there with his weekend bag and goes to him, urgently

Potter Ah, good! You're here at last!
Rodney (*puzzled*) Who are *you*?
Potter I'm Mr Potter! The manager! Where have you been? We were expecting you.
Rodney I'm only two hours late.
Potter Never mind. You're here, that's the main thing. So don't hang about! Get on with what you came here to do.
Rodney (*amused*) Get on with it *now*?
Potter Well, you don't want to waste any *more* time, do you?
Rodney No, but I didn't think——
Potter You have brought your spanner with you?
Rodney I'm sorry?
Potter So you should be! We've all been overheating in here. I'm quite flushed. So you'd better get on with the plumbing.
Rodney *You're* talking about plumbing, as well!
Potter What?
Rodney *He* mentioned pipes.
Potter Who did?
Rodney A man who was over there. Wrapped in a towel. He's gone now, but——

Potter Well, I hope he hasn't gone far. (*He looks at his wrist-watch*) He's due to be lying down with Mrs Maddock in fifteen minutes.

Rodney He went in there. (*In disbelief*) He said it led to the steam baths and sauna.

Potter Yes—that's where the trouble is! So you get in there and see to it! (*He urges Rodney on his way*)

Rodney But I'm not here for that!

Potter Not here for the plumbing?

Rodney No.

Potter Then why have you got your spanner with you?

Rodney I haven't!

Potter (*pointing, suspiciously*) Well, you've got a very big bag. A big bag and no spanner? What *have* you got in there, then? (*He tries to look*)

Rodney (*witholding his bag*) This and that.

Potter This and *that*? This and *what*?

Rodney Well... T-shirts, jeans, toothbrush. The usual things the things people want.

Potter You can't come here selling things that people want!

Rodney I'm not selling things!

Potter Then what are you doing here?

Rodney (*uncertainly*) I... I think I'm a guest...

Potter You mean you've got a booking?

Rodney Yes. I think so...

Potter *Here*?

Rodney Yes!

Potter (*unimpressed*) You don't look like our usual clientèle. I'll have to look you up. (*He opens the register*) Let's see if we can find you in here, shall we? (*The register has emitted some dust, which he shies away from*) Oh, they must get a new one of these. That dust gets right up my trachea. Right. Name?

Rodney Rodney.

Potter Just Rodney? Nothing to follow?

Rodney Sorry?

Potter Rodney *what*?

Rodney Yes!

Potter Oh, my head's spinning...! (*He tries to be patient*) Let's try again, shall we?

Rodney If you must.

Potter *Second* name!

Rodney Watt! Watt!

Potter If you're hard of hearing you'd better see a doctor.

Rodney That's my name—Watt!

Potter Watt?

Rodney Now *you*'re doing it!
Potter Rodney Watt?
Rodney Yes!
Potter Oh, good. We made it at last. (*He looks in the register*) I don't think there's a Rodney Watt in here.
Rodney No. There isn't.

Rodney shuts the register, abruptly. More dust. Potter splutters a little

Potter You said you were expected.
Rodney Yes, I am, but——
Potter If you're not in the register then you're not expected. And if you're not expected, then you must be an infiltrator. (*He glares at him accusingly*)
Rodney (*blankly*) Infiltrator?
Potter One who permeates. One who filters in. Is that what you're doing? Permeating?
Rodney I don't even know what it means!
Potter We don't allow infiltrators in here. Not with people in dressing-gowns and leotards.
Rodney You don't understand! I'm looking for a girl!

Potter gives him a withering look

Potter Then you'd better look elsewhere. This is a health farm, not a bordello.

Potter trit-trots out the way he came as—

Linda comes in from the bedrooms. She is a pretty girl dressed in a short towelling bathrobe over her bikini. She sees Rodney

Linda Rodney!
Rodney Aaaah! (*He jumps and turns, holding his weekend bag up in front of his chest like a shield*)
Linda You're late! Where have you been?
Rodney Don't *you* start! Why did you take your clothes off when I wasn't here?
Linda It's a health farm. Here *every*body takes their clothes off.
Rodney Blimey…!
Linda Oh darling! (*She runs to embrace him but his weekend bag is between them. She backs off to try again*)

As she approaches, he lifts the bag above his head to let her in

I expected you hours ago.
Rodney I was looking for an hotel. You never said you were going to book us into a place like this.
Linda Well, I told you what my father's like!
Rodney What's your father got to do with you and me going away on a dirty weekend?
Linda He's very fussy about who I go out with.
Rodney Ah! So *that's* why I've never met him? Because he wouldn't approve of you having it away with a window-cleaner?
Linda I did warn you...
Rodney And because of that you booked us into *this* dump?
Linda I thought it would be more discreet. Daddy doesn't know about health farms so he'd never find us here.
Rodney Thank God for that!
Linda Come on, then! (*She takes his hand and starts to lead him away*)
Rodney Where are we going?
Linda Now *you*'re going to take your clothes off.
Rodney I thought you'd never ask!

They laugh as Linda leads Rodney out towards the bedrooms

A swell of lush romantic music heralds the arrival of Sandra from the swimming pool. She's a jolly girl, very pretty, though a little on the plump side. Not that this bothers Sandra who sees herself as slim and sexy. She picks up her towel from the wicker chair and starts to dry herself

Gerald almost falls out of the steam baths, gasping for breath and staggering unsteadily, relieved to be out of the inferno and trying to regain his composure

Sandra sees him and smiles delightedly

Sandra Mr Corby!

The music stops

Gerald What? (*He steadies himself and focuses on her*) Sandra! What the hell are *you* doing here?
Sandra That's not much of a welcome. I thought you'd be pleased.
Gerald Well, I'm *not* pleased! You shouldn't be here! You should be elsewhere—and elsewhere isn't here!

Sandra moves in, smiling secretively

Sandra Fancy you and me coming to the same health farm…

Gerald Yes—what a coincidence!

Sandra What will they think in the office when they hear what we've been up to? (*She giggles*)

Gerald We haven't been up to *anything*!

Sandra They never guessed that we were going away together, did they?

Gerald We didn't go away together!

Sandra (*romantically*) Mind you, they could probably tell from the way we behaved that we wanted to spend some time together…

Gerald We're not *going* to spend some time together!

Sandra We *might*…

Gerald We mustn't!

Sandra We spend a lot of time together in the office.

Gerald That's different. You're sitting at a computer with your clothes on and I'm not dressed in a bath towel.

Sandra (*giggling*) Wouldn't it be funny if we dressed like this in the office?

Gerald Yes. *Very* funny. We could charge admission. Sandra! You've got to go!

Sandra Why?

Gerald Because I'm supposed to be relaxing, that's why! I came here for peace and quiet. To recharge my batteries.

Sandra I'll soon recharge your batteries…!

Gerald No, you won't! (*He clutches his towel defensively and sinks on to the sun lounger in disarray*)

Sandra smiles happily, enjoying the romantic moment

Sandra I couldn't believe it when I saw you here. It was such a lovely surprise.

Gerald It wasn't a surprise! You *knew* I was coming here.

Sandra (*feigning innocence*) No, I didn't…

Gerald You faxed the letter confirming my reservation!

Sandra You would have been so lonely all on your own, Mr Corby. You'll soon get used to the idea. I'll fetch you a nice cool drink. You look as if you could do with one.

Gerald I don't want a nice cool drink!

Sandra 'Course you do! Stay where you are. I'll be back in a minute.

Sandra giggles and runs out towards the offices

Gerald Oh my God…! (*He lies back on the sun lounger in despair and covers his face with his towel*)

Potter (*off*) Mr Corby!

Potter comes in urgently, looking for Gerald

Mr Corby! (*He spots the towelling figure*) Ah! (*He hastens across to Gerald and calls again*) Mr Corby!

Gerald lies doggo, hoping Potter will go away

It's no good pretending. I know you're in there somewhere. (*He tries to pull the towelling apart, searching for Gerald*)

Gerald resists his attempts

Gerald (*muffled*) Go away!
Potter But what about Mrs Maddock? You don't want to keep Mrs Maddock waiting, now do you?
Gerald (*muffled*) Yes, I do...!
Potter But she's so good for you! You know you always feel better when you've been lying down with Mrs Maddock.

Gerald's head appears

Gerald Couldn't I give her a miss? Just this once? I'm not in the mood for Mrs Maddock! Not *now*...
Potter Mrs Maddock's massage is part of the treatment. It's what you're paying us for. We can't take your money if you don't have the treatment, now can we?
Gerald Well, knock ten per cent off the bill and cancel the massage! (*He disappears back under his towel*)
Potter (*with a bleak smile*) Oh, Mr Corby, you will have your little joke...!
Gerald (*reappearing*) Look, Potter—being here is supposed to be a pleasure.

Potter hastily quietens him, appalled by the word

Potter S'sh! S'sh! (*He glances about, fearful that Gerald may have been overheard*) I hope you didn't come here looking for pleasure?
Gerald (*guiltily*) No! No, of course not!

Potter closes his eyes sorrowfully

Potter I hope *not*, sir. This is a health farm, not a holiday camp. Enjoyment here comes from physical fitness. (*He runs on the spot for a moment*)

Gerald watches him balefully

Gerald That's enough, Potter…

Potter continues running on the spot

Potter!!

Potter stops

Are you telling me that I'm supposed to suffer?
Potter A small price to pay for physical health. (*He leans close to Gerald*) And physical health—as you and I know, sir—is the first step to *moral* health.
Gerald There's nothing wrong with *my* morals!
Potter Ah, no! Of course not! I didn't mean to suggest——
Gerald Anyhow, I don't think I've got the strength to face Mrs Maddock's massage. Not after that steam bath! It's like a blasted inferno in there. You'll have people passing out soon. I thought you were getting a plumber?
Potter I have tried, sir. But plumbers' promises are paper thin. (*Hopefully*) So, Mr Corby? Are you ready? Shall we … er…? (*He moves his arms from side to side, encouragingly*) Shall we … er…?
Gerald Dance?
Potter No, no!
Gerald *What*, then?
Potter Mrs Maddock's waiting!
Gerald Well, she can go *on* waiting, I'd rather stay here.

Potter flutters about like an agitated butterfly. Desperately he pulls the astonished Gerald to his feet

Potter Come along, Mr Corby! You can do it!

Potter tries to pull Gerald away, but each time Gerald resists and pulls Potter back

Gerald No, I can't!
Potter Yes, you can!
Gerald No, I can't!
Potter Yes, you can!

The to-ing and fro-ing becomes rhythmical and they find themselves unconsciously going into a neat but simple dance. Finally, Gerald realizes what is happening and pushes Potter aside

Gerald Potter! What are you doing?
Potter I got carried away…
Gerald I should think you did! Well, I'm not going to see Mrs Maddock and that's that. (*He sits down*)
Potter But it's all a balanced programme! It has to go like clockwork!
Gerald Potter…
Potter People have got to do what I ask them to do and at the time I ask them to do it!
Gerald Potter!
Potter And if they don't, then my whole edifice will start to crumble!
Gerald (*loudly*) Potter!!

Potter controls himself. Gerald gets up reluctantly

All right. If I must, I must.
Potter (*cheering up immediately*) Oh, thank you, sir! Follow me!

They start to go

Gerald I'd rather be massaged by Mrs Maddock than stay here and watch your edifice crumbling…

Gerald and Potter go off towards the massage parlour

The Lights come up in the bedroom

Rodney and Linda come in. We see the number "10" on the outside of the door

Rodney puts his weekend bag down on the bed

Linda Well? What do you think of it?
Rodney (*grinning*) I don't know yet, do I?
Linda The room!
Rodney (*looking about*) Oh. Yes. Very nice. I've never done this before, you know.
Linda I bet you have!
Rodney Not on a health farm! (*He laughs and moves away to look out of the window. He sees something that alarms him*) What the hell are they doing out there?

Linda joins him to look out

Linda Exercises, of course.

Rodney Exercises?!

Linda It's good for you. *I* should be out there with them, but I said I was waiting for you.

Rodney (*appalled*) You mean *we* have to do that?

Linda Every afternoon.

Rodney I don't think I'm going to like it here. If you'd left it to me I'd have booked us into the Holiday Inn. (*He starts to unpack some of his things untidily on to the bed, including a pair of colourful pyjamas*)

Linda If I'd left it to *you* we'd still be in the back of your car! (*She goes to him*) You will like it, Rodney…

Rodney (*busy*) Will I?

Linda Well … we are *together*, aren't we? Just the two of us.

Rodney glances around to confirm

Rodney So we are! (*He abandons his unpacking*)

They kiss. He tries to guide her towards the bed, but she restrains him

Linda No.

Rodney What?

Linda You can't do that now.

Rodney I thought that was what we came here for.

Linda There's plenty of time!

Rodney No, there isn't. Tomorrow we'll be out there doing exercises! (*He tries again*)

Linda No, Rodney! You're not allowed to.

Rodney Sorry?

Linda You've only just arrived.

Rodney What's that got to do with it?

Linda Well … you've got to be weighed first.

Rodney considers this and smiles in disbelief

Rodney Beg your pardon?

Linda They weigh you first.

Rodney Do they?

Linda Yes. Before and after.

Rodney Before and after?!

Linda Yes.

Rodney laughs, uncertainly

Rodney Don't be daft!

Linda They have to know how much you weigh before you start and when you finish.

Rodney They'd never do that at the Holiday Inn…!

Linda And they have to keep an eye on your blood pressure.

Rodney Well, there's bound to be a bit of heavy breathing…

Linda Then they enter it all on your card.

Rodney What card?

Linda Your record card.

Rodney You mean they're going to keep a record?!

Linda Rodney, that's what we're paying them for.

Rodney To keep a record of everything we do?

Linda It won't make any difference to *us*.

Rodney Won't it?

Linda No, of course not.

Rodney Oh. Well, that's all right, then.

Linda So now go in there and take your clothes off.

Rodney grins

Rodney That's more like it! I'll do it now. (*He starts to take off his shirt*)

Linda (*picking up her beach towel*) I'll be downstairs by the swimming-pool. (*She starts to go*)

Rodney But I'm just taking my clothes off.

Linda Yes.

Rodney Well … don't you want to stay?

Linda Why? Do you need an audience?

Rodney I … I just thought you'd be staying.

Linda Can't you manage on your own?

Rodney Of course I can manage! I just thought——

Linda That's all right, then. As soon as you're undressed go downstairs and get yourself weighed. (*She opens the door*) See you later!

Linda blows him a kiss and goes, closing the door behind her

Rodney (*unhappily*) Oh, my God…

Rodney picks up his weekend bag and his pyjamas and goes miserably into the bathroom

Lights out in the bedroom

In the pool area, Sandra returns with a cold drink, expecting to find Gerald where she left him

Sandra There! That didn't take long, did it? (*She stops, seeing no sign of him*) Oh...

Potter comes in briskly, carrying his clipboard

You seen Mr Corby anywhere?
Potter Yes. He's lying down with Mrs Maddock. And they mustn't be disturbed.
Sandra (*her eyes on stalks*) Lying down with *who*?
Potter Mrs Maddock. He tries to do it every afternoon if he can. And he always feels much better for it.
Sandra (*pathetically*) He never told *me* he was going to lie down with someone. I've brought him a cold drink. (*She holds up the cold drink for him to see*)
Potter Well, I'm sure he'll be glad of it when Mrs Maddock's finished with him. And then *you* must have a session with her. (*He consults his clipboard*) Let's see. Yes, I can fit you in after Mr Corby.
Sandra No, you can't!
Potter It's all part of the treatment. Mrs Maddock's famous for her massage.
Sandra Massage? (*Realizing*) Oh, I see...! (*She laughs*)

Potter gives her a severe moral look

Potter You naughty girl. What *were* you thinking? I'll have you know this is a moral establishment. We don't go in for hanky-panky here! (*He continues on his way*)
Sandra (*quietly*) That's what *you* think...!
Potter (*hesitating*) Sorry?
Sandra I said, "So I should think".

Potter gives her another disapproving moral look

Potter You'll find the massage parlour through the yellow door on the right.

Potter trit-trots out towards the bedrooms

Sandra sits down forlornly and sips the cold drink she brought in for Gerald

Linda comes in, carrying her towel. She sees Sandra

Linda Hullo!
Sandra (*looking up*) Oh, hullo. You just arrived?
Linda Yes. (*She takes off her bathrobe*)

14   In at the Deep End

Sandra Been here before, have you?
Linda No. It's my first time.
Sandra Me too. (*A beat*) On your own, are you?
Linda No. I'm... I'm here with a friend.
Sandra Me too. But mine seems to have disappeared...
Linda (*puzzled*) Sorry?
Sandra He didn't know I was going to be here. It was meant to be a sort of a surprise.
Linda He must have been very pleased to see you, then.
Sandra I'm not sure...
Linda How long have you known him?
Sandra Oh, years! (*A little sheepish*) He's my boss.
Linda (*with a smile*) Oh, I see...!
Sandra So he's quite a bit older than me. But very nice. Is *yours* an older man, too?
Linda No. I think he's quite young, actually.
Sandra Did you pick him up *here*?
Linda (*laughing*) No. I brought him with me!
Sandra Well, where is he? Don't say *yours* has disappeared, as well?
Linda Oh, no. He's upstairs taking his clothes off.
Sandra (*surprised*) And you're down *here*?
Linda Yes, I'm going for a swim. You want to join me?
Sandra No, thanks. I think I'd better go and see if mine's still lying down with Mrs Maddock.

Sandra goes

Linda reacts to this and goes off for her swim, taking her towel with her

Lights up in the bedroom

There is a knock at the door. No response

The door opens and Potter peers in

Potter Are you there?

No reply, so he comes in, tentatively

Is anybody there?

Rodney walks in from the bathroom. He is now wearing only a short lady's dressing gown (Linda's). He pirouettes to show it off, not yet seeing Potter

Rodney There! How about that?

Potter looks aghast. Rodney completes his turn and sees him

Oh my God...! (*He clutches the dressing gown to his throat, modestly*)
Potter I wasn't expecting to find *you* in here!
Rodney And *I* wasn't expecting to find *you*...!
Potter I knew you were an infiltrator. The minute I set eyes on you without
your spanner I knew yow were up to no good. How did you get in here?
I never gave you a key.
Rodney *She* let me in, of course.
Potter (*appalled*) You haven't found a girl *already*?! You've only been here
five minutes!
Rodney No, no—I was meeting her here. That's why you couldn't find me
in the register.
Potter You mean you came here with...?
Rodney Linda—yes!
Potter I hope you haven't arranged an assignation. This is a respectable
institution. We don't approve of assignations here!

Rodney assumes immense astonishment

Rodney *Really*? I didn't know that, Mr Potter.
Potter It's part of our policy.
Rodney (*adjusting his moral outlook*) And so it *should* be! Well, you don't
have to worry in *this* case, Mr Potter. (*He smiles a nice moral smile*) She's
my *wife*.
Potter Your *wife*? (*He smiles delightedly*) Well, why didn't you say so?
(*Then his enthusiasm fades*) But in the register her name is down as Smith.
You said you were Watt.
Rodney Ah—yes—that was her maiden name! Before we were married.
She must have forgotten.
Potter Forgotten that she's married?
Rodney Forgotten that she'd changed her name. We haven't been married
very long, you see, so she hasn't got used to it yet.
Potter Why are you wearing a lady's dressing-gown?
Rodney Sorry? Ah—yes! I didn't think you'd noticed!
Potter You can't go downstairs in a lady's dressing-gown without raising
eyebrows.
Rodney Oh, it's not mine! It's Linda's.
Potter Didn't you bring a dressing-gown of your own?
Rodney I didn't think I was going to need one. Does everyone here wear
dressing-gowns *all* the time? Don't they even dress for dinner?

Potter Oh, dinner here is hardly worth dressing up for. Thin soup. A little fruit. Not exactly cordon bleu.
Rodney Oh, I see! More Garden of Eden.
Potter Garden of Eden?
Rodney Yes. An apple and a lot of heavy breathing! (*He laughs*)
Potter (*ignoring such vulgarity*) Anyway, now you're here we'd better get on with it.
Rodney Get on with what?
Potter (*playfully, reprimanding*) You didn't come to see me, did you?
Rodney I—I didn't know I had to.
Potter When you first arrive we have to have a little talk.
Rodney You and me?
Potter Well, I am the manager.
Rodney A little talk about what?
Potter About the things you'll be getting up to here.
Rodney What's it got to do with *you* what I get up to?
Potter I have to explain exactly what it is that you'll be trying to achieve while you're here.
Rodney I *know* what I'll be trying to achieve!
Potter And after we've had *our* little talk I shall pass you on to the doctor.
Rodney Doctor?!
Potter We've got to be sure that you're fit for all the various activities.
Rodney Sorry?
Potter Well, we can't have you over-exerting yourself if you're not up to it.
Rodney I *am* up to it! I don't need a doctor!
Potter I'm afraid it's one of the rules here. We have to give you a check-up before you start.
Rodney What?!
Potter And if you're not completely fit there may be some things that we won't allow you to do.
Rodney It's none of your business what I do!

Potter gives a wan smile

Potter But we're responsible for you while you're here. We can't have you dropping dead halfway through, now can we?
Rodney (*grinning*) No—that *would* be embarrassing! All right, then. Lead on! Let's get it over with.

Potter starts to go, then hesitates and indicates the dressing-gown Rodney is wearing

Potter Couldn't you find something a little more ... substantial? This is not the Folies Bergères. (*He opens the door*)

Rodney All right. I'll put my clothes back *on* again! I'll be down in five
minutes.
Potter (*on a breath*) You'll find *me* behind a green door marked "Private",
it's next to a blue door marked "Doctor", that's where you'll find the
doctor.

Potter goes, closing the door behind him

Rodney I'd never have guessed...! (*He opens the bathroom door*)

Potter re-appears

Potter What?
Rodney Never mind!
Potter Right!

*Potter and Rodney both go, slamming their respective doors behind them
in complete unison*

Lights out in the bedroom

*In the pool area, Gerald returns from his massage. He is now wearing a
colourful towelling bathrobe and is carrying a glass of orange juice. He
sits on the sun lounger and sips his drink as—*

*Linda returns from her swim, putting her bathrobe back on. She sees
Gerald and reacts with alarm*

Linda Daddy!
Gerald (*jumping a mile*) What?! (*He sees her*) Linda!
Linda I—I don't believe it! It *is* you, isn't it?
Gerald I wish it *wasn't*...!
Linda What are you doing here?
Gerald I *was* trying to relax...
Linda You never said you were going to a health farm!
Gerald Neither did you!
Linda (*anxiously*) Are you here for long?
Gerald Not any more, I'm not...! (*He leaps up, falling over the table and
spilling the rest of his orange juice as he tries to escape*)

*Potter comes in and sees Gerald in a state of disarray. He goes to him
urgently*

Potter Oh, Mr Corby, what *are* you doing? You're supposed to be resting after Mrs Maddock's massage. (*He sits Gerald down again and tidies him, perfunctorily*) And you've knocked over your orange juice! (*He takes out a napkin and mops up*) You must try to relax.

Gerald I was relaxed! Then I ran into someone I know...

Potter *Here*?

Gerald Yes.

Potter Where? (*He looks about and sees Linda*) You?

Linda Yes...!

Potter Well! What a lovely surprise for you both. Fancy coming here and meeting an old friend!

Linda He's not a friend. He's my father.

Potter Your *father*?

Linda (*unhappily*) Yes...

Potter (*to Gerald*) Your *daughter*?

Gerald (*unhappily*) Yes...

Potter claps his hands together, ecstatically

Potter Oh, I do so enjoy a happy family reunion!

But the family looks far from happy. He notices

You don't seem very pleased to see each other.

Linda Well, it was so unexpected.

Gerald (*quietly*) It certainly was...!

Linda Did Mummy know you were coming here?

Gerald Of course she did!

Linda (*quietly*) Well. I wish she'd told *me*...!

Gerald You here with a girlfriend?

Linda Er—not exactly, no...

Gerald So *you*'re here on your own as well?

Potter (*smiling happily*) Oh, no, sir! She's not on her own.

Linda Yes, I am!

Potter (*surprised*) Sorry?

Linda (*going to him, urgently*) You know very well I'm on my own!

Potter No, I don't. You're here with your——

Linda No. I'm not!

Potter What?

Linda I haven't got one!

Potter But I met him!

Linda No, you didn't!

Potter Yes! Upstairs! He was wearing a... (*He mimes a short skirt*)

Linda No, he wasn't!

Potter He came out of the bathroom——

Linda No, he didn't!
Potter I was sure I saw a——
Linda You must have gone into the wrong room! You're mixing me up with someone else.
Potter Am I?
Linda Yes! Yes! I'm not here with *anyone!*

Potter is bemused

Gerald Wanted to be on your own and have a bit of peace and quiet, was that it? Time to relax. Read a book. Have a few early nights.
Linda Yes. That *was* the idea...
Gerald Got a nice room, have you?
Linda Yes. Very nice.
Gerald That's good. (*Ingratiating himself*) And don't you worry about the expense. It'll be my treat. (*To Potter*) You make sure she gets what she wants up there!
Potter I think she already *has*...!
Linda Yes! A lovely view of the garden! (*She glares at Potter*)
Gerald (*a little put out*) The garden? *My* room looks over the car park... Still, I'm glad for you. I always want the best for my little girl. I'll pop up and have a look at it, shall I? (*He starts to get up*)

Linda pushes him firmly back into his seat

Linda No!!
Gerald What?
Linda It—it's rather untidy! Isn't it, Mr Potter?
Potter Well, yes, there are ... *things* lying about...
Gerald That doesn't matter. I only want to see the view of the garden. (*He starts to get up again*)

Potter pushes him firmly back into his seat

Potter No!!
Gerald Potter!
Linda I'll go and tidy it up a bit. *Then* you can have a look.
Gerald I can't think what you're making such a fuss about...
Potter *I* can...!
Linda I shan't be long. (*She starts to go*)
Potter She'll let you know when it's all clear.
Gerald All *clear?*
Linda All clean!
Potter Yes—all clean. Clean and tidy. (*He joins Linda*)

Linda (*aside to Potter*) Don't let him know that I'm here with a man!

Potter (*aside to Linda*) But wasn't he at the wedding?

Linda (*aside to Potter*) What wedding? (*She calls to Gerald*) Lovely to see you, Daddy! Yes. What a surprise!

Linda gives Potter a hectic look and races out towards the bedrooms

Potter is all at sea. Gerald gets up and goes to Potter angrily

Gerald You never told me my daughter was here!

Potter I—I—I didn't know, did I? (*He backs away*)

Gerald (*pursuing him around the sun lounger*) You didn't think it was a coincidence that you had two people booked in here with the same surname?

Potter (*blankly*) What?

Gerald Two Corbys!

Potter *Two* Corbys?

Gerald Me and my daughter!

Potter I thought *her* name was... (*He stops just in time*)

Gerald What?

Potter No, not Watt!

Gerald It's Corby!

Potter Is it?

Gerald Well, she's unmarried, isn't she?

Potter Is she?

Gerald Potter—if she was married, I'd have given her away, wouldn't I?

Potter Yes, that's what *I* thought...!

Gerald *And* paid for the wedding! And I didn't do either, did I?

Potter If you say so, Mr Corby. Oh dear—I think I've got one of my headaches coming on...! (*He flees towards the archway*)

Gerald Potter!

Potter puts on the brakes

Potter Yes, Mr Corby?

Gerald Surely you noticed that there were two Corbys in the register?

Potter I'm sure I'm sickening for something incurable... (*He starts to go again*)

Gerald Potter!

Potter puts on the brakes again

Potter Yes, Mr Corby?

Gerald She must be using another name...

Potter Sorry?

Gerald In the register! Why should she be using another name in the register?

Potter *I* don't know…! (*He starts to go again*)

Gerald Potter!

Potter (*stopping again*) Yes, Mr Corby?

Gerald She must have something to hide…

Potter No! No!

Gerald Yes! Yes! If she has nothing to hide why is she travelling incognito?

Potter You mustn't ask *me*! I'm only the manager!

Potter darts out quickly before Gerald can stop him again

Gerald picks up his empty glass and goes off in search of orange juice

Lights up in the bedroom

The door bursts open and Linda races in

Linda Rodney! Quickly!

Rodney comes out of the bathroom. He is now back in his T-shirt and jeans

Rodney Whatever's the matter?

Linda You've got to go!

Rodney I've only just arrived.

Linda You can't stay here! (*She races around collecting up his things*)

Rodney Can't I?

Linda Not in *this* room.

Rodney Don't say they've given us the wrong room?

Linda No. This is the right room.

Rodney Oh, good.

Linda But you can't stay in it.

Rodney Then it must be the *wrong* room.

Linda No. It's the right room. But *you*'ve got to go. And you mustn't come back here!

Rodney Where are we going to, then?

Linda We're not going anywhere.

Rodney But you said…!

Linda I'm staying here.

Rodney You said we had to go.

Linda No. *You*'ve got to go!

Rodney Even though this is the right room?

Linda It's the right room for *me*, but the wrong room for *you*.

Linda races out into the bathroom

Rodney tries to work this out

Linda returns with his weekend bag and puts his things into it

Rodney You mean … we aren't going to sleep in the same room?
Linda Not any more.
Rodney But isn't that what we came here for?
Linda Yes.
Rodney That's what I thought.
Linda But now we can't.
Rodney So where shall *I* be sleeping?
Linda *I* don't know! You'll have to find another room!
Rodney One room each?
Linda Yes.
Rodney Isn't that rather unusual?
Linda There's no time to argue!
Rodney But if I stay in another room, won't people hear me creaking along the landing to *this* room?
Linda You won't be.
Rodney Of course I will!
Linda No.
Rodney Not just once?
Linda No! (*Desperately*) Rodney—please go! (*She hands him his weekend bag*)
Rodney (*looking at it*) You've packed my bag…
Linda I can't explain now. Just go! And whatever happens—you don't know me!
Rodney Don't I?
Linda No.
Rodney Oh. Right. I hope you remembered to pack my toothbrush.

Rodney goes in a daze

Linda closes the door after him, relieved but fed up

Linda Oh, hell…!

Linda goes into the bathroom

Lights out in the bedroom

In the pool area, Gerald returns with a fresh glass of orange juice

Rodney comes in, carrying his weekend bag

Gerald sees him

Gerald You don't look very happy! Hasn't your girlfriend turned up yet?
    (*He sits down*)
Rodney (*gloomily*) Oh, yes, she turned up. But she won't let me in.
Gerald Sorry?
Rodney She's locked me out of the bedroom!
Gerald (*appalled*) She hasn't!
Rodney Yes. And she says whatever happens I don't know her.

Gerald begins to philosophize

Gerald Funny blokes, women. Unpredictable. Play hard to get sometimes.
    You want my advice?
Rodney (*uncertainly*) Well…
Gerald Of course you do! Don't take no for an answer.
Rodney But she won't let me in!
Gerald That's all part of her game, isn't it?
Rodney Is it?
Gerald Oh, yes. I know the signs. She wants you to take her by storm.
Rodney That wasn't the impression *I* got… (*He sits down in despair*)
Gerald Because she's playing her game! Women always play games to get
    what they want.
Rodney Do they?
Gerald Oh, yes. So now it's all down to you.
Rodney Is it?
Gerald You'll have to storm her battlements.
Rodney How do I storm her battlements when the door's locked?
Gerald Use your initiative.
Rodney Initiative? I'll need a battering ram!
Gerald You'll have to find another way to gain access.
Rodney Yes, but what?
Gerald That's up to you. You'll have to put on your thinking cap. (*He smiles
    encouragingly*)

But Rodney looks remarkably short of inspiration

*Potter comes in. He sees Rodney and Gerald together and reacts in alarm,
fearing a confrontation*

Potter Aaah!

Gerald and Rodney look at him in surprise

Gerald What's the matter, Potter?
Potter You're here!
Gerald Of course I'm here!
Potter And so is *he*...
Gerald Yes.
Potter You're *both* here.
Gerald Yes.
Potter Together.
Gerald Yes!
Potter You haven't been ... talking to each other, have you?
Gerald Of course we've been talking to each other!

Potter shies like a nervous horse

Potter Ah! What about?
Gerald I was just giving him a bit of advice.

Potter shies again

Potter Ah! What about?
Gerald About his girlfriend.

Potter shies again

Potter Ah! What girlfriend? (*To Rodney*) You haven't got a girlfriend!
Rodney I had before she locked me out...
Potter No!
Rodney What?
Potter You're here on your own!
Rodney No. I'm not!
Potter Yes! *Yes!*
Gerald Are you going potty, Potter?
Potter Very likely! (*To Rodney*) You shouldn't be in here, you should be out
    there! The doctor's waiting for you! (*He urges him on his way*)
Rodney I'm not in the mood for the doctor...
Potter But he's expecting you! You can't keep the doctor waiting! (*He
    indicates*) Go straight down the corridor and you'll see a green door
    marked "Private"——
Rodney (*wearily*) Yes—you told me!
Potter | (*together*) —it's next to a blue door marked "Doctor", that's
Rodney | where you'll find the doctor!

Potter pushes him on his way, energetically, with his weekend bag

Potter is breathing heavily from all the excitement

Gerald Calm down, Potter! You go on like this and you'll do yourself a mischief. (*He gets up and starts to go*)

Potter shies, nervously

Potter Ah! Where are you going?
Gerald To speak to my daughter—if that's all right with you. She must have tidied her room up by now? (*He continues on his way*)
Potter Oh, do you *have* to speak to her?
Gerald Yes, I do! I want to know why she's using a false name in the register.

Gerald goes out towards the bedrooms with a determined tread

Potter Oh, dear—the pillars of morality already appear to be trembling...

Potter hastens out towards his office

Lights up in the bedroom. A smart rat-a-tat on the door

Linda comes out of the bathroom anxiously. She has changed into a sun-dress. She calls out, thinking Rodney has returned

Linda Go away! You can't come in!
Gerald (*off*) It's only me!

Relieved, Linda goes to open the door

Linda Daddy! I didn't know it was you.
Gerald Who did you think it was, then?
Linda Oh—er—nobody.
Gerald You said, "Go away, you can't come in!" to *nobody*?
Linda The—the chambermaid! She keeps trying to get in. To see to things.
Gerald That's what she's paid for. To see to things.
Linda But she *keeps* trying to see to them!
Gerald (*moving into the room*) Well, if you'd have let her in to see to them she'd have seen to them, wouldn't she? Then she wouldn't have had to see to them again. (*He looks about*)

While he is looking the other way, Linda hastily looks into the corridor to make sure there is no sign of Rodney, closes the door and joins her father

You tidied the place up, then?
Linda Oh, yes.
Gerald Got rid of the rubbish?
Linda I hope so...!
Gerald Very nice room.
Linda Yes.
Gerald Nice big bed.
Linda Yes.
Gerald I've only got a single bed in *my* room...
Linda Really?
Gerald How long ago did you book?
Linda Last week.
Gerald Last week?! I booked a month ago and all I got was a small single room overlooking the car park! Did you *ask* for a double room?
Linda No! But they hadn't got a single room left. So I had to have a double.
Gerald I see... (*He studies the view from the window, enviously*) You have got a nice view of the garden, haven't you? (*A beat*) Did you ask for a view of the garden?
Linda No. I ... I don't think so.
Gerald Then they can't charge you extra for it! I'm not paying for a room with a view that you didn't ask for. (*He chuckles*) I'll have a word with Potter about it. (*He heads for the phone*)
Linda No! No, Daddy! (*She runs after him*)

They struggle for possession of the phone. She succeeds in getting the receiver from him and replaces it, abruptly

I don't want any fuss!

Gerald looks at her with growing suspicion

Gerald You've got something to hide, haven't you?
Linda W-what?
Gerald Some dark secret?
Linda No—no, of course not! (*She moves away*)

Gerald delivers the coup de grâce

Gerald Then why are you staying here under an assumed name?
Linda Am ... am I?
Gerald (*with a sly, profound smile*) There's only one Corby in the register.
Linda Is—is there?
Gerald Oh, yes. And you know who that is?
Linda No...

Gerald It's *me*! I'm the only Corby in the register. And yet there are two Corbys staying here.

Linda I … I didn't want anyone to know that I was here.

Gerald Ah! Why not?

Linda It was like you said. I came here for a bit of…

Gerald A bit of what?!

Linda Peace and quiet. (*She acts in a pathetic mode*) I've been working so hard lately…

Gerald Of course you have! *I* know that…

Linda So I needed rest. Rest and peace and quiet. And I couldn't have had peace and quiet if friends had been ringing me up all the time, now could I? So I… (*lowering her head impressively*) I decided I'd call myself … Smith.

Gerald smiles at her, proudly, and pats her shoulders, marvelling at her brilliance

Gerald *What* a good idea! I'd never have thought of that.

Linda (*gently remonstrating*) And you thought I had something to hide…!

Gerald (*heavily ashamed*) I should have known better. (*He gives her a noble, forgiving kiss*) Can I have a look at your bathroom?

Linda (*surprised*) It's a perfectly ordinary bathroom.

Gerald I want to see if it's better than mine…

Gerald goes into the bathroom

Linda sinks on to the bed, relieved. Lights out in the bedroom

In the pool area, Rodney returns from the doctor, carrying his weekend bag. He looks about furtively, and sets off towards the bedrooms

Potter races in at high speed, carrying the register, and catches him

Potter Mr Watt!

Rodney stops nervously

Rodney | (*together*) | Why are you following me?
Potter | | Where are you going?

Rodney I started first! Why are you following me?

Potter Because I want to know where you're going.

Rodney Well, I've seen the doctor. And now I'm going (*he gestures vaguely*) … elsewhere.

Potter (*suspiciously*) *Elsewhere*? Which way is that?
Rodney Er—*this* way. (*He indicates*)
Potter (*indicating*) *That* way?
Rodney Yes.
Potter That's not the way to elsewhere, that's the way to the bedrooms.
Rodney Is it? Good Lord. I'd forgotten. I'm a stranger here, you see.
Potter I know what *you*'re trying to do. And you can't do it here!
Rodney I … I just want to see if I'm still locked out.
Potter You *are*!
Rodney She might have changed her mind.
Potter She hasn't! So you go and sit in the garden and wait. It's a beautiful garden so why don't you go and sit in it? (*He tries to urge him on his way*)
Rodney (*not keen*) On my own?
Potter If you're lonely you can talk to the gardener. He's out there. He'd like a little chat. It's very lonely gardening, so he'll be glad of the company. He can tell you all about the birds and the bees. (*He pushes Rodney towards the main entrance, and calls after him*) I'll send out a pot of tea for two!

Rodney staggers out towards the garden with his bag

Potter races at high speed towards the bedrooms, jumping over the sun lounger as he goes

Lights up in the bedroom

Gerald comes out of the bathroom, holding up Rodney's pyjamas

Gerald What the hell's this?

Linda sees what he is brandishing

Linda It … it looks like a pair of pyjamas.
Gerald It *is*! A pair of *men*'s pyjamas!
Linda (*playing for time*) Are they yours?
Gerald Of course they're not mine!
Linda Where did you find them?
Gerald In there! Hanging up behind the door! What's a pair of man's pyjamas doing in your bathroom?
Linda He must have left them behind.
Gerald What?!
Linda The last guest! When he went. He was probably in a hurry and left them behind.
Gerald Well, there you are, you see. If you had let the chambermaid in she'd have removed them, wouldn't she?

There is a knock at the door, Linda is alarmed

Linda Oh, no…!
Gerald I'll see who it is. (*He puts the pyjamas down and starts to go*)
Linda No! I'll go! That's probably the chambermaid now. (*She calls out to the door*) My *father* wants to know who it is!
Potter (*off*) It's me! Mr Potter!
Linda (*relieved*) It's Potter! (*She opens the door*)

Potter is there, carrying the register

Gerald Come on in, Potter! I want a word with you.
Potter (*going to him*) It's time for your sauna, sir.
Gerald No, it isn't. There's half an hour yet. There are a couple of things I want to get straight. All right?
Potter Couldn't we talk in my office? (*He starts to go*)

Gerald grabs his arm and pulls him back abruptly

Gerald My daughter asked for a single room.
Potter (*shaking his head*) No, no…!
Gerald (*nodding his head*) Yes, yes!
Potter I don't *think* so… (*He consults the register*)
Gerald I *know* so!
Potter I thought so! This is Number Ten. And Number Ten is designated as a double room with bathroom en suite. And Number Ten is the room reserved for your daughter. (*He smiles, sagely, and snaps the register shut. It emits a small cloud of dust which makes him splutter a little*)
Gerald But she only asked for a single room!
Potter Are you sure? (*Turning to Linda*) I could have sworn——
Linda Yes! I did! But all the single rooms were occupied. (*Nodding in time to the words*) Surely you re*mem*ber?
Potter (*shaking his head in time to the words*) No, I don't re*mem*ber!
Linda (*nodding in time*) Yes, you *do* re*mem*ber! (*She looks at him desperately*)
Potter (*relenting*) Oh, very well…! (*Turning to Gerald and nodding in time again*) Yes, I *do* re*mem*ber…!
Gerald Are you telling me that all the single rooms were occupied?
Potter Yes. So your daughter had to have a double room with bathroom en suite.
Gerald I hope you don't expect me to pay for a double room with bathroom en suite for my daughter when all she wanted was a small single room?
Potter I'll have to ask the register… (*He dives into the register again*)

Gerald Never mind the register! (*He snaps the register shut, emitting another puff of dust*)

Again Potter splutters

And there's another thing! (*He goes to the window*)
Potter I thought there might be...
Gerald Come and look at this!

Potter exchanges a look with Linda, then trots across to join Gerald at the window. Gerald nods, indicating something outside

You see that out there?
Potter (*peering out*) What?
Gerald The view! The view of the bloody garden!
Potter (*enthusiastically*) Oh, yes! It's lovely at this time of the year, isn't it? Lupins, gaillardias, delphiniums... Much better view than over the car park.
Gerald Well, she's not paying for *that*, either!
Potter The car park?
Gerald The view!
Potter Oh, I think the view comes with the room. I don't think you can have the room without the view. (*Without realizing, he begins to sing*) "A room without a view, and you, and no-one to worry us..."

Gerald joins in automatically

Gerald | (*singing together*) "No-one to hurry us through this dream we've
Potter | found..."

Gerald realizes what he is doing, and stops

Gerald Potter!
Potter (*singing*) "We'll sit and we'll coo-oo-oo..."
Gerald (*loudly*) Potter!!

Potter stops singing, and is embarrassed by what he has allowed to happen

You got carried away again, didn't you?
Potter Just a little, yes. I do apologise. I'll see what the register says about rooms with unrequested views. (*He opens the register*)
Gerald Never mind what the register says! It's what *I* say that matters! (*He snaps the register shut. A bigger cloud of dust*)

Again poor Potter splutters

Potter Oh, dear. I shall be coughing all night after this. And I never can find my linctus.
Gerald I'll make a note about this and then you'll remember. (*He takes the register from Potter and opens it, helping himself to the pen from Potter's pocket*)

Linda looks alarmed and grabs Potter's arm

Linda (*whispering, urgently*) Don't let him look in there...!
Potter What?
Linda The register...!

But it is too late

Gerald Wait a minute! What's this? "Room Ten—Mr and Mrs Smith". (*He looks at them*) Mr and Mrs?!
Linda Ah! Er—*you* can explain that, can't you, Mr Potter?
Potter No!
Linda Yes!
Potter (*miserably*) No-o-o...!
Linda (*pleading, quietly*) *Please*, Mr Potter...!

Potter is silent

Gerald (*glaring at him*) Well, Potter?

Potter looks at Linda. She nods encouragingly, so he relents and tries to think of something

Potter Ah—well, you see, it ... it's ... it's for the records.
Gerald Records?! What records?

Potter looks at Linda again. She nods encouragingly again. Potter succumbs to subterfuge and plunges in recklessly, gradually gathering momentum

Potter Oh, they're very fond of records at Head Office, and this *is* a double room—although on this occasion occupied by a single client due to lack of availability of single accommodation—but to Head Office it is still designated as a double, and "double" meaning "two", Head Office will expect *two* names to be entered in the register for Number Ten, although on this particular occasion your daughter Miss Corby is the sole occupant thereof. (*He is left breathless*)

Linda smiles at him gratefully. Gerald gazes at Potter, astonished by this speedy exposition. After a moment...

Gerald I beg your pardon?
Potter I'm not saying all *that* again...!
Linda I don't know what Mr Potter must think of you, Daddy. All these questions. Surely you aren't suspicious of your own daughter?
Gerald No—no, of course not. But I was bound to wonder, wasn't I, when I found ... *what* I found ... in the bathroom?
Potter (*to Linda*) You naughty girl! What *have* you left lying about?
Gerald I mean—what was I supposed to think? Look at this! (*He picks up the pyjamas and holds them aloft*) A man's pyjamas!

Potter stares at the pyjamas in horror

You still haven't explained how these came to be here!

A dreadful pause. Then Linda thinks of a way out

Linda They belong to Mr Potter.

Potter and Gerald react

Gerald ⎫ (*together*) What?
Potter ⎭

Gerald glares at Potter

Gerald *Yours*?!
Potter No!
Linda Yes!
Potter No! I've never seen them before!
Linda Yes, you have! Don't you remember? You left them in here.
Gerald (*apoplectic*) You left your pyjamas in my daughter's bedroom?
Potter No!
Linda Of course he did!
Gerald Then why is he saying "No"?
Linda Well, he's bound to say "No" now, isn't he?
Gerald (*to Potter*) Have you got something to hide? .
Potter No! I'm a very moral man!
Gerald But my daughter says you left your pyjamas in her bedroom.
Potter She made a mistake.
Gerald Are you calling her a liar?
Potter No, but——

Gerald So you *did* leave these here?

Potter No!

Linda Yes!

Gerald You took off your pyjamas in my daughter's bedroom?

Linda Don't be silly, Daddy. He wasn't wearing them at the time.

Gerald He wasn't wearing them?!

Linda Of course not.

Potter Thank God for that!

Gerald Then what *was* he wearing?

Linda He was dressed like he is now.

Gerald Fully clothed?

Linda Of course.

Potter Saved by the bell…!

Gerald Then why did he leave his pyjamas in here?

Linda I told him he could.

Gerald What for? (*To Potter*) What for, Potter?

Potter That's what I'm waiting to hear…!

Linda He'd lost a button off the jacket.

Gerald In his hurry to get it off?

Linda For heaven's sake. I wasn't there when he did it, Daddy.

Potter That *is* a relief…!

Linda So I said I'd sew it back on for him.

Gerald Why couldn't he sew it on himself?

Linda You could hardly expect the manager of a health farm to sew on his own buttons! So *I* said I'd do it *for* him. (*She grabs the pyjamas from Gerald and thrusts them into Potter's hands*) There you are, Mr Potter. The button's back on again.

Potter (*gazing at it, deeply moved*) Ah… So it is. You'd think it had never been off.

Gerald But, Linda—how did you know he'd lost a button off his pyjamas in the first place?

But before Linda can think of a suitable reply, Rodney climbs in through the window and puts his weekend bag down on the floor

They all look at the intruder in astonishment

Potter And now Peter Pan's arrived!

Rodney looks up and sees not only Linda as he expected but also Potter and Gerald. He is deeply embarrassed

Linda realizes that she must warn Rodney and calls out to her father, dramatically

Linda Oh, *Daddy*! (*She runs to him*)
Rodney (*fearfully*) D-d-daddy…?
Linda There's a burglar in my bedroom!
Gerald (*amused*) He's not a burglar!
Linda Then why is he coming through my bedroom window?
Potter I expect he's looking for the Lost Boys.
Gerald I'll *ask* him what he's doing! (*He goes to Rodney*)

Rodney cowers as Gerald approaches

Potter Oh, dear. The pillars of morality are on the move again…
Gerald What the hell are you doing in *here*?
Potter I expect he's come to clean the windows.
Rodney Yes! That's right!
Gerald But *you*'re not a window-cleaner!
Rodney Yes, I am!
Potter (*quietly, to Linda*) Is he?
Linda Yes!
Potter I *thought* he seemed at home on a ladder.
Gerald (*chuckling*) You're a funny sort of window-cleaner arriving without
your bucket.
Rodney I knew I'd forgotten something. (*He starts to climb out of the
window again*)
Gerald Where are you going?
Linda Don't stop him!
Rodney To get my bucket. I must have left it at the bottom of the ladder.
Gerald No, no! Wait a minute!

Rodney stops nervously

Whatever made you come into *this* room?
Potter He told you—he's here to clean the windows! (*Without realizing, he
begins to sing again*) "He goes cleaning windows to earn an honest bob…"
Gerald (*patiently*) Potter…
Potter (*singing*) "For a nosey-parker it's an interesting job…"
Gerald (*loudly*) Potter!!

Potter stops singing

Potter Sorry, Mr Corby. I got carried away again.
Gerald (*indicating Rodney*) He's the one who ought to be carried away! (*To
Rodney, with a big smile*) I know what you're doing, don't I?
Rodney (*nervously*) Do you?
Gerald You're storming the battlements!

Rodney I'll just go and get my bucket. (*He tries to escape*)
Gerald (*laughing*) You are an idiot!
Rodney Yes. I know!
Gerald The intention was good, son. Finding a ladder and all that.
Rodney I borrowed it from the gardener.
Potter They'd been having a pot of tea together in the shrubbery.
Rodney He said he'd been cutting back the ivy.
Gerald Full marks! E for Effort. Only thing is—you came into the wrong room, didn't you?
Rodney Did I?
Linda (*to Potter*) What are they talking about?
Potter Don't ask me! I've lost track of the conversation.
Gerald I can understand your mistake. All the windows look alike from outside. In the heat of the moment—passion running high—difficult to pinpoint the right room, eh?
Rodney Yes, it was rather difficult…
Gerald So if I were you—you don't mind me making a suggestion?
Rodney No. I'd be glad of your help.
Gerald I think you should go back down the ladder.
Potter (*to Linda*) Good idea! Back down the ladder…
Rodney Right! I'll go *now*——
Gerald Hang on!
Rodney (*hesitating*) Not yet?
Gerald In a minute.
Rodney Right. There's no hurry.
Potter (*aside to Linda*) Yes, there *is*…!
Gerald Go down the ladder…
Potter (*aside to Linda*) It's all right—we're off again.
Rodney Yes? Down the ladder. And then?
Potter Try not to put your foot in the bucket.
Rodney I'll be careful.
Gerald Move the ladder.
Rodney Move it. Yes.
Gerald Along a bit.
Rodney Which way?
Potter What does it matter which way!
Gerald That's up to you.
Potter (*impatiently*) Do you *have* to give him a choice?
Gerald Along to *your* room. (*He grins knowingly*)
Rodney But how do I know which that is?
Potter Well, it's not *this* one…!
Linda No, it's certainly not…!
Gerald I should try the one next door.
Rodney Good idea. Shall I do it now?

Gerald Why not?
Rodney (*quietly*) Thank goodness for that…! (*He starts to go*)
Gerald Wait a minute!
Potter (*aside to Linda*) I *thought* things were going too well…
Linda (*loudly, going to them*) Don't stop him!

They look at her in surprise

Gerald What?
Linda I don't want a burglar in my bedroom!
Gerald He's not a burglar!
Potter No. He's a window-cleaner.
Linda (*to Rodney, urgently*) You can't stay in here! Go on! Get out!
Rodney I'm *trying* to…!
Potter Yes, he is! He keeps popping in and out like the cuckoo in a clock.

Rodney has suddenly noticed something. He stares hard at Potter and points to him

Rodney Mr Potter, what are you doing with my pyjamas?

They all freeze. Potter stares at the pyjamas, at a loss

Gerald *Your* pyjamas?
Rodney Yes!
Gerald (*to Linda*) You said they were *Potter*'s pyjamas.
Linda Yes! They are!
Gerald Potter…?
Potter (*looking up at the sky*) Did somebody call?
Gerald You're very quiet.
Potter I'm trying to remember the Lord's Prayer.
Linda Mr Potter must have lent them to him.
Potter No, I didn't!
Linda Yes, you did! (*To Rodney*) Yes, he *did*!
Rodney (*realizing*) Did he?

Linda nods urgently

Gerald You lent him your pyjamas?

Potter sees Linda's look and relents

Potter Apparently…
Gerald Why?

Potter He hadn't got any of his own.
Gerald (*to Rodney*) You came to this place without your pyjamas?
Rodney Yes.
Gerald Why?
Rodney I didn't think I was going to need them.
Gerald *I* brought *my* pyjamas.
Potter Well, next time you can lend him *yours*...!
Rodney Thank you, Mr Potter. It was very kind of you.
Potter It's all part of the service. I trust the colour's to your liking?
Rodney Oh, yes. My favourite. Couldn't be better.
Potter We aim to please.
Rodney I've got a pair just like them at home.
Gerald (*to Rodney*) Well, go on, then! You're losing your momentum.
Rodney (*having forgotten*) Sorry?
Gerald You're not supposed to *be* in this room. Remember?
Rodney Of course! I'd forgotten for a minute.
Gerald So go and storm the battlements in the *right* room! (*He grins encouragingly*)
Rodney Yes—right.

Rodney glances briefly at Linda and disappears hastily down the ladder, leaving his bag behind

Gerald Poor chap. He's in a bit of a state.
Potter He's not the only one...! (*He starts to go*)
Gerald Where are you going, Potter?
Potter (*holding up the pyjamas*) I thought I'd better put these in the *right* room. (*Quietly as he goes*) Wherever that may be...!

Potter gives Linda a hectic look and goes quickly

Linda Have you met him before, then, Daddy?
Gerald Potter?
Linda The man on the ladder!
Gerald Oh. Yes. Downstairs. We had a bit of a chat. He came here to meet a girl.
Linda (*assuming surprise*) He *didn't*!
Gerald He did! But she's locked him out of their room! (*He laughs*)
Linda She *hasn't*! (*She laughs also*)
Gerald She has! So I gave him a bit of advice. As a man of the world. I told him to storm the battlements. But the idiot went and picked the wrong room! (*He looks at his wrist-watch*) I'd better go and get ready for my sauna before Potter goes ballistic. (*He opens the door, then looks back at her, thoughtfully*) I'll tell you one thing, though.

Linda (*nervously*) What?
Gerald *I* wouldn't like to borrow Potter's pyjamas!

Gerald laughs at the thought, and goes, closing the door behind him

The moment Gerald has gone, Rodney appears outside and starts to come in through the window

Linda sees him and panics

Linda (*in a horrified whisper*) Rodney...! (*She goes quickly to lock the bedroom door*)

Rodney climbs in through the window

(*Going to him*) Why do you keep coming in through my bedroom window? I told you we mustn't be seen together!
Rodney You never told me your father was here! You said we'd be safe from him on a health farm.
Linda I didn't know then that he was going to *be* here, did I?
Rodney (*sulking a little*) I knew we should have gone to the Holiday Inn...
Linda Oh Rodney... (*She embraces him comfortingly, then finds that she likes it, kisses him and tries to make it develop*)

Rodney holds back, surprised by her bravado

Rodney What *are* you doing?
Linda I'm kissing you.
Rodney But we mustn't do that! Remember?
Linda Then why have you come back?
Rodney I left my bag behind! (*He picks it up*) I'm not staying here now your father's arrived!
Linda But Daddy's gone to hava a sauna. We've got plenty of time.

Rodney considers this for a moment

Rodney How long does it take to have a sauna?
Linda Half an hour? (*She smiles encouragingly*) And I've locked the door.

Rodney holds her look for a second, then capitulates

Rodney Oh, all right, then! (*He puts his bag down again*)

They embrace and fall back on to the bed

Lights out in the bedroom

> *In the pool area, Potter comes in, carrying the pyjamas, and meets Sandra, arriving from the other direction. She is now wearing shorts and a shirt*

Sandra Have you seen Mr Corby?

Potter shies nervously

Potter No! Why?
Sandra I've got a nice surprise for him.
Potter No! Please! No more surprises! You keep away from him. The moral fabric of this place is already in disarray... (*He starts to go*)
Sandra Mr Potter...?

Potter hesitates

Potter Now what?
Sandra Why are you carrying a pair of men's pyjamas?

Potter looks down at the pyjamas, having forgotten all about them. Then he clutches them to his chest protectingly

Potter I'm looking after them for a friend.

> *Potter trit-trots out towards his office*

Sandra watches him go, amused

> *Gerald comes in from the bedrooms*

Sandra I've been looking for you everywhere! What *have* you been doing?
Gerald You'd never believe me if I told you...!
Sandra Anyway, you're here, that's the main thing. (*She advances seductively*) So now we can carry on from where we left off.
Gerald We weren't doing anything to *leave* off!
Sandra Then we'd better start *doing* something, hadn't we? (*She closes in on him with a big smile*)

Gerald backs away

Gerald No! Go away! I want to be on my own!
Sandra But you wouldn't like it on your own, Mr Corby.

Gerald I don't know what's come over you, Sandra. You're never like this when we're in the office together.

Sandra But we're not in the office *now*, are we? (*She lunges at him*)

He falls back on to the sun lounger with Sandra on top of him. Gerald struggles manfully

Potter enters and sees them

Potter Mr Corby!

Gerald and Sandra leap up and sort themselves out. Potter stares at Gerald in moral outrage

Gerald It's not as bad as it looks, Potter.

Potter I hope not, sir! But the pillars of morality appear to be trembling.

Gerald You needn't worry about *my* morals! She's my secretary!

Potter (*appalled by such decadence*) Oh, no—you haven't gone away with your *secretary*! I shall have to go and search for my smelling salts…! (*He sinks his face into his hand in despair*)

Gerald I didn't know she was going to be here!

Potter You can hardly expect anyone to believe that. A man travelling with his secretary is certain to raise eyebrows.

Potter goes unhappily

Gerald Now see what you've done! What's Potter going to think?

Sandra What does it matter what Potter thinks?

Gerald He's the manager!

Sandra So?

Gerald He's a very moral manager. I don't want him getting hold of the wrong end of the stick. He might talk. Moral people always talk.

Sandra What about?

Gerald About other people's morals!

Sandra What does that matter? There's nobody here who knows you, is there?

Gerald No!! No—of course there isn't!

Sandra Anyway, I've got some good news. Mr Potter's found you a better bedroom.

Gerald (*puzzled*) He never mentioned it just now.

Sandra I expect that was because he had morals on his mind. But he told me that there'd been a cancellation and now *you* can have Number Fourteen. So you won't be overlooking the car park any more.

Gerald (*pleased*) Really?

Sandra *And* he said you can move in *now* if you want to.

Gerald Well that *is* good news! Number Fourteen, eh?

Sandra I'll come and help you.

Gerald No, you won't! I'm in enough trouble as it is!

Gerald looks around quickly for an escape route and has no choice but to hasten into the steam baths to get away from her

Sandra giggles mischievously, and runs out after him

Sandra (*as she goes*) Mr Corby…!

Marion walks in from the main entrance. She is a forceful woman in her fifties. Potter is fluttering along behind her, still carrying the pyjamas

Marion Why are you following me about waving your pyjamas in the air?

Potter They're not my pyjamas!

Marion Well, whose pyjamas are they?

Potter *I* don't know!

Marion Then I suggest you give them to the manager.

Potter I am the manager! Mr Potter!

Marion Ah! Then perhaps you can help me? I'm Mrs Corby. I'm looking for my husband.

Potter Oh my God!

Gerald comes running out of the steam bath, a towel over his head, hotly pursued by Sandra

Potter hastily grabs Marion and clutches her to his chest

She struggles, but is unable to see Gerald and Sandra as they race across, without noticing Marion and Potter, and disappear out the other side

Marion escapes from Potter's clutches, appalled

Marion Mr Potter!! (*She pushes him away abruptly*)

Potter falls back on to the sun lounger, the picture of misery

Black-out

ACT II

The same. A few minutes later

In the bedroom, Linda and Rodney are lying on the bed kissing each other. After a moment, Rodney extricates himself

Rodney It's no good. I can't do it.
Linda (*insulted*) Why not?
Rodney I can't concentrate. Your father might walk in.
Linda He can't. The door's locked.
Rodney Well, the *window*'s open! (*He gets off the bed*) I'm going home. (*He collects his weekend bag and starts to climb out of the window*)
Linda Rodney...!

He hesitates

Rodney Well, I didn't think it was going to be like this...!

Linda gets off the bed and runs to him

Linda I'm sorry. It's all my fault. Next time we'll go to the Holiday Inn.
Rodney If there *is* a next time...
Linda What?!
Rodney I don't think my nerves would stand a second attempt. (*He starts to go down the ladder with his bag*)
Linda Rodney!

Rodney stops

Rodney What?
Linda (*with a touch of melodrama*) Goodbye, then... (*She kisses him gently*)
Rodney Goodbye. (*He starts to go*)
Linda Rodney!

He stops again, a little irritated

Rodney What?

Linda Goodbye… (*She kisses him again*)
Rodney Goodbye!

Rodney disappears down the ladder

Linda looks out of the window and calls to him again

Linda Rodney!
Rodney (*off*) What now?
Linda (*calling*) I love you! (*She comes back inside*) Oh, hell!

Linda goes into the bathroom, closing the door behind her with a bang

Lights out in the bedroom

In the pool area, Gerald comes in DL, *looking about furtively for signs of Sandra. At the same time Potter appears from the main entrance, urgently. They do not see each other until they collide*

Gerald ⎫
              ⎬ (*together; jumping in unison*) Ah!
Potter ⎭

They see each other

Gerald Have you seen her anywhere?
Potter Which one, sir?
Gerald What?
Potter I hope you're looking for the right one…
Gerald Is there *more* than one?
Potter Certainly. Didn't you see the other one?
Gerald What other one?
Potter Standing here! Just now!
Gerald I couldn't see *anything* with Sandra after me!
Potter Well, there *was* one.
Gerald In here?
Potter She *was* in here. But now she's out there. Having a cup of tea in the garden. That's why I'm looking for you. I didn't want her to see you if the other one was still about. I wouldn't want you to get off on the wrong foot with *this* one.
Gerald Which one?
Potter The one having tea. She's just arrived.
Gerald What's that got to do with me?
Potter She's come to see you.

Gerald Has she?

Potter Yes. (*He smiles happily*) So that's good news, isn't it, Mr Corby?

Gerald Is it?

Potter Of course. And I'm so glad!

Gerald You?

Potter Yes.

Gerald Why you?

Potter Because she seems to have arrived just in time to restore the temporarily tottering pillars of respectability.

Gerald What are you talking about?

Potter Your *wife*, sir!

Gerald What wife?

Potter Don't tell me you haven't got a wife?

Gerald Yes. But she's at home.

Potter Not any more. She's here.

Gerald What?!

Potter Out there.

Gerald Having tea?

Potter In the garden.

Gerald She didn't see Sandra chasing me, did she?

Potter Oh, no. I was embracing her at the time.

Gerald What?!

Potter To prevent her from seeing you and Sandra.

Gerald Oh, well done, Potter! I wouldn't like her to get the wrong impression. What the hell's she doing here, anyway?

Potter (*smiling benignly*) I knew you'd be pleased to see her!

Gerald Did you?

Potter And so am I!

Gerald You?

Potter Yes.

Gerald Why you?

Potter Because I'm a manager who's very keen on morals.

Gerald And quite right, too. So whatever happens—keep Sandra out of the way! I don't want my wife thinking the worst.

Potter I'll do my best, sir.

Gerald Oh, and Potter...

Potter Yes?

Gerald (*shaking Potter's hand vigorously*) Thank you! I'm very pleased!

Potter (*moved*) Aah—about your wife. I knew you would be...

Gerald No, no!

Potter No?

Gerald About my room.

Potter Pleased about your room? I thought you didn't like it.

Gerald I didn't like the *old* one, but I shall like *this* one.
Potter Which one?
Gerald The new one.
Potter New one?
Gerald I mustn't hang about here in case Sandra spots me—so when my wife's finished her tea, send her up to Number Fourteen.
Potter (*puzzled*) Fourteen?
Gerald That's where I'll be.
Potter You can't go into Number Fourteen!
Gerald Don't be daft, Potter! You've just put me in there!
Potter Into Number Fourteen?
Gerald Yes! And I'm very grateful!

Gerald embraces the astonished Potter and goes marching out to the bedrooms

Potter is left bewildered as Marion comes in from the garden with her cup of tea

Marion I've just seen a young man climbing down a ladder carrying a bag. Do you suppose he's a burglar?
Potter No. He's a window-cleaner.
Marion Oh, that *is* a relief! What's the number of his room?
Potter The window-cleaner's room?
Marion No, no! My husband's! You told me he was here. So what room is he in?
Potter Ah—er—I'm not sure.
Marion I thought you were the manager.
Potter Yes, but I'm not managing very well! (*He takes the spoon from her saucer and stirs her tea briskly*)

Marion glares at him

Marion You must know which room he's in!
Potter (*quietly*) I wish I didn't...! Now, look... (*He grabs her shoulders*)
Marion You're embracing me again!
Potter It was a mistake.
Marion It certainly was!

To Marion's surprise Potter pushes her down on to the seat

Potter You stay here! I'll go and warn him—er—*find* him!—and bring him to you—down here—*now*!

Marion Very well. But don't keep embracing me!

Potter runs out towards the bedrooms

Marion sighs impatiently and goes back into the garden with her tea

Lights up in the bedroom

Gerald comes in, carrying an armful of clothes and a travel bag. As the door opens we see there is now a number "14" on the outside. Gerald looks at the number to check

Gerald Fourteen... Right! (*He pushes the door shut with his foot and dumps his belongings on the bed. He looks about approvingly*) Oh, yes—this is more like it! (*He looks out of the window*) Oh, yes—very nice indeed.

Potter bursts in desperately

Potter Mr Corby! You can't move in here!
Gerald Only too glad to get away from that car park, I can tell you. (*He chuckles happily*)
Potter But this is Number Fourteen!
Gerald I know, and I'm very grateful. (*He reaches in his back pocket*) Here you are. I should have thought of it before.
Potter Sorry?

Gerald holds out a note to him. Potter hesitates

Gerald Go on. Take it.
Potter No. I can't!
Gerald Don't be daft! You deserve it. Here... (*He takes Potter's hand and puts the note into it*)

Potter leaves his arm extended, the note still sticking out of his clenched fist like a small flag

This room is *much* better...
Potter Yes. But you can't stay here!

Gerald immediately snatches back his money and returns it to his pocket

Gerald What do you mean I can't stay here?
Potter You've got to go back to your *own* room!

Gerald This *is* my room.

Potter No! You've got to get out of here!

Gerald But I've only just got *in* here!

Potter This is no time for argument. (*He picks up Geralds clothes from the bed*) Come on!

Gerald Give those to me! (*He snatches them back and puts them on the bed again*)

Potter I'm trying to keep you out of trouble, sir.

Gerald What are you talking about?

Potter Your wife's downstairs!

Gerald Yes. So why didn't you bring her *up*stairs?

Potter (*appalled*) She mustn't find you in here! (*He picks the clothes up again*)

Gerald snatches the clothes back

Gerald Why not?

Potter snatches the clothes back from Gerald

Potter Because this is a double room!

Gerald snatches the clothes back

Gerald What's wrong with that? I'm the only person in it!

Potter (*quietly*) That's what *you* think…!

Gerald What?

Potter Please, sir—go back to Number Six over the car park where you belong! Your wife mustn't find you in here with another woman.

Gerald Have you been drinking?

Potter I wish I had, but I'm teetotal…!

Gerald Now look here, Potter—I'm not going backwards and forwards, changing rooms like a husband in a French farce! (*He dumps his clothes back on the bed*) I'm here now—in Number Fourteen—and that's where I'm staying! (*He picks up his travel bag and starts to go into the bathroom*) Oh, very nice bathroom…

Gerald disappears, closing the bathroom door behind him

Potter hastily picks up Geralds clothes again, opens the door to the corridor, then hesitates

Potter Ah! *Now* I remember—"Our Father which art in Heaven, hallowed be Thy name…"

Potter goes, praying, closing the door behind him

Lights out in the bedroom

In the pool area, Marion enters from the garden, impatiently

Potter races in, carrying Geralds clothes, and goes to Marion, grim-faced

Bad news, I fear, Mrs Corby.
Marion Don't say you're going to embrace me again!
Potter Your husband says he's awfully sorry—he'd like to have seen you and all that—had a little chat—a cup of tea, perhaps—but he is here for the treatment, you see—so he's going jogging now and after that it'll be hot soup, a few grapes and off to bed. He sends you his good wishes.
Marion (*thundering*) Good wishes?!
Potter And he'll tell you all about it when he gets back home. (*He turns to go*)

Marion sees the clothes he is carrying

Marion Where did you get those clothes from?
Potter What? (*He remembers the clothes*) Oh—*these*? Ah! These! Yes...
(*He hides them behind his back*)
Marion I've seen them somewhere before.
Potter Oh, surely not?
Marion Let me have a look!
Potter No! Please! You mustn't!

Marion tries to see them. Potter dodges this way and that, and as his shoes hit the ground rhythmically he gradually begins to execute a small Spanish dance. Marion starts to join in, and they clap their hands and stamp their feet enthusiastically, finally throwing up their arms and shouting—

Potter ⎫ (*together*) Olé!
Marion ⎭

But in throwing up his arms, Potter also throws up the clothes—high into the air! They fall around him. He goes on to his hands and knees to gather them up, frantically. Marion stands over him, triumphantly

Marion I thought so! What are you doing with my husband's clothes?
Potter Taking them to the cleaners.
Marion They've only just come *back* from the cleaners!
Potter He's very keen on personal hygiene.
Marion I'll go and see what he's up to...

Potter Oh, no! You mustn't do that!

Marion I'll catch him before he goes jogging. (*Glaring at him*) Well, Mr Manager? Have you managed to remember the number of his room?

Potter (*seeing a way out*) Ah—yes! I *do* remember now! It's Number Six. Yes, that's it—Number Six! The one overlooking the car park.

Marion Right! I'll find him there!

Marion marches determinedly out towards the bedrooms

Potter (*quietly*) No, you won't…! (*He looks in despair at the clothes he has gathered up*) Now I'll have to get rid of the dirty linen…

Potter goes out towards his office

Lights up in the bedroom

The door opens on a swell of lush, romantic music, which continues until the dialogue starts. Sandra comes in. We see the number "14" is still on the outside of the door

She is carrying a bottle of red wine which she puts down on the armchair table. Then she gets a perfume atomiser from the drawer of the bedside table, sprays the atmosphere and herself liberally, replaces the atomiser and draws the curtains. The room darkens a little

She turns the bedside light on and is pleased with the effect. Then she lies down on the bed, decoratively, smiling in wicked anticipation

Gerald comes out of the bathroom. He is wearing brightly-coloured boxer shorts and a blue vest, and is carrying his dressing-gown which he puts down on the armchair. Then he turns and sees Sandra. He reacts with alarm

The music stops

Gerald Sandra! (*He pulls in his stomach with masculine pride*) What are you doing in here?

Sandra Waiting for you.

Gerald You can't lie down there!

Sandra Nobody can see us. I've drawn the curtains.

Gerald glances briefly at the curtains and is a little aggrieved

Gerald I can't see the view now…

Sandra There's a better one over here…
Gerald (*clapping his hands, imperiously*) Come on! Off you go—back to your own room!
Sandra This *is* my room.
Gerald No, it isn't. It's mine!
Sandra Whatever gave you that idea?
Gerald I've been moved! Don't you remember? Into Number Fourteen.
Sandra But Number Fourteen is *my* room.
Gerald Now look, Sandra—I enjoy a joke as much as the next man, and we've had a good laugh, the two of us, haven't we? (*He laughs briefly then claps his hands again*) But now—up you get and off you go! (*He pulls her up off the bed*)

Sandra smiles and goes towards the bathroom

Sandra Why don't you look at the room card on the bedside table? See whose name is on it.

Sandra goes into the bathroom

Gerald hesitates for a second then hastens to the bedside table and looks at the room card

Gerald Oh, my God…!

Sandra returns with two plastic glasses and puts them down with the wine

(*appalled*) It's *your* room!
Sandra I told you it was.
Gerald I'm in my secretary's bedroom…!
Sandra Yes…
Gerald (*like a man awaiting the gallows*) What am I doing in my secretary's bedroom?
Sandra Well, let's have a glass of wine and then you might *think* of something…
Gerald You said Mr Potter had found me a better room.
Sandra It *is* a better room.
Gerald You made it up!
Sandra Aren't you pleased?
Gerald No. I'm not! This is a health farm. I'm supposed to go home feeling better for it!
Sandra You *will*…!

A knock at the door

Gerald Oh, my God! (*He whispers to her urgently*) You'll have to get out of here!

Sandra It'll only be Mr Potter.

Marion (*off*) Gerald!

Gerald Doesn't sound like Mr Potter.

Marion (*off*) Gerald!!

Sandra (*with a big smile*) Sounds like somebody who knows you.

Gerald It *is*! Come on—quickly! (*He hustles her towards the bathroom*)

Sandra Where are we going?

Gerald *You*'re going into the bathroom. (*He opens the bathroom door*)

Sandra (*giggling*) Oo, hide and seek! What fun!

Gerald does not think it is fun and pushes her abruptly into the bathroom and closes the door

> *In the pool area, Potter comes in busily from the main entrance and goes out towards the bedrooms, stepping over the sun lounger on his way*

> *Gerald opens the door to the corridor. Marion is there. She looks at his attire in surprise*

Marion I see you're all ready for it!

Gerald Sorry?

Marion Jogging! Mr Potter said you were going jogging.

Gerald looks down, sees his vest and coloured shorts

Gerald Ah—yes! That's why I'm dressed like this. (*He hastily grabs his dressing gown and puts it on*)

Marion closes the door and looks around

Marion It's very dark in here. Are you having a séance?

Gerald runs across to draw back the curtains and switch off the bedside lamp. The room lightens

You took a long time opening the door.

Gerald I was lying down.

Marion In the middle of the afternoon?

Gerald It's all part of the treatment.

Marion You were supposed to be jogging, not lying down! It smells like a tart's boudoir in here. Have you changed your aftershave?

Gerald It's the air freshener! It's the same in all the rooms.

Marion Very sexy for an air freshener. No wonder you all go to bed in the afternoons. I was told you were in Number Six over the car park.

Gerald Yes. I was. But I've been moved. So how did you know where to find me?

Marion A man in shorts saw you coming in here with a bundle of clothes and a smile on your face.

Gerald What are *you* doing here anyway? I left you at home.

Marion I was nearby——

Gerald (*quietly*) Yes, I bet you were...!

Marion —so I thought I'd look in and see what it's like. I've never been to a health farm.

Gerald You won't like it! (*He propels her towards the door*) Go and speak to Linda!

Marion Linda?

Gerald Yes.

Marion *Our* Linda?

Gerald Yes!

Marion (*puzzled*) Is she on the telephone?

Gerald She's staying here!

Marion I didn't know that.

Gerald Neither did I...!

Marion You must have been very surprised to see her.

Gerald Yes. I was!

Marion And then I turned up! Quite a family reunion. We ought to be on *This is Your Life*.

A rat-a-tat at the door

What a very busy bedroom.

Gerald opens the door

   Potter comes in

Potter Good heavens! It smells like a tart's boudoir in here!

Gerald When were *you* last in a tart's boudoir?

Potter (*seeing Marion*) So you found him, Mrs Corby...

Marion (*severely*) *You* told me he was in Number Six.

Potter I wish he *was*...!

Gerald So do I...!

Marion Why? This is a very nice room.

Potter Yes. But he doesn't like it. Do you, sir?

Gerald No. I don't like it at all.

Potter He prefers Number Six.

Marion Over the car park?

Gerald Yes. I miss the smell of petrol.

Potter So we're going to move him back in there.

Marion Gerry, you can't keep moving from place to place like a gypsy. This is a lovely room. You should be pleased.

Gerald Yes. I know. I thought I would be. But I'm not.

Marion Such a big bed.

Gerald Far *too* big.

Marion You like a big bed to stretch in. And you'll have plenty of room in this one.

Potter (*quietly*) No, he won't…!

Gerald It faces north!

Marion (*puzzled*) What?

Gerald The bed. I'll have dreams if I face north.

Potter You certainly will…!

Gerald That's settled, then. Off we all go! Back to Number Six!

Gerald and Potter start to go

Marion Good heavens! There's a bottle of wine, over here!

Gerald and Potter stop

Gerald What?

Potter (*aghast*) Wine? We don't allow alcohol on the premises! This is a health farm, not an off-licence.

Marion Well, there's some over here.

Potter looks at Gerald deeply disillusioned

Potter Oh, Mr Corby … the pillars of morality appear to be trembling again…

Gerald It's not mine!

Marion And two glasses. Were you expecting a guest?

Gerald No! No!

Marion *Two* noes?

Potter One for each glass.

Marion Then why is there a bottle of red wine in your bedroom?

Gerald has sudden inspiration and goes to her urgently

Gerald Ah—yes—of course—I forgot!

Marion Forgot what?

Gerald That's not red wine.

Marion Looks like red wine to me.

Gerald Yes, but it isn't. Is it, Potter?

Potter Isn't it?

Gerald Of course it isn't!

Marion Well, if it's not red wine what is it?

Gerald Well, it's … it's medicinal. Isn't it, Potter?

Potter Is it?

Gerald Yes! Good for the blood! That's what you told me! "That's why it's red," you said.

Potter Did *I* say that?

Gerald Of course you did! Go on—you're the manager. (*To Marion*) He's the manager. He knows all about it. Go on, Potter. Tell her all about it.

Against his better judgement, Potter reluctantly tries to get Gerald off the hook

Potter Well, it's … it's made by monks. Often used in health farms.

Gerald Exactly! (*To Potter impatiently*) Go on!

Potter It's a … a sort of … syrup. A cordial. Full of iron.

Gerald (*to Marion*) Yes. Very good for the nerves.

Potter (*quietly*) It'll need to be…!

Gerald And that's it, really—(*recapitulating briefly*) red liquid, good for health, made by monks, sort of cordial.

Potter So what do you think, Mrs Corby? True or bluff?

Gerald glares at Potter

Marion But what exactly are the ingredients?

Gerald Potter! What are the ingredients?

Potter Nobody knows.

Marion Why don't you ask the monks?

Potter It's a silent order. (*He smiles, enjoying his witticism*)

Gerald gives him a push

Marion (*looking at the label*) But why does the label say Beaujolais?

Gerald (*in huge astonishment*) Beaujolais? (*He goes to inspect the bottle, then turns to glare at Potter*) Potter! How the hell did this get in here?

Potter *I* don't know…

Gerald Well, you're the manager! Think of something!

Potter tries to think of something

Potter I … I can only assume … that there must be a … a secret drinker on the staff. (*He lowers his head in shame, having uttered another lie*)

Gerald smiles broadly, takes Potter's face in his hands and kisses him on the forehead

Gerald Of course! Why didn't *I* think of that? (*To Marion*) Did you hear that, darling? A secret drinker. (*He kisses her on the forehead for good measure*) Well, well! Now we know, eh? (*He laughs, relieved*)

Marion That doesn't explain why there's a bottle of wine in your bedroom.

Gerald Doesn't it? Oh. (*He turns to Potter again*) Got anything for that, Potter?

Potter (*defiantly*) No…!

Gerald Yes, you have!

Reluctantly, Potter proceeds to put another nail in his moral coffin

Potter Well … presumably … the secret drinker… (*He falters*)

Gerald (*helpfully*) Had too much to drink?

Potter Very possibly.

Gerald Yes? *And*? (*He nods encouragingly*)

Potter And left red wine in here … in mistake for the monks' medicinal cordial…

Gerald takes Potter's face in his hands and kisses him on the forehead again

Gerald There! That wasn't very difficult, was it? (*To Marion*) There you are, you see? I knew there was a simple explanation.

He makes to kiss her also, but Marion sees it coming and takes avoiding action. The lavatory in the bathroom flushes, noisily. They all freeze, astonished by this

Marion Gerry…?

Gerald Yes?

Marion There's someone in your bathroom.

Gerald (*hopefully*) Perhaps it's a plumber! (*To Potter*) Plumber, Potter?

Marion Let's see, shall we? (*She goes towards the bathroom*)

Gerald looks at Potter, who shakes his head, mournfully

Potter Oh, no, sir—she *isn't*…?

Gerald (*nodding in despair*) Oh, yes, sir—she *is*…!

Marion opens the bathroom door and looks inside

Marion No. I don't *think* it's a plumber... (*To Sandra inside*) Perhaps you'd like to come in and join the party?

Sandra comes in apprehensively

Sandra Hullo...
Marion (*thoughtfully*) No, she doesn't look like a plumber to me... (*She turns to Gerald*) Well, Gerry?

Gerald turns to Potter hopefully

Gerald Well, Potter?
Potter I think I'll pass on this one...
Marion Aren't you going to introduce us?
Gerald Ah—yes. Right. This is Marion.
Marion I know who *I* am! I want to know who *she* is!
Sandra Who's Marion?
Marion *I* am! And I'm his wife.
Sandra Wife?!
Marion Don't you know what a wife is?
Sandra Yes, but I didn't think he'd brought one with him.
Marion Well, he has—and it's me! Who the hell are you, and why are you hiding in my husband's bathroom?
Gerald Oh, I don't think she was hiding. Was she, Potter?
Potter Wasn't she?
Gerald You know very well she wasn't!
Marion Well, if she wasn't hiding what *was* she doing?
Gerald (*hopefully*) Potter...?
Potter (*with a shrug*) Cleaning?
Gerald Of course! (*To Marion*) Cleaning!
Marion ⎫ (*together*) Cleaning?!
Sandra ⎭
Gerald Yes! She's on the staff here. Isn't she, Potter?
Potter You mustn't ask *me*! I'm too depressed...
Marion (*to Sandra*) And that's why you were in the bathroom?
Sandra Yes. I'm the chambermaid.
Marion Of course you are! I should have realized. You're wearing the new summer uniform.
Gerald Anyway, you've finished the cleaning now, haven't you, Sandra? (*He grabs her and pushes her towards the door*)
Marion Sandra? Is that her name?
Gerald Yes. (*A beat*) Isn't it?

Marion I didn't think you'd know.

Gerald Ah—well—er… (*He turns to Potter hopefully*) Potter…?

Potter Perhaps she was wearing her staff name badge when you arrived, sir. (*He smiles sagely*)

Gerald Quite right, Potter! (*To Marion*) She was wearing her staff name badge. On her chest. (*He starts to indicate Sandra's chest, but quickly decides it safer to indicate his own*)

Marion And you noticed it, of course?

Potter He couldn't miss it…!

Gerald glares at Potter

Marion I'm sure he couldn't.

Gerald (*to Sandra*) If you've finished you may as well go. It's all right if she goes now, isn't it, Potter? To get on with her work—elsewhere?

Potter Yes. I'm sure she can find plenty to do elsewhere…

Sandra I'll be on my way then. Nice to meet you, Mrs Corby. (*She starts to leave, then remembers something. She runs across and picks up the bottle of wine. With a cheerful smile*) I mustn't leave *this* behind, must I?

Sandra runs out with the bottle of wine

Gerald puts his arm around Potter, proudly

Gerald You see? Potter was right! There *was* a secret drinker on the staff. And it was Sandra!

Marion Yes. Wasn't that lucky?

Gerald What?

Marion picks up the two plastic glasses

Marion Shall I put these back in the bathroom? You won't be needing them now, will you?

Gerald Are you *going* into the bathroom, then?

Marion I thought I'd freshen up before I leave. Is that all right? Or have you got any *more* young ladies hidden away?

Gerald Oh, darling, you are funny! Young ladies! (*He turns to Potter*) Isn't she funny, Potter? (*He sees Potter's stony face*) No—never mind. (*To Marion*) You carry on, darling. There's nobody else in there.

Marion There'd better not be!

Marion goes into the bathroom, taking the plastic glasses with her, and closes the door behind her

Gerald (*delightedly*) Well done, Potter!

Potter I'm a moral man and I disapprove of lies...

Gerald You're a genius!

Potter I'm a liar! A stranger to the truth. I shall never be able to set foot in the Conservative Club again.

Gerald You'd better go and have a word with her!

Potter I can't do that! She's in the bathroom.

Gerald Not my wife! Sandra! Tell her to keep out of sight.

Potter Why?

Gerald casts a quick, anxious glance towards the bathroom

Gerald Because we can't have my wife seeing Sandra sitting by the swimming-pool when she's supposed to be on the staff. So keep her out of the way until my wife's gone. (*He urges him towards the door*)

Potter The moral fabric of this establishment has suddenly become threadbare...

Gerald pushes Potter out of the door and closes it abruptly after him

Marion returns from the bathroom

Gerald goes to her, anxious for her to be on her way

Gerald It was good of you to pop in and see how I was getting on. A kind thought. And such a nice surprise. But I've got to move my things back into Number Six now, so I'll say goodbye. Goodbye. (*He kisses her briefly*) I'll see you back at home. (*He hastens towards the bathroom*)

Marion She's got quite a pretty face...

Gerald (*hesitating*) H'm? Who?

Marion The secret-drinking chambermaid.

Gerald (*deliberately vague*) Really? I hadn't noticed.

Gerald goes into the bathroom, Marion goes into the corridor. They shut their respective doors abruptly and in unison

Lights out in the bedroom

In the pool area, Linda and Sandra come in from opposite directions. Sandra is carrying the bottle of wine. They stop when they see each other

Sandra *You* don't look very happy.

Linda Neither do you...

Sandra His wife's turned up. (*She sits on the sun lounger, miserably*)
Linda Oh, dear. (*She sits beside her*)
Sandra How about *your* feller?
Linda Gone…
Sandra Gone?
Linda He thought my father might catch him.
Sandra You mean your *father*'s staying here, as well?
Linda Yes…
Sandra Well, that's that, then, isn't it?
Linda Yes…
Sandra What are we going to do?
Linda (*unhappily*) I suppose we'll just have to concentrate on the treatment…
Sandra Saunas and swimming and no sex?
Linda Well, we are British…

They contemplate the thought without enthusiasm

Potter runs in from the bedrooms, grabs the astonished Sandra by the arm and pulls her to her feet

Potter Come along! You can't stay here!
Sandra Why not?
Potter (*distractedly*) You mustn't be seen sitting by the swimming-pool as if you were a guest!
Linda She *is* a guest!
Potter Yes. *You* know that, and *I* know that—but some people *don't* know that! (*He sees the bottle of wine and grabs it from her*) Give that to me!
Sandra But it's mine! I bought it.
Potter Well, you can't have it! Not in this place. (*He hands the bottle to Linda*) Take that away and hide it in your room. Whatever happens, it mustn't be seen on the premises.
Linda (*bewildered*) But surely…?
Potter Do as I say! (*He pushes her on her way*)

Linda staggers out towards the bedrooms with the bottle of wine

Potter (*grabbing Sandra's arm*) Come along!
Sandra Where are we going?
Potter To my office. *You*'ve got to keep out of sight!

Potter drags the bewildered Sandra out towards his office

Sandra (*as they go*) But when can I go back into *my* room?

Lights up in the bedroom

   Linda comes in. We see that the number "10" is now on the door

She puts the bottle of wine down and goes towards the bathroom

   Rodney climbs in through the open window, carrying a plastic bag

Linda runs to him, delightedly

Linda Rodney! You came back again!
Rodney (*sheepishly*) Yes... I got as far as the village, then I thought to
   myself—why am I leaving without doing what I came here to do? So I
   came back.
Linda I'm glad you did! Because *I*'ve got something that'll cheer you up.
Rodney (*grinning*) Yes—I know you have! That's why I came back.
Linda You'll never guess what it is.
Rodney I bet I will...! *I*'ve got something to cheer *you* up, too! You're not
   going to believe what I found. (*He holds up the plastic bag*)
Linda (*intrigued*) What is it? (*She tries to look*)
Rodney (*hiding the plastic bag behind his back, playfully*) No! You show
   me yours first!

Linda giggles, fetches the wine and hands it to him. He looks at it in surprise

   I thought you weren't allowed booze in this place.
Linda Well, *I* won't tell if *you* don't! Now you show me yours.

Rodney gives the bag to her. She hesitates

Rodney Go on—look inside!

Linda looks inside the bag

Linda (*incredulously*) It *isn't*!
Rodney It *is*!
Linda Chinese food?
Rodney Yes! There's a take-away in the village.
Linda You can't bring Chinese food in here!
Rodney Well, *I* won't tell if *you* don't! You see to the food. I'll open the wine.
   (*He stops*) Oh my God! We haven't got an opener!

*Linda starts to take the silver foil containers out of the plastic bag on to the
armchair table*

Linda Ring reception. They'll send one up.

Rodney And let them know we're drinking wine? Oh, well—here I go again…! (*He puts the wine down and starts to climb out of the window*)

Linda Where are you going?

Rodney To borrow one from the Chinese take-away.

Rodney starts going down the ladder

Linda (*calling after him*) Bring some chopsticks while you're at it!

Rodney (*off*) Righto…!

Linda smiles happily and continues to sort out the containers. The aroma is obviously delicious. There is a knock at the door. Linda freezes in alarm

Linda (*calling*) Who is it?

Marion (*off*) It's your mother!

Linda Oh, no…! (*Calling*) Just a minute! (*She hastily puts the containers of food back into the plastic bag, dithers with it uncertainly, then shoves it under the bed*)

Marion (*off*) Come on! Let me in!

Linda goes to open the door

Marion is there

Surprise! Surprise! (*She sails in*)

Linda It certainly is…! (*She shuts the door*) What are *you* doing here?

Marion I'm visiting an old friend.

Linda Don't tell me you've got an old friend staying *here*?

Marion Not *here*! *Near* here! So as I was passing I thought I'd pop in and see what your father was up to. You never told me *you* were coming here as well.

Linda And *you* never told me that *he* was coming here…!

Marion (*looking around*) This room's just like the one your father's got.

Linda I thought he was overlooking the car park.

Marion Then he must have moved. Have *you* got a nice view? (*She goes to the window*)

Linda No, Mummy—I'd rather you——

Marion (*looking out*) Good heavens! There's a ladder outside your window!

Linda I-Is there?

Marion You mean you hadn't noticed? The window-cleaner must have left it there. We'd better have it taken away.

Linda No!

Marion What?

Linda He … he might need it.

Marion You can't have a ladder outside your bedroom window all night. Somebody might get in. I'll tell reception to have it removed. (*She heads for the phone*)

Linda No! No—*I'll* tell them!

Marion (*returning to Linda*) Darling…?

Linda Yes?

Marion You'll probably think I'm being awfully silly, but—(*she sniffs the air a little*) I think I can smell cooking.

Linda Cooking?!

They both freeze

Black-out bedroom lighting

> *In the pool area, Gerald comes in from the bedrooms, carrying his travel bag, as Potter appears from the opposite side, urgently, and sees him*

Potter Ah, Mr Corby! I fear there's been a change of plan.

Gerald Yes, I know! I'm just going to get my key.

Potter Which key?

Gerald The key to Number Six!

Potter Your old room over the car park?

Gerald (*impatiently*) Well, that's where I'm going, isn't it?

Potter Ah. Yes. It *was*. But it *isn't*.

Gerald Was but isn't?

Potter That *was* the plan, but now it *isn't*!

Gerald But you *wanted* me to go back to Number Six!

Potter Yes. I did. I wanted it more than I can say. But now it's too late. Number Six is occupied.

Gerald Occupied?

Potter Did you tell Miss Figgis at reception that you were moving into Number Fourteen?

Gerald Yes, but I didn't know then that it was Sandra's room!

Potter Well, Miss Figgis naturally assumed that you had no further use for Number Six.

Gerald Are you trying to tell me that someone *else* is in my old room?

Potter Yes…

Gerald Who?

Potter The plumber.

Gerald Ah! Well done, Potter! You've found a plumber, then?

Potter Yes, and he's in your room.

Gerald He's supposed to be mending the steam bath not going to bed!

Potter He was so tired. Poor man. Miss Figgis took pity on him. She's got a heart of gold, Miss Figgis. He'd cycled fifty miles to get here. So he needs to rest before he starts unpacking his tools.

Gerald Then you'll just have to find another one, won't you?

Potter Another plumber? Oh, I don't think that's on the agenda——

Gerald Another room!

Potter Impossible! All the rooms are taken.

Gerald So you're saying that either I share a double room with Sandra or a single room with the plumber?

Potter That does appear to be the choice…

Gerald Well, it's not a choice I'm going to make, Potter. If you can't find me another room I'm going to throw the plumber and his tools out of the window of Number Six!

Gerald storms out towards the bedrooms, carrying his bag

Potter (*calling after him*) No! You mustn't disturb his equilibrium! If he doesn't get his sleep he'll refuse to see to the pipes! (*In despair*) Oh, dear! How am I going to find another room…? (*He has an idea*) Ah—yes!

Potter runs out after Gerald

Lights up in the bedroom

Marion and Linda activate themselves

Marion There's definitely a smell of cooking…

Linda It—it'll be the fumes from the kitchen!

Marion I didn't think they did a lot of cooking on a health farm. I thought you lived on raw vegetables.

Linda They cook soup! Yes—that's what you can smell! Chicken soup! Coming through the window.

Marion I don't think it's coming through the window. (*She goes to check*)

Linda grabs her mother by the arm and swings her round recklessly, diverting her from the window. Naturally, Marion is astonished by this

Linda It was lovely to see you, Mummy—such a nice surprise—but I mustn't hold you up any longer! (*She urges her towards the door*)

Marion You're very keen to get rid of me. I've only just arrived! (*She escapes from Linda and moves back into the room*)

Linda But you hate driving in the dark!

Marion It's summertime! It won't be dark for ages! (*She notices the bottle of red wine*) Ah! I see *you*'ve got some of the monks' medicinal cordial as well. (*She picks up the bottle and looks at it*)

Linda (*puzzled*) Medicinal cordial? It's red wine!

Marion Then it shouldn't be here! (*Confidentially*) There's a secret drinker on the staff, you know…

Linda What *are* you talking about?

A rap at the door, and Potter walks in, urgently, to Linda

Potter Miss Corby! Miss Corby!

Linda Whatever's the matter, Mr Potter?

Potter Bad news, I fear.

Linda *More* bad news?

Potter You have to move out of this room at once!

Linda But I've only just moved in!

Marion (*moving in, imperiously*) And you can't expect my daughter to move out when she's only just moved in.

Potter sees Marion, and bounces with fury

Potter You're still here, Mrs Corby! You should have gone by now!

Marion Everyone wants to get rid of me. (*Suspiciously*) I wonder *why*…?

Potter (*to Linda*) So if you'd just collect up your belongings… (*He gestures, encouragingly*)

Linda But *why* have I got to move?

Potter Because this room is due to be decorated.

Linda Then why was I booked in here in the first place?

Potter Clerical error. I fear Miss Figgis is not as alert as she was.

Linda So where am I going?

Potter You'll have to share with the chambermaid.

Marion The secret-drinking chambermaid?

Potter The very same.

Marion My daughter didn't come here to share a room with a secret-drinking chambermaid!

Potter But this is an emergency! And in an emergency we all have to pull together. I need this room! The decorator will be arriving any minute!

At that moment Rodney leans in through the window with a big smile

Rodney (*announcing proudly*) There we are! Chopsticks and a bottle opener! (*He holds the items up delightedly. Then he sees them all and freezes in horror*)

They all stare at him in surprise. Potter points at Rodney triumphantly

Potter There, you see! I told you the decorator would be arriving any minute!

Marion Decorator? You told me he was the window-cleaner.

Potter Well, he's a window-cleaner during the day and a decorator at night.

Linda (*to Marion*) You mean you've seen this man before?

Marion Yes. He was climbing down his ladder when I was having my tea. (*Turning to Potter*) Mr Potter—if he's a decorator and a window-cleaner, why is he carrying chopsticks and a bottle opener?

Potter You mustn't keep asking me questions!

Rodney I think I've come into the wrong room *again*...! (*He starts to descend*)

Potter races across to prevent him leaving

Potter No! No, you haven't! This is the right room! (*He struggles with Rodney, trying to pull him into the room*)

Linda No, it isn't! It's the wrong room and he's got to go!

Potter He can't go *now*! This room has got to be decorated!

Desperately, Linda tries to urge her mother on her way

Linda Don't you think you should go now, Mummy? Your friend will be wondering where you are.

Rodney (*to Potter*) Mummy?!

Potter (*nodding, frantically*) Yes—Mummy!

Rodney *Her* Mummy?

Potter Yes...! *Her* Mummy!

Rodney Oh God...!

Potter It's too late now for prayers. Just remember you're a decorator. (*He returns to Linda*) Come along, Miss Corby! I'll show you to your new room. (*He goes to open the door*)

Linda No, Mr Potter! *This* is my room and this is where I'm staying!

Marion Yes, it certainly is!

Gerald walks in through the open doorway and sees Potter

Gerald Potter! What the hell are you doing? You're supposed to be finding me another room.

Potter I am *trying*, sir...

Gerald Well, try a little harder!

Potter (*pointedly*) I'm trying to move your daughter into *Number Fourteen*...

Gerald Number Fourteen? You mean with—er...?

Potter (*nodding wildly*) Yes—exactly! Leaving *this* room ... *empty*! (*He smiles triumphantly*)

Marion For the decorator.

Gerald Decorator?

Marion (*indicating Rodney*) *This* decorator!

Gerald sees Rodney half in and half out of the window, and chuckles delightedly

Gerald Good heavens! Are you here *again*? (*To Potter*) I thought he was a window-cleaner.

Potter ⎫ (*together*) Yes. He's a window-cleaner during the day and a
Marion ⎭ decorator at night.

Potter is surprised by Marion's collaboration

Gerald (*to Marion*) Why are *you* still here? You should have gone by now.
Marion I came to say hullo to Linda.
Linda Yes. And now she's leaving!
Marion (*to Gerald, puzzled*) I thought you were moving back into your old room over the car park?
Gerald I was. But that damn plumber refuses to leave! He's barricaded himself in.
Potter (*in despair*) Oh, you shouldn't have disturbed him, Mr Corby. Now we'll *never* persuade him to get his spanner out!
Marion What on earth was a plumber doing in your bedroom?
Gerald Never mind. It's a long story. (*He crosses to Rodney with a smile*) You keep coming into the wrong room!
Rodney Yes. I never was good at geography.
Gerald Your girlfriend will be wondering what's happened to you.
Potter (*quietly*) No, she won't…!
Marion What *are* you talking about, Gerry? He can't possibly have a girlfriend.
Gerald Why? What's he done to himself?
Marion If he's a window-cleaner during the day and a decorator at night, he'll be far too busy to think about girls! (*Patiently*) Gerry, he's here to decorate the bedroom.
Gerald (*laughing*) No, he's not! *I* know what he's here for and it's not to decorate a bedroom!
Potter (*suffering*) Oh, no, Mr Corby…!
Gerald (*to Marion*) He told me all about it!
Potter (*quietly*) Well, please don't tell *us* all about it…!
Gerald He's been having trouble with his girlfriend!

Linda grabs Marion and pushes her towards the door abruptly

Linda Come along, Mother! Your friend is expecting you. You mustn't keep her waiting!

Marion All right! All right! I'm going! I'll leave you to get on with it, then, Gerry.
Gerald Get on with what?
Marion (*with dark suspicion*) Whatever it was that you came here to do.
Gerald Ah—the treatment! Yes—right. (*He laughs nervously*)

Marion gives him a severe look and goes out with Linda

(*To Rodney*) Off you go then! Don't keep your girlfriend waiting any longer! (*He assists him out of the window*)

Potter is standing very still, concentrating on something

Potter Mr Corby...
Gerald What is it, Potter?
Potter I think I can smell cooking...
Gerald Cooking?!

Potter's eyes are moving from left to right, his nostrils twitching as he sniffs the air like a rabbit. He moves about slowly, gradually going lower and lower as he follows the scent. Gerald and Rodney watch him: Gerald in surprise, Rodney in fear (one leg out of the window). Potter goes on to his hands and knees, his face almost touching the carpet, then he reaches under the bed with one outstretched hand. Gerald goes to him, intrigued

Gerald What are you looking for?
Potter I don't know. But whatever it is I've found it! (*He produces the plastic shopping bag containing Chinese food*)

He and Gerald look at it in surprise. Rodney is frozen with fear. Potter opens the top of the bag and looks inside. He looks up at Gerald perplexed

No wonder he wanted chopsticks.
Gerald It's *not*?
Potter It *is*!
Gerald ⎤
           ⎟ (*together*) Chinese food!
Potter ⎦

Rodney falls, spectacularly, off the ladder, disappearing from sight outside, calling as he goes

Rodney A-a-a-a-ah...!

Potter and Gerald look at each other in alarm

Gerald Now he's fallen off his bloody ladder!

Gerald races out of the room

Potter starts to follow with the Chinese food, then remembers the bottle of wine. In appalled disapproval he grabs the offending bottle and hastens out after Gerald closing the door behind him

Lights out in the bedroom

In the pool area, Gerald comes running in from the bedrooms, muttering despairingly

Oh dear, oh dear, oh dear, oh dear…!

Gerald disappears out to the garden

Potter races in. He hesitates, looks at the bottle of wine and the Chinese food, disapprovingly, and echoes Gerald

Potter Oh dear, oh dear, oh dear, oh dear…!

Potter runs out after Gerald

Marion and Linda come in from the bedrooms

Marion I can't think what's got into your father. Why on earth did he come to a health farm? It doesn't seem to be doing his health any good at all.

Sandra looks in uncertainly, from the direction of Potter's office, not yet seeing them

Sandra Mr Potter? Can I come out now?

Marion sees her and whispers to Linda

Marion There she is!
Linda Who?
Marion The secret-drinking chambermaid!
Linda (*looking*) Don't be silly! That's Sandra!

Sandra sees them

Sandra Oh—sorry. I'm not supposed to be here. (*She starts to go*)

Linda Don't go!

Sandra hesitates

Marion (*to Linda*) You *know* this girl?
Linda Yes, I met her this afternoon. Come on in, Sandra. Let me introduce you.
Marion I *think* we've already met. (*She glares at Sandra*)

Sandra decides it best to continue as a member of the staff and bobs a curtsy

Sandra Can I get you anything, madam? A pot of tea? Glass of orange juice?
Linda (*amused*) Sandra, what are you playing at?
Marion I told you—she's a chambermaid. With a secret penchant for red wine. (*She gives Sandra a stern look*)
Linda Of course she isn't! She came here to see her boss. Didn't you, Sandra? (*She grins at Sandra playfully*)
Marion Her ... boss?
Linda Yes! She's his secretary and she decided to come here and give him a nice surprise. But—(*she giggles*) unfortunately his wife turned up unexpectedly!
Marion (*icily*) Did she really? (*To Sandra*) So *that*'s why you were hiding in my husband's bathroom!

Linda realizes she has put her foot in it

Linda Oh, no...!

Marion starts to go towards the bedrooms

Where are you going?
Marion I'm going to find Gerry and give him *another* nice surprise!

Marion sails out, decisively

Linda turns to Sandra, feeling rather guilty

Linda Sorry, Sandra. I—I didn't realize.

Sandra looks puzzled

Sandra Do you *know* that lady, then?
Linda Know her? She's my mother!

Sandra (*realizing*) Oh, no! So—so my boss is … is your…?
Linda *Father!* Yes!
Sandra Oh my God…!

They both look appalled. Then they see the funny side and start to laugh, collapsing on to the sun lounger together

> *Gerald strides in urgently from the garden. He stops when he sees them laughing together and goes to them, uncertainly*

Gerald Have … have you two met, then?
Linda Of course we have, Daddy!
Sandra Of course we have, Daddy!

They laugh louder

Linda You never told me your secretary was here.
Gerald D-didn't I?
Linda Did you bring her along to take down notes?
Gerald No!
Sandra Well, he brought me along do take down *some*thing…!

The girls giggle at this, which infuriates Gerald

Gerald I didn't bring her! Did I, Sandra?
Sandra (*deliberately vague*) Didn't you, Mr Corby?
Gerald You know very well I didn't! (*To Linda*) We met here by accident!
  (*He starts to go*)
Linda That doesn't seem likely…

Gerald stops

  Does it, Sandra?
Sandra No…
Linda Bit of a coincidence… Isn't it, Sandra?
Sandra Yes…
Gerald Sandra! You know very well what happened!
Linda Ah! Something did happen, then?
Gerald No! Nothing! That's what happened—nothing!
Sandra Well, don't worry, Mr Corby. There's still time!
Linda Anyway, it doesn't really matter whether anything happened, does it?
Gerald (*relieved*) Doesn't it?
Linda It's what people will *think* happened that matters.

Gerald is far from reassured

Potter comes in from the garden, urgently

Potter Mr Corby! What *are* you doing? I've got a man lying on his back out there!

Sandra Think yourself lucky. I wish *I* had!

Potter (*to Sandra*) You're not supposed to be here! I left you in my office with the dirty linen.

Linda It's all right, Mr Potter. My mother knows what's been going on.

Potter I knew when I got out of bed this morning that it was going to be one of those days…! (*To Gerald*) You were supposed to be fetching a blanket, Mr Corby, not fraternising with the clientèle.

Sandra Why do you need a blanket?

Potter To cover the poor boy until the doctor's examined him, of course!

Linda Doctor?

Potter Yes! He fell off his ladder! Call himself a window-cleaner…

Linda (*without thinking*) Oh, the poor darling!

Gerald Poor darling? (*He laughs*) Anyone would think *you* were his girlfriend!

Linda Is he all right, Mr Potter?

Potter Well, I don't think anything's broken. Fortunately for him he landed on top of the kitchen refuse.

Linda
Sandra } (*together*) What?!

Rodney comes in unsteadily from the garden. His face and clothes are streaked with dirt and he is adorned by a few pieces of stale salad

Potter goes to him anxiously

You shouldn't be standing up! I left you lying down!

Rodney Go away! I'm all right! (*He goes weak at the knees*) No, I'm not…

Potter supports him, perilously. Gerald goes to assist

Sandra (*quietly, to Linda*) Is *this* your fella?

Linda Yes…

Sandra I thought he'd gone.

Linda He came back.

Sandra I bet he wishes he hadn't!

Gerald Right, son! We'd better get you up to your room.

Potter (*quietly, in despair*) Oh, *now* where are we going to put him…?

Gerald and Potter pick Rodney up, one on either side

Gerald And we'd better make sure you get into the *right* room this time, eh?
(*He laughs*) What's the number of your room?
Linda He can't remember!
Gerald How do *you* know?
Linda He's just fallen off a ladder!
Potter Yes! Probably got amnesia!
Gerald (*to Potter*) Well, *you* can remember! You haven't got amnesia!
Potter Yes, I have! I felt it coming on a moment ago.

They put Rodney down on the sun lounger

Gerald Then go and look in the register!
Potter I can't! Miss Figgis has locked up the office for the night.
Gerald Well, we can't leave him *here*, can we?
Linda I know!

They all look at her

(*Innocently*) He can lie down in *my* room if he wants to.
Gerald Yes! *What* a good idea!
Potter No! *Not* a good idea!
Gerald Well, there's nowhere else to put him until you find the number of
his *own* room.
Potter No, no! I won't have immorality on the premises!
Gerald Don't be daft! There won't be anything immoral about it.
Linda (*disappointed*) Won't there?
Gerald Of course not! *He* can go into *your* room—and you can move in with
Sandra like Potter said!

Which does not please Linda and Sandra at all

Sandra ⎱ (*together*) Ooh…!
Linda ⎰
Sandra But if Linda's in *my* room where are *you* going to be, Mr Corby?

Gerald glares at her

Linda (*in assumed outrage*) Daddy! What will my poor mother think when
she finds out?
Gerald She's not *going* to find out! I mean—there's nothing to find out!
Potter's sorting it out. Aren't you, Potter?

Potter I'm trying to…! (*He concentrates*)
Linda (*happily*) That's settled, then! (*To Rodney*) Come along!

Rodney looks up, still dazed from his fall

Rodney Where am I going?
Linda *You're* going to lie down in *my* room.
Rodney Am I?
Linda (*as if just realizing*) Oh. I'm sorry! We haven't been introduced, have we? I'm Linda. And you're…?
Rodney Rodney…
Linda Come along, then, Rodney.

Linda leads the weary Rodney off towards the bedrooms

Gerald (*glaring at Sandra*) What did you have to go and say that for? Now my daughter thinks I'm sharing a bedroom with *you*!
Sandra Well, that's better than thinking you're sharing with the plumber.
Gerald I'm not sharing with anyone!
Sandra Well, your toothbrush is still in my bathroom…
Gerald (*alarmed*) Is it?
Sandra Yes—(*romantically*) I saw it—right next to mine…
Potter (*coming out of his reverie*) I've *got* it, Mr Corby!
Gerald Yes?
Potter For the time being you'll have to move into your daughter's room with the window-cleaner.
Sandra Oh, no…!
Gerald Well done, Potter! (*He kisses him on the forehead*) So I'll just go and get my toothbrush out of Number Fourteen. (*He starts to go*)
Sandra You don't have to be in such a hurry.
Potter Oh, yes, he does…!

Gerald goes, speedily

Sandra Spoilsport! (*She calls*) Mr Corby!

Sandra runs out after Gerald

Potter watches her go, miserably

Potter Oh, dear. The pillars of morality are starting to tremble again…

Potter hastens out towards his office

Lights up in the bedroom

Linda leads Rodney in. We see the number "10" on the outside of the door

Rodney is still dazed after his escapade. He sinks on to the bed and tries to gather himself. Linda closes the door and goes to draw the curtains. The room darkens a little. She turns on the bedside lamp. He clocks this, apprehensively. Linda snuggles up to him, sexily

Linda Oh, Rodney…
Rodney H'm?
Linda Alone at last…
Rodney (*the picture of dejection*) Sorry?
Linda Wet've got nothing to worry about *now*, have we?
Rodney Haven't we?
Linda Daddy's got other things on his mind.
Rodney Has he?
Linda So … that's all right, isn't it?
Rodney Is it?
Linda (*trying to be patient*) Rodney … what did we come here for?

Rodney tries to remember

Rodney I can't remember.
Linda This is the moment we've been waiting for! We're all alone and my father's out of the way!
Rodney (*plaintively*) But I've just fallen off a ladder…
Linda (*impatiently*) Well, you haven't broken anything *vital*, have you?
Rodney I don't *know* yet, do I? But after you fall off a ladder you do tend not to feel quite so … "romantic" as you might…

Linda gets up abruptly and glares at him

Linda You don't fancy me any more, is that it?
Rodney No!
Linda You *don't*?!
Rodney I mean no it isn't that! Of course I fancy you! But at the moment … I'm littered with lettuce… (*He has an idea*) I tell you what we *could* do, though…
Linda (*smiling, hopefully*) Yes…?
Rodney We could eat our Chinese food.
Linda (*livid again*) How can you think of food at a time like this?
Rodney I'm hungry… It must be around here somewhere. (*He looks about*) Where the hell did he put it?

Linda What are you talking about?
Rodney Potter found our Chinese food! He must have taken it with him!
Linda (*sulking a little*) It would have been cold by now, anyway…
Rodney *I* wouldn't have mindeed…
Linda You mean you'd rather have cold Chinese food than hot *me*?
Rodney It's not that…!
Linda If food is all you fancy I'll go and find some!

Linda goes, furious, slamming the door behind her

Rodney sighs and goes, aching, into the bathroom

Lights out in the bedroom

In the pool area, Potter comes in, carrying Gerald's clothes, as Marion returns, impatiently

Marion Mr Potter!
Potter Are you *still* here?
Marion Where is he?
Potter Sorry?
Marion My husband! Where is he hiding? I tried to catch him in Number Fourteen but he wasn't there.
Potter Why should you catch him in Number Fourteen? That's the chambermaid's room. You wouldn't catch Mr Corby in the chambermaid's room, now would you?
Marion You needn't pretend, Potter! I know what's going on here.
Potter Oh, I hope *not*, Mrs Corby…
Marion You're not running a health farm at all. You're running a…!
Potter (*hiding his face in the clothes*) No! Please! Don't utter that word in my presence!

Marion recognizes the clothes Potter is carrying

Marion You've got my husband's clothes again!
Potter What?
Marion You said you were taking them to the cleaners.
Potter I did. And now they're back.
Marion You must have sent them express.
Potter All part of the service, madam.
Marion So where are you taking them now?
Potter To Number Ten.
Marion Number Ten's my daughter's room.

Potter Not any longer! *She*'s moving into Number Fourteen.
Marion With the chambermaid?!
Potter Yes. And your husband is going into Number Ten with the window-cleaner.
Marion You don't expect me to believe that, do you? *I* know what my husband's up to, and I'm going to catch him when he's up to it!

Marion storms out

Potter This is beginning to feel like the longest day of my life… (*He calls*) Mrs Corby!

Potter hastens out after her

Lights up in the bedroom

Gerald comes in, urgently. We see the number "14" on the door. He rushes into the bathroom and returns with his toothbrush

Sandra comes in and shuts the door

Sandra You don't have to be in such a hurry!
Gerald Oh, yes, I do! Keep away! (*He holds up his toothbrush as if trying to repel a vampire*) I only came back for my toothbrush.
Sandra Then why have you drawn the curtains?
Gerald What? (*He looks and sees that the curtains are indeed drawn*) How on earth did *that* happen…? (*He races across and draws back the curtains*)

The room lightens. He switches off the bedside lamp

Thank God my wife isn't here to see this!
Sandra But she *is*!
Gerald What?!
Sandra (*advancing*) *And* she knows all about *us*…
Gerald There's nothing to know about us! Nothing happened!
Sandra (*sweetly logical*) She'll never believe that, though, will she? So it may as well happen! (*She grabs him and pulls him on to the bed on top of her*)

Gerald struggles, valiantly

The door opens and Marion walks in and sees the struggling mass on the bed

Marion Gerald!

Gerald Aaaah! (*He hastily extricates himself from Sandra's clutches and tries to regain his equilibrium*)

Sandra smiles, enjoying the situation. Marion waits for an explanation

Marion *Well*?

Gerald I … I was looking for my toothbrush. (*He holds up his toothbrush*)

Marion I knew you were looking for *something*! What was your toothbrush doing in your secretary's bedroom?

Gerald It was a mistake.

Marion It certainly was!

Gerald There *is* a reasonable explanation——

Marion When you can think of it?

Gerald When I can think of—no, no! I've got what I came here for.

Marion Yes, I'm sure you have!

Gerald My toothbrush! (*He waves it at her*)

Potter bursts in, carrying Gerald's clothes

Potter Ready to move into Number Ten, Mr Corby?

Gerald Ah—yes, Potter—I was just on my way!

Marion You certainly were! Why don't you tell us exactly what you were doing in your secretary's bedroom?

Sandra He was only giving me dictation…

Marion Do you *always* take dictation lying down on a bed together?

Potter (*aghast*) Oh, Mr Corby…! And you'd only been in here for two minutes!

Gerald I wouldn't have been in here at all if it hadn't been for the plumber.

Marion What's the plumber got to do with it?

Potter He was so tired, poor man. Fifty miles he'd travelled. On his bicycle!

Marion What has a pedalling plumber got to do with my husband cavorting about on a bed with his secretary?

Potter After fifty miles he was too tired to see to the pipes.

Gerald So Miss Figgis popped the plumber into *my* room.

Marion And you popped into Sandra's room?

Gerald I didn't know it was Sandra's room then!

Marion It didn't take you long to find out.

Potter Shall we go, then, sir? (*He moves his armful of clothes forward and back indicating the door, hopefully*)

Gerald Ah—yes—right! (*To Marion*) Mr Potter's found me another room.

Potter (*to Marion, sagely*) You see, madam? It's all change here now.

Potter smiles faintly and goes

Gerald turns to Marion, his confidence returning

Gerald Shouldn't you be on your way, darling? Your old friend will be wondering where you are. What time was she expecting you?

Marion smiles enigmatically

Marion She? Whatever gave you the idea it was a woman?
Gerald What?! (*He suspects the worst*)

Marion goes, closing the door behind her

Sandra closes in on Gerald, smiling hopefully

Sandra Mr Corby … if your wife's got another fella *we* can carry on from where we left off.
Gerald No, we can't! (*He holds up his toothbrush*) *This* is all I came here for!

Gerald escapes quickly, closing the door behind him abruptly

Sandra Oh, hell…!

Fed up, Sandra goes into the bathroom, closing the door equally abruptly

A brief musical glissando

Someone knocks loudly on the door to the corridor

Rodney comes out of the bathroom. He has cleaned himself up and regained enthusiasm for what he came here to do

Rodney (*calling*) Just coming, darling! (*Smiling happily as he opens the door*) I'm feeling much more like it now!

But it is Marion who is there. Rodney's smile fades quickly. We see that the number "10" is now on the outside of the door

Marion walks in, surprised to see him

Marion What are *you* doing here?
Rodney Sorry?
Marion You're in my daughter's bedroom!

Rodney Am I?

Marion This *is* Number Ten, isn't it?

Rodney Is it? (*He looks to see*) Good Lord, so it is! (*He shuts the door*)

Marion So what are you this time? A window-cleaner or a decorator?

Rodney Ah—well, I——

Marion Or perhaps you're a gigolo? Is that it? Perhaps you're in the habit of climbing ladders to get into ladies' bedrooms?

Rodney I didn't climb up a ladder this time! I was invited.

Marion *Invited*?! Are you saying that my daughter invited you into her bedroom?

Rodney Yes. She said I could lie down for a bit.

Marion Lie down for a bit?!

Rodney I had to rest, you see. After what had happened. (*Rather put out*) Didn't they tell you about it?

Marion I don't need to be told about it. I can imagine what happened!

Rodney I fell off a ladder, that's what happened!

Marion After you'd appeared through my daughter's bedroom window with chopsticks and a bottle opener?

Rodney Yes, I picked the wrong room, you see. Anyone can pick the wrong room, can't they?

Marion *I*'ve never picked a wrong room in my life!

Rodney (*quietly*) I can believe that…!

She glares at him

It was a mistake!

Marion It certainly was!

Rodney It's a long way down if you're at the top of a ladder. I was in agony! I could hardly walk. Mr Potter had to help me. So your daughter—er— what's her name?

Marion Linda!

Rodney Yes—Linda! That's it! I remember now—what a nice name. Anyhow, Linda took pity on me and kindly lent me *her* room. *This* room. To lie down and rest.

Marion And *have* you?

Rodney What?

Marion Rested!

Rodney Oh, yes.

Marion And that's why you're "feeling more like it now"?

Rodney (*grinning*) Yes! (*He adds quickly*) *Walking*, that is!

Marion So Linda's not your girlfriend, then?

Rodney (*vehemently*) No, of course not! Whatever gave you that idea? She's just a good Samaritan. I'm here on my own!

Marion Are you sure?
Rodney 'Course I'm sure! I'm all alone! Definitely! All alone!

So Marion has an idea...

Marion Oh, good...! (*She advances towards him*)
Rodney (*nervously*) Here—what's *your* game?
Marion What's the matter? You're not frightened of older women, are you?
   (*She pushes him down on to the bed and throws herself enthusiastically on
   top of him*)

Whereupon Gerald walks in, carrying a bunch of grapes

Gerald I thought I'd bring you a bunch of grapes.
Marion No, thank you, Gerry. I think we've *got* everything we want.

Gerald sees them

Gerald Marion!!

*Rodney hastily escapes from Marion's clutches, deeply embarrassed. Marion
remains sitting serenely on the bed and tidying her hair*

   I thought you'd gone to meet your "gentleman friend"!
Marion I was just on my way.
Gerald I could see that!
Marion (*innocently*) I only popped in to say goodbye to Linda.
Gerald And said hullo to *him* instead!

Rodney intervenes nervously

Rodney It ... it wasn't as bad as you think.
Gerald Oh, good! Then perhaps you'll give her a reference! What the hell
   do you think you were doing?
Marion (*enjoying his discomfort*) Wasn't that obvious?
Gerald (*to Rodney*) You were lent this room to recover from your fall, not
   to attack defenceless unaccompanied married females!
Marion Oh, dear. Is that what I am?
Gerald (*glaring at her*) Had you forgotten that you'd got a husband here?
Marion Well, you've got a *wife* here and it didn't bother *you.*

*The door opens and Potter comes in, carrying Gerald's clothes and a
bunch of grapes*

Potter I thought the young man might feel better for some grapes. (*He sees Marion*) Mrs Corby! You're still here!
Marion I'm just leaving!

Potter puts down the clothes and goes to Rodney with the grapes

Potter You're supposed to be lying down.
Gerald He *was*! Lying down on the bed with my wife!
Potter (*appalled*) A window-cleaner taking advantage of an unaccompanied married female?
Marion Don't *you* start!

Potter goes to Marion sympathetically

Potter Poor Mrs Corby. What an ordeal… Oh, I shall have to sit down. (*He sits down with Marion on the bed and eats a grape*)
Marion You don't have to worry, Mr Potter. My husband came in before anything happened.
Potter But the shock! Would *you* like a grape, Mrs Corby? I'm sure you're ready for one.
Marion Oh, thank you, Mr Potter. I'm glad to see that you're a gentleman, after all.

She and Potter eat grapes

The door opens and Linda comes in with a bunch of grapes

Linda Here you are! Perhaps *these* will make you feel a bit sexier! (*She holds out the grapes. Then she sees them all*)

And they see her. Reactions

I … I brought him some grapes…
Potter It'll soon be like a vineyard in here.
Linda Mummy, you're still here!
Marion (*to Potter, suffering*) Everyone wants to get rid of me.
Potter You come with me, Mrs Corby.

They start to go

Perhaps you'd like a nice cup of tea before you go? It'll settle your nerves. They must be in ribbons. I know mine are.

Potter and Marion go, he taking the grapes with him

Linda looks at Gerald hopefully, reconciliation in her mind

Linda Aren't *you* going too, Daddy?
Gerald Going? I'm moving in here with *him*!
Linda What?!
Gerald And you're supposed to be moving into Number Fourteen—remember? I'm not leaving you here with this sex maniac!
Linda I thought he was a window-cleaner.
Gerald Yes—a sex-mad window-cleaner!
Linda Oh, I'm sure he's not that! I don't expect he's feeling very sexy now he's fallen off his ladder. (*She gives Rodney a cold look*)
Gerald Well, just now he was rolling about on the bad with your mother!
Linda What?! (*To Rodney*) *Were* you?
Rodney Well ... yes, but——
Linda Yes?!
Rodney But *she* was on top!
Linda Ooooh!!

Linda races out, noisily, slamming the door behind her

Gerald naturally finds this reaction hard to understand

Gerald I can't think why *she*'s so upset. You were lucky your *girlfriend* didn't find out what you were up to!
Rodney I wasn't up to anything!
Gerald Now look, son—you take my advice——
Rodney I took your advice last time and see where it landed me!

Rodney races out after Linda

Gerald shrugs, puzzled, picks up his clothes and goes into the bathroom

Lights out in the bedroom

In the pool area, Potter and Marion wander in from DL, eating grapes

Potter We'll get you a nice strong cup of tea, Mrs Corby. It must have been such a shock for you.
Marion (*suffering suitably*) Oh, it *was*, Mr Potter...
Potter And for *me*...
Marion Why you?
Potter I never thought I'd live to see the day when the moral supports of this establishment were on the brink of collapse...

Linda comes storming in. She sees Marion and glares at her

Linda No wonder you didn't want to leave!
Potter Your mother's had a very nasty shock.
Linda So have I...! Aaaah...!

Without thinking, Linda runs into the steam baths

Potter considers this

Potter I didn't think Miss Corby was due for a steam bath at this time...

Rodney runs in from the bedrooms, looking for Linda

Marion sees him, grabs Potter and clings to him in mock fear

Marion Ooh! He's after me again!

Rodney stops, sees there is no sign of Linda and runs out the way he came in

Marion is a little aggrieved

Oh. He must have changed his mind.
Potter Then you've had a lucky escape. (*He extricates himself from Marion*)

Linda bursts out from the steam baths

Linda There's a man in there with his clothes on!

Linda runs out through the archway to the bedrooms

Potter That must be the plumber. Perhaps the poor man couldn't sleep.

As they continue on their way, Potter looks down at the grapes despondently

Oh, Mrs Corby, you've squashed my grapes...

Potter and Marion disappear out to the offices

Lights up in the bedroom

Rodney comes in. We see the number "14" on the door. He looks about hopefully

Rodney Linda? Are you there?

No response

   (*Calling*) Oh, come on! Let's stop messing about and get on with it, eh?

Sandra comes out of the bathroom. She sees him and smiles delightedly

Sandra Oo, what a lovely surprise! This *is* good news! I thought you were
   spoken for.
Rodney I *am*!
Sandra Then what are you doing in my bedroom?
Rodney Mr Corby said it was *Linda*'s bedroom *now*!
Sandra (*laughing*) You expect me to believe that? (*She moves towards him*)
   You came to see *me*, didn't you?

Rodney backs away nervously

Rodney No! No! I didn't! Honestly!

Sandra follows him with a big smile

Sandra You don't have to play hard to get, Rodney. I heard you say you
   wanted to get on with it. Well, that's what *I*'ve been trying to do all day!
   (*She grabs him and clings on like a limpet*)
Rodney Sandra! No! (*He struggles valiantly*)

   Whereupon Linda walks in, of course. And sees them

Linda Rodney!!

Rodney hastily escapes from Sandra's clutches

   You're at it again! Daddy was right! You *are* a sex-mad window-cleaner!
Rodney It wasn't me! It was *her*!
Linda Sandra! What *did* you think you were doing?

Sandra tries to think what she was doing

Sandra I was trying to teach him the tango. He's very quick on his feet.
Linda He'll *need* to be! (*She glares at Rodney*)
Sandra (*with a sudden thought*) Wait a minute! If you're both here in
   Number Fourteen, your father must be all alone in Number Ten!

Linda Yes…!
Sandra Brilliant!

Sandra scuttles out, hopefully

Linda looks at Rodney with dark suspicion

Linda The tango? Is that *all* she was trying to do with you?
Rodney (*with a shrug*) I can't help it if I'm irresistible.
Linda Oh Rodney!

They laugh. She embraces him and they fall back on to the bed

The door opens and Gerald walks in, talking as he arrives

Gerald Linda, I wonder if… (*He stops, seeing them*) What the hell are you doing?!

They remain where they are and look up at him patiently

Linda We're two adults consenting, and we *thought* we were in private.
Gerald (*glaring at Rodney*) I don't understand you. First you're on a bed with my wife and now with my daughter! Are you trying to get into the *Guinness Book of Records*?

In the pool area, Potter and Marion come in from the offices. Potter is carrying a small tray of tea things

Potter Here we are, Mrs Corby. A small pot of tea. You sit down and make yourself comfortable. (*He puts the tray down on the garden table*)

Marion sits on the padded seat. Potter carries the garden table down to her. He puts it down and sits beside her

You'll feel much better for a nice cup of tea. I know *I* will. (*He briskly stirs the tea in the tiny pot and starts to pour two cups*)
Gerald (*to Rodney*) You aren't even ashamed!
Rodney (*getting up off the bed*) Why should I be?
Potter Sugar, Mrs Corby?
Gerald You told me you'd already *got* a girlfriend here!
Marion No, thank you, Mr Potter.
Linda He has! It's me!
Potter Just one for me, then. (*He empties the contents of the tin sugar bowl into his cup and stirs vigorously*)

Gerald You?!

Linda Yes.

Gerald You mean you *didn't* come here on your own?

Linda No. I came here with *him*. (*She gets up and joins Rodney*)

Gerald With *him*?

Linda Yes.

Gerald With a window-cleaner? You cannot be serious!

Rodney But we *are*, Mr Corby. *Very* serious.

Linda (*surprised and delighted*) Are we? Oh, good!

Sandra comes in and sees Gerald

Sandra Where were you, Mr Corby? I looked for you in Number Ten but you'd gone.

Linda Yes—he came back *here* and surprised us…!

Marion Very nice tea, Mr Potter.

Potter I'm glad you like it, Mrs Corby. I always use one spoonful for each person… (*he lifts up the tiny teapot*) …and just a *half* for the pot!

Potter and Marion laugh happily

Gerald (*to Sandra*) You're not going to believe this, but Linda and the window-cleaner came here *together*!

Sandra Yes! I know! Just like *we* did.

Gerald Sandra! You *know* we didn't come here together!

Sandra Yes. *I* know that and *you* know that, but your *wife* doesn't know that, does she?

Potter Perhaps you'd like a Marie biscuit, Mrs Corby? I always think they go so well with afternoon tea.

Marion Oh, no, Mr Potter! You mustn't spoil me any more.

Gerald (*staring at Sandra, aghast*) You wouldn't tell my wife something that wasn't true?

Sandra Well, not if you give Linda and Rodney your blessing.

Gerald That's blackmail!

Sandra Oh, good! I've never done that before.

Sandra grins at Gerald and runs out of the room

Gerald panics

Gerald Oh my God…! Wait! Sandra…!

Gerald runs out after her

Linda looks happily at Rodney

Linda You never said you were serious.
Rodney I'm a window-cleaner. I'm always serious.

Linda and Rodney laugh and follow the others

Lights out in the bedroom

Potter and Marion look up from their tea as Sandra races in, with Gerald in hot pursuit

Marion Gerald—you're not chasing her *again*, are you?
Gerald No, I'm not! (*He pretends to be skipping*)
Potter I hope you're not expecting tea. I only made a pot for two...
Sandra Mrs Corby, there's something I've *got* to tell you!
Gerald (*loudly*) No, there isn't!!

Potter and Marion look at him in surprise

Marion Whatever's the matter?

Linda and Rodney arrive

Potter Oh, dear. Two more! I should have made a larger pot...
Sandra Or do *you* prefer to tell her, Mr Corby? (*She grins at him*)
Gerald (*after a moment, a beaten man*) Oh, very well... If I must. (*He glares at her*)
Marion Tell me what, Gerry?
Potter Oh, do tell her! My nerves can't stand the suspense...
Sandra It's good news. Isn't it, Mr Corby?
Gerald (*giving her a baleful look*) I suppose so...
Potter Oh, that *is* a relief! My pulse was racing.
Marion Well, go on, then—tell me what it is!

Gerald prepares himself

Gerald Linda didn't come here alone. She came here ... with *Rodney*! (*He smiles at Rodney in exaggerated delight*)
Marion Rodney?
Potter The window-cleaner!
Marion Oh my God...! (*She jumps to her feet in embarrassment, spilling the remains of her tea over Potter in the process*)

Potter hastily mops up

Potter Oh Mrs Corby…! All over my trousers!

Marion (*indicating*) *This* window-cleaner?

Linda Yes. *My* window-cleaner… (*She gazes at Rodney adoringly*)

Marion Oh, no…!

Potter And just when we were enjoying our Earl Grey…

Sandra (*enjoying Gerald's discomfort*) And Mr Corby's very pleased about it. Aren't you, Mr Corby?

Gerald Yes, I suppose so…

Marion (*surprised*) You mean you don't mind?

Gerald (*putting a brave face on it*) Of *course* I don't mind! I've always wanted to have a window-cleaner in the family! It'll save me a fortune.

Marion (*to Linda*) So you and … Rodney … came here together?

Linda ⎫ (*together*) Yes!
Rodney ⎭

Potter I knew he was up to no good the minute I saw him in a lady's dressing-gown…

Sandra Yes—*they* came here together, but *we* didn't, did we, Mr Corby?

Gerald grins at her gratefully and points her out to Marion, jumping about in nervous relief

Gerald There! You see? Did you hear that? (*He kisses Marion on the forehead*) Did you hear what she said? We didn't come here together! What did I tell you? (*He kisses Sandra on the forehead, realizes who he is kissing and hastily backs off*)

Marion Gerry, there's no need to get so excited.

Gerald Isn't there?

Marion I *know* you didn't come here together.

Gerald You do? Oh, good!

Potter There, Mr Corby! Isn't that a relief for us both? I know *I*'ve been on tenterhooks.

Marion (*to Gerald, severe again*) But you still ended up in her bedroom!

Potter Shall I get you some fresh tea, Mrs Corby? Your nerves must be in shreds. I know mine are…

Gerald Wait a minute! Why should *I* feel guilty? (*Glaring at Marion*) What about *you*? Who is this "gentleman friend" you came to see?

Potter (*distressed*) Oh, no, Mrs Corby! Not you as well…!

Gerald Who *is* he?

Marion Do you *really* want to know?

Gerald Yes, I do!

Marion It'll be a bit embarrassing.

Gerald Who *is* it?
Marion You promise not to get angry and start shouting?
Gerald (*loudly*) Who *is* it?!
Marion Well, it … it's Mr Potter, of course.

Gerald and Potter both react

Gerald Mr *Potter*?! (*He points at Potter in disbelief*) *This* Mr Potter?
Marion Yes—*my* Mr Potter… (*She gazes at him adoringly*)
Potter Oh, Mrs Corby—why did you have to go and tell him that?
Gerald (*erupting*) Potter!!

Potter starts to make his getaway with Gerald in hot pursuit, the others laughing, as music swells and——

                    —the CURTAIN *falls*

FURNITURE AND PROPERTY LIST

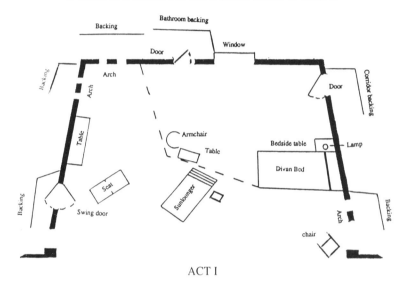

ACT I

On stage: POOLSIDE AREA:
Sun lounger
Large towel
Low coffee table
Colourful padded seat
Light garden table
Wicker chair. *On it*: towel
Signs "To the Doctor" and "To Massage Parlour"

BEDROOM:
Divan bed with bedding
Bedside table. *On it*: lamp, telephone, room card. *In drawer*: perfume atomiser
Small armchair
Small table
Door numbers 10 and 14 (interchangeable)
Linda's beach towel
Window curtains (open)
Carpet

Off stage: Weekend bag. *In it*: items of clothing, washbag, pyjamas (**Rodney**)
Register containing dust (**Potter**)
Cold drink (**Sandra**)
Clipboard (**Potter**)
Towel (**Linda**)
Short feminine dressing-gown (**Rodney**)
Colourful towelling bathrobe, glass of orange juice (**Gerald**)
Glass of orange juice (**Gerald**)
Men's pyjamas (**Gerald**)

Personal: **Rodney:** wrist-watch
Gerald: wrist-watch
Potter: napkin, pen, wrist-watch
Gerald: towel over his head

ACT II

On stage: As before

Off stage: Half full cup of tea, saucer, teaspoon (**Marion**)
Handbag (**Marion**)
Armful of clothes, travel bag (**Gerald**)
Bottle of red wine (**Sandra**)
Dressing-gown (**Gerald**)
2 plastic glasses (**Sandra**)
Plastic bag with silver foil containers (**Rodney**)
2 pairs chopsticks, bottle opener (**Rodney**)
Toothbrush (**Gerald**)
Bunch of grapes (**Gerald**)
Gerald's clothes, bunch of grapes (**Potter**)
Bunch of grapes (**Linda**)
Small tray of tea things inc. tiny pot and 2 cups (**Potter**)

Personal: **Gerald:** £5 note
Rodney: dirt and stale salad

LIGHTING PLOT

Practical fittings required: bedside lamp
Interior. Composite set of swimming-pool area and bedroom. The same throughout

ACT I

To open: Lights up in swimming-pool area

Cue 1	**Gerald** and **Potter** exit to massage parlour	(Page 10)
	Bring up lights in bedroom	
Cue 2	**Rodney** exits into bathroom	(Page 12)
	Lights out in bedroom	
Cue 3	**Linda** exits	(Page 14)
	Bring up lights in bedroom	
Cue 4	**Potter** and **Rodney** exit	(Page 17)
	Lights out in bedroom	
Cue 5	**Gerald** exits	(Page 21)
	Bring up lights in bedroom	
Cue 6	**Linda** exits to bathroom	(Page 22)
	Lights out in bedroom	
Cue 7	**Potter** exits to office	(Page 25)
	Bring up lights in bedroom	
Cue 8	**Linda** sinks on to bed	(Page 27)
	Lights out in bedroom	
Cue 9	**Potter** exits	(Page 28)
	Bring up lights in bedroom	
Cue 10	**Rodney** and **Linda** fall on to bed	(Page 38)
	Lights out in bedroom	

Cue 11   **Potter** falls back on to sun lounger   (Page 41)
Black-out

ACT II

To open: Overall general lighting

Cue 12   **Linda** exits to bathroom   (Page 43)
Lights out in bedroom

Cue 13   **Marion** exits to garden   (Page 46)
Bring up lights in bedroom

Cue 14   **Potter** exits   (Page 48)
Lights out in bedroom

Cue 15   **Potter** exits to office   (Page 49)
Bring up lights in bedroom

Cue 16   **Sandra** draws the curtains   (Page 49)
Darken bedroom slightly

Cue 17   **Sandra** switches on bedside lamp   (Page 49)
Switch on lamp lighting

Cue 18   **Gerald** draws back the curtains   (Page 51)
Return bedroom lighting to normal

Cue 19   **Gerald** switches off bedside lamp   (Page 51)
Switch off lamp lighting

Cue 20   **Gerald** and **Marion** exit   (Page 58)
Lights out in bedroom

Cue 21   **Sandra**: "…go back into my room?"   (Page 59)
Bring up lights in bedroom

Cue 22   **Marion** and **Linda** freeze   (Page 62)
Black-out bedroom lighting

Cue 23   **Potter** runs out after **Gerald**   (Page 63)
Bring up lights in bedroom

Cue 24   **Potter** exits   (Page 68)
              Lights out in bedroom

Cue 25   **Potter** exits to office   (Page 73)
              Bring up lights in bedroom

Cue 26   **Linda** draws the curtains   (Page 74)
              Darken bedroom lighting slightly

Cue 27   **Linda** switche on bedside lamp   (Page 74)
              Switch on lamp lighting

Cue 28   **Rodney** exits to bathroom   (Page 75)
              Lights out in bedroom

Cue 29   **Potter** exits   (Page 76)
              Bring up subdued lighting in bedroom

Cue 30   **Gerald** draws back the curtains   (Page 76)
              Return bedroom lighting to normal

Cue 31   **Gerald** switches off bedside lamp   (Page 76)
              Switch off lamp lighting

Cue 32   **Gerald** exits to bathroom   (Page 82)
              Lights out in bedroom

Cue 33   **Potter** and **Marion** exit to offices   (Page 83)
              Bring up lights in bedroom

Cue 34   **Rodney** and **Linda** exit   (Page 87)
              Lights out in bedroom

Cue 35   **Potter** runs away pursued by **Gerald**   (Page 89)
              Fade lights to black-out

EFFECTS PLOT

ACT I

Cue 1	As CURTAIN rises *Play peaceful, relaxing music*	(Page 1)
Cue 2	**Rodney** jumps and turns *Cut music*	(Page 2)
Cue 3	**Linda** and **Rodney** go out *Play lush, romantic music, preferably* *"Love is a Many-splendoured Thing"*	(Page 6)
Cue 4	**Sandra**: "Mr Corby!" *Cut music*	(Page 6)

ACT II

Cue 5	**Potter** goes *Play lush, romantic music as before*	(Page 49)
Cue 6	**Gerald** sees **Sandra** on bed *Cut music*	(Page 49)
Cue 7	**Marion** avoids **Gerald**'s kiss *Sound of lavatory flushing noisily in bathroom*	(Page 55)
Cue 8	**Sandra** goes into bathroom *Play brief musical glissando*	(Page 78)
Cue 9	**Potter** starts to run away from **Gerald** *Play "hurry" music*	(Page 89)

MADE AND PRINTED IN GREAT BRITAIN BY
LATIMER TREND & COMPANY LTD PLYMOUTH
MADE IN ENGLAND